AF326976

FOR
LOVE
OF THE
LAND

FOR LOVE OF THE LAND

A History of the National Association of Conservation Districts

R. Neil Sampson

National Association of Conservation Districts
League City, Texas

Copyright © 1985 by the National Association of Conservation Districts
League City, Texas

Cover design by Carol Crosby Black

Extensive quote from Robert J. Morgan, *Governing Soil Conservation:
Thirty Years of the New Decentralization,* used with express
permission of the publisher. The book was published for Resources for
the Future, Inc., by the Johns Hopkins University Press.

Library of Congress Cataloging in Publication Data
Sampson, R. Neil.
   For love of the land.

   Includes index.
   1. National Association of Conservation Districts—History. 2. Soil
conservation—United States—History. 3. Water conservation—United
States—History.
 I. National Association of Conservation Districts.
II. Title.
S622.N273S36 1985   333.7'2'0973   84-16617
ISBN 0-9614178-0-3
Printed in the United States of America

This book
is dedicated to
the thousands of men
and women who have served
as soil and water conservation
district officials, and who, in
that service, have demonstrated
the meaning of responsible
stewardship for God's
creation, based on
love for the
land.

Contents

10 — Expanding the Agenda 233

11 — NACD Today 253

12 — Issues of the 1980's 273

Appendices 293

Notes and References Cited 320

Index 326

Foreword

Organizations, like people, need a sense of their history in order to move forward with confidence. For the National Association of Conservation Districts (NACD), that history involves the major achievements, issues, debates and turning points of the soil and water conservation movement in this country. Since 1937, when the first conservation districts were founded in this country, those associations of men and women have been in the forefront of the work to protect our natural resources in a vigorous way. Since 1946, NACD has represented those groups on the national level, and has been involved in the work to gain and keep a strong national resource policy.

This book tells the story of that effort. From its beginning, it is alive with the strong voices of the people who led and are leading the conservation movement. Reading it, we can deepen our own convictions about the importance of resource conservation and take pride in the leadership of this movement.

We can also clearly mark the accomplishments for conservation. The work at the national level to develop and maintain federal programs of assistance to land and water conservation through conservation districts is a first achievement. Other actions of NACD have also been vital to conservation: the founding of a national newsletter, sponsorship of conservation education programs, the establishment of a Washington office and regional offices, and the building of a service capability to assist districts. Together, those achievements have built conservation districts' capacity to "speak with one voice" on the national level -- an aim of the first founders of NACD.

Along with marking success, a good history also shows the outline of unfinished business. The work to control nonpoint pollution and to develop conservation programs related to commodity programs are an effort in which conservation districts and NACD have been deeply involved for more than a decade. In studying that effort, we can clearly see the political difficulties in building a solid, long-range national conservation policy. Strengthening that policy so that our resources are adequately protected will take much effort in the years to come.

This book should help every district official and conservation professional grasp a sense of their own place in the 50-year history of the movement. It should also help every citizen interested in the conservation of our resources to locate what has been done and what yet remains to be done. It belongs on the bookshelf of all 17,000 district officials, of every serious conservationist, every friend of conservation districts, every library across the country -- especially the libraries of schools, colleges, and universities.

I would like especially to thank the Board of Directors of NACD for authorizing the publication of this book. Hal Jenkins, the retired SCS conservationist who began the first version of this manuscript more than 10 years ago, and Gordon Zimmerman, who began revision of that work before his death, also deserve appreciation for their contributions. Neil Sampson began with those early drafts of the first portion of this book and has woven them into a fascinating story of NACD. In addition, I would like to acknowledge with appreciation the work of NACD Service Department Manager David Stewart for supervising the publication and the Review Committee for their hours of work in reading the early drafts and making suggestions for the final copy.

It gives me great pleasure to see this book completed, for I treasure the knowledge that understanding our history brings. By charting the past, this book provides the challenge for our future.

Milton E. Mekelburg

President, NACD

Preface

It has been a half-century since the United States embarked on an effort to devise a national program for soil and water conservation. The resulting program has been copied the world over, with particular emphasis on the science and art of proper land use management that has been learned in both laboratory and field experience.

The soil and water conservation program in the United States was not, however, just an exercise in science and technology. Instead, it has been an experiment in developing institutions and shaping government to be effective in dealing with the nation's private landowners and operators. It has been said many times, but it bears repeating: government programs and government employees do not apply soil conservation practices to private land. Farmers, ranchers, foresters, homeowners and all kinds of citizens do. The question is, how are those people going to know how to do good soil conservation management, and be encouraged to take the extra time and effort, or make the extra investment, that such management demands?

The answer that emerged in the mid-1930's was a new unit of local government. It is a special-purpose unit of government, with a limited charter and powers. It was (and is) called a soil conservation district or some similar name. It was (and is) operated by locally-elected or appointed officials who are responsible for managing the district's program under the laws of each state. It can do many things under the state code to encourage, educate, coordinate, and take action to assist the land users within its boundaries. What actually occurs is often largely a reflection of the dedication, vision and commitment of those officials.

It is said today, somewhat cynically, that wherever you have two of anything, it won't be long before you have an association. Back in the late 1930's and early 1940's, that was true, as well. It took a little longer, with a major depression from which to recover and a war to fight, but it happened, just the same. This book is the story of that association -- how it came into being, who shaped it, what it fought for over the years, and where it exists today.

In a sense, it is also the story of the broader conservation streams that have flowed through American life for 5 decades. No major resource battle was fought without involving or affecting the interests of the thousands of lay conservation leaders brought into public life by the soil conservation district movement. This story, then, also tracks their participation and, hopefully, measures some of their effect on the issues.

The initial research and writing on this manuscript was done in 1971 by Hal Jenkins, who had retired after a distinguished career in the Soil Conservation Service. Hal did a great deal of research, particularly into the earliest history of SCS and NACD, and wrote a manuscript for NACD, but time and events prevented its publication. We owe much of the insight into early leaders such as Bennett, McArthur and Leavitt, to Hal's work. He was a friend of many of the early participants in the story, and captured their ideas and thoughts very well. Had we waited until now to begin, we would have lost those fine contributions.

Later, Gordon Zimmerman worked on the manuscript, making some marginal notes for later consideration. After his retirement in 1977, Gordon contracted with NACD to finish the book. Tragically, he was stricken with cancer before he had the chance to get started, and once again the project went dormant.

In 1983, with the 50th anniversary of the soil conservation movement approaching, the officers and staff of NACD decided that it was time to dust off the old manuscript, bring it up to date, and publish it as a contribution to the 50-year celebration. Thus began a project that started out nights and weekends, and finally ended up in a 3-month full-time effort that resulted in the completed book.

Many, many hands were involved along the way. A Review Committee read all the early drafts of the manuscript, and their contributions changed, in many places, the cold, impersonal contents of the official record into a warm, personal story. I owe deepest thanks to George and Barbara Bagley, Lyle and Glenda Bauer, Norm Berg, George and Marion Cason, Nolen Fuqua, Mary Garner, Philip Glick, Bud Mekelburg, David Stewart, Lucille Thompson, David Unger, Sue Wilkinson and Bob Williams. These people lived this history, and their assistance has been vital in seeing the project through.

Chris Berger, Charles Boothby, Debi Callahan, Sara Ebenreck, and Shirley Parks of the NACD staff have been tremendously helpful in hundreds of ways, from word processing to proofreading, editing, assisting with layout, and managing portions of the effort. Each of them has offered insight into the issues, and helped with research of specific topics. A special word of appreciation is due to David Stewart, who has served as the publisher, and Sara Ebenreck, who has been the editor. Both of them have been marvelous. Chris Parent worked in the early part of the project as a research assistant, and was a great help as well.

The hardest part of writing a book like this is facing the fact that many stories must be left out, and many people not given the credit that they deserve. An organization like NACD has only a few officers, directors and staff members, but it has thousands of active contributors. Some of their stories would make a good book in itself, but space and time make one draw boundaries, and we had to leave many out. It was particularly hard to find space for more than just a glimpse at the results achieved at the local and state level by conservation district leaders over the years. It was also hard to accurately portray the thousands of miles and hundreds of days contributed as people came to Washington to testify, or served on an NACD committee, or attended state, regional and national meetings.

Every effort, whether it was working with the Boy Scouts, testifying in Washington, starting the Small Watershed Program, gaining support for urban interests, responding to public lands issues, studying forestry problems, spurring research, giving to NACD when it needed organizational or financial help, or reaching out to environmental organizations, had its leaders and advocates. These people -- numbering in the hundreds, if not the thousands -- are largely unsung. To each and every one of them, the people of America owe a debt. To those who could not be mentioned in this brief historical overview, I give my apologies, as well as a hearty "thank you."

No one can foretell what the next 50 years may bring, but one thing is certain: it will start with what we have, and where we are today. That is the value of this history. Harry Truman was once quoted as saying that the only thing new in this world is the history we have forgotten. Much in this book will bear that out. Most of the newest and hottest issues of 1985 will be found lurking in the shadows of 1935, or 1955, or some other time in the past. How we solve them in 1985 is not likely to differ too greatly from how we solved them then, either. The values that Americans hold concerning the rights of the individual, the rights of property, the limits of government, and the ethics that guide our interaction with one another have not shifted dramatically over the years. So long as that remains true, we are well advised to read history, and understand it, for it holds the key to understanding the present and being prepared to move from where we are today into the future.

Neil Sampson

July 1, 1984

Hugh Bennett's Idea 1

The spring of 1935 was not a very cheerful time in America. A Great Depression had the country in its grip, and the problems of jobless, homeless people preoccupied the nation's leadership. To make matters worse, the Midwest was going through a serious drought, and wind-blown topsoil from Texas and Oklahoma had been seen as far as 300 miles out in the Atlantic Ocean.

Among the ideas being considered by Congress was a new national soil conservation program. The expert witness that the Senate Public Lands Committee called on April 2, 1935, to testify on the bill before them was Hugh Hammond Bennett, a soil scientist who had been active in the Department of Agriculture's soil survey work since 1903, and who headed up the soil erosion work that had been ongoing in the Interior Department since 1933. Bennett was widely known as a knowledgable, articulate and dedicated spokesman on the problems of soil erosion.

Bennett was in no hurry as he testified. Fact after fact was brought forth to convince the Senators of the seriousness of the problem. That Bennett knew the facts to back his case was not in doubt, and, for that matter, neither was the seriousness of the situation. But Bennett was not content to win his case with mere facts; his was the heart of a showman. He knew that another major dust storm was on its way, and he orchestrated his testimony accordingly. Slowly, he proceeded through his material, all the while hoping that the storm would hurry up and arrive.

Finally, the room began to darken. As the Senators, staff and assembled witnesses gathered at the window, the billowing, roiling clouds of soil blotted out the sun, and the fine grit could be felt between the teeth. It was nature that really testified that day; Hugh Bennett just timed the show. The result, of course, was that Congress speedily passed Public Law 46, the soil conservation act that has been the basis for the most extensive and aggressive soil conservation program in the world.[1]

The soil conservation story cannot be told without telling the story of Hugh Bennett, the man who brought the issue of soil erosion to the

It was dust storms like this one in Springfield, Colorado, that helped awaken the nation to the threat of soil erosion.

nation's attention and whose leadership resulted in a national soil conservation program of tremendous dimensions. But while Bennett and his skills are a logical focal point for the beginning of the story, the soil conservation movement has been characterized by the active involvement of thousands of people: scientists, farmers, politicians, agency administrators, writers, educators, business leaders, and just plain ordinary citizens who were concerned with the future of their land and who felt strongly enough to become actively involved. This, then, is their story as well; the story of all who have served to save this land.

Ideas promoting soil and water conservation in the United States date back to Colonial times, when Thomas Jefferson extolled the soil-saving virtues of cultivating his corn on the contour rather than running the rows up and down the hills, and public programs can trace their roots back to early work in the Department of Agriculture and the colleges of agriculture of the land-grant universities.

USDA established a Division of Chemistry in 1862, a Division of Agricultural Soils in 1894, and a soil survey program in 1898.[2] Bulletins on soil washing were published by state agricultural experiment stations in the 1890's and many state extension programs included education on soil erosion, soil conservation and the application of conservation measures. One estimate was that, between 1915 and 1932, some 18 million acres of land on some 600,000 farms had been terraced through the efforts of the state extension services.[3]

But this activity was too simplistic in its approach, and was proceeding much too slowly to suit Hugh Bennett, who had seen serious soil erosion at work in virtually every state in the nation during his more than 20 years as a field surveyor. Bennett's concern for the menace of soil erosion dated back to the realization, gained in 1905, that sheet erosion -- the insidious but largely unseen washing away of thin layers of topsoil -- had quietly stolen eight or nine inches of Virginia topsoil from a field that he and his partner were surveying.

Two soils, Bennett would later say, had been formed under identical conditions of geology, slope, and rainfall, lying side-by-side on a hillside, but on that day they were vastly different. The soil on one piece of land was mellow, loamy and moist, even in dry weather; but the other was hard, dry unworkable clay. The first had been protected by forest, but the other was a crop field, where soil erosion had removed the topsoil completely to

---

In his ruthless exploitation of land and water resources, Man has violated basic arrangements in a manner which Nature will not tolerate.

Through countless centuries there has been built up a balanced, fruitful relationship among waters, soils, grasses, and forests. Each dependent on and helpful to the others, they have learned to work together, through physical, chemical, and biological processes, to create and maintain a continent of abundant, useful resources for the habitation and sustenance of Man.

Then came the settlers -- vigorous, keen, and intelligent with respect to matters of the moment, but unforeseeing and destructive with respect to matters of the future. Unwittingly, for present gains they sacrificed the birthright they believed they were actually increasing for their descendants.

Blindly and ruthlessly they shattered that balance of Nature's forces which created and maintained the land and water resources that they assumed would last forever.

Impoverishment of these resources, in part by unwise selection for use, in part by improper methods of use, has become a real danger.

This danger is a vital concern to everyone. It is as significant to merchant, manufacturer, and banker as to those who work immediately on the land. Nature's gifts are the basis of all economic life. All conversion and interchange of goods rest on the application of human activity to the earth's materials. This is the basic reality. Progress or decadence of a people is determined by the manner in which it accepts and utilizes these gifts of Nature. Soils and waters may be so used as to remain permanent assets yielding a perpetual income. On the other hand they may be destroyed as sources of income; may even be so used as to make them essentially self-destructive. A people must choose.

H.S. Person, *Little Waters*
(Washington: U.S. Gov't. Printing Office, 1935).

expose the underlying subsoil. It had been, for all practical purposes, damaged beyond use as cropland.[4]

A Crusade Begins

From then on Bennett never stopped talking and writing about what was happening to the American land. But it was not until 1928, when he persuaded the Department of Agriculture to publish his (and William R. Chapline's) pamphlet, "Soil Erosion A National Menace," that he attracted much attention. One of the people who listened to Bennett's story was E. H. (Zack) Taylor, an editor of *The Country Gentleman,* who gave Bennett his first national audience in a major magazine. That action opened the gates for other magazine articles and editorial support.

Early in 1929 Bennett gained public support for his cause when the agricultural appropriations for fiscal year 1930 included $160,000 for soil erosion investigations -- the first federal funds ever appropriated for soil conservation. This came about after Representative James P. Buchanan of Texas, a member of the Appropriations Subcommittee on Agriculture, called on Bennett to testify at a subcommittee hearing. Bennett was not a budget spokesman for the Department of Agriculture. He "just happened" to be there. Indeed, Buchanan interrupted the testimony of the Department's official spokesman to call on Bennett. Bennett, as usual, was not at a loss for words, and the effort was worth $160,000.[5]

Using these funds, the first erosion experiment station was established at Guthrie, Oklahoma, in 1929 and nine others quickly followed. The Agricultural Appropriations Act of February, 1931, added $330,000 to expand this work, and the result was a rapid increase in knowledge and understanding of the soil erosion process and the problems it could create.[6]

Bennett had a large hand in the establishment and work of these stations. He selected most of the sites and outlined most of the studies. A vast amount of information was acquired and made public. More than 300,000 quantitative measurements were made of soil and water losses under differing conditions of land use, management, treatment, and cover.[7]

Out of these studies, as well as a national Reconnaissance Erosion Survey completed in 1934 by the Soil Erosion Service, came a grim picture of spreading damage to the American land, a picture which was skillfully exploited (some critics have argued that it was overexploited) by Bennett and his staff.

But despite the growing evidence of soil erosion's damage to the American land, there was no national action program specifically organized to combat it. In 1930, Bennett delivered a paper to the American Society of Agronomy in which a national program proposal was outlined in some detail. The action Bennett sought was a move from research to

Eroded hill pastures and orchards led to abandoned homesteads (top) and huge, gnawing gullies such as this one in Mississippi (bottom) led people to despair of ever being able to use the land again. (SCS photos)

demonstration projects, where farmers could learn to apply the conservation methods being developed by the research efforts.[8]

In the meantime, both the national economic situation and the weather were at work building Bennett's case. The Great Depression of the 1930's was coupled with severe drought, particularly in the Great Plains, where the expansion of wheat plantings in the 1920's had opened up millions of acres of droughty, unstable soils to the ravages of the wind. In the face of crop failures and bankruptcy, thousands of farmers and ranchers simply abandoned their lands and sought better conditions elsewhere. John Steinbeck, in his classic novel, *The Grapes of Wrath*, portrayed these "Okies" as victims of a land destroyed by attempts to do more than was possible.

In its December, 1934 report, the National Resources Board estimated that 35 million acres had been completely destroyed in terms of usefulness for farming, that the topsoil had been largely or completely removed from an additional 125 million acres, and that another 100 million acres were suffering lesser, but increasing damage.[9]

The Dust Bowl of the Plains, and the black blizzards it spread over much of the nation, was a significant contributor to public alarm over the soil erosion problem, but it was far from the only example. In the Southeast, it was gullies that made the headlines. Stuart Chase described the situation in Stewart County, Georgia, as follows:

"Presently the road approached a kind of isthmus, perhaps 100 yards wide. A plowed field was on the left and beyond it a sickening void. A battered church stood on the right, a few pines about it, then another void.

"We got out of the car and approached the brink. The land fell away almost sheer for 200 feet. We stood over one of the gully's arms and far down caught a glimpse of the central basin. Shaped like an octopus, it covered more than 3,000 acres. A red gash on a little hill a mile away marked the tip of another tentacle of the same gully.

"It was something like looking into the crater of a volcano, only instead of eruption one feared a cave-in. The good earth had given up the struggle."[10]

Portraits such as these, coupled with the growing need to lift the country out of Depression with a major public works program, led to the inclusion of two sections (202 & 203) in the National Industrial Recovery Act of 1933 which proposed to step up the erosion control program as a means of increasing employment and addressing the erosion problem at the same time.[11]

In 1933, Bennett, his antennae ever alert to rumblings relating to his first and only concern, heard that a program of terracing, to be carried out under this Act, had been approved in his own Department of Agriculture. It was pending in the Public Works Administration, which had been established as an independent agency and was headed by a member of the cabinet --Secretary of the Interior Harold L. Ickes. The terracing program was to be administered by the USDA's Bureau of Agricultural Engineering, where the proposal originated.

Bennett immediately drafted a counter-proposal. He argued that more than terraces and trees were needed to control erosion; vegetative cover was equally important and often far superior to mechanical measures and structures. Strip cropping, contour plowing, grassed waterways, and crop rotations were needed in addition to terracing in its proper place. Usually, a combination of measures was necessary because land differed from field to field and even within fields.

Bennett started his proposal through his regular channels in the Department of Agriculture, where it languished for six weeks before reaching Secretary Henry A. Wallace. In fact, Bennett's proposal did not get to Wallace until shortly after the terracing project had been approved by Ickes' Special Board of Public Works.

To combat the delay of his proposal through the channels of Agriculture, Bennett bypassed his own department and conveyed his ideas directly to Ickes. He confided to his friend, Bryce C. Browning of Ohio, that he expected to be reprimanded, at the very least, and might even be forced to give up his position for "getting out of channels". He also bypassed his superiors and went directly to Rexford G. Tugwell, Undersecretary of Agriculture, who became an active advocate of Bennett's proposal. Tugwell maneuvered behind the scenes and may have played an important, if largely unseen, role in getting Bennett's program, with Bennett in charge, established in the Department of the Interior.

Ickes was familiar with Bennett's proposal, which did not get out of the Department of Agriculture officially, and he had talked to Bennett personally. He evidently liked both the ideas and the man. Besides, he might have had another reason for wanting the new program under his wing. Many believed that Ickes planned to establish a Department of Conservation, and wanted the erosion control program as an opening wedge.

As for Tugwell's interest and support, some felt that he wanted the program to be in Interior so it could steer clear of the conflicts and jealousies of the bureaus in Agriculture. At least that is the way several authors have told the story, using interviews with Hugh Bennett as the source.[12]

Another version of this story, however, comes from Charles Collier, who was intimately involved in setting up the Soil Erosion Service while working as a $1-a-year assistant to his father, John Collier, the Commissioner of Indian Affairs under Harold Ickes. Collier is convinced, and others who were in Interior at the time agree, that Tugwell was never involved at all -- that the SES idea sprang mainly from the contact that Bennett had with Charles Collier during an erosion survey of the Navajo Reservation. That report, according to Collier, led to the idea of creating a Soil Erosion Service using Public Works Funds. The proposal was presented to Secretary Ickes by John Collier along with the recommendation that Hugh Bennett be chosen to head the activity. Bennett immediately chose Charles Collier as his special assistant, making him the second employee of the SES.[13]

The Soil Erosion Service

The Bennett-Tugwell-Ickes (or Collier-Collier-Ickes) efforts came to light when Ickes' Special Board of Public Works amended the minutes of the meeting in which it had approved the terracing program offered by the engineers in Agriculture, and approved a new and historic undertaking that was to lead to a permanent national program.[14]

In a press release dated September 13, 1933, the Department of the Interior said in part:

"Establishment of a new division of the Department of the Interior and appointment of its director was announced today by Harold L. Ickes, Secretary of the Interior. The new office will be known as the Division of Erosion, and will be headed by H. H. Bennett, regarded as the country's leading authority on soil erosion problems. Mr. Bennett began his new duties today. The new division will operate with a fund of $5,000,000 allotted by the Public Works Administration."

The new agency quickly became known as the Soil Erosion Service (SES). Bennett began assembling a staff and developing a program of erosion control demonstrations in representative areas of the country. He needed a ready-made approach that would enable him to get underway quickly so that he could provide jobs for unemployed persons through the Works Progress Administration (WPA) and the Civilian Conservation Corps (CCC). Demonstrations were a tried and accepted way to introduce new ideas in agriculture. The state extension services had used them for many years, and modern agriculture owes much to this system. The theory is that concerned people are attracted to the scene, impressed by the logic and value of what they see, and motivated to incorporate the activity into their own operations.

Bennett was concerned with the vast area of the nation's lands, and he needed to prove his theories on a big scale, so he selected large areas for his demonstrations. The demonstration project areas averaged 25,000 acres; some of them were 30,000 acres or more. The CCC camp demonstration areas averaged 15,000 acres. Watersheds were the basis for each demonstration, because Bennett felt he needed to prove that soil conservation and water conservation could not be separated, for the surface movement of uncontrolled water across unprotected or improperly used land was the chief cause of soil erosion.[15]

Bennett's goal was to apply the best known methods of erosion control in a large watershed and encourage inspection by farmers in an effort to spread the conservation work to other areas. Bennett and his staff called the demonstration areas "showcases".

In assembling his staff, Bennett, for the first time, had the opportunity to test his unique concept that soil conservation could not be achieved by any single approach or by any one of the sciences, but only through a proper combination of all the physical and biological sciences. He recruited soil scientists, agronomists, agricultural and civil engineers, foresters, biologists, wildlife management specialists, economists, hydrologists and others. Their job was to work together in planning the use of land and in applying combinations of vegetative and mechanical practices as needed to protect and improve it.

In a demonstration area, the landowner was only required to sign an agreement and furnish what he was able to in the way of labor and materials. The SES did the technical planning, provided large amounts of labor through the WPA and the CCC, furnished materials, and did most of the construction. This included building check dams, terraces, and new fences, laying out contour strips, planting trees, seeding eroded areas, and other operations.

Work got under way quickly, but there were problems. Harry Hopkins, aide to President Franklin D. Roosevelt and head of the Federal Emergency Relief Administration, clashed frequently with Bennett over the low number of people being taken off the relief rolls. Bennett argued that he was doing the best he could, and needed competent people to operate the projects.

At one point the infant program was about to die a sudden death. Hopkins had objected to the SES request for $25 million on the ground that the cost per man employed was too high. This was at a meeting of the Allotment Board set up by FDR, and with which he always met, to handle public works allotments. As Bennett later told the story: "It looked like the end, but at this point Morris L. Cooke, a member of the board (later the first head of the Rural Electrification Administration), asked the President for two weeks in which to prepare a special report." Cooke's comprehensive report on the value of soil conservation to the nation overrode the objections made by Hopkins, and the program was saved.[16]

Secretary Ickes was very proud of the program and fretted over it like a mother hen. He was sensitive to criticisms of it and took a personal interest in all details of the operation, even minor items of day to day activities. He kept Bennett and his staff busy responding to a steady flow of memoranda.

The work progressed and gained in popularity. In 18 months, 41 soil and water conservation demonstration projects were established and about 50 Civilian Conservation Corps camps were assigned to the work. The program's popularity was not restricted to those living in the demonstration projects who were the direct beneficiaries. The first in a continuing series of attempts to "take over" began almost as soon as the program proved itself. In one such instance, Bennett was summoned to the White House a few months after the SES program started and told by President Roosevelt: "Bennett, I want to congratulate you and your technicians in the Soil Erosion Service for doing a good job. They're after you, Bennett, and when they are after somebody, he's usually doing a bang-up job."[17]

Bennett had discussed the proposal of moving the SES to Agriculture with Secretary Ickes in November, 1934, but made it clear that more important than where the agency was located was the need for all erosion control activities to be coordinated through one agency. And FDR, in the same conversation in which he told Bennett "they're after you," had asked Bennett if he objected to moving the program to Agriculture. Bennett said he had no objections to Agriculture, since he had "spent most of my life there."

Secretary Ickes' concern over the fate of the program led him to set up a special committee called "The Soil Erosion Service and a Permanent Coordinating Program of Soil Erosion Control." As chairman he named Ward Shepard, a forester in the Bureau of Indian Affairs, who later was to write *Food or Famine,* one of the significant early books on soil conservation, published by MacMillan in 1945. Shepard's committee members were Charlie F. Shaw and W.W. Johnston, also of the Interior Department.

Shepard's report, submitted December 18, 1934, must have disappointed Ickes, for it recommended transfer of the SES to Agriculture and consolidation of all erosion-control activities in one agency as well.[18]

The die had been cast. Over the objections of Secretary Ickes, President Roosevelt issued an order on March 25, 1935, transferred the SES, its funds, property, and equipment to the Department of Agriculture. When Ickes, who was in Florida at the time, sent a telegram of protest, FDR wrote him a note saying that "I had to decide the matter from the point of view of common sense administrative layout and charting and there is no question that Soil Erosion has more to do with Agriculture activities than with Interior activities. I know you will understand."[19]

Two days later, Secretary Henry Wallace, in Department of Agriculture Memorandum 665, ordered the consolidation, effective April 1, of all USDA erosion-control work. This order expanded the SES to include the erosion-control experiment stations of the Bureau of Chemistry and Soils and the Bureau of Agricultural Engineering, the erosion nurseries of the Bureau of Plant Industry, and the CCC camps previously assigned to the Forest Service for erosion-control work on agricultural lands.

And so it happened that after an absence of 18 months, Hugh Bennett came "home" to USDA, bringing with him an agency that seemed to pose a threat to the prerogatives of many old line bureaus in the Department of Agriculture.

National Policy Declared

In the early months of 1935, several bills were introduced in the Congress to create a permanent agency for soil erosion control. Some, calling for the agency to be in the Department of Interior, were introduced in both the House and the Senate. A bill by Representative Marvin Jones of Texas, Chairman of the House Agriculture Committee, specified that the new agency be in the Department of Agriculture.

The President's transfer of SES to Agriculture solidified sentiment in the Congress, and action thereafter was swift. On March 27, Representatives John J. Dempsey of New Mexico and Marvin Jones introduced new bills to create the Soil Conservation Service in Agriculture. On March 29, on motion of Representative Jones to suspend the rules, the House passed the bill. On April 19, the Senate, with Senator Carl Hatch of New Mexico in the role of chief advocate, passed the bill on a voice vote. The bill became the Soil Conservation Act of 1935, Public Law 46, and was approved by President Roosevelt on April 27, 1935.

The Act both created the Soil Conservation Service and established a national policy. Thus, the Secretary of Agriculture was armed with broad authority to carry out a national program of soil and water conservation, with a great deal of latitude in choosing the way he would do it. Although Public Law 46, "To provide for the protection of land resources against soil erosion, and other purposes," was the major milestone in American conservation history, its entire contents can be completly reproduced on two typewritten pages. A testimony to the vision of its drafters lies in the fact that for nearly half a century, no substantive amendments have been considered necessary to meet the nation's changing and expanding conservation needs.

> Be it enacted by the Senate and House of Representatives of the United States of America in Congress Assembled, That it is hereby recognized that the wastage of soil and moisture resources on farm, grazing, and forest lands of the nation, resulting from soil erosion, is a menace to the national welfare and that it is hereby declared to be the policy of Congress to provide permanently for the control and prevention of soil erosion and thereby preserve natural resources, control floods, prevent impairment of reservoirs, and maintain the navigability of rivers and harbors, protect public lands and relieve unemployment, and the Secretary of Agriculture, from now on, shall coordinate and direct all activities with relation to soil erosion and in order to effectuate this policy is hereby authorized, from time to time--
>
> (1) to conduct surveys, investigations, and research relating to the character of soil erosion and the preventive measures needed, to publish the results of any such surveys, investigations, or research, to disseminate information concerning such methods, and to conduct demonstrational projects in areas subject to erosion by wind or water;
>
> (2) to carry out preventive measures, including but not limited to engineering operations, methods of cultivation, the growing of vegetation, and changes in use of land;
>
> (3) to cooperate or enter into agreements with, or to furnish financial or other aid to, any agency, governmental or otherwise, or any persons, subject to such conditions as he may deem necessary, for the purpose of this Act; and,
>
> (4) to acquire lands, or rights or interests therein, by purchase, gift, condemnation, or otherwise, whenever necessary for the purposes of this Act.
>
> Declaration of Policy,
> Public Law 75-46, April 27, 1935.

Since Public Law 46 specifically established the Soil Conservation Service within the Department of Agriculture and provided that existing facilities should be used in forming the new agency, the Acting Secretary of Agriculture, in Memorandum 673, April 27, 1935, ordered that the Soil Erosion Service become the Soil Conservation Service, with status as a regular bureau of the Department.

Broadening of the program began with the transfer of 150 CCC camps from the Forest Service and assignment of more than 300 additional CCC camps to the SCS in the summer of 1935 to extend demonstrations to wider areas.

By June 30, 1936, the SCS had in operation 147 demonstration projects, 48 soil conservation nurseries, 23 research stations, and 454 CCC camps, down from an apparent high level of 498 in December of 1935. Some 50,000 farmers in the demonstration areas had applied conservation plans on about 5 million acres. The program was popular; thousands more were asking for a chance to participate.[20]

The CCC program was of immense and lasting importance to the emerging conservation program in SCS. In addition to leaving physical monuments to conservation behind, the CCC experience made thousands of young men conscious of the need for proper land use and conservation. Enrollees could attend classes on conservation taught by SCS technicians at night. Those that were interested in a career in conservation could often join the service, and more than 1,000 availed themselves of that opportunity during 1937-38. The CCC camp administrators, scientists and technicians became the backbone of the emerging SCS leadership at the field, regional and national level.

Early Problems in USDA

The work of the agency, as developed in Interior, crossed many of the established bureau lines in the Department of Agriculture, especially those of the Bureau of Plant Industry, Bureau of Agricultural Engineering, Forest Service, Federal Extenison Service and its associated state extension services and colleges of agriculture of the land grant college system, and the Agricultural Adjustment Administration.

Especially critical were the state extension services. They believed, and had some two decades of precedent in their corner, that all "extension" work of the Department of Agriculture should be carried out through them. The erosion control program, they maintained, was extension work, largely "educational," and SES and its successor, SCS, should not work directly with farmers. That was extension's "prerogative."

Clyde W. Warburton, who was USDA's Director of Extension Work, argued strongly that the "1914 Agreement" meant that all "extension work" within USDA would be done through the state extension services. It was Extension's view, he said, that the SCS work in demonstration projects "is in large part extension, and it is without question extension so far as efforts are made to get farmers outside these areas to adopt the practices followed thereon."[21] It was therefore proposed that the new program be channeled through the state universities rather than become an independent action agency within USDA.

The state extension services, the colleges of agriculture, and many bureaus in USDA had another gripe. SES began and SCS continued to hire some of their best men. The depression had hit the extension services and old line bureaus hard. Employment and salaries were down. The new program seemed to offer a better career opportunity, plus higher salaries to start, and jobs for men trained and experienced in the agricultural sciences at this stage were more plentiful in the new agency than in the old line federal bureaus and in the states.

Secretary Wallace, in a move to integrate the new agency into a somewhat hostile Department of Agriculture, set up the Secretary's Committee on Soil Conservation. The committee, in its report of June 5, 1935, recommended that the SCS carry out its program on private lands by turning over its funds to the state extension services, which would provide educational and technical help through assistant county agents. Direct SCS help would be limited to areas where an "organized association" had been established.

The advocates of this method of operation apparently considered the recommendations to be binding on the Secretary. In any event, for years to come, they referred to the committee's report as official USDA policy despite the Secretary's early actions indicating that he considered the committee's job was to make recommendations to him -- not decisions for him.

The situation was complicated by the passage of the Soil Conservation and Domestic Allotment Act in February, 1936, which made soil conservation a major function of the Agricultural Adjustment Administration. Under this program, payments were made to farmers willing to take lands out of the production of surplus crops and place them in a "conservation use." The cost of installing certain conservation practices on the land was partially reimbursed through a new "cost-sharing" program administered by AAA.

This act brought new programs that impacted upon both the Extension Service and the SCS. For Extension, it meant a new action program within the Department; one that they would either have to administer at the local level with extension agents or allow to function as an independent action agency. At the outset, the AAA programs were administered by the state extension services, but this arrangement did not prove satisfactory to either the state universities or the Department officials in charge of the program.[22]

In 1936, H. R. Tolley, head of AAA, began efforts to separate the AAA from the state extension services in order to establish a more direct line of administrative authority for the programs. This effort resulted in an agreement, ratified by USDA and the Policy Committee of the Association of Land-Grant Colleges and Universities in 1938, which established that USDA would administer action programs directly, but cooperate with the land-grant colleges in establishing state and county land-use planning committees which could advise and comment on the work of the action agencies.

Thus, for Extension, the creation and rapid growth of both the SCS and AAA programs, along with other New Deal efforts such as the Resettlement Administration, posed a serious threat to the tenuous balance of federal-state relations which, in agricultural matters, had been firmly tilted toward the states since the passage of the Hatch Act in 1914. The federal government was taking a more active role, and the land-grant universities lacked the political power to prevent it from happening.

For SCS, the creation of the AAA programs meant a rival soil conservation program within USDA, setting out to do the same job with different methods. SCS was largely working through education and demonstration, with on-site technical planning and installation assistance to farmers as a key element. Under the AAA program, farmers were given subsidies for shifting land out of "soil-depleting" crops and installing conservation measures on their land. In addition to conservation, this program's goals included the reduction of the acreages of surplus crops and the creation of a legal, publicly-supported reason (conservation) for shifting public funds to farmers as a means of helping prop them up financially.

What had been created, then, was a multi-agency, multi-objective set of soil conservation programs within USDA where competition and strife were virtually assured.

Demonstrations Display Problems

The SCS demonstration program achieved popularity in a few months, recorded tangible accomplishments, and was destined to continue for several years. It was apparent as early as mid-1936, however, that "the spread of practices" objective -- keystone of the demonstration theory -- was a failure. Without a new approach, the purposes of P.L. 46 would not be achieved as rapidly as many hoped.

For one thing, the demonstration system simply would not work when applied to planning and installing soil and water conservation systems on agricultural land. There was a growing awareness that soil and water conservation was so complex that it could not be accomplished without on-site technical help. Farmers who saw the demonstration work liked what they saw, but they could seldom adapt the theories and practice combinations on their own lands without assistance.

In addition, they were in the midst of the Depression, and it was difficult to contemplate paying for conservation practices when there was scarcely even food for the table. Farmers faced with the problem of providing a family's living on 160 acres of eroded, run-down land had little opportunity to do anything but continue to till every acre and pray for better times.

One of the most significant accomplishments in the project and camp areas was the on-the-job training of personnel, many of whom someday would become conservation leaders. During the summers of 1934 and 1935, a large number of young college graduates were employed as trainees. Also, personnel for the operation of the camps were, for the most part, recent college graduates.

Three significant developments came from these early activities. First, it was demonstrated that soil erosion could be controlled -- and was not a natural process to be accepted passively along with the thunder and lightning.

Second, the men who worked in early demonstration projects and camp areas developed a measure of self-confidence which they may not otherwise have acquired. After checking with their own hands the flow of water falling into a 30-foot gully, they were not alarmed by the relatively small quantity discharged at the end of a terrace. They knew they could manage it!

Third, a new science was brought into being: Soil and Water Conservation. This science resulted from synthesizing segments of many other sciences into a new whole. It was not unlike the efforts of an inquisitive and inventive metallurgist who blends different metals to form a new alloy with properties and advantages previously unknown.

W. B. Wilkerson, et. al., *Keepers of the Land: A History of Soil and Water Conservation Districts in South Carolina* (Columbia:SCASCD, 1972).

One major problem was that the farmers in the demonstration areas had little or no part in the program. Most of them merely gave their consent, signed an agreement and sat back while technical help, labor, and materials were supplied free of charge. When something went wrong with an installed measure, it was not uncommon for the SES technical men to receive a call that "your" terrace "needs fixing." As a result, too few of the demonstrated practices were duplicated, even on the farm where their effectiveness had been proven.

There was a great deal of misinformation about the new conservation program, as well. One description of the situation in Oklahoma goes as follows:

"Some farmers had the impression that conservation practices were being forced upon them. To many of the pioneering, independent thinking

Oklahoma farmers, the situation smelled like Federal intervention in their rights as free landowners. The problems of overcoming the suspicions of these farmers -- many of whom were down on their luck anyway -- was not an easy task. One promoter of conservation programs recalls having looked down the barrel of more than one shotgun in the hands of farmers who were fearful that the Federal Government was making an effort to force more laws and regulations on the people."[23]

But the demonstrations were successful in many ways. They proved that Bennett's ideas were more than unfounded theories -- they were practical solutions to practical problems. The projects proved that the information obtained from the erosion experiment stations could be translated into action on the land. They provided worthwhile work for thousands of otherwise unemployed WPA clients and CCC youth in a depressed time.

Many questions, however, remained unanswered. It was clear that demonstrations would never reach all the lands needing conservation treatment. It was equally clear, particularly to M.L. Wilson of USDA, that the costs were too high, particularly if landowners had to consider matching those costs on their own farms. "You will never be able to control erosion on millions of farms in 48 states out of an office in Washington, D.C.," Wilson told Philip Glick, a young USDA attorney, in 1934. "How are we going to get around that problem?"[24]

The Gospel According to Bennett

Hugh Bennett expressed his deep feeling about productive land and its value to mankind many times, and he built the SCS in accordance with these strong beliefs and ideas: land is a complex resource within a complex environment, and soil is but one part of land. To protect and improve the land for permanent, productive use, it must be considered in terms of all its parts: soil, slope, climate, and susceptibility to depreciation by erosion, overcropping, or other processes of deterioration. There is no easy way to soil and water conservation, no panacea such as terracing or any other single practice indiscriminately applied. Land varies from field to field and can be classified as to its capability. Each farm or branch or watershed must be considered as a whole and not planned or treated piecemeal.

It was Bennett's idea that neither the engineers, the agronomists, the foresters, nor any of the other technical specialists had all the answers. Working together, however, they could diagnose and prescribe, much as a medical team. Thus, while building a new kind of federal agency that differed from any previous agency in that it worked directly with private landowners, and creating a new science and art, Bennett also created a new kind of professional -- the soil conservationist -- a man trained to bring to focus on individual farms and ranches and in small watersheds the combined skills of all the physical and biological sciences. Backing up this new breed of technician were small groups of specialists in engineering, wildlife management, soils, the plant sciences, economics and others, as needed, for training, advice, and consultation on special problems.

The heart of the soil and water conservation job in conservation districts was the conservation plan, a guide to land use and conservation treatment. Tailored to each farm or land unit, it is developed by the farmer and a professional conservationist working together. It is based on a soil survey, from which a land capability map is developed. The map shows the capability of each field. The capability classes (Bennett and his staff developed eight, and they are still in use) indicate the suitability of each field for various uses and the conservation treatment required for the various uses to avoid losses of soil and water.

Hugh Bennett led thousands into the fields of America to view the ravages of soil erosion. In this Texas field Lewis P. Merrill, Willis Nolan and Bennett view the results of one rainstorm.

Developing the conservation plan is actually a process whereby the individual land user selects, from several alternatives within the capability of the land, what they wish to do, based on the type of operation to be carried out, and the individual's or family's needs and preferences.

"Productive land is unlike any other natural resource. It is characterized by the element of life placed by Nature in the thin mantle of fruitful soil occurring over a limited portion of the earth's surface. It is this life-producing quality that makes some lands productive, and it is the absence of this quality that makes some lands barren. Productive land is further differentiated from other natural resources in that it must be maintained and used simultaneously; it must be kept intact while in use. All other natural resources, with very few exceptions, must be taken from the earth -- separated from it -- in order to be used by man. The exceptions are certain forms of wildlife and those natural areas which, because of their aesthetic values, are kept in the original state.

"Productive land is much more limited than commonly has been supposed. It occurs only on the surface of the earth, and only on part of this surface. It is not permanent. Once the fertile topsoil is washed or blown away, it cannot be restored or replaced in any practical way for generations. And what is left -- subsoil -- usually is far less productive, or sterile, and less stable. There are no undiscovered reserves of productive land of any substantial area. We cannot dig deeper into the earth and find new productive soil. We cannot pump it from wells, plant it with seeds, or dig it from mines. We must keep what we have or do without, for when soil has been washed or blown into the oceans it is not recoverable. Assorted residues of sand and gravel left stranded along streamways are of small value. Productive land is the only natural resource without which we cannot live."

> Hugh H. Bennett, speech at the Engineering
> and Human Affairs Conference at Princeton
> University, October 2, 1946.

These conservation plans, based as they are on soils and their proper treatment, have been the basis of a great deal of criticism of Bennett's approach. Critics from the extension services were quick to assert that the plans neglected economic analysis, failing to plan the farm from the standpoint of production economics.[25] Others pointed out that the plans were too complex, took too much technical time to develop, and were of limited value to farmers.

But despite these criticisms, which have continued from time to time over the years, no alternative approach has come forth to displace the idea that a planned approach to the installation of an integrated conservation management system is both sensible and workable. Bennett's approach to conservation planning, although under constant scrutiny, debate and revision, remains as a basic feature of the soil and water conservation program in the 1980's, a half-century after its introduction.

Conservation Districts Proposed

The conservation district idea emerged in the mid-1930's when it became apparent that the demonstration program could not go on forever, and, even so, that it could never reach all the lands in the nation needing conservation treatment. As one student of the district movement said, "Society, in undertaking soil conservation as a goal, had to require more of the farmer-citizen than the mere refraining from doing an illegal act. Rather, as in the achievement of so many of the new tasks for which society has made government responsible, the citizen had to share positively in the performance of soil conservation."[26]

The demonstration program had shown that the control measures developed through research were practicable and could be applied on any land if only the necessary information and technical assistance could be provided in a way acceptable to the people who owned and operated the land.

It had also shown, however, that there needed to be some way to enforce the five-year agreements which SCS made with farmers; some way that did not impose federal regulations directly on the farmer. Because of similar problems, the Bureau of Reclamation had begun to work with irrigation districts authorized and operated under state laws. A local soil conservation district might play this role, in addition to being able to raise some local financing to assist in the installation of projects.[27]

The idea of establishing local special-purpose districts to bridge the gap between federal technicians and private land owners had a gestation period of at least three years. No one can be certain as to the parentage, but midwives and godfathers were plentiful.

In a report prepared in November, 1934, for the National Resources Board, one of the recommendations made by Hugh Bennett, as Director of the Soil Erosion Service, was "that states should be encouraged to pass legislation authorizing: (a) cooperation with the federal government in erosion control; (b) the organization of conservancy districts or similar legal sub-divisions with authority to carry out measures of erosion control; and (c) the establishment of state or local land-use zoning ordinances where lack of voluntary cooperation makes such ordinances necessary."[28]

A month later, Ward Shepard's committee in Interior, in the report that also recommended transfer of SES to the USDA, suggested an organization of landowners in these words: ". . . the work of the Soil Erosion Service would be more valuable if the landowners in the demonstration area had a more active part in the establishment of the project, in working out the general plan for erosion control, and in the continuation and expansion of the erosion control program beyond the demonstration stage. Also it is believed that close cooperation would result in a more substantial part of the program being carried out at the landowner's expense than is now the case."

"The committee recommends that as a condition precedent to the establishment of any new demonstration area, the Soil Erosion Service require that the landowners organize and set up the machinery for active cooperation in the demonstration project and in the continuation of the whole program. The committee further recommends that new projects be initiated only after a convincing showing that a sufficiently large number of landowners are willing to execute contracts to insure an effective demonstration."[29]

One of Bennett's first requests to Secretary Wallace after transfer of SES from Interior to Agriculture in March, 1935, was for legal assistance to analyze state legislation authorizing the formation of "conservancy" districts. At about the same time, in testimony before the Subcommittee on Public Lands of the House of Representatives, Bennett said provisions should be made for "carrying out practical erosion control measures . . . in cooperation with conservancy districts or other subdivisions of states and other erosion control associations or similar organizations."[30] Secretary Wallace's Committee on Soil Conservation, in its June, 1935, report, recommended; "That on or after July 1, 1937 . . . all erosion control work on private lands, including new demonstration projects, be undertaken by the Soil Conservation Service only through legally constituted soil conservation associations."[31]

Public Law 46 authorized the Secretary of Agriculture to require enactment of safeguards for the enforcement of state and local laws imposing suitable permanent restrictions on land use for erosion control; agreements as to the permanent use of such lands; and contributions in money, services or materials.

The conservation district idea was evolving. The next step was to develop a proposal for state legislation that could put the idea into action. The result was the development of a model, or standard act, for use as a guide by the state legislatures.

Standard State Districts Act

The Standard State Soil Conservation Districts Act reflected the thinking of many, but the principal architect was probably M. L. Wilson, Assistant Secretary of Agriculture, USDA's representative on the Land Planning Committee of the National Resources Board, and Chairman of the USDA Land Policy Committee. Wilson had often discussed with

Bennett the pros and cons of how to tackle the erosion control job. He told Robert J. Morgan that he got the idea of soil conservation districts in a talk with Representative Jones, Chairman of the House Agriculture Committee, during a discussion of allotting AAA funds to proposed wind erosion districts in Texas if the legislature passed enabling legislation.[32]

The man responsible for the actual drafting of a standard act that would be constitutional in all states and embody the thinking of those holding differing views was Philip M. Glick, Chief of the Land Policy Division in the USDA Solicitor's office.

A draft of Glick's standard state act for creating soil conservation districts was submitted to the National Resources Committee by Assistant Secretary Wilson in October, 1935. The final version was published May 13, 1936. The standard act provided that land occupiers could organize soil conservation districts as local governmental subdivisions of the state. It set up procedures for establishing districts, and defined their duties and powers.

The steps to establish a district included a petition to a state soil conservation committee signed by at least 25 land occupiers, to be followed by a public hearing by the committee, which would define the boundaries of the district and conduct a referendum on whether the district should be formed. A majority of the votes cast in the referendum had to be favorable.

The standard act provided districts with powers to carry out research in erosion control; conduct demonstration projects; direct prevention and control measures; make agreements with land occupiers and give them various kinds of assistance; make loans of equipment and conservation materials; take over federal and state projects; build and maintain structures; accept contributions of money, services, and materials; and propose land-use regulations.

The act recommended that a state soil conservation committee should consist of the heads of extension and the experiment station, the state secretary or commissioner of agriculture, and a member to be appointed by the Secretary of Agriculture. The committee's major function was to encourage the formation of districts and to carry out the steps needed to create them. The act provided that districts would be governed by five supervisors -- two appointed by the state committee and three selected by the land occupiers in the district.

Secretary Wallace did not accept the recommendation of his soil conservation committee to handle the soil conservation program largely through the state extension services. He chose instead to carry out his authorities under Public Law 46 through soil conservation districts.

Why did Wallace make this decision? Robert Morgan said, "Wallace did so for several reasons, but three stand out." Morgan wrote:

"First, under the 1914 agreement, state extension services were not effectively responsible to the Secretary for program planning and execution. Second, the President and Congress had directed the Secretary of Agriculture to plan and execute a new program which would consist not merely of techniques which farmers might adopt or ignore as they chose. Rather, it should be based on national, district, and individual farm conservation plans to be enforced, ultimately, by the police power of the states. And, third, the state extension services had valuable contributions of a technical character to make to the program, but the Secretary could not always rely on them to carry out the Department's objectives, regardless of the political party in control of the national administration. He feared that if the traditional pattern of relations with extension were followed, the power of the extension services and the American Farm Bureau Federation as interest groups would be vastly increased relative to his own."[33]

The state extension services and the land grant colleges, and their ally, the American Farm Bureau Federation, headed by Ed O'Neal of Alabama, vigorously opposed the standard act. O'Neal argued that such districts were not needed and would infringe upon the exclusive right of the state extension services to carry all agricultural programs direct to the farmers. It was hard for extension to accept the fact that a federal agency should be demonstrating soil conservation and providing technical assistance directly to farmers -- a function previously carried out by the land-grant universities and state extension services.

At a series of meetings in October and November of 1936, various committees of the Association of Land Grant Colleges argued against the idea of districts and also registered opposition to the SCS regional offices. So formidable was the attack that even Hugh Bennett was alarmed. After all the years of frustration, he finally had a good thing and he began to fear breaking more new ground. He suggested substituting certain existing state laws for the standard act, but the Secretary's office held firm.

In January, 1937, the land grant college group made another direct effort to stem the tide. Bennett was summoned to Wallace's office to face an impressive array of officials from the USDA and the agricultural colleges. Bennett recalled that several state extension directors were in the group. The objective was to sell the Secretary, and get Bennett's approval, on an amendment to Public Law 46 that was in the hands of Senator John Bankhead of Alabama. The amendment would remove from the SCS all its functions except research and surveys and give Bennett more time to "rest, write, and think."[34]

Bennett told Wallace, in front of the group, that he didn't like any part of the proposal, that it had taken three decades to develop and sell a soil conservation program that was acceptable to farmers, and he was sorely

Shocked by the trend of events, the American Farm Bureau Federation and the Committee on Extension Organization and Policy made common cause against the New Deal's Department of Agriculture. From this time forward, the Farm Bureau made the extension services of the land-grant colleges its official "chosen instrument" for administering some agricultural programs. Frightened by drastic losses of membership, the American Farm Bureau Federation turned to the colleges and demanded that they use their county agents to organize a Farm Bureau in every state to the point where the Federation would have no serious rival as the voice of American agriculture. The college extension directors, frightened by the rise of the AAA, the Resettlement Administration, and the Soil Conservation Service as rivals with superior fiscal resources and popular programs, committed the extension apparatus to the task of increasing the membership of the American Farm Bureau Federation. The alliance, which had existed legally or in fact in more than half the states, by this exchange of telegrams, was made a national alliance. In the years which followed, this alliance waged a determined, often muted, battle to "decentralize" the Department's soil conservation program.

This move on the part of the college and Farm Bureau leadership signalled a lack of confidence in the Department at the very time when Wallace and his associates were beginning to understand the difficulties of administering "action" programs through extension. The dominance of a single party in rural county governments, especially in the Republican Northeast and Midwest, made extension unreliable. If the Farm Bureau and extension alliance could control the conservation program with the understanding that the county agents were to encourage farmers to join the Farm Bureau, the Department would soon be faced with a single axis of power in agriculture capable of exercising a paralyzing influence over national policy.

Robert J. Morgan, *Governing Soil Conservation*, pp. 48-49.

disappointed at the attempt to disrupt a successful, on-going program just because another group claimed it could do the job better without offering any proof that it could. The next day, after the visitors had returned to their home bases, Wallace again summoned Bennett and confided that he "hadn't slept much" the night before. He told Bennett that the amendment in the hands of Senator Bankhead would not receive his support, and that so far as he was concerned, the SCS would continue as it was.[35]

The growing pressures finally brought help from the White House. Franklin D. Roosevelt had been overwhelmingly re-elected in 1936, much to the surprise of some opponents of the conservation district idea and of the New Deal as well, and his power and prestige were at a new high.

Late in February, 1937, President Roosevelt sent the governors of the states a copy of the Standard State Districts Act and a letter that said in part: "To supplement the Federal programs, and safeguard their results, state legislation is needed. At the request of a number of states, and in cooperation with them, the Department of Agriculture has prepared a standard form of suitable state legislation for this purpose . . . . The Act provides for the organization of 'soil conservation districts' as governmental sub-divisions of the state . . . . I hope you will see fit to make the adoption of legislation along the lines of the Standard Act part of the agricultural program for your state."

The states began to act on the recommended legislation in early 1937. The federal soil conservation effort began to shift from a program of demonstrating conservation techniques to one of reaching out to involve farmers and others in the design and operation of the program itself. Perhaps more importantly, in terms of the ultimate directions the program would take, USDA was promoting the creation of a new set of operational and political allies at the local and state level; allies that would often find themselves in a competitive position with the Department's traditional friends in the land-grant universities, as well as with other units in USDA and the rest of the federal government. The new program would be not just an experiment in conserving natural resources; it would be an experiment in the application of government to natural resource problems in a democracy.

The Emergence of Districts

2

Within a week after President Roosevelt's letter reached the Governors, Arkansas became the first state to enact enabling legislation. The House passed the bill by 81 to 3, and the Senate acted by a vote of 30 to 0. Governor Carl E. Bailey signed the bill on March 3, 1937. Gordon J. Swearingen credited the bill's passage to "tireless and effective lobbying" by a Russellville attorney, Reece Caudle, who later became a prominent state and national leader in the conservation district movement.[1]

Twenty-seven states passed conservation district enabling acts in 1937 and 1938, but only 12 of the laws fully met the goals of the standard enabling legislation, according to an evaluation sent from SCS to Secretary Wallace on December 1, 1938.[2] Ten more states enacted legislation in 1939. In many states, the laws were opposed vigorously by the state extension services and the Farm Bureau. In others, token opposition was expressed, or support merely denied. A few extension leaders let it be known that they did not oppose the legislation and a very few expressed themselves as favorable.

In Kentucky, the battle lines were drawn squarely. Opposed were Dean Thomas P. Cooper of the College of Agriculture, University of Kentucky, and Director of the State Extension Service and the State Experiment Station; Ben Niles and Ben Kilgore, President and Secretary, respectively, of the Kentucky Farm Bureau Federation; and Hubert Meredith, Attorney General of Kentucky and a large farm owner. On the pro side were "Uncle Joe" Robinson of Lancaster, floor leader of the House of Representatives; Representative J. Wood Vance of Glasgow, sponsor of the bill in the House; Senator H. Stanley Blake of Carlisle, sponsor of the bill in the Senate; the *Louisville Courier-Journal* and the *Louisville Times*; and many local Grange and county Farm Bureau leaders, including August Threlkeld of Corinth, a Farm Bureau director who later helped to organize the National Association of Soil Conservation Districts.

Representative Robinson, whose name was attached to the legislation by amendment, had been injured in an automobile accident and was on crutches. He masterminded the legislative activities from a chair command post, using staff aides to scurry here and there to this and that trouble spot.

County extension agents flocked to the capitol at Frankfort to buttonhole their legislators. The *Courier-Journal* and the *Times* published almost daily news stories and frequent strong editorials. Their letters-to-the-editor columns were loaded with pro and con statements. Stormy hearings were held, at which charges and counter-charges flew. SCS employees were accused of lobbying.

Through it all, Robinson remained unperturbed. His strategy was to bottle up every single piece of agricultural legislation. "When our bill passes, I'll let some of yours out," he told the opponents. And that's the way it was. The battle was finally concluded with the passage of the legislation, and it was signed into law by Governor Keen Johnson in March, 1940.

Ohio had a long history of conservation legislation and action. It had enacted the first state conservancy act in 1914 under the leadership of Governor James M. Cox, who was later the Democratic candidate for President, leading the ticket that included Franklin D. Roosevelt as the Vice-Presidential candidate in the 1920 election. Ohio had established two great conservancy district projects, one mainly for flood control in the Miami Valley, and the other for multiple-purpose water management, with accent on flood control, in the Muskingum Valley. And it had amended and modernized its pioneering 1914 conservancy act in 1937.

The Ohio Farm Bureau Federation, long known for its independence in the American Farm Bureau Federation, took exception to the national group's stand on soil conservation districts enabling legislation and became the main sponsor of the bill. The job was turned over to the Federation's veteran legislative representative, Ed Bath. Stocky, white-haired Bath, a man whose booming voice belied his short stature, "took charge" of the district bill.

The Ohio Extension Service did not oppose the legislation. In fact, its leaders generally expressed support for it. Oddly enough, the main opposition came from the Ohio Grange through its State Master, Walter Kirk. The Grange, in most states, had supported or at least had not opposed legislation for districts.

Ed Bath wore a hearing aid of sizeable proportions, and was so sensitive to the actions and prospective actions of committee members and others that he was often accused of being able to "tune in" across the room. Bath and his helpers had to get the districts bill passed twice. After the first enactment, it was vetoed in a surprising move by Governor Martin L. Davey, who attacked it as "trespassing on the rights of farmers by forcing them into land-use regulations controlled by the federal government." The bill passed the second time around, with Ed Bath still in the driver's seat. Ohio, once districts were authorized, organized them at a rapid rate.

An outstanding example of unusual state cooperation in the enactment of conservation districts enabling legislation was in Maryland. H. C. (Curly) Byrd, President of the University of Maryland, personally went before the state legislative committees and asked them to enact the districts law. He gave it his personal guarantee and said it was a good thing for the state. Byrd often said he was influenced in this by his long-time friend and former faculty member, Oscar C. Bruce, then SCS State Coordinator for Maryland, and had always been proud of his action.

For many years, conservation districts were kept out of the Tennessee Valley Authority territory, embracing portions of seven states, through an arrangement between the TVA Board of Directors and the land grant colleges.

TVA contracted with the land-grant colleges in each state to carry out all aspects of agricultural work, including soil conservation. This consisted largely of improved uses of fertilizers, a TVA product. TVA provided funds to the colleges to hire assistant county agents for soil "improvement" work. The TVA-college combine was successful in opposing the creation of conservation districts. Their arrangement not only kept out SCS and conservation districts but other USDA "action" programs as well, a point of controversy between at least three Secretaries of Agriculture and several TVA Boards of Directors.

While the organizational competition to the new soil conservation district law was significant, it was far from the only problem facing sponsors of the district idea. In many states, the opposition was plainly partisan -- and the problem was Secretary of Agriculture Henry Wallace and the New Deal Democrats. Wallace did little to hide his distrust of the rural Republicans that ran the courthouses in much of rural America, and they, in turn, were as adamantly opposed to everything the New Deal stood for. In Missouri, for example, internal correspondence in SCS during 1937 pointed out that the most significant opposition to the district law came from the leader of the Missouri Farmers Association who was said to be "absolutely against all measures which he thinks Secretary Wallace has approved."[3] In later years, soil conservation issues have been notably non-partisan in nature, but this was far from the case in the first few years.

In addition, there is considerable evidence that not all SCS people were 100 percent supporters of the district idea. In 1936, SCS was operating 141 demonstration projects and 450 CCC camps. These activities were highly popular, and new demands for projects and camps were regularly received in Washington, a fact not lost upon either Hugh Bennett or the Members of Congress whose districts were benefitting from the SCS work. Bennett was a pragmatist. His goal was to get conservation practices on the land. If the political opposition to conservation districts threatened to impede that process, Bennett was willing to look for other organizational options.

As a result, Bennett tried to get the Department to relax its request for conservation district legislation and allow other state laws or state-created special districts to suffice. The Department held its ground, and Secretary Wallace finally imposed a deadline on SCS: after July 1, 1937, states with satisfactory state district laws would be eligible for new SCS demonstration projects; those without would not.[4]

Legislative Patterns Emerge

In spite of considerable opposition in many places, by July 1, 1945, all 48 states had passed districts enabling acts. Puerto Rico and the Virgin Islands passed district laws in 1946; Hawaii and Alaska followed in 1947. During the eight-year period (1937-1945) in which states were passing district laws, many changes were made in the standard act. While most states followed the general outline of the federally-suggested bill, many of them differed in certain particulars. Considering the pioneering nature of the legislation, and the forces arrayed against its passage in many states, it seems surprising today that so many state laws adhered so closely to the standard act.

Some eliminated or thoroughly watered down the provisions for land-use regulations. Some enabling acts required a simple majority in a referendum to establish a district. Others required up to a two-thirds majority. Some provided for an appointed governing body to operate the district, others an elected body, and still others a part-appointed, part-elected body. Wisconsin pioneered in eliminating the referendum, giving authority to the county governing body to create a district, a procedure adopted later in New York and Pennsylvania.

New Hampshire created the entire state as a district, allowing the counties to become "sub-districts." Alaska did likewise. Some states provided for district organization by watersheds, others by counties. West Virginia specified 13 districts for the state and prescribed the boundaries, authorizing counties within the boundaries to join "their" district through a referendum. Only two states, Colorado and California, included the power to levy tax assessments among the authorities of districts, but the tax power was tightly circumscribed.

Land Use Regulations -- A Major Issue

There is no doubt that the initial thinking behind conservation districts was based in large measure on the hoped-for value of these new units in establishing and enforcing land use regulations as a parallel activity that could support and protect the conservation work being recommended by USDA technicians (and cost-shared by public funds).

One of the efforts to address the land use problems of the 1930's was a significant national land use planning thrust. A National Planning Board had been established in 1933; to be followed by a National Resources Board which would, in turn, be succeeded in 1935 by a National Resources Committee. USDA had been an active participant in these activities and some of the names so prominent in early SCS and district history, Rexford G. Tugwell, M. L. Wilson, and Milton Eisenhower, for example, are also widely remembered for their role in the national land use efforts of the era.

It is well to remember, however, that the type of land use regulation foreseen in USDA (the ability to regulate certain types of conservation treatment on certain lands) is different, and considerably more narrow, than land use regulations such as zoning, which establish the permissible uses on a parcel of land.

As explained by Wilson, a key feature of the district enabling legislation was the requirement that each district prepare a comprehensive erosion control plan which could serve as the basis for proposed land use regulations. The regulations would be subject to a vote of the landowners in the district; if favorably approved, they would be imposed and administered by the district.[5]

As late as 1942, SCS divided states into three categories to decide how to "target" SCS assistance. States in the first category were eligible for the full range of SCS services; those in the second received reduced help, and those in the third none at all. The adequacy of the state's legislation in regard to land use regulations was the major factor in deciding to which category each state was assigned.[6] But land use regulation of any kind was then -- as now -- a contentious idea in rural America, and few state legislatures were ready for such a law.

Some of the state legislatures that enacted district enabling acts in 1937-1938 amended their laws in the 1939 legislative session. The North Dakota act, which restricted the application of land use regulations to lands under written agreement between the district governing body and the land user, was amended to make the regulations applicable to all lands in the district.

The California legislature gave districts the power to adopt regulations by amending its act of 1938, which did not authorize land use regulations. New Mexico amended its act to provide for establishment of a "range land zone" and a "farm land zone" in each district that contains both grazing land and cultivated land. The amendment provided: Two of the three elected supervisors to be elected by the owners of the land in that zone containing the larger proportion of the total number of landowners of the district, and one to be elected by the landowners of the other zone. Land use regulations were to be separately submitted for each zone, and landowners could vote only on the regulations applicable to their zone.

By July, 1951, 33 of the state laws included the authority for districts to adopt land use regulations or conservation ordinances, but by 1967 the authority had been used in only three states -- in several districts in Colorado, one in North Dakota, and one in Oregon. Colorado, in particular, was active in this area and quite a few court cases ensued over this issue -- one going to the State Supreme Court. The issue lay dormant for decades, and not until 1982 -- in response to tremendous problems created by huge acreages of fragile grasslands being plowed up and planted to wheat -- would land use regulations return to active use in a few conservation districts.

There are several reasons, it would seem, why the early emphasis on the need for land use regulations to achieve widespread adoption of conservation measures on private lands never resulted in actual controls in more than a few locations.

Philip Glick, the author of the Standard State Districts Act, has said that these regulatory powers have remained largely unused because, "the number of private landowners that want to cooperate with their districts and request assistance from them has always exceeded the manpower and equipment the districts have been able to call upon to satisfy these requests. The districts naturally choose to stretch all their resources to satisfy these requests, leaving them no time, or motivation, to deal with the enactment and enforcement of ordinances that would compel the unwilling landowners to join in conservation efforts."[7]

D. Harper Simms wrote that "the land-use regulations aspect of the standard act proved to be an obstacle to its passage in many states and was often dropped before enactment of the measure. What is more significant is that conservation districts found they did not need such power . . . they found persuasion and the force of local sentiment much more effective in obtaining compliance with the local program."[8]

There is considerable evidence then, in retrospect, that there may have been two significant reasons why land use regulation was never accepted as a significant part of the conservation district movement. First, it was politically unacceptable, both at the state and local levels. Secondly, it was clearly not the first thing, nor the most important thing, needed in the fight against soil erosion. The first thing was the challenge to educate people to the need for erosion control, and convince them that practical measures to combat it were, in fact, available. Once that realization had been accepted by the majority of farmers, regulations to reach a "recalcitrant minority" might be acceptable. For many decades, however, it was not the "recalcitrant minority," but the "well-meaning majority," who laid claim to all of the service and attention the new program could muster.

First Conservation Districts

The first soil conservation district in the world was chartered August 4, 1937. It was the Brown Creek District in North Carolina, and it included Hugh Bennett's native home.

Fourteen other districts in six states were organized that same year. Many of them later split into county-size districts from multiple-county districts. The 14 other "first" districts were Upper Savannah and Edisto,

THE BROWN CREEK SOIL CONSERVATION DISTRICT -
FIRST IN AMERICA

Here was established the first district in America for a systematic program of land erosion control. Known as the Brown Creek District because it embraced the area of the Brown Creek Watershed, it heralded the beginning of a national program of soil conservation districts.

The Brown Creek District included the plantation birthplace of Hugh H. Bennett, "father of soil conservation" (A). Bennett, born in 1881, graduated from the University of North Carolina in 1903, and became a soil surveyor in the Bureau of Soils, Department of Agriculture. Observing that soil erosion ruined much good land throughout the United States, Bennett slowly initiated a program to prevent this waste. On April 27, 1935, Bennett became director of the Soil Conservation Service, a position which he held until his retirement in 1952. By this time soil conservation was a national concern, largely because of the work of Hugh Bennett and his associates.

The success of the soil conservation district program was due to local participation by farmers and landowners. Conservation districts were created throughout the United States. Bennett and his specialists worked with the farmers in the districts for an effective program.

The Brown Creek District was established in 1937. In May thirty local property-owners petitioned the State Soil Conservation Committee "That there is need, in the interest of the public health, safety, and welfare, for a soil conservation district to function in the territory hereinafter described." The district would embrace 120,000 acres, much of it badly eroded. The petition was approved on May 31. A public hearing, held on July 3 at Wadesboro and followed by the mailing of ballots to the local farmers, resulted in an overwhelmingly favorable vote for creating the district. The North Carolina Secretary of State issued a certificate setting up the district on August 4. The Brown Creek District became the example for districts of the future.

This marker stands today to mark the historic spot where the first conservation district in America was created.

South Carolina; Coosa River and Broad River, Georgia; Tri-County and Brown-Marshall, South Dakota; Minersville, Utah; Lower East Saline, Mine Creek, East Central Arkansas, Magazine, and Green County-Crowley Ridge, Arkansas; and Moapa and Virgin Valley, Nevada.

By 1940, more than 300 districts covering 190 million acres had been organized. "Billion acre day" was achieved on June 9, 1947. On that day the San Juan Soil Conservation District in Colorado was chartered, bringing the total land in districts to a billion acres. By 1950, the number of districts had climbed to 2,164.

From Demonstrations to Districts

Although the SCS began to work with conservation districts in 1937, its demonstration program continued during a transition period of several years. Between August, 1937, and July 30, 1944, when all demonstration projects were terminated, SCS was engaged in a gradual phasing out of its demonstration work. Emphasis was then placed on technical assistance to landowners who cooperated with their conservation districts.

The basis of SCS assistance to conservation districts was a memorandum of understanding between the individual district and the Secretary of Agriculture following development by the district's governing body and presentation to the Secretary of a work program in which the district

> "Conservation districts will unify a number of the different action programs which the Department is now authorized to carry on. Through local soil conservation districts the Department should be able to assist farmers in formulating and executing comprehensive plans for bringing about wise land use. I think it is important, therefore, that the districts should not come to be looked upon as having significance only for the program of the Soil Conservation Service, but that they should be seen as local governmental units, organized democratically . . . and possessing the necessary governmental power to . . . carry on well-rounded agricultural programs. The districts will need the help of most of the agencies of the Department and, in turn, they can help the Department as a whole to carry out more effectively the various programs it is administering."
>
> Henry A. Wallace, in a letter
> to Hugh Bennett dated December 10, 1937,
> quoted in *Governing Soil Conservation*,
> pp. 82-83.

outlined its problems and what it proposed to do about them. The departmental agreement authorized all agencies of the USDA to help districts in whatever way they could.

SCS, the only agency receiving funds from Congress earmarked for assistance to conservation districts, normally signed a supplemental working agreement with each district. This agreement spelled out what SCS and the district would do. In broad terms, SCS provided professional conservationists to help plan and carry out the district's conservation program and the district determined the recipients of services and set priorities for the kind and amount of work.

The district is charged with the preparation of a long-range program and work plan which spells out the general outline of what the district will do, and what each of the cooperating agencies will be asked to contribute. In the first years, each district's program and work plan was reviewed within USDA by the Department of the Solicitor, the Coordinator of Land Use Planning, and the SCS. This was a sore point with Extension, however, who argued successfully that this constituted federal control over the local programs. In 1940, after several meetings between SCS and Extension, as well as internal staff meetings within SCS, Secretary of Agriculture Claude R. Wickard issued a new policy that abandoned the requirement for Departmental clearance of the district plans. Thus ended the short era when local districts were required to meet the standards of a federal agency in order to be recognized by USDA.[9]

The district, in turn, signed a cooperative agreement with land users who asked for help. This form, too, was prescribed by SCS in the beginning, but many people criticized this as too much standardization, left over from the old demonstration project days. As a result, the form of this agreement was allowed to vary from state to state. In general, it provided that the land user prepare and follow a conservation plan, and that the district would furnish technical assistance, a soil and land-capability map, and other materials and services needed to help the cooperator carry out his plan.

The early results of the district programs were evident in many communities around the country. In Arkansas, the Louisiana Bankers Association visited the Sylvania community in Lonoke County in July of 1947. Afterward, this was the way their magazine described what had happened as a result of the conservation district program in that community:

"The community was going broke 10 years ago. Soil erosion was cracking the land wide open and soil depletion had relentlessly cut down production until it took 4 or 5 acres to make a bale of cotton. The school district was in debt. Teachers made as little as $40 a month. Most of the farmers owed money. It was hard for many operators to pay the interest

Farm plans were the basis for the district's assistance to landowners. This is the site of the first farm plan developed in the nation's first conservation district.

on their loans, and some didn't.

"But since that time has come a complete shift in the use Sylvania folks make of their land. They used to farm, now they dairy. Their Soil Conservation District is responsible for the change."[10] The programs of districts were making a difference -- and changing entire communities.

A major new factor in the equation was the district governing body, and the men and women who were chosen to serve in the early districts had to establish what this new type of public entity would entail. This was a new adventure for, as George Bagley, NACD Past President, has observed, "at the time of their beginning, they (districts) represented a totally new concept in the relationships between federal, state and local units of government."[11] There was no precedent.

The state law gave them authority, but no guidance. The districts were empowered to conduct surveys, investigations, and research relating to soil erosion and control, carry out preventative and control measures, develop comprehensive plans for the prevention of soil erosion, and enter into agreements which landowners and other units of government. In 33 states they could adopt land use regulations, using procedures that were usually complex and cumbersome. But few people knew what all that really meant, and how to translate it into action on the local level.

In contrast with the county and community committeemen serving the ASCS (then called AAA or PMA) programs of USDA, who received a per diem payment for every day they worked on the federal programs, the vast majority of conservation district officials were unpaid, and in many states the districts did not even have enough money to reimburse super-

> "Action by American farmers marks the beginning of a movement
> that can insure the permanency of our nation. It provides for the
> permanent security of a basic resource of our nation -- productive soil
> -- without which it cannot survive. Until this step was taken, it could
> not be rightly said that our country was the most progressive nation
> on earth -- with respect to the care of the land -- but I see no reason
> why we cannot say it now.
>
> Soil conservation districts are non-political. They serve all lands
> within their boundaries. Local governing bodies control district affairs
> without personal profit or financial gain. No soil conservation district
> is responsible to any federal agency. This is a voluntary farmer
> movement for the common good of all the people, both agricultural
> and industrial. These facts are enough, it would seem, to convince
> anyone that the American people have found a way of solving their
> land problems. Such locally-organized, locally-managed districts can
> handle the agricultural lands of this country in the best interests of the
> entire nation."
>
> Hugh Bennett, "Report to the Secretary
> of Agriculture," July 16, 1947.

visors for their out-of-pocket expenses except in rare situations. So
district officials, in the main, donated their time, paid for what needed
paying for, and also exerted the patience, resourcefulness, ingenuity and
perseverance that any new enterprise demands.[12]

One of their most vexing duties was try to make peace between the
local representatives of the SCS, Extension Service, Forest Service, and
the AAA. They realized that the conservation program would never work
unless all agencies cooperated, but they were not neutral parties in the
fray, since it was the very existence of the district that was at issue in some
situations.

In the process, there needed to be a defined role for the district
officials. As lay persons, they were not trained in the technical sciences of
conservation; that role was carried out by the SCS person serving the
district. However, in many cases, the technical role was seen as the only
function for the district, and the question then became "why a district?"

The answer that was expressed by many of the pioneering district
officials, and that has come down over the years, is that the districts have
provided the guiding hand, the practical touch, that mediated between the
technical orientation of SCS and other agency technicians, the often-
confusing methods of operation common to government agencies and
programs, and the pragmatism of farmers. Carried further by far-seeing
district officials, the concept of the district has been extended toward the

fuller potential embodied in the enabling legislation -- a locally-operated "department of natural resources and conservation," seeking help from a variety of sources and coordinating a program that results in maximum benefit to the people and the land of the district.

But even today, evidence demonstrates that this progress has been neither swift nor universal, and there have been many times during the intervening years when the question "why a district" has come up for debate. That districts have not only survived, but prospered in this crucible of testing is a tribute both to the insight of the original creators of the district concept and to those pioneering lay people who put the concept into action.

1944 Districts Study

By January 15, 1944, when 45 states had enacted district enabling legislation, and about 900 districts including more than 500 million acres had been organized, USDA initiated a study to determine how the philosophy underlying the district laws was actually working out.

In the spring of 1944, the SCS, the Federal Extension Service, and 19 state extension services made individual studies of the administration of 69 soil conservation districts in 19 states. The objective was to find "how effectively the state extension services and the SCS were lending strength to district administration." The study was conducted in California, Iowa, Kansas, Maryland, Michigan, Mississippi, New Mexico, New York, Oklahoma, Pennsylvania, South Carolina, South Dakota, Utah, Vermont, Virginia, Washington, West Virginia, Wisconsin, and Wyoming.

A few highlights from the report indicate how the district movement was evaluated after six years of activity.

"1. The concept of governing bodies as to their responsibilities varies from those who consider themselves advisory bodies to those who believe they are in charge of soil and water conservation work and should initiate and direct all such work in their districts.

"2. Governing bodies are capable of assuming greater responsibilities.

"3. Extension services do their educational work in steps leading to district organization and in initial stages of operation but have only partially met the need for continuing education after districts have been formed.

"4. SCS employees sometimes exercise undue influence in district administration, partly because they work full time and need to make frequent decisions. Sometimes they take action in matters for which the board is responsible.

"5. More assistance is needed by districts from the state soil conservation committees (boards or commissions) after districts are organized."

It was evident that in a few years conservation districts had become prominent on the national scene. No other agricultural movement in American history had escalated so rapidly from birth to general acceptance. It was apparent by the early 1940's that conservation districts were here to stay -- that a new way had been found to cope with the nation's land and water problems -- and that the new way was, despite its imperfections, a way that worked.

"One question, of a dual nature, seems to be dominant. Half of the question is, how far should assisting agencies go in influencing or affecting district administration? The other half is, how far should district supervisors go in guiding agency representatives?

In some instances, agencies are becoming concerned lest district supervisors influence too much the activities of agency representatives. Many boards of supervisors, on the other hand, are awakening to their full powers and responsibilities, and occasionally a board becomes restless in the belief that it is too much restricted by agency policies or practices.

Let us hope that history will show that district supervisors and cooperating agencies were able together to determine accurately their respective functions, maintain the right balance in all phases of operations and administration, and make soil and water conservation endure through democratic processes."

USDA Study on Districts, 1944.

"Perhaps the most encouraging dimension in supervisor administration is that, within so brief a period as ten years, so much progress has been made in developing processes, organizational devices, and techniques for a productive operational merging of the skills of the conservation technician and the farmer supervisor. The resulting cross-fertilization of national and local experiences promises increasingly to produce a sounder and better proportioned approach than if either technicians or farmers were attempting to go it alone."

W. Robert Parks, "Effort to
Synthesize National Programming with
Local Administration in Soil
Conservation Districts," PhD Thesis,
U. of Wisconsin, 1948, p. 133.

State Soil Conservation Agencies

An integral part of the Standard Enabling Act drafted in USDA was the creation of a state agency to oversee the establishment and operation of districts. The Enabling Act called the agency a "State Soil Conservation Committee," and many states adopted that name. Others, to retain consistency with state governmental structure, called the new agency a "Commission," "Board" or "Council." Many observers found it hard to distinguish this agency from the other agencies that worked in the district movement -- SCS, Extension Service, or, for that matter, from the districts themselves.

The Standard Enabling Act called for the Director of the State Extension Service, the Director of the State Experiment Station, and other un-named people to be members of the committee, along with an invitee from USDA. Again, there were many variations as states adopted the act, but it was common for the early committees to be composed entirely of state and federal officials -- usually 4-6 in number.

The committee's major task in the beginning was to assist in the formation of soil conservation districts. In the typical state, they were to receive the petition signed by at least 25 land occupiers and then officially designate the boundaries of the proposed district. They then arranged the necessary public hearings and referenda called for under the state's act. In most states, once the district formation process was complete, the committee duly certified that the district was in existence and named at least two district supervisors to the first district board. Normally, an election was held to choose three others for a full board of five, but this, too, varied somewhat by states.

Clearly, the personalities on the first state committees had much to do with the progress of district formation in the state. In most states, the committee had little or no appropriation with which to operate, so it was up to the members to function as best they could. Where the state's Extension Director was fully in support of the district concept, extension staff people were named to aid district formation, letters went out to encourage county agents to begin the educational process, and applications from localities were processed fairly rapidly. Where the Extension Director opposed districts and used his committee position to create obstacles, a different process emerged. Both situations, as well as many in between, existed.

Funding became an immediate problem, as many states had created the committee with little or no appropriation. Public hearings, legal advertising, and conducting elections cost money, and took skilled people. As more and more districts were formed, another need emerged -- funding for assistance to the districts themselves. State soil conservation agencies were called upon to provide training for district officials, or field men who could visit the districts and explain district law and operating procedures. In many states, districts were eager to begin their own action programs at the local level, but there needed to be a source of funding for that, if it were to happen, and virtually no states had granted taxing powers to districts as part of the original law.

All these pressures began to move district officials toward the amendment of their state's district law to create a stronger, more politically aligned state committee, with the authority resting in lay leaders rather than agency officials. Many of these changes were not easily gained, and took a few years, along with some strong leadership by district officials themselves. Nolen J. Fuqua, in an oral history interview with Douglas Helms, SCS historian, told of a fairly contentious battle in Oklahoma in about 1940 to switch from a committee of state agency representatives to a committee made up of a district official from each congressional district in the state. "We weren't getting anything done," Fuqua relates. "So we decided the best thing for us to do was some more reorganizing."[13]

The outcome was a state committee, in Oklahoma as in most states, with members appointed by the Governor on rotating terms. The State Association of Districts is normally asked for nominations, but the Governor is usually free to ignore them if he chooses. The state committee (or commission, board, etc.) then oversees a professional staff who function as state employees, either within a larger state department or as an independent state agency.

These state agencies were able to be more closely tied in to the state's normal budgeting cycle than were the original interagency committees, and could provide not only the direct service to districts, but also serve as the advocate of an active state role in the soil conservation program.

As more and more districts were formed, and states became completely covered, it became common for the state agency to direct its energies more to action programs of its own. In addition to helping districts with training, operational guidance, and funding support, many state agencies gained state funds to assist in watershed planning, conservation education, soil surveys, and a variety of other activities.

The soil conservation movement thus was transformed from a totally federal activity to a truly intergovernmental program involving local and state efforts in a significant way. These involvements are never very clearly defined, and efforts to separate them into neat categories are usually futile. As Philip Glick is fond of saying, "Ours is not a layer-cake form of government but a marble cake. Each layer of government makes indispensible contributions."[14] Every task is woven back and forth between and among the three layers: federal, state and local.

With the states and territories serving as different, and often, unique, laboratories for the political development of the program and the districts working to keep the technical and administrative standards associated with soil conservation from being so burdensome as to be unacceptable to people in the local setting, a truly national soil conservation effort could become a reality. Without the contributions of the state and local partners, the federal effort would have been short-lived. Without a vigorous, active, centrally-directed technical program from SCS, however, the evidence strongly suggests that nothing significant would have happened to address the soil erosion problem. It is this seeming enigma that baffles many who try to make a clear categorization of the soil conservation program.

Robert Parks put it this way: "The peculiar value of the district lies in the fact that it is a hybrid in government. The test of its worth is its capacity to merge the best values of local government and national planning in its operation."[15] Thus, as districts attempted to fulfill their difficult and rather ill-defined role of pulling together all of the agencies into an ordered, effective local conservation program, the role of the state agency in helping them understand and accomplish that difficult mission was a critical one.

State Associations

Conservation district officials keenly felt the need to exchange ideas with each other and to work together in an organized way, for they were breaking new ground, and guidelines were few. And, since most of them served without pay and usually at some out-of-pocket cost and at considerable personal sacrifice, they needed all the help they could get from colleagues in other areas who were trying to cope with problems similar to their own.

The first known state-wide meeting of conservation district officials was held at the University of Arkansas in Fayetteville on May 31, 1938. It was called as a training meeting, not an organizational meeting, by the Arkansas State Soil Conservation Committee and the State Extension Service. Thirty-six supervisors of the state's 10 conservation districts participated in an all-day discussion of their duties and responsibilities. After listening to lectures all day, they decided to meet that evening by themselves. As a result, they organized the nation's first State Association of District Supervisors, and elected Reece Caudle of Russellville, Chairman; Dr. F. W. Cox of Pocahontas, Vice-President; and Fred Williams of Yellville, Secretary-Treasurer.[16]

By 1941, many states had organized state associations. Today, all 50 states and Puerto Rico have active state associations of conservation district officials. The Virgin Islands and the District of Columbia, each with only one conservation district, function as an association by themselves.

In a 1970 year-end message, NACD President John S. Wilder said the state associations "are steadily becoming stronger, more effective, and more useful in advancing the purposes of the nation's 3,000 individual districts." He called the state associations "an indispensable link in the chain of district work to improve our land, water, forest, fish, and wildlife resources for the benefit of people" and said "their operations provide the opportunity for district officials to act in concert to achieve needed state legislative action, secure necessary appropriations, develop resolutions leading to national policy, and achieve educational and other vital objectives."

Regional Associations

The first officially recorded effort to organize beyond the state level was made by a small group of conservation district supervisors from Arkansas, Oklahoma, Louisiana, and Texas. Meeting September 23, 1941, at the Grim Hotel in Texarkana, Texas, they formed the "Affiliated Association of Soil Conservation District Supervisors." E. T. Powell of Marion, Louisiana, Chairman of his state association, presided. The group adopted a constitution and bylaws so far-seeing that much of the language and the ideas were included in the basic documents of the national association several years later.[17]

The new regional association adopted these major objectives: "(1) to promote to the utmost the conservation of soil and water resources for the good of our country and its people; (2) to bring about exchange of information that will insure a constructive conservation program; (3) to encourage uniformity of basic policies and objectives in soil conservation work; (4) to assist in securing coordinated assistance from all available sources on local, state or national levels to the end that the greatest possible permanent benefit to the lands and people within the districts may be obtained; (5) to foster and develop active farmer participation and leadership in conservation and in the affairs of soil conservation districts; and (6) to assist the districts in the conservation program in all manners possible."

The constitution limited membership to soil conservation district supervisors and to state associations, thus establishing the principle that no general membership organization was contemplated. The officers elected at the Texarkana meeting were Dan C. Sparks, Texarkana, Texas, President; Nolen J. Fuqua, Duncan, Oklahoma, First Vice-President; and David B. Means, Gloster, Louisiana, Second Vice-President.

In addition to the officers and Powell, the following participated in this historic "first"; Walter W. Cardwell, Luling, Texas; Vernon Howell, Stillwater, Oklahoma; W. E. Moncrief, Arlington, Texas; C. E. Martin, Velma, Oklahoma; V. C. Marshall, Temple, Texas; Reece Caudle, Russellville, Arkansas; and Glenn T. Wallace, Nashville, Arkansas.

Another meeting was held in Spartanburg, S.C., on February 4, 1942, with representatives from Alabama, North and South Carolina, and Virginia attending. E.C. McArthur of South Carolina pushed hard for a regional or national association, but the war was in progress and the time did not seem right.[18]

Nolen Fuqua recalls a meeting at Auburn, Alabama, probably in 1942, called by SCS Chief Hugh Bennett to get SCS, districts and AAA together to iron out their differences. As Fuqua relates the story, they broke up into committees to present their points of view and, at the end of the day, left the meeting with their organizational differences largely unresolved. The district officials present, however, met afterwards and determined that some kind of national association was going to be needed if they were to be able to get their views heard.[19]

The need for a national association of district supervisors had been discussed, then, in several meetings over a period of two years or so. This idea evidently appealed strongly to Fuqua, then Chairman of the Oklahoma State Association, for in drumming up attendance to the second meeting of the "Affiliated" association to be held at the Youree Hotel in Shreveport, Louisiana, on March 30, 1942, he referred to it as the "annual meeting of the National Association of Soil Conservation District Supervisors," in a letter to R.C. Longmire, Pauls Valley, Oklahoma, dated March 20, 1942.

Fifty-five district officials from the four states attended the second meeting of the "Affiliated" association at Shreveport, as well as the following: Louis P. Merrill, Fort Worth, SCS Regional Conservator for the region; J.W. Sargent, Merrill's assistant; Dr. J.G. Lee, Jr., Dean of Agriculture, Louisiana State University and Chairman of the Louisiana State Soil Conservation Committee; E.H. Hudson, SCS State Coordinator, Arkansas; H.B. (Joe) Martin, SCS State Coordinator, Louisiana; Paul Walser, SCS State Coordinator, Texas; and J.L. Jordon, SCS Area Conservationist, Natchitoches, Louisiana.

Nolen Fuqua, one of the speakers, said that, in his opinion, the people of Oklahoma were in favor of a national organization of districts and, at his suggestion, a resolution recommending that a national organization of conservation district supervisors be organized for the "purpose of further advancing the soil and water conservation program," was adopted.[20]

Sam H. Burchard of Gonzales, Texas, Chairman of the Middle Guadalupe Soil Conservation District, was elected President of the regional group, and the representatives of each state elected the following Vice-Presidents: Reece Caudle, Arkansas; David B. Means, Louisiana; R. C. Wood, Texas; and Nolen Fuqua, Oklahoma. Each supervisor of districts in the four-state region was assessed $1, with 25 cents of each dollar assigned to remain in each state. The assessment was levied by the state vice-presidents by mail.

The Soil Conservation Society of America

It was not just the district officials who felt the need to organize; that urge was running through the professional corps in SCS as well. Professional soil conservationists by then numbered in the thousands, but had no communications network outside the formal bureaucracy of SCS. As the first President of the Soil Conservation Society of America (SCSA), Ralph H. Musser explained it, professional soil conservationists, "had no common meeting ground, no medium for joint expression, and no unified strength for advancement."[21]

As a result, the SCSA was formed in Chicago on November 11, 1941. Due to the war and other circumstances, nearly two years elapsed, however, before the founders proclaimed its formal organization on September 1, 1943. The goals of SCSA were to provide a forum where soil conservationists could seek agreement and unity on professional standards, as well as scientific objectives. Among its early missions, as outlined by Musser, were:

(1) "To undertake to stimulate, collect, and put to use the best scientific thought, in and out of government circles, on soil and water conservation;

(2) "To present the professional soil conservationists' point of view, whenever that seems advisable, to the public, to appropriate branches of government, and to other societies; and,

(3) "To evolve certain professional standards, as guides, for the conduct of soil and water conservation work."

The SCSA, by the time it published its first issue of the *Journal of Soil and Water Conservation* in 1946, boasted 14 chapters, and a steadily increasing membership of over 1,700.[22]

Failure of a Mission

Conservation districts had become a potent force in the states by the mid-1940's. As World War II ended, enterprising district officials, adopting the "swords into plowshares" theory, urged transfer of heavy-duty military equipment to peacetime uses such as protection and development of the nation's soil and water resources in conservation districts. They convinced the governors of a majority of the states to appoint representatives, mostly conservation district officials, to represent the state at a meeting in Washington, D.C., in support of surplus equipment transfer legislation introduced by Representative W. R. Poage of Texas.

Fifty-eight men, 49 of them conservation district officials, from 40 states, went to the nation's capital in January, 1946, to urge the enactment of legislation authorizing transfer of military equipment to conservation districts. They met with House and Senate members and, with the help of Governor (later Senator) Robert Kerr of Oklahoma, unofficial leader of the mission, had a conference with President Harry S. Truman. But the bill providing for the transfer of equipment died before it could get out of committee. The districts had failed.

The failure of the first national legislative effort was an eye-opener. The lesson learned was that it was quite possible to be treated cordially by members of Congress, and even by the President of the United States, and still fail to win support. It was apparent that they lost simply because they were in an unorganized group speaking with many voices rather than one. They had no "national muscle." The setback was made to order for those who for several years had been urging formation of a national organization.

And so, before they left Washington, D.C., those of the delegation who were conservation district officials met at the Statler Hotel to talk about the need for a national organization and a national office to coordinate the activities of districts. Out of these discussions came a course of action. The group authorized E. C. McArthur of Gaffney, South Carolina, to select a committee to begin the work of organizing a national association of conservation districts.[23]

Assignment for McArthur

The choice of McArthur (Mr. Mac) was a happy one. A gentle, pleasant man who had a sly sense of humor, he nevertheless was not one who could be pushed around, and this was a quality he sought first of all in others. Mr.

E.C. McArthur was born in Gaffney, South Carolina, on March 7, 1882. He became a leading farmer and auto dealer, and one of the pioneers who promoted the formation of soil conservation districts.

By 1938, McArthur was calling for the formal organization of a state-wide association of the people who, like himself, were trying to learn how best to serve as a conser-

vation district official. When the state association was formed, McArthur was elected as its first President.

E.C. McArthur was a charter member and President of the Gaffney Lions Club and an active member of the Buford Street Methodist Church. He was a Supervisor and Chairman of the Broad River Soil Conservation District of South Carolina from February 28, 1938, until his death.

He was elected to assemble a committee to establish a national association of soil conservation district supervisors, and upon formation of the National Association of Soil Conservation Districts, was elected its first President. His letters, speeches and pamphlets on soil conservation were filled with compelling prose to promote the soil conservation cause. He died in an auto accident on September 8, 1947.

Mac, one of six children, worked on his father's farm in Cherokee County, South Carolina, until he was 21. Then he bought 140 acres and worked in a laundry, a store, a bakery, and a cotton gin for the money to pay for it. In 10 years he owned his farm free and clear, and also was the successful owner-operator of an automobile agency. He was an original member of the board of supervisors of the Broad River Conservation District and was perhaps the prime mover in organizing the South Carolina State Association of District Supervisors.

An idealist and something of a philosopher, Mr. Mac expressed himself in words that became familiar to thousands as he traversed the country: "Where there is a need, there is an opportunity and a great responsiblity;" "plan your work and work your plan;" "the philosophy of soil conservation districts is the basis of democracy: the people know what is best for them and when they make up their minds they can get whatever they want, for the people are the most potent force in any nation."

When President R. F. Poole of Clemson College, South Carolina, accepted a portrait of Mr. Mac at ceremonies in the college chapel on August 17, 1950, he called the subject "a fearless leader and searcher for truth" and said the painting would be an inspiration to future generations as the portrait of "a great teacher and a great missionary."

Ellen S. Cobb of Spartanburg, South Carolina, first Executive Secretary of the NASCD who worked with Mr. Mac from 1938 until his death in September 1947, knew him perhaps better than anyone outside his family. Mrs. Cobb said: "Soil conservation was Ed McArthur's religion. To save the soil was an obsession with him. He accepted it as his mission. He worried over barren hillsides and steep slopes and the streams that run red with the lifeblood of the land."

T. Lee Gaston, a long-time aide of Hugh Bennett and close personal acquaintance of McArthur's, recalled to Hal Jenkins of SCS that McArthur had told him several times in 1947 that if he were elected again as President, at the 1948 annual meeting, he would not accept. Gaston said that when he asked him why, Mr. Mac replied: "The possibilities and the job are too big for my abilities; I was able to get it started, but after that I knew it was too big for me."

Mr. Mac began selecting his organizing committee with great caution. He wrote to many, and he double-checked and triple-checked each name suggested. His correspondence was handled by Ellen Cobb, much of it actually written by her, and it was voluminous.

Mr. Mac made it clear his main requirement was for dedicated soil conservationists, men who believed without reservation in the conservation district idea, men whose first loyalty was to the soil and water conservation movement, men who were not interested in using the movement as a means of self-advancement. "I realized the committee should be composed of men with a love of the soil in their hearts, men of character, ability, aggressiveness, and purpose," Mr. Mac said.

During the committee formulation period, Mr. Mac was also busy in another area: trying to raise money to defray the expense of postage, printing, travel and other incidentals. The first two important contributors, $1,000 each, were General Motors in March, 1946, and International Harvester in May, 1946. Both responded to letters from Mr. Mac.

McArthur's letter must have been a masterpiece -- at least an undated note from Ellen Cobb to David Stewart of NACD indicates that it was -- but copies have not been found. In the response from General Motors Corporation, dated March 15, 1946, John F. Daneke, Department of Public Relations, said:

"While I have always been convinced myself of the importance of soil conservation, I was so impressed with what you said in your letter, that I immediately reviewed the subject again with our executives. I am delighted to report that they were glad to authorize a contribution of $1,000, and our check is enclosed." Many professional fundraisers today would love to pen a letter that elicited such a response!

Other contributions made up to the time of the first annual meeting in February, 1947, were listed in the minutes of that meeting along with GMC and IH. The first list of contributors included John Deere and Co., and Martel Mills Corp. $500 each; Pacelet Mfg. Co., $250; South Carolina Bankers Assn., Virginia-Carolina Chemical Corp., Sunny Slope Farm, Avondale Mills of Alabama, International Minerals and Chemicals of Alabama, and Ernest Burwell of Spartanburg, SC, $100 each. Contributors of amounts less than $100, including several of $50 and $75, were Long Island Produce Fertilizer Co., Robertson Chemical Co., Chilean Nitrate Co., Cooperative Grange League Federation Soil Building Service, and the Herald-Journal of Spartanburg, SC.

Mr. Mac, over a six-month period, found not only some money with which to operate for a little while; he also identified 17 men who passed his personal muster, and he invited them to participate in an organization meeting in Chicago at the Morrison Hotel on July 24-25, 1946. The conservation district movement was about to grow beyond local and state boundaries; it was headed toward national prominence. The major questions were how, under whose guidance, and to what ends.

Birth of an Organization

3

Including E. C. McArthur, the district officials assembled at Chicago to organize the national association represented 17 states. "They were a working committee if ever I saw one," McArthur said of them later. Eleven of the eighteen organizers had attended the Washington, D.C. meeting in January, 1946, when the decision was made to go ahead with a national association.

The evening before the first session, the committee met with invited representatives of business and industry in the Chicago area. The group discussed soil erosion control and its importance to the nation, the duties and responsibilities of soil conservation district officials, and the need for a national organization to speak for them. The meeting minutes list the firms represented: Allis Chalmers, Oliver Plow Co., J. I. Case Co., International Harvester, John Deere & Co., General Motors, The Burlington Lines, The Burlington Railroad, The Milwaukee Railroad, Natural Gas Pipe Line Co. and Sears Roebuck.[1]

At the opening session of the meeting, Mr. Mac set the stage by briefly tracing the development of the soil conservation district movement:

"After the fanfare of appointing and electing us as district supervisors in our own communities was over, we were a pretty bewildered group . . . . Some of us realized we were merely acting in the capacity of rubber stamps and became very dissatisfied, for we were responsible men and wanted to carry out the obligation we had accepted. Therefore, some of us began an aggressive effort to see what our duties are and how we should go about fulfilling our obligation . . . . Many of us older heads . . . were somewhat wary lest our soil-saving program eventually become compulsory by government dictum. We believed that soil conservation districts were based on the democratic idea that the masses are capable of planning and carrying out their plans.

"Many of us have seen the need to approach the Secretary of

The 18 NASCD Founders, left to right around the table -- Everett M. Barr, Liberty, NE; D. T. Paugh, Phillipi, WV; Allen Craig, Springfield, OH; W. A. Groom, Grand Junction, CO; Frank Gyberg, Cornville, AZ; R. L. Rutter, Jr., Ellensburg, WA; E. C. McArthur, Gaffney, SC; Mrs. Ellen Cobb, Spartanburg, SC; R. M. Boswell, Kenedy, TX; William A. Benitt, Hastings, MN; Lloyd Arbuckle, Morocco, IN; Walter Burrall, New Market, MD; Dennis Getchell, Limestone, ME; R. D. Conly, Ringgold, LA; Fred Prell, Bremen, KS; August Threlkeld, Corinth, KY; P. G. Compton, Demopolis, AL; W. M. Hodgson, Bay Minette, AL; and R. Lester Hill, Caro, MI.

The first NASCD Officers and Directors. Front row (l. to r.) -R.L. Rutter, Jr., E.C. McArthur, Dennis Getchell. Back row (l to r.) Allen Craig, R. M. Boswell, Walter Groom, and Fred Prell.

Agriculture, the Congress, and even the President of the United States on affairs of districts. We believe it will be a distinct advantage over individual and state association approaches to be able to present a united front of district governing officials of the United States when dealing with Washington on soil conservation districts' problems.

"It certainly is not our desire to build a powerful political pressure group through which we may unduly influence any other group or the Congress. But we need and want a united body of men who represent the agriculture of our nation to press for and with each other, farmers, agriculture agencies, businessmen, bankers, and individual citizens toward that goal, the conservation and maintenance of our soil, which will mean a better life for this and succeeding generations."

Mrs. Cobb recalls that it "was hot as Hades when those 17 men, plus McArthur, plus little me, sat around a table in the Morrison Hotel, and discussed the merits of a national organization, and I won't deny that some of them were doubtful; but after much talk, that great leader, McArthur, sold his idea."

In two full days of work the committee organized what they called the National Association of Soil Conservation District Governing Officials, elected temporary directors and officers, and adopted the constitution that had been drafted under supervision of William A. Benitt of Minnesota. The committee also adopted a slogan, "Nail Down the Topsoil," suggested by R. M. Boswell of Texas and W. A. Groom of Colorado. Temporary officers and directors elected were McArthur, President; R. L. Rutter, Jr. of Washington, Vice-President; and Allen Craig of Ohio, Fred Prell of Kansas, Dennis Getchell of Maine, Groom and Boswell, Directors. Mr. Mac was authorized to employ Mrs. Cobb as Executive Secretary.

There was some argument during the discussion preceding the adoption of the constitution over the name of the organization. Groom and Benitt felt that membership should not be restricted to district governing officials. The original suggestion of "American" Association was changed to "National" at the suggestion of Frank Gyberg of Arizona.

The Chicago papers covered the organizational meeting and the press associations picked up the news and sent it across the country to the daily press, especially in the home areas of the 18 organizers. The *Chicago Daily News* covered the story under a two-column head that included a picture of McArthur.

The *Alabama Journal* of Montgomery, Alabama, lauded McArthur in an editorial that said in part:

"Mr. McArthur believes fervently that he is engaged in a crusade against an enemy more deadly than the Axis powers; that national salvation and hope depend even more completely upon conquering this enemy; that humanity itself is at stake and human life in the balance. The

> . . . The purpose of the district is to save soil and water by bringing all available assistance to farmers through the district channel and then multiply that assistance by coordinating the efforts of technical representatives of agricultural agencies, civic groups, clubs, businessmen, bankers, legislators, churches, schools, and each individual citizen. The purpose of our proposed national association is to do that same thing on a much bigger scale -- always with the idea in mind of making this a better country in which to live . . .
>
> E.C. McArthur, speaking to the
> organizational meeting of NASCD, 1946.

enemy is soil erosion. Mankind depends on the 7 inches of soil that covers the surface of the earth. One-third of that soil has already been washed and blown away in the United States. Nothing is so precious to man as that soil. Nothing is so valuable as the soil upon which man depends for food to keep him alive, clothes to wear, and shelter over his head. Gold is nothing in comparison. Platinum, iron, uranium, oil, coal -- all amount to nothing if soil is lost and if man loses the means of maintaining life. No one can plead the cause of soil conservation more eloquently or more convincingly than Mr. McArthur."

The *Spartanburg (S.C.) Herald-Journal* quoted McArthur as saying "Get this information out to the people -- erosion and soil conservation comprise the greatest problem confronting this nation, foreign questions notwithstanding."

Mr. Mac wanted dedicated men of the soil for his organizing committee, and he got them, in more ways than one. One story that has been told many times in NASCD circles happened as the 18 delegates were checking out of the Morrison Hotel. The manager approached McArthur with the bill for the meeting room -- $1,000 that no one had contemplated. As McArthur was protesting that he had no money to pay such a sum, a man standing nearby said, "It's all right. Put it on my bill," and the International Harvester Company saw to it that the bill was paid.

If Frank Gyberg of Arizona accurately reflected the sentiments of the founders in a letter written to McArthur a few days after arriving home from Chicago, then Mr. Mac had indeed selected a dedicated group.

"I think we took a great step -- and maybe posterity will be building monuments to us. But if we only staved off hunger for this nation a couple of hundred years or two, the effort will be mighty worthwhile. A man can get damn hungry in 48 hours, which, unfortunately, is about all the average citizen is interested in . . . .

"Sometimes our case looks pretty hopeless until I think of the man Christ, and Him going around almost alone in the beginning, preaching a doctrine of gentleness in the most brutal age (barring our own) in the annals of time. Imagine trying to put over something like that to the Roman centurion or Caesar or the private in the ranks whose whole idea of worth and respectability was war booty and trampling on the weak. So maybe we have something; let's hope we don't get too weary in well doing or discouraged when there be those who by specious arrangement of words and argument can often make a horse chestnut seem to be a right smart chestnut horse.

"The Roman Legions have been out of the picture for some little time now as have a good many of the others with the same idea, but the doctrine of the Son of the Carpenter is still a pretty potent force for those who know how to use it -- I wish I did. It strikes me we're going to have to learn to use it if we want to continue sticking around.

"It was a real pleasure to meet you and your good wife and Mrs. Cobb. I hope I may have that pleasure again sometime. And as for me and you, we have got a helluva lot of work ahead. It now only remains to see how much we can get done. But I guess I don't have to tell you that! It's a real pleasure to meet folks like E. C. McArthur. God bless you."

First Publication

The "Chicago 18" returned to their home bases to begin the hard task of helping to build a new national organization. The job, first of all, was to persuade their colleagues -- in the several states for which they, as temporary directors, were responsible -- that a national association was needed. Other jobs were to help gather finances, to collect dues from those eligible for membership, to encourage formation of active associations, and to arouse interest in the first national meeting, which they had scheduled for February in Chicago -- barely seven months away.

One of the first efforts of the new organization was publication of a pamphlet explaining the purposes of the association, and including the constitution and a statement from Mr. Mac. The pamphlet, titled "National Association of Soil Conservation District Governing Officials," with a sub-title, "An association of men who manage soil conservation districts, democratically organized and operated for the public good," carried on the cover a map of the nation overprinted by the slogan, "Nail Down the Topsoil." It came off the press in August, 1946, just a month after the organizational meeting.

The publication listed the association's major purposes as follows:

(1) To facilitate the exchange of information, knowledge, and experience among soil conservation district governing bodies.

(2) To collect, compile, and disseminate information relating to the organization and effective functioning of soil conservation districts.

(3) To further the functioning of state associations, or other organized groups of members of soil conservation district governing bodies.

(4) To advance generally the organization and functioning of soil conservation districts, including matters relating to applied sciences, processes of administration and management arts used by them.

The constitution specified that the Association would be managed by a Council and a Board of Directors, the Council to consist of one member designated by the membership in each state, and the Board of Directors to consist of seven persons elected by the Council -- one from each of the geographical divisions of the country as designated by the Council. The Directors would elect a President and a Vice President from its members. Members of the Council, Directors, President and Vice President would serve without pay but would be entitled to expenses.

Soil conservation district governing officials and state associations of such officials were cited as eligible for membership and the dues were set at $1 a year per member.

From the Ground Up

The next few months were busy ones for McArthur. In addition to carrying on a voluminous correspondence, he attended many meetings and invariably left behind a more enthusiastic group of district officials than he found. During the few months between the organizational session in July and the first annual convention in February, he participated in meetings in Montana, Illinois, Mississippi, several New England states, New York, Pennsylvania, North Carolina, Alabama, Tennessee, and Colorado. Mrs. Cobb represented him at a meeting in Georgia.

The Directors were busy, too. The activities of Dennis Getchell, Director for the Northeast, are an example. Getchell corresponded with the chairmen of district governing bodies, urging support for the national association. He arranged a meeting of district officials at Springfield, Massachusetts, that was attended by 35 supervisors from New Hampshire, Vermont, Massachusetts, Rhode Island, and Connecticut. Getchell reported that those who attended were "greatly impressed by Mr. McArthur and his masterful presentation." Mr. Mac later assisted in completing the

"Unless you do your job well, and unless districts succeed, we run the risk of losing our soil. We also run the risk of inviting government land regulation or of reverting to the old and ineffectual demonstration methods of the past. Neither of the alternatives is anywhere near as desirable as success with the program we now have in conservation districts.

"Our job is to keep what we have by making it work better than any agricultural undertaking ever before attempted. So far we are doing just that. We have made an excellent beginning. We are conserving our land. We are on the right road. We, the farmers and ranchers, control this conservation program ourselves -- instead of some state or federal agency.

"We must help each other in order to do an even better job. We must help each other so that the work of each one of us will be more effective, easier, and surer. Working together is the American way of doing things.

"Join your fellow district officials. Work with us. Let us work with you. All of us -- each of us -- want the same things. We want to protect the soil and water resources of our district -- and use them better than they've ever been used before -- so that all our friends and neighbors in the district will have a better life. And so that our children will have a chance to prosper too.

"Through the National Association of Soil Conservation District Governing Officials you can keep in touch with what is going on in other districts all over the country. You can benefit -- your district can benefit -- from this information.

"By joining the national association your district will be helping in doing a better job. Your district, in turn, will help others. By joining the national association your district will help build the strength that comes with numbers. This is a big job. It will take great strength to complete it. The strength of all of us -- WORKING TOGETHER."

E.C. McArthur, National Association of
Soil Conservation District Governing Officials

organization of the Maine state association at a meeting in Bangor. As a direct result of the Springfield meeting, according to Getchell, state associations were organized in New Hampshire, Connecticut, and Vermont the following month.

At year's end, district officials were sending in membership dues slowly. In a December 30, 1946, letter to Allan J. Collins, SCS State Conservationist for New Hampshire (and presumably to many others), McArthur, after saying that the first national meeting had been postponed from February 18 to February 25, 1947, listed 114 districts from 32 states that had paid membership dues to date. Leading the list was Tennessee, with 13; followed by Oklahoma, 12; South Carolina, 10; and Texas, with 7 districts paid.

In this letter Mr. Mac also said: "We are concerned with the need for each state to select a member of the Council who will be able to attend the meeting in Chicago February 25, and the need for each state to pay the expenses incurred by the Council member in attending this meeting . . . . We hope eventually to raise enough money to pay expenses of Council members but have not been able to do so yet. Therefore, it will be necessary for you to impress upon supervisors the need for each state bearing this expense for the February 25 meeting."

Name Change

The name of the organization was shortened from National Association of Soil Conservation District Governing Officials to National Association of Soil Conservation Districts shortly before the first annual meeting.

Apparently no one knows when this action was taken, or how. The original name was still in use late in 1946. And the minutes of the first annual meeting do not record an action to change the name. None of the surviving members of the organizing committee can recall details about the name change, and the files accumulated by Mr. Mac from early 1946 to the first annual meeting in February, 1947 have disappeared.

The best guess is that the change was made informally, probably by Mr. Mac with the concurrence of some of the temporary directors. In any event, the National Association of Soil Conservation Districts -- the second of four names the organization was to have -- was the official name when delegates assembled for the first annual meeting. This name was retained until 1962, when it was enlarged to the National Association of Soil and Water Conservation Districts. At the 1970 convention in San Francisco, the name was shortened to its current form, the National Association of Conservation Districts.

First Annual Meeting

Forty-two of the then 48 states were represented at the first annual meeting in Chicago when 69 delegates convened for a two-day session on February 25, 1947 -- a testament to the diligence of Mr. Mac and the association's temporary Directors. Once again the Morrison Hotel was the locale.

Louisiana was the leader with 10 delegates, followed by Alabama with five, and Georgia and Wisconsin with four. Ohio had three. Arkansas, Indiana, Minnesota, Virginia, West Virginia, and North Dakota were represented by two each. Thirty-one states were represented by one each. Two future Presidents were registered: Kent Leavitt of New York and Nolen Fuqua of Oklahoma.

There was a lot of talk at the first meeting, mostly centered on the conservation program and its progress and problems in the various states. These men had to get acquainted, and everyone was asked to speak freely. The program was informal; the agenda flexible. A rough count of the minutes of the meeting indicates that at least 48 of the 69 delegates spoke during the meeting, which included an unscheduled two-hour night session on the opening day.

The Directors elected Mr. Mac President, Rutter First Vice-President, and Boswell Second Vice-President -- all by acclamation. The elected Directors "drew" for length of term with the following results: One year - McArthur; Guy Van Cleve, Montana; Lloyd Arbuckle, Indiana; and Irving Hudson, Delaware; Two years - Parley P. Smith, Utah; August Threlkeld, Kentucky; A. N. Chamness, California; and Reece Caudle, Arkansas; Three years Getchell; Rutter; Everett Barr, Nebraska; Gyberg; Boswell; and Alfred Wiger, Minnesota.

TELEGRAM

The Honorable Harry Truman
The President of the United States
Washington, D.C.

In the first meeting of the National Association of Soil Conservation Districts, representing nearly 1800 districts in the 48 states of the Union, we respectfully call attention to the tenth anniversary of the establishment of soil conservation districts and request the spotlighting of this momentous event in United States agriculture by designating the week of August 4 as National Soil and Water Conservation Week for our Nation, to the end that our country shall never forget its responsibility for conservation. Pledging our cooperation in this worthwhile matter, we are respectfully,

            THE NATIONAL ASSOCIATION OF
            SOIL CONSERVATION DISTRICTS
            E.C. McArthur, President

By geographic areas the Directors were paired as follows: Northeastern - Getchell and Hudson; Southeastern - McArthur and Threlkeld; Upper Mississippi - Wiger and Arbuckle; South Central - Caudle and Boswell; Northern Great Plains - Barr and Van Cleve; Southwestern - Smith and Gyberg; Pacific - Rutter and Chamness.

Des Moines, Iowa, was selected for the second meeting. This was after invitations had also been extended from California, Mississippi, Texas, Utah, South Dakota, Florida, Tennessee, and South Carolina. All recommendations were withdrawn when McArthur suggested that Iowa be selected because of its central location and the need to make the meeting as inexpensive as possible for those who must "pay their own expenses."

A discussion of continuing problems with the Farm Bureau and Extension was inevitable. Reece Caudle brought it up. "Under the district program we are going along and doing a good job. We are having some trouble, and let's talk about what that trouble is," he said. Caudle continued: "There are some agencies who should help do this job, but they are pulling back. There is a place for all agencies with no overlapping. I am opposed to the suggestion that some agencies take over the duties of other agencies . . . . This association should get in touch with O'Neal, sit across the table from him and see what can be done about it. Let's stop this." Caudle was referring to Mr. Ed O'Neal, President of the American Farm Bureau Federation, who had proposed assigning the SCS programs to the state extension services. The major SCS program, of course, was technical assistance to conservation districts.

Rt. Rev. Msgr. George J. Hildner of Missouri, who had introduced himself earlier as having "hitch-hiked here; we passed the plate a second time," said, "You can't pussyfoot forever. Let's not sit around and be afraid of stepping on somebody's toes. This is a war to defend our largest inheritance . . . . It's time all this quarreling is over. In some states things are fine; others are in a terrible fix . . . . Gentlemen, walk out of here with your heads up, chest out, with determination that this thing must be done and every American citizen must be urged to do something concrete about it."

August Threlkeld of Kentucky: "I was on the mission to Washington to get surplus equipment, and the sad thing was that a leader of a national farm organization was working to see that we should not have it; the bill was killed in the Rules Committee. We could not get it out. This farm organization contributed to holding that bill in the Rules Committee."

Dave Johnson of Alabama: "A group of district supervisors attended that last annual meeting of the Farm Bureau in California and we said that we did not want the bill where you are going to turn this over to the Extension Service. We were told, 'you just don't know what you are talking about. You are poor misled fools.' Ed O'Neal said he was going to push for a bill and that it would have the support of the American farmers."

Frank Feser, South Dakota: "Let's get to the grass roots. You hold the destiny of soil conservation in your hands. Senators and Representatives also hold this destiny in their hands. Those are the ones we should

> "If we fail to conserve our soil, the government will enforce land use regulations upon us. This is regimentation and regimentation leads to dictatorship. We can regulate all this through organization that is real democracy in action. Within a period of ten years, all states in the United States have recognized this thing and have taken steps to do something about it . . . . 1,760 individual districts have tried, independently of each other, to win the fight against erosion. That battle was equal to guerilla warfare, with little accomplished. Then the districts within the states began to organize into state associations. Organization was the answer. Immediately, soil conservation speeded up as supervisors profited by an interchange of advice and experience and activities and as they joined themselves together to deal with agencies on a state level. Now, we have a national association to do, on a national scale, what individual districts and states have been doing. The National Association is composed of supervisors of all the states who have banded themselves together to render assistance to each individual district and each individual district bending its efforts to render assistance to the National Association to protect America's basic asset, her soil."
>
> E. C. McArthur, Speech at
> First Meeting of NASCD, Chicago, IL,
> Feb. 25, 1947.

work with. To the dickens with Ed O'Neal! If we sell those men on it, we will save it . . . . Get hold of your representatives. This is the solution to this problem. Get action. Go home and work with your Senators and Congressmen!"

The discussion ended with the delegates voting favorably on a motion by Measell of Mississippi, seconded by Paugh of West Virginia, to have McArthur name a committee to meet with a Farm Bureau committee and "representatives of any other organizations that seem appropriate," to seek a solution.

Mr. Mac pledged his services full time for the next 12 months. He urged the governing bodies to "run their districts" and said "you can't afford to let bureaucratic agencies rob you of this opportunity and right. It is your responsibility. Let me urge you to take this thing seriously . . . . If we go back home with the determination to make our districts succeed, they will succeed. Organize your districts to the grass roots of each community."

A Plan of Action

Mr. Mac's first communication to the Directors and the Council following the first annual meeting was dated April, 1947. It transmitted a copy of the minutes of that meeting, a preliminary draft of "Plan of Action for the National Association of Soil Conservation Districts," and membership application forms. Following are excerpts from the plan of action that Mr. Mac had prepared and revised after consultation by mail with the Directors:

On membership: All members of the association, and the officers, the directors and council members, and others are expected to explain the association, its purposes, and its work to others. Thereby those interested will know of the association and those eligible may desire to become members.

On state associations: Activities of the national association leading toward exchange of information, knowledge and experience among soil conservation districts will be most effective and efficient if carried out, at least largely, through alert and well operated state associations.

On assistance to districts: The soil conservation districts need, and can wisely use, more assistance for helping landowners and operators plan, apply, and maintain soil and water conservation on their lands. Assistance is needed from all sources - federal, state and local, and private.

On credit: The association will work towards developing sources of sound credit for the districts throughout the country.

On finances: Current estimates are that the national association will need from forty to forty-five thousand dollars a year to effectively carry on its work. Paid annual membership dues of voting members are estimated to be from four to five thousand dollars. Dues from non-voting affiliate members and contributions will, therefore, be necessary if the association performs the work that is essential.

On bulletins and information letters: As an aid to exchange of information and experiences, the association intends to prepare and distribute (a) a bi-monthly or quarterly news bulletin; and, (b) non-periodic information letters containing special information that directors and council members should receive.

First Information Letters

Mr. Mac's Information Letter No. 1, dated April 30, 1947, was largely an account of the SCS budget situation and a report of his (and Kent Leavitt's) appearance before the House Subcommittee on Agricultural Appropriations on April 22. A copy of McArthur's testimony was attached. Mr. Mac warned of a rumored $5 million cut in SCS appropriations and pointed out how this would affect conservation districts.

In appearing before the House committee, McArthur introduced himself as President of NASCD, a farmer, a supervisor of the Broad River (South Carolina) Conservation District for nine years, a member of the Grange, and President of the Farm Bureau in his county. He said he was proud to represent men who "are giving their time and efforts gratis, in the interest of their communities, states, and nation." He emphasized that SCS is the main source of district assistance -- and that districts believe it should continue to be the main source. He pointed out that too many people "think and talk conservation in terms of conservation practices such as terracing, contouring, strip cropping, and so on, but these are only segments of a conservation program."

Mr. Mac also spoke for Extension Service appropriations. "The soil conservation districts need, desire, and can make good use of assistance from the state extension services in carrying on conservation educational activities," he said.

McArthur took a strong stand against transfer or consolidation of soil conservation responsibilities at the federal level. He said:

"The soil conservation districts need, appreciate, and desire assistance from the various state extension services, particularly county agents, but the districts and their national association recognize the necessity of a national agency working on soil conservation and giving the kind of assistance to districts throughout the country that the SCS is now giving. We are strongly opposed to any combining or consolidation of the SCS with the Extension Service or with any other agency. There is more than enough for both services to do, each in their respective fields. We want to see them working harmoniously side by side, assisting the districts to get this great conservation job done for the good of our nation and its citizens."

Information Letter No. 2, dated May 7, 1947, was devoted entirely to an explanation of the differing conservation activities of each of the four main public organizations engaged in soil conservation -- conservation districts, SCS (technical help), state extension services (education), and the Production and Marketing Administration's agricultural conservation program (cost sharing).

In a note to Robert Farnum, New Hampshire Council member, dated May 27, 1947, McArthur suggested that the campaign for affiliate members, highly necessary to support the association, could be more gracefully supported by district governing officials if they, themselves, were members. Almost as an aside, he added: "no dues have been received from districts in New Hampshire."

"The key features of the Farm Bureau-extension plan of reorganization for SCS were plain. A small staff to give 'advice' would be retained in the Department of Agriculture in Washington; this would be similar to the federal Extension Service. The regional, state, and district offices of SCS would be abolished. The work of technicians on the county level would be 'decentralized' to the state extension services and placed under the county agents, as in the TVA area. The PMA would be continued to administer the conservation payments through the county committees. Under this plan, the extension services, at long last, would be solely responsible for all the technical phases of soil conservation and would no longer have to battle with SCS over practices and specifications. The final wisdom in matters agricultural would again filter down to the American farmer exclusively from his land-grant agricultural college. The landscape of rural America would once again be at peace."

Robert J. Morgan, *Governing Soil Conservation*, p. 133.

In Information Letter No. 3, July 24, 1947, McArthur broke the news that legislation had been introduced in the Congress to eliminate the SCS and transfer its functions to the state extension services. The legislation was in the form of three identical bills, H.R. 4150 by Representative Cooley of North Carolina; H.R. 4151 by Representative Hill of Colorado; and S. 1621 by Senators Reed of Kansas and Stewart of Tennessee.

Mr. Mac wrote: "These bills are now being publicized throughout the country by release from Washington. These bills are the old Ed O'Neal -Farm Bureau proposals which I have long been convinced neither are sound nor represent the rank and file of Farm Bureau members. Under the guise of coordination and decentralization, they would eliminate the SCS and turn the funds over to the already overloaded and separate 48 state extension services which were set up solely for educational purposes in all phases of agriculture."

Mr. Mac attached a copy of the Cooley Bill. He said the assumption was that the bills would not be acted upon until the session beginning in January, 1948. He suggested: "Districts in each state, through their state association or otherwise, should get the board of trustees, or other governing body, and the president of the Land Grant College, to provide a written statement or letter as to their position on these bills. Since they have long maintained, and rightfully so, that the scope of these colleges in all three branches -- teaching, research, and extension -- is educational, now is the time for them to restate their position."

In the same Information Letter, Mr. Mac called attention to the 12 percent cut in SCS appropriations for the current fiscal year and said it meant less assistance to districts. He recommended a three-point program: (1) make every effort to get the maximum amount of planned conservation work actually applied on the land; (2) between adjournment of Congress and January, through personal conversations, tours, and otherwise, be sure that members of the House and Senate Committees on both Agriculture and Appropriations understand conservation needs and the work of the districts; and (3) through the President of each Land Grant College and the State Director of Extension, arrange for more and sounder educational assistance to the districts throughout the county agent system, thus lessening the time SCS men have to spend with a farmer and providing more of their time for conservation surveying, planning, and applying conservation on the land.

Information Letter, No. 4, dated August 5, 1947, concerned financing. "We have spent and are spending money for secretarial help, stationery, printing, postage, and travel, and our funds are low," he wrote. He advocated a special campaign for affiliate members. "I suggest that members of each governing body discuss the association with a local banker, equipment dealer, or other leader interested in the district and its work. Such a person, or his business firm, may desire to become an affiliate member and each can, no doubt, give valuable suggestions as to other possible affiliate members."

Mr. Mac's last broadside was addressed, not to Directors and Council members, but to State Conservationists of the SCS. On August 22, 1947, he addressed a "personal-confidential" memorandum to the SCS state officials transmitting a copy of an August 5 editorial from the *Fort Worth (Texas) Press* that blasted the proposed legislation to transfer SCS to Extension. McArthur asked the State Conservationists to "get some Director, Council member, or supervisor in your state to have this editorial reprinted in as many local papers as possible."

The editorial was headed "A Dangerous Plan," and it made the point that "the SCS has provided leadership of a high order, free of politics, and directed solely at one goal . . . often described as the gravest problem facing the nation. To emasculate it would be folly of the highest order." The editorial concluded: "Senators Reed and Stewart, the Farm Bureau and other selfish interests sparking this attack against the soundest agency of the national government are rendering the United States a great disservice."

Death of a Leader

While preparations were being completed for the September 11-13, 1947, meeting of NASCD Directors in Chicago, Mr. Mac was killed in an automobile accident as he was returning to Gaffney from his office in Spartanburg, South Carolina. The meeting took place as scheduled, three days after his death, with the entire first day spent in discussing how to carry on the programs initiated by the first President.

A committee of Directors -- Getchell of Maine, Smith of Utah, and Caudle of Arkansas -- drafted a statement concerning Mr. Mac's death in which they said, in part: "His was the leading influence in the formation of the national association and his profound leadership was an inspiration to all of us . . . We mutually pledge our time and resources to carry on the principles of the association founded under his able leadership . . . We feel a personal sense of loss in his passing."

August Threlkeld of Kentucky, in a letter to Joe Douthit, President of the South Carolina Soil Conservation District Association of Supervisors, on September 22, added this tribute to Mr. Mac: "He will go down in history as one of our men of vision, and I am sure posterity will look on him as being one of our greatest outstanding pioneers in the welfare of our nation."

The Directors elected Kent Leavitt of Millbrook, New York, to fill McArthur's unexpired term. Directors present, in addition to Leavitt, were: Rutter of Washington, Getchell of Maine, Threlkeld of Kentucky, Caudle of Arkansas, Smith of Utah, Boswell of Texas, Barr of Nebraska, Wiger of Minnesota, Gyberg of Arizona, and Chamness of California. Mrs. Cobb was also present.

On the final day of the Chicago meeting a committee of NASCD Directors met with a Farm Bureau committee headed by Ed O'Neal. NASCD officials who attended were Leavitt, Rutter, Threlkeld, Caudle, Smith, Boswell, Barr, and Mrs. Cobb.

Vice-President Rutter, the spokesman, asked the Farm Bureau to support establishment of a new national land policy based on proper land use. He declared NASCD in favor of H.R. 4417, introduced by Representative Ben Jensen of Iowa, that would provide for such a policy, strengthen local administration of the program through soil conservation districts and continue the SCS as an independent agency in Agriculture to give technical assistance to soil conservaton districts. The Jensen Bill also provided for expanded educational help from the state extension services.

The NASCD representatives declared their opposition to the Cooley-Hill, Reed-Stewart Bills that would give SCS functions to the state extension services. They said such legislation, supported by O'Neal,

Kent Leavitt of Millbrook, New York, owned and operated a dairy and beef cattle farm, Fraleigh Hill Farm, for 35 years. A graduate of Milton Academy and Harvard University, he was President of the National Association of Soil Conservation Districts in 1948-49.

He organized the Northeast Duchess County Open Space Committee, which is dedicated to preserving open space and the natural environment. Serving on the Board of Directors and as President of this group led to other endeavors, including the Nature Conservancy and various planning commissions such as Mid-Hudson Pattern for Progress.

Leavitt had been a Director of the Fresh Air Fund for many years and was serving on the executive committee at the time of his death in 1973. He was instrumental in setting up a camp for children, providing healthy outdoor living and education in many aspects of nature. He was in constant demand for advisory bodies and had worked with such organizations as the Town of Stanford Conservation Council, New York Farmers, and the Land Advisory Committee.

An authority on bassets and beagles, Leavitt raised a special strain of small beagles which hunted with all the verve of the large ones.

"would destroy the national soil conservation district program." These bills would create a Farm Bureau-Extension monopoly and result in 48 different weakened programs instead of one strong national one which is adapted to local needs and administered by the farmers' and ranchers' own district," Vice President Rutter said.

No agreement was reached by the two committees, as might be expected from the polarity of the positions. Leavitt labeled the discussions "futile."

The Style of Leadership Changes

Leavitt and McArthur were opposites in almost every respect except in their devotion to the land, belief in the NASCD and its mission, and earnest desire for it to become a potent force in conservation.

Mr. Mac was slow and soft-spoken, rather short and stout, courtly, inclined to be cautious and reserved, and a true son of the South. His successor was a tall, handsome, brusk, aggressive Yankee -- a Harvard graduate who spent three years in banking and five years in the U.S. Consular Service before deciding to become a farmer in 1935. Leavitt was Chairman of the Dutchess County Soil Conservation District, President of the New York State Association, which he had helped organize, and a member of the New York State Soil Conservation Committee by appointment of Governor Thomas E. Dewey.

On Fraleigh Hill's 400 acres in the uplands of Dutchess County, near Millbrook, Leavitt had established an outstanding farm and developed a two-fold retail business -- milk and cheese. Built for a fast pace -- like a football end -- Leavitt seldom relaxed. He always worked at top speed no matter what the job. He didn't believe in wasting time. If he got home from a meeting or trip and half an hour remained before supper, he was more likely to wheel out a piece of equipment and head for the nearest field that needed attention than he was to sit down with the evening paper.

Leavitt was to demonstrate his tremendous energy in succeeding months as he held together the infant organization and built on the foundation laid by Mr. Mac and the organizing committee. He took over the presidency of an organization that had little in the way of funds, files, or office. Mrs. Cobb was the only person who knew all that McArthur had done and had proposed. She was persuaded to move from Spartanburg to Millbrook, New York, and soon was established in a house rented by Leavitt that provided both an office for NASCD and a home for her. Leavitt recalls that substantial financial support from Alabama and Maine and from "other good friends of NASCD" kept the hard-pressed association in business. In addition to ongoing expenses, NASCD owed $2,000 to Mr. Mac's estate.

The six months between September, 1947, and the second annual meeting at Des Moines in February, 1948, were spent in laying the foundation of the NASCD. The new President attended every state association meeting to which he was invited, trying to gain an understanding of the problems that faced districts in the many diverse areas of the country. He also tried to build a picture of what the NASCD could do for state associations and local districts, and to focus the attention of the Directors and the state associations on the problems that were ahead.

NASCD's new office was a rented room in this home in Millbrook, New York.

"Everywhere I met men who were dedicated to solving these problems, both state and national," Leavitt said.

Leavitt was able to report in his first newsletter, Information Letter No. 5, November 1, 1947, that the activities of the association had doubled and tripled in recent months. He wrote: "Letters and requests for information about districts are coming in from all over the country -- from farmers, newspapers, magazines, members of Congress, business concerns of many kinds, and just plain citizens. Officers of the association have appeared before Congressional groups to explain the needs for soil conservation work and the role of districts in our present-day agriculture. Officers of the association have also undertaken to represent the districts in talks and negotiations with the National Grange, the Farmers Union, the American Farm Bureau Federation, departments of the federal and state governments and a wide variety of business concerns."

Leavitt's first newsletter was a long one -- 15 pages in rather small type printed by photo-offset. About half of the issue was devoted to an analysis of the Jensen Bill, to establish a new national land policy, which had NASCD support, and of the Cooley, Hill and Reed-Stewart Bills, to abolish the SCS and turn over its functions to the state extension services, which was opposed by the NASCD but supported by the American Farm Bureau Federation.

The newsletter also included a resolution by the Dutchess County (NY) Farm Bureau, of which Leavitt had long been a member, supporting the further development of soil conservation districts, the maintenance of the SCS as an independent bureau to assist them, and an intensified soil conservation educational program to be supplied by the extension services. Leavitt commented: "I know, and so do you, that the national leaders of the Farm Bureau did not seek the opinion of the rank and file membership before taking their stand to ruin districts and wipe out the national soil conservation program. If you are a member of the Farm

Bureau and feel about this issue as I do, I urge you to seek the adoption of a similar resolution by your own bureau."

Bankers Association Manual

A well-illustrated, 35-page manual, "What Bankers Can Do About Soil Conservation," published in 1947 by the Agricultural Commission of the American Bankers Association, emerged at a perfect time to advance the soil conservation district movement. Despite long-established ties with the Colleges of Agriculture, the state extension services, and the Farm Bureau, the Commission had the courage to publish the manual over the objections to much of its contents by members of its advisory council, all of whom were associated with the Land Grant Colleges.

A. G. Brown, Director of the Commission, C. W. Bailey, President of the First National Bank of Clarksville, Tennessee, and President of the American Bankers Association, and Charles T. O'Neill of the National Bank and Trust Company, Charlottesville, Virginia, and Chairman of the Commission, were the guiding spirits behind issuance of the manual. The author, although not credited, was Gordon K. Zimmerman, who worked a great deal with Leavitt, on loan from Hugh Bennett's staff in Washington.[2] Zimmerman, who later served as NASCD's Executive Secretary, was widely acclaimed as one of the best writers on conservation subjects in America, and was a key member of Bennett's staff. His service with Leavitt was indicative of the degree of support for the new organization within SCS, and his anonymity may have been an indication of the reluctance of either SCS or NASCD to admit that, at this period, the fledgling organization lacked the resources to provide its own staff support.

The first chapter of the manual, "The What, Why, and How of Soil Conservation," gave the current land use picture, and was based on SCS figures that had been disputed by the Land Grant College-Farm Bureau group. Chapter 2, was titled "Conservation Questions Bankers Ask About Soil Conservation Districts."

Chapter 3 covered "Making Conservation Equipment and Trained Personnel Available to the Farmer." Here, the manual discussed the financing of specialized equipment impractical for individual farmers to own, such as graders, bulldozers, ditching machines, slip-scrapers, dibbles and grass sowers.

Chapter 4 dealt with "Bank Loans For Soil Conservation." It pointed out that banks are interested in soil conservation not primarily for the new loan business which can directly result, desirable as any "sound loan may be at the present time, but rather because of the importance of productive soil as a foundation for the prosperity of their community and their customers."

In Chapter 5, "What Banks Can Do About It -- Developing Community Interest in Soil Conservation," the manual recommended that the banker should consider the following as a part of his bank's public relations program: (1) make or arrange for speeches on soil conservation at meetings of bankers or farmers; (2) hold special banker-farmer meetings; (3) give awards for farmers with outstanding performance, and to soil conservation districts; (4) sponsor soil conservation demonstration projects; (5) sponsor farm tours; (6) show exhibits or displays at fairs, in the bank lobby, or windows, or other places; (7) advertise in publications or through direct distribution of mailing pieces; (8) sponsor essay writing contests or other educational projects in schools; (9) show or sponsor motion pictures on soil conservation; (10) distribute literature; and, (11) sponsor erosion and conservation inspections by air.

Des Moines Meeting

Most of the states (40) were represented when 165 delegates came together at the Hotel Savery in Des Moines for the second annual meeting, February 27-28, 1948. Some of the delegates were from states having active state associations that had functioned for several years. Others were from states having only a few recently organized districts and, therefore, little knowledge of problems existing beyond their own boundaries. Here, for the first time, they had the opportunity to discuss the problems that had to be faced if the movement was to become of national importance.

The 13 committees named by Leavitt held separate sessions and the chairmen reported to the entire group at a general session where each report was discussed from the floor. Major conclusions of the general session covered the recommendations of several committees and a wide range of topics.

To bolster the sagging finances of the association, the delegates decided that each state having a state association should pay $5 per district to the national; that in a state having no state association, each district should pay $5 dues to the national, and each district should obtain one or more affiliate members ($25 for an individual and $100 for a corporation).

The delegates advocated three days for the annual meeting instead of two. They resolved that the soil conservation district program be confined to the specific problems of applying the techniques of soil conservation to the land and that other programs designed to bring economic aid to agriculture should be clearly differentiated from the soil conservation program as carried out by the districts. They urged continuance of cost-sharing for soil conservation practices.

In the legislative area, the delegates expressed belief that the SCS should continue as an independent agency in USDA, that it should have funds sufficient to furnish adequate assistance to districts; that an adequate research program, properly financed, was essential to progress; that an adequate program of education through the land grant colleges and vocational agriculture was necessary and should be properly financed; and, that the general principles of the Jensen Bill (for a national land policy) were desirable.

The delegates commended the legislatures of 45 states and Puerto Rico for appropriating nearly $3 million for the district program, but emphasized that as only a beginning for meeting the nation's need. They recommended that an agreement be developed between the soil conservation districts of each state and the forestry commission or similar bodies of the state in order to develop a definitely planned program of reforestation, including the propagation of necessary seedlings. They recommended that, in order to prevent floods, control erosion, conserve water and prevent damage to reservoirs and valuable land, the agencies of the federal government and valley authorities should cooperate with the various states and soil conservation districts in formulating a long-range plan of land and water utilization and erosion control, and that the state and federal governments should bear the total expense of erosion control and land utilization on federal and state owned and controlled land.

Representative Ben Jensen and Iowa Governor Robert Blue met with the delegates at the banquet session.

Following the meeting, seventeen of the more affluent delegates took off in a chartered plane from Des Moines to Chicago and then to Washington via a scheduled flight to appear before the House Agriculture Committee to oppose the Cooley Bill. Eight other delegates went to Washington by train and regular air travel from the Des Moines meeting, also at their own expense. The two groups were joined by delegations from several states, and they spent the week in Washington answering questions, making statements, reviewing hearing proceedings, and spending a lot of time with their Congressmen.

In their visits with members of Congress and testimony before the House Agriculture Committee, the NASCD delegates made the following major points: (1) additional technical assistance to districts is vital; (2) SCS must remain independent of the Extension Service; (3) a new land policy that will keep the soil conservation activities of the government free and clear from any other work is a basic need.

These contacts, perhaps more than any single foregoing action, established the NASCD as an independent group of conservation farmers and ranchers who were determined to promote the democratic use of land and water resources under local control -- and they were not about to let anything stand in the way of this program.

Leavitt was re-elected at the Des Moines and Denver annual meetings, and drove himself unmercifully the balance of 1948 and through 1949. He sent informative and challenging newsletters at regular intervals to every district. He was "on the go" almost constantly, attending state association meetings, making new contacts and new friends for conservation districts.

Mrs. Cobb, at the Des Moines Board meetings, after tributes had been paid to Leavitt by Boswell of Texas and Barr of Nebraska, said: "I want to tell you how much time he has given -- every day and every Saturday and Sunday and nearly every night, sometimes all night. I don't know when the man sleeps."

Mrs. Cobb resigned in June, 1948, and returned to Spartanburg. Morris E. Fonda, long-time SCS employee in Illinois and of the regional office at Milwaukee and later briefly with Friends of the Land, succeeded Mrs. Cobb but left in October to accept a position in industry. He was succeeded by Robert S. Calkins, SCS conservation engineer on the regional office staff at Upper Darby, Pennsylvania. Calkins served until mid-1950.

The Hope Bill

The post-war years saw renewed efforts to "reform" the soil conservation programs, with proposals ranging from transferring all the educational, demonstrational and technical services of SCS to Extension (the Hill-Cooley Bill of 1947) to shifting virtually all the land use, soils and related activities of the Department to the SCS (The Jensen Bill of 1947).[3] Out of this debate came a far more comprehensive proposal to not only centralize many of the USDA conservation functions in SCS, but also provide a policy setting that would expand upon and solidify the policy contained in Public Law 74-46, the basic enabling law under which SCS was operating.

On March 30, 1948, Representative Clifford R. Hope of Kansas, Chairman of the House Agriculture Committee, introduced H.R. 6054,

"The National Land Policy Act." The bill was an outgrowth of the thinking in the Jensen Bill, the writings and speeches of *Country Gentleman's* "Zack" Taylor, and the drafting skill of Gordon Zimmerman, in concert with staff from the House Agriculture Committee.[4]

Leavitt devoted most of his April, 1948, newsletter to an analysis of the bill and urged district officials to study it and give it their support. "In our opinion," he wrote, "this bill makes the soil conservation district one of the cornerstones of the proposed national land policy."

The Hope Bill called for establishing, as national policy, the sound conservation and orderly use and development of the nation's resources, instead of a policy of year to year expediency. It provided for an integrated conservation program and concentration of responsiblity in one agency --SCS. Farmers, through their soil conservation districts and local committees, were to be given a large share of responsiblity for and control over conservation programs.

Organizationally, the bill established the Agricultural Resource Administration in the Department of Agriculture and also an advisory group on conservation, the National Agricultural Land and Water Resources Advisory Board, with the Secretary of Agriculture as Chairman.

The new Agricultural Resources Administration would be made up of three constituent agencies: Agricultural Land Service, Forest Service, and Fish and Wildlife Service. The bill proposed that the Soil Conservation Service, all related functions and activities of the Production and Marketing Administration and the Bureau of Plant Industry, Soils, and Engineering be brought into the Agricultural Land Service.

It provided for outright transfer of the Fish and Wildlife Service from the Department of the Interior to the Agricultural Resources Administration, an action that would return to USDA a function it had lost several years before when the Fish and Wildlife Service was created by transferring the old Bureau of Biological Survey from USDA to Interior and combining it with the Bureau of Fisheries. It was, as Gordon Zimmerman told an interviewer 33 years later, "pretty revolutionary."[5]

Over a period of two weeks, beginning May 5, district officials from all over the country testified before the House Committee on Agriculture on the Hope Bill. They went to Washington in most cases at their own expense and at personal sacrifice of time, and they supported the bill strongly.[6]

The Hope Bill never became law, but it served some useful purposes. It focused attention on the need for a national land policy, or at least a need to think about land policy in a structured way. It influenced the thinking of many political leaders in the legislative and executive ares of state and federal government. A more immediate benefit to NASCD and the conservation districts was its offsetting effect on legislation such as the

Cooley Bill. With the Chairman of the House Agriculture Committee offering a strong pro-SCS bill, those wishing to dismantle the agency had a significantly more difficult battle to face.

The Cooley Bill was killed, due in some measure, no doubt, to the testimony of the conservation district people who came from all parts of America to tell the benefits that districts and SCS assistance had brought to them and their farming endeavors.

Historians of the conservation movement differ, however, on how important the young NASCD group was in this battle. Charles M. Hardin of the University of California, in discussing the political allies of the Soil Conservation Service in 1952, said, "by all odds the most important is the National Association of Soil Conservation Districts (NASCD)."[7] A much lesser role was attributed by Robert J. Morgan of Resources for the Future, who wrote in 1965 that, "The National Association of Soil Conservation Districts did not play an important role in blocking the American Farm Bureau's plan of reorganization in 1948. It (NASCD) was still quite new . . . ."[8]

The Third Meeting at Denver

A convention of 400 or more enthusiastic district officials and their families and friends was not surprising to the Colorado soil conservationists, for they often attracted that many to their state association meetings. But a rousing meeting of that size was an eye-opener to district officers who came from across the land for the third annual NASCD meeting in Denver February 15-17, 1949.

Leavitt found the meeting "a most stimulating and wonderful experience." Registered were 334 district officials from 42 states. The meeting followed the Des Moines pattern. Seventeen major committees reported on a comprehensive array of subjects. Major speakers were Robert S. Wilson, Vice-President of Goodyear, and Palmer Hoyt, Editor and Publisher of the *Denver Post*. Both stressed the importance of the work being done by conservation districts and linked it with the future of the nation.

A major decision was that Directors serve for two-year terms and be elected by the Council from the seven areas so that their terms would expire on alternate years.

The following month Leavitt addressed the 14th North American Wildlife Conference in Washington, DC. The speech attracted national notice and focused favorable attention on NASCD. The speech, "Watershed Management," was published in the Congressional Record of March 15, 1949, at the request of Representative Jay Le Fevre of New York.

"The United States is on the threshold of the greatest conservation progress the world has ever seen," Leavitt told the assembled conservationists. "Consider some of our assets. We, as conservationists, are better organized today than ever before. Numerically we are stronger. We have made a great deal of progress in actual conservation work. Our technology is steadily improving. We have more friends than we have ever had, and they represent all walks of life. More people understand what we are talking about and doing. More people share our aspirations. And perhaps most important of all, we are learning to make common cause.

"The time is about past when the forester thinks only of forestry, the soil conservationist only of the land, the engineer only of his structures, and the biologist only of birds, fish, game, and other forms of life. We are all coming to understand the interdependence of land, water, forests, and wildlife. They all fail or prosper together. The same is true of human beings. Our part in this situation is the most vital of all. . . .

"Watershed management, based on use of the land in accordance with its capabilities and treatment of it in accordance with its needs, means improved agriculture, improved water supplies, reduced sedimentation, reduced flood hazards, protection for downstream engineering structures, more and better wildlife habitats, and improvements in range and woodlands . . . .

"I hope those of you who are in wildlife, forestry, and water-conservation organizations will recognize that you have a new and strong ally in soil conservation districts. The men in soil conservation districts are with you, and for you. They realize that all of us must stand together . . . .

"There is a middle ground between regimentation and rugged individualism. This middle ground is a partnership shared by the individual and government, without any loss of integrity on either side. There is an almost unlimited opportunity for development of this partnership in the watersheds of the country.

"We need to provide for the comprehensive development of the nation's major river basins on the basis of a unified plan developed and carried out by existing federal and state agencies, including soil conservation districts, and without recourse to the delegation of extreme authorities to new agencies . . . . The public so far has been asked to choose between a valley authority approach on the one hand and a laissez-faire approach on the other. The choice is too limited . . . . Somewhere between the two extremes we must find our solution.

"The question today is no longer over the wisdom of watershed management. Its value in the conservation of resources is widely accepted. The question now is whether we shall participate in the management or be the object of it."

Leavitt was speaking, of course, of the new idea of a partnership approach on the nation's thousands of small watersheds, and his speech came five years and five months ahead of enactment by the Congress of comprehensive legislation to serve this need -- P.L.566, the Watershed Protection and Flood Prevention Act. Perhaps the speech helped move that program ahead. Perhaps it helped lay the foundation for the National Watershed Congress, a coalition of organizations that supported the concept of watershed management for 25 years.

At the very least it alerted the country's leading conservationists attending the most prestigious of all conservation conferences that here was a new national organization representing the owners of private lands, the key to all resource development, and that its leadership was competent and responsible. It also, no doubt, had the effect of building friends and support for NASCD among the wildlife and conservation organizations, some of whom -- particularly the Wildlife Management Institute -- came to the new organization's aid in many ways during its formative years.

The Denver convention, as you know, adopted a $60,000 budget for the National Association, making it necessary that each district pay its dues of $5 and at least one affiliate membership of $25 or more by July 1. The attached report shows our income for the first quarter is slightly less than $7,200, whereas as of this date it should be $30,000, or half of the budgeted amount. It should not be forgotten that about one-half of the 1948 income was raised by President Leavitt in large amounts from private or corporate organizations. We can not be sure that these funds will again be available. Therefore we must exert our efforts to get many more smaller contributions in the form of affiliate memberships of $25 or more. To function effectively we must have travel funds for officers and directors, postage, office supplies, rent, payroll, and $400 for each issue of our Information Letter.

— Excerpts from a
letter, April 7, 1949,
to State Association Presidents by
Robert S. Calkins, NASCD Executive Secretary.

The Fourth Meeting at Atlanta

The first major internal crisis of the NASCD occurred at the fourth annual meeting in Atlanta in February, 1950. Some old-timers refer to this as the "Second Battle of Atlanta." The meeting was the biggest annual meeting so far, being the first in the "home country" -- the South -- the origin of the district movement and of the NASCD itself. More than 1,200 delegates signed in from every state and Puerto Rico as well.

The delegates wrote a new constitution, a major provision of which was to provide for the election of seven Area Vice Presidents who would make up the national executive committee along with the President and the national Vice President.

The first storm signals were raised at the Board meeting on February 27 when Leavitt proposed that he be paid a salary if he were to continue as President, on the grounds that his personal affairs had suffered to such an extent that he could no longer continue in the job without financial assistance.

The Board did not take kindly to this proposal, it having been part and parcel of the philosophy of the association, from the organizational meeting onward, that all officers should serve without compensation other than expenses.

Leavitt's proposal, and the reaction to it, threw the convention into a tizzy, and backstage maneuverings and "smoke-filled" room discussions were everywhere in evidence. It was the first "internal politics" incident for NASCD, and it left a few scars. Rumors flew thick and fast that SCS had men on the scene promoting the interests of this or that presidential candidate.

Out of near chaos, a gruff, burly Texan -- Waters S. Davis, Jr. -- emerged as President, and Clay Stackhouse of Ohio as national Vice President. The seven elected to the new position of Area Vice President were: Northeastern - George Heidrich, West Virginia; Southeastern - William F. Hall, Georgia; Upper Mississippi - Herbert Eagon, Ohio; South Central - R. M. Boswell, Texas; Northern Great Plains - Everett Barr, Nebraska; Southwestern - Walter A. Groom, Colorado; Pacific - J. Max Wilson, California.

Waters S. Davis, Jr.

The new President had been active in soil conservation district work for six years, having agreed to run for district supervisor in 1944 . . . "because I felt sorry for the fellow who asked me after he'd been turned down by nine other men."

Upon his election, Davis got a copy of the state law that authorized the establishment of soil conservation districts and went over it closely. "That law put the responsibility for soil conservation right square on the

Waters S. Davis, Jr., was born in Galveston, TX, in 1899. His family had a significant influence on the history and economic development of the Texas Gulf Coast. League City was named after his maternal grandfather, J. C. League.

After graduating from Williams College, he entered business as a Vice President in the Comet Rice Company, a family enterprise. He held a seat on the New York Stock Exchange and was a member of the brokerage firm of Lapham and Davis for many years.

In 1940, he returned to League City and assumed management of his family's ranch holdings which included extensive operations in timber, grain, cotton and cattle in several Texas counties. In 1944, he was elected a supervisor of the Brazoria-Galveston Soil Conservation District and became an ardent promoter of the district movement. He was elected President of the Texas Association of Soil Conservation Districts in 1947 and began writing *Texas Topsoil,* probably the first newsletter devoted to the development of soil conservation districts.

In 1950, Davis was elected President of the National Association of Soil Conservation Districts, a position he held for five consecutive terms. Thereafter, he served as Treasurer and Director of NASCD until his death in 1959. He was general Chairman of five National Watershed Congresses.

Davis was honored with many awards for his work, including the Hugh Hammond Bennett gold medalion, presented in 1958 by Friends of the Land; the Fort Worth Press Award, in 1956; and an honorary life membership presented in 1952 by the Soil Conservation Society of America.

shoulders of farmers," he would later say. "I couldn't see any way for a government agency to move in and tell us what we had to do or how we had to do it. It made the best sense of any law I ever read. So I went to work."

And work he did. When elected NASCD President, Davis was

President-Manager of the Association of Texas State Conservation District Supervisors, Editor of its *Texas Topsoil,* and Chairman of the Brazoria-Galveston SCD Board. His comical, chiding comments in *Texas Topsoil* about farmers who were "letting George" run their soil conservation districts made that monthly letter a best seller among Texas readers. Typically, for him, he was author, typist, editor, proofreader and circulation manager of *Texas Topsoil.* Besides his "volunteer" duties, he was an active cooperator with five districts: Brazoria-Galveston, Mc-Lennan County, Wichita-Brazos, Lower Trinity, and Upper West Fork.

Davis spent many of his early years in the east. He graduated from Hotchkiss School in Connecticut and Williams College in Massachusetts where "I majored in German literature, so help me," he often quipped. During his years in the east, Davis visited his home state frequently and returned to Texas in 1940 to take over his family's ranch holdings, which included the home ranch near League City and grain, timber, and grazing lands near Waco, Wichita Falls, Newcastle, and in east Texas.

Davis often recalled that when he took over active management of the 4,000 acre home ranch, he was dismayed at the toll taken by poor soil care, erosion, and dwindling soil fertility. He sought the best agricultural advice available, but decided to get some of the answers himself. At one time his ranch was known as "the Waters Davis experiment station." He brought in grasses and legumes from faraway places and planted them in test plots. The experts assured him they would never grow. But some did, and he put them to work on his land and soon they were putting big gains on his cattle. In a few years he had quadrupled beef production.

He put the same drive and enthusiasm into rebuilding his other ranch holdings, insisting that his managers and foremen work out and follow systematic plans of soil conservation and soil improvement. Results were generally spectacular. Davis became a crusader hell bent on saving the soil of America in a hurry. The only thing wrong with soil conservation districts, he often said, is "too darn few people have the foggiest notion of what they are." He was to spend the next five years trying to correct that situation and in the process establish soil conservation districts, and the NASCD, as a potent part of the American scene.

Growth in Service

4

The decade of the 1950's will long be remembered by many of the participants in the soil conservation movement as the "fighting 50's," and Waters Davis established a national reputation as a dedicated and skillful fighter for conservation districts. But what is less well known outside the inner circle of district people are the tremendous gains made by the young organization in improving communications between district people, improving the quality of service to districts, and helping district officials improve the capability of their districts. In many ways, NASCD "came of age" as a service organization under Davis' leadership.

Program For Greater Service

The Program for Greater Service came out of a conversation between Waters Davis and Gordon Zimmerman, then Chief of SCS Information, early in 1950, not long after Davis had become NASCD President. Davis and Zimmerman reasoned that the way to improve district operations was to get outsiders active in the program at the district and state association levels. This would serve two other purposes: relieve the volunteer district and state association officials of jobs that most of them did not have the time or the experience to plan and carry out, and, at the same time, help them develop the skills that many of them lacked.

The proposal provided that each district and state association official head a key committee and that each select as a committee member an expert or professional who would do most of the work and guide the chairman into new skills.

Publicity, for example, would be a committee including a newspaper

editor, farm reporter or radio station director. He would attend board or
state association meetings, be a full-fledged "staff member," and see to it
that the affairs of the district or the state association were properly
publicized. The Finance Committee could include a bank president or
other knowledgable bank official, and the Education Committee could
include a professional educator.

The proposal was presented in a first-class promotional brochure, long
since out of print, "A Suggested Program for Greater Service."

President Davis pushed the program vigorously. By October, 1950, he
had conducted seven area meetings with representatives of state
associations in an effort to get the program started. At these meetings,
Davis pointed out that working alone, district supervisors can accomplish
their objectives only with extreme difficulty. With the help of the advisory
committees at both state association and local district levels, the task
would be greatly simplified. "We need to split the job up into little pieces,"
he said.

And he always added: "There is another important reason for bringing
to our assistance the people suggested in the Program For Greater
Service. This reason is that since ours is a movement of landowning
farmers and ranchers for the benefit of all, it is essential that everybody
understands what districts are and what they are doing."

The program never reached its potential, although successes were
reported in many states for the next year or so. Today, however, districts
are carrying on the same concepts in many ways and under a variety of
names. Many districts now have committees that include professional
advisors. Some have "associate" members of district boards chosen for
their special skills and professional know-how, and some have youth
supervisors, mostly teenage high schoolers, who are given specific jobs to
plan and carry out.

The Program For Greater Service did not die except in name; its first
transformation was a shift of emphasis to the District-Dealer Program,
which Nolen Fuqua called "the Program For Greater Service in Action."

District-Dealer Program

The District-Dealer Program had its genesis in 1951 when the Farm
Equipment Institute published a brochure entitled "The Farm Equipment
Dealer and His Soil Conservation District." This brochure explained what
districts are and how they operate and how farm equipment dealers
should and could help in district activities. Waters Davis called it "the
opening gun in a campaign for closer relationships between equipment

dealers and districts." The emphasis in the beginning was active participation in the committee work of the Program For Greater Service.

Nolen Fuqua was the NASCD sparkplug in getting the program underway in 1952. When Fuqua became President in 1955, he appointed William E. "Bill" Richards of Nebraska as liaison officer between NASCD and the Farm Equipment Institute and the National Retail Farm Equipment Dealers Association.

Fred O'Hair directed the program for the industry. He described the program as having four objectives for equipment dealers: (1) go to the district and get acquainted with the officers and district operations; (2) take on a specific job to help the district; (3) get equipment customers to complete the conservation job on their farm or ranch; and, (4) help publicize the district by distributing literature from the NASCD and other conservation groups. Philip Noland, Chairman of the Conservation Committee of the Farm Equipment Institute, was equally articulate in support of the program through the manufacturers.

Much the same as the Program for Greater Service, the value of the District Dealer Program can not be assessed in tangible accomplishments alone. Its value was in bringing people together around the common goal of striving to preserve the nation's soil and water resources through local initiative, both to secure an enhanced quality of life for agricultural people and to assure future economic stability for local businesses.

Incorporation of NASCD was first suggested at a Council meeting at the national convention in Cleveland, February 25, 1952, by Alf Larson of Minnesota. C.R. (Pink) Gutermuth, Wildlife Management Institute, speaking from the floor by permission, urged incorporation, saying (1) it relieves personal liability of officers and directors; (2) fixes the name of the organization; and (3) prevents infringement. NASCD was incorporated under the laws of Wisconsin on November 6, 1953.

Speaking Contest

NASCD initiated a National Speaking Contest in 1950, with the Dow Chemical Company as the sponsor. Participants spoke on an assigned topic, some aspect of the soil and water conservation program, and competed on the state and regional levels in pursuit of a national prize. All bona fide conservation district cooperators, including district officials, were eligible to compete.

The Spencer Chemical Company became the sponsor in 1952 and

continued through 1956, when the activity was terminated. First prize became $1,000, plus an expense-paid trip to the NASCD Convention to deliver the speech and pick up the prize. In addition, seven area winners received $100 each and state winners received a certificate.

The subject for 1953, for example, was "Democracy at Work in my Soil Conservation District," and entrants were told that talks should cover such things as when and how the district was formed; who the officials were and what they did for the district; and how the district worked on the local level. The subject and the instructions, along with a full reprint of the previous year's winning talk, were printed in a pamphlet that was distributed to all conservation districts.

Waters Davis was a strong promoter of the program, calling it "without a doubt, the most powerful tool any Soil Conservation District or State Association can use to get our movement SOLD to the general public."

Winners after McKnight were D.A. Woodfin of Oklahoma, 1951; Billy Howard of Georgia, 1952; Mrs. W. L. Spears of Oklahoma, 1953; Clarence M. Rogers of West Virginia, 1954; George Carr Ganter of Kentucky, 1955; and Harold Scanlan of Kansas, 1956.

The first winner of the NASCD Speaking Contest, Donald McKnight of Maryland, received $500 at the 1951 annual meeting.

Ladies Auxiliary

The wives of district officials had usually accompanied their husbands to the annual conventions, which for many had become the annual family vacation. In addition, most had listened to (or been involved in) endless hours of kitchen table meetings and discussions on the subject of soil conservation. Few, however, were directly involved in conservation district work itself. Idaho SCS State Conservationist, R. Neil Irving, thought the women could do more, both at the district and state level, by forming an auxiliary whose members would be the wives of district officials.

At Irving's encouragement, thirteen women established the first State Auxiliary at the 6th Annual Convention of the Idaho Association of Conservation Districts, in November of 1948.[1]

In 1949, Idaho Auxiliary President Mrs. Glen Henderson of Nez Perce was invited to attend the 4th national convention in Atlanta. She could not attend, but plans were started for an organizational meeting in connection with the annual meeting to be held the following year.

At the 1951 annual meeting in Oklahoma, 58 women from 24 states decided to form a National Auxiliary. Only three states -- Idaho, Minnesota and Washington -- had formed a State Auxiliary prior to the meeting. Officers elected for the new organization were Mrs. Don Fredericksen of Gooding, Idaho, President; Mrs. James Lane of Xenia, Ohio, Vice President; Mrs. E. E. Adams, Jerome, Idaho, Secretary-Treasurer.

A committee was established under the leadership of Mrs. J. W. Cornwall of Washington to draw up a constitution and bylaws, and a request to hold a meeting at the 1952 NASCD Convention was approved by the NASCD Board.

The major objectives of the organization were: encourage development of auxiliaries in every state; hold an annual meeting coinciding with that of NASCD; promote conservation education in the public schools; assist local districts and state associations in planning and observing Soil Stewardship Week; and, assist local districts in every way possible on request.

The Auxiliary Officers after their re-election at the 1962 Convention in Philadelphia were Mrs. James Setters, WA, Vice President; Mrs. Oscar Hippe, MT, Secretary-Treasurer; Mrs. Charles Gotthard, MI, President; Mrs. Paul Pancoast, OK, Nominations; and Mrs. Archie McIntosh, IL, Second Vice President.

Attendance was up to 100 in 1952, as the Auxiliary met for the second time in Cleveland, Ohio. Five new states had joined the ranks of state auxiliaries -- Oregon, Nebraska, Indiana, Michigan and California. The constitution and bylaws were presented by Mrs. Cornwall and her committee, and adopted.

In 1953, at the Omaha, Nebraska, NASCD Convention, the Auxiliary established a dues structure of $1.50 per member per year and adopted conservation education as their major project for the coming year. Mrs. J. E. Conklin of Hubbell, Nebraska, was elected President and Mrs. Elmer Warner of Michigan was elected Secretary-Treasurer.

The Auxiliary had achieved major status by 1954 when 600 women attended the fourth annual meeting at New Orleans. Effective work on conservation education was reported from many states. In 1955, the Auxiliary heard Dave Doneen, NASCD Director from Washington and Chairman of the Soil Stewardship Committee, explain the Soil Stewardship program and the major role the Auxiliary could play in encouraging local observances.

Since 1956 the annual meetings of the Auxiliary have been reported in the proceedings of the annual convention, and since October, 1962, the President of the Auxiliary has been invited to speak to the NACD Board meetings. Mrs. Charles Gotthard of Traverse City, Mich. was the first to have that honor. The Auxiliary became an affiliate organization of NACD in 1963.

Beginning with Mrs. Don G. Fredericksen of Idaho, in 1951-53, twelve have served the Ladies Auxiliary as president: Mrs J. E. Conklin of Nebraska, 1953-55; Mrs. Elmer Warner of Michigan, 1955-57; Mrs. Paul Mungle of Oklahoma, 1957-59; Mrs. Henry W. Bethea of Florida, 1959-61; Mrs. Charles Gotthard of Michigan, 1961-63; Mrs. Oscar Hippe of Montana, 1963-67; Mrs. Del Krenik of Minnesota, 1967-71; Mrs. Earl M. McClellan of Idaho, 1971-75; Mrs. Lyle Bauer of Kansas, 1975-79; Mrs. Hugh A. Jones of Kentucky, 1979-83; and Mrs. Richard Thompson of Louisiana.

The President receives an expense allowance from NACD and each year travels thousands of miles to attend meetings, and make talks and radio and television appearances. The organization receives NACD help in issuing a quarterly newsletter, The Chatterbox, which keeps members informed on Auxiliary activities and projects.

Activities of the Ladies Auxiliary and the state and local auxiliaries include: providing scholarships in resource education to teachers; sponsoring conservation contests such as speaking, posters, and essays; promoting outdoor conservation laboratories for schools; participating in Soil Stewardship Week by giving talks, distributing literature and even occupying church pulpits; sponsoring conservation tours; giving awards for individual conservation achievements; making cash contributions to the Davis Conservation Library; conducting fund-raising projects, public exhibits and displays; donating conservation books to public and school libraries; helping to publish and sell state conservation district histories.

Auxiliary activities have had a positive effect on conservation districts by encouraging the interest and support of thousands of women, many who otherwise might never have become involved in soil conservation. The NACD Auxiliary and its sister state and local groups have had a healthy influence on conservation educational work in the schools and among youth groups and have helped bring women to the fore of what had previously been considered all-male conservation activities.

The Tuesday Letter

The *Tuesday Letter*, NASCD's weekly newsletter, made its first appearance October 21, 1952. It was on one 8-1/2" by 14" page, printed in green ink, with a caricature of Waters Davis at the top and a cartoon-type "balloon" telling the reader what to look for in that issue.

The first issue said, "Hey, here's a new gimmick!" and went on to tell how the newsletter was mimeographed, folded, put through an automatic addressing machine and mailed (for a penny apiece) without needing any envelopes, hand folding or hand stuffing. "We can do the same for you," Davis offered. "Our printer can fix up a letterhead similar to this for your State Association or your District. This same kind of a job will cost so little that no Association or District can afford NOT to have a regular bulletin or newsletter. How about it?"

As a result of that invitation, many districts began to publish a regular newsletter, using the services of NASCD for printing, addressing and mailing. Few, however, would have the kind of spicy news that characterized the *Tuesday Letter* under the pen of Waters Davis and, occasionally, Bill Southworth. Southworth had been an Information Specialist with SCS prior to coming with NASCD, and was a skilled writer who served as Davis' "right-hand man" from 1953 until 1956, when he left to go into private business.

Even Clair Guess, then Executive Director of the South Carolina Soil Conservation Committee, got roped into the act. He wrote the third issue of *Tuesday Letter*, dated November 4, 1952 "while Bill and Waters are in the next room scratching together the last touches on plans of the National meeting in Omaha."

Guess was clearly impressed with the activity and spirit at the NASCD office at League City. "Any District Supervisor that could see this organization at work would be proud of the part he has had in building such an efficient clearinghouse for our common problems," he said. "The pulse of a District in Florida and the skip of a District heartbeat in California can both be felt in this one spot."

Costs for attending the Annual Meeting in Omaha were the subject of a letter from Director Alf Larson to supervisors in Minnesota and Wisconsin that Guess reprinted for the rest of the *Tuesday Letter* readers: "Rooms in the Fontenelle Hotel or nearby hotels can be had for $3.50 up. You better plan on three nights. When you register you can get a book of tickets for $14.50 which includes registration fee, two luncheons and two banquets. We cut the registration fee in half this year. There won't be any registration fee at all for wives."

Finally, a note on the politics of the day (election day, 1952): "I'll bet the calmest spot (politically) in the U.S. today is your national headquarters at League City. The only 'politics' you hear down here is Soil Conservation Districts. And with both 'Ike' and 'Adlai' on the record with strong approval of Districts, how can you stir up an argument?"

"Hope your man won. But if he didn't, don't feel too bad. Your District will have a friend in the White House regardless of the winner."

On March 24, 1953, *Tuesday Letter* distribution was expanded to all district chairmen as well as state and national association officers. Within a month, Davis reported that "Getting this TUESDAY LETTER to all Soil Conservation District Chairmen put our old mimeographing machine on the obsolete list. With this issue we begin using a brand new Multigraph Model 1250 with the Multilith Offset process. In time it will pay for itself through a number of economies. Right now, though, it puts a $2,935 crimp in the bank balance."

With that kind of direct, folksy news, *Tuesday Letter* quickly became established as a spicy, informative letter that "told it like it was." Whether it was Davis giving district officials a peek at his busy schedule -- "It's Pocatello, Idaho, and back this week for a talk to the Idaho Cattlemen's Association. (Anybody want a copy?)" -- or exhorting them to send in their districts NASCD quota -- "Puleeze, send in your quota early this year. It is costly in time and money to have to keep sending statements. That time and that money can be spent much better WORKING FOR YOU." -- each week's *Tuesday Letter* was another thread in the fabric that drew district officials closer together in a national organization.

Goodyear Conservation Awards Program

The Goodyear Conservation Awards Program grew out of the

leadership of Robert S. Wilson, Goodyear Vice President in charge of sales. He had purchased a run-down farm during World War II and joined as a cooperator with the Charlevoix County Soil Conservation District in Michigan. As he learned more, the district and its supervisors impressed him as a model of local self-government, with its local leaders performing a valuable public service for their community without pay.

Wilson began to ask what he and Goodyear could do to further this young and viable idea, to help districts better serve their communities. He and his aides held discussions with district leaders and with Ralph Musser, SCS Regional Conservator for the Upper Mississippi Region at Milwaukee; Leslie R. Combs and Morris E. Fonda of Musser's staff; Russell G. Hill, Secretary of the Michigan State Soil Conservation Committee, and many others.

The major need seemed to be better management of the district's programs and activities by the supervisors. A contest was devised where the awards are based on a comprehensive score sheet upon which the district boards are graded as to how well they administer district affairs during the year. Thus, what was started was a competition between district boards to see who could develop and operate the best district program.

The first awards program began August 1, 1947, just six months after the first NASCD convention at Chicago, and closed July 1, 1948. It was limited to the eight states -- Minnesota, Michigan, Missouri, Indiana, Illinois, Wisconsin, Iowa, and Ohio. Wilson thought a regional program would best serve to iron out the "bugs" and the program would be easier for Goodyear to administer in its early stages if competing districts were not too far from company headquarters at Akron, Ohio.

Grand awards were bronze plaques to the top winner in each state and a five-day vacation-study trip to Goodyear's 14,000 acre subsidiary and guest resort, "The Wigwam," at Litchfield Park, Arizona, for all members of first-place district boards and three outstanding cooperators selected by the board in each first-place district.

The program was repeated in 1948-1949, with the vacation trip replaced by cash awards. This brought a resounding response from district leaders in favor of the trip, and it was restored to the regular program permanently.

In 1950-1951, the test program was expanded to include Arkansas, Kansas, Louisiana, Montana, Nebraska, North Dakota, Oklahoma, South Dakota, and Wyoming. The program continued in the original eight states, but plaques and luncheons were awarded in place of a trip to Goodyear farms.

With the full-scale awards limited to the southwestern states during the testing period, four states in the original group adopted a program of their own. In Illinois and Iowa the state associations sponsored a modified Goodyear program, and in Indiana the State Farm Bureau sponsored one. In Missouri, Henry Blesi, State Association President, Howard C. Jackson, SCS Assistant State Conservationist, and Robert S. McClelland, Executive Secretary of the Missouri State Soil Districts Commission, persuaded the *St. Louis Globe Democrat* to become a sponsor. The newspaper continued the program through 1956.

McClelland recalled in later years that when the committee met at Columbia to get the program started, the *Globe Democrat* representative opened the discussion by asking: "Tell me, before we get into this, what in the hell is a soil district?"

The national program began in 1953-54 in the 48 contiguous states on the basis of 50 competing units, established in order to balance the numerical distribution of conservation districts and farms in certain states. Puerto Rico was added in 1959-1960, Hawaii in 1960-1961, and Alaska in 1965. The grand awards now go to 106 individuals in the 53 winning conservation districts. The award is a four-day vacation trip to the Goodyear farms.

During their stay the guests study conservation practices at the Goodyear farms; vegetable, feed, and fruit production; and irrigation systems. Since 1965, the program has included an all-day tour of the desert and high mountain country around Phoenix. The opportunity to exchange views with fellow conservationists from every part of the country is the part of the program many district officials find most useful and enjoyable.

Over the years many changes have evolved, primarily in the mode of travel. From 1948 through 1957, the guests travelled by train to and from Phoenix, congregating at Chicago, Kansas City, and New Orleans. Pullman cars leaving Chicago were joined by other pullmans at Kansas City, Clovis, N.M., and Flagstaff. From that point on, it was an all-Goodyear train into Phoenix.

In 1958, the change was made to air transportation, which saved up to 4 days travel for many of the winners. For several years after the switch to air travel, the flight to Arizona was the very first plane trip for more than half of the district officials involved. At first the guests were flown to Chicago, St. Louis, and Kansas City by regular flights, and then taken by charter flight to Phoenix. As universal jet transport developed, the winners, beginning in 1967, travelled by regular commercial flights from their homes to Phoenix.

Goodyear's first Program Director was W. E. Still, who served in 1947-1949. Jim Kearney was Director in 1949-1951, and Art Morrill in 1951-1955. A. H. (Don) Settle took over in 1954 and became one of conservation's best known figures at state, area and national meetings of districts during his long tenure. Settle retired in August, 1969, and was succeeded by the present Director, Ray Oviatt, who has become equally well known in over 15 years of service.

This group picture shows the Goodyear Award winners all decked out in their new cowboy outfits, standing on a map representing their home states.

The impact of the Goodyear program on the quality of conservation district programs has been significant, but may defy measurement. Over 90 percent of all districts have participated for one or more years, and even one year's enrollment has been shown to have a beneficial effect on the district board. The Goodyear score sheet is a valuable training guide for both old and new supervisors, and keeping it current for the year makes the board more aware of its strengths and opportunities for improvement. No district board can win a top award without being strong in each of the elements making up its total responsibilities.

An additional benefit is that Goodyear invites leaders of the National Association of Farm Broadcasters, the Newspaper Farm Editors of America, and the American Agricultural Editors Association to the annual tour at Litchfield Park. The media representatives have this additional opportunity, in a congenial vacation atmosphere, to learn about districts and their leaders, which undoubtedly has helped the movement in many ways during the past quarter century.

Expanding the Service Department

When Waters Davis took over the leadership of NASCD, he wasted little time in expanding the communications capability of the national organization. By 1952, when the first *Tuesday Letter* was published, it was clear that Davis had expanded the NASCD office far more than any of his predecessors. That would, for the first time, raise the question of what to do with the office when the President's term expired.

The first office was in a little one-room house across the railroad tracks from the current Service Department, where one typewriter and a mimeograph machine were Davis' tools to reach his constituents. As the *Tuesday Letter* circulation expanded, and as districts ordered more and more printing, both staff and space were enlarged. By May of 1953, Davis was ordering paper in 5,000 lb. lots and offering districts a price of $3.10 per hundred newsletters, printed, folded and postage-paid. Before long, NASCD was said to be the largest user of green ink in the South!

In League City, a sleepy country town of some 2,000 at the time, the new organization was a pretty substantial operation. Up until the early 1960's, when the Johnson Space Center was built at nearby Clear Lake, NASCD was the second- or third-largest employer in town (after the school system and, perhaps, the bank). It was by far the biggest postal patron, producing over 75 percent of the outgoing mail from the local Post Office. The Post Office was upgraded, it has been said, to a First Class Post Office on the basis of the NASCD-generated mail volume.

In 1956, Davis built a new 9,300 square-foot masonry building on League City's Main Street. Because of the controversy within NASCD as to whether or not the office should be moved to the new President's hometown after each election, Davis waited until the Board had decided to establish a permanent Service Department in League City, then he donated the building to NASCD. Later, to provide space for future expansion, Davis purchased adjoining property which was willed to the organization upon his death.

This one-room house in League City was where Waters Davis wrote and distributed the Tuesday Letter and established a full-scale service facility to serve the nation's soil conservation districts.

The Service Department provides a central location to give districts and their associations fast, economical service to meet their needs for printed materials, signs, awards and office supplies. It handles around 1,000 orders per month, ranging in size from a few business cards to several thousand copies of a multiple-page booklet, brochure or report.

The Conservation Districts Foundation

The Conservation Districts Foundation was incorporated in 1954 under the laws of Wisconsin as a nonprofit, nonpartisan research and educational institution. It was felt at the time that such a foundation could provide financial security to NASCD by helping to attract outside contributions to an endowment that could be invested for steady income. In addition, a foundation could provide a vehicle for accepting tax-free contributions and carrying out functions that might be questioned if they were done under the name of the more political basic organization.

Francis E. Coxe, President of the South Carolina Association of Soil Conservation District Supervisors, started the Foundation in South Carolina early in 1952. W. Joe McArthur, son of the first NASCD President, and Coxe were the first contributors with donations of $500 and $100, respectively. In his annual report to the South Carolina State Association on December 31, 1952, Coxe spoke of the Foundation, acknowledged McArthur's gift as a memorial to his father, said Attorney W. Croft Jennings of Columbia, S.C. was preparing a proposed charter and bylaws, and said that the idea would be presented to the national association at its next convention for launching on a national scale.

At Omaha, February 5, 1953, the NASCD Council adopted the proposed charter for the Foundation as presented by Coxe, and referred it to the Directors for action. The following day the Directors discussed the proposal but reached no agreement on the make-up of the Foundation's management. At the meeting, Coxe presented a check for $1,825 which he said had been donated to the Foundation by SCS personnel and others, mostly in the Southeast. When the questions of administration had been cleared up to the Board's satisfaction, the Foundation's charter was finally approved by Board action on February 24, 1954.

The Foundation made its first major contribution by publication, in 1956, of the first of a series of annual guidebooks for district officials to use in planning their year's program. President Fuqua said: "I've never seen any part of our work more widely accepted anywhere in the states I have visited than this guidebook."

But the dream of substantial outside contributions to an endowment was never realized, and the Foundation continued in a state of suspended animation. Treasurer Marion Monk deplored the situation at a meeting in Louisville, February 4, 1960, and the Directors decided to develop and announce a program of activity and take "appropriate steps" to obtain donations. Objectives proposed for 1960 were financing and implementing the Watershed Development Committee, preparing and distributing the Guidebook, printing and selling the NASCD history, and taking specific steps to invite contributions. Monk circularized Officers, Directors, Council members and NASCD friends asking for their suggestions and comments on proposals for "a rebirth" of the Foundation.

Monk argued that the Foundation, "properly handled, can add untold strength and stature to the soil and water conservation movement; it has possibilities of assuring more direct help to districts; it can give a new opportunity to many who may desire to leave a portion of their estate to a great cause; and small personal contributions from a growing number of conservation-minded people will build a reserve that will be of lasting value." Prospective donors were urged to become "original contributors" who would have their names recorded on a permanent roll of honor at League City.

In 1961, the Foundation reported that *Land, Water & People,* a history of the NASCD, had been published; that the Davis Conservation Library was nearing completion; and that the Guidebook for District Officials had been issued for the fifth consecutive year. *Land, Water & People* was prepared under the direction of Otis Tossett of North Dakota, assisted by Joe Douthit of South Carolina. Tossett enlisted the help of Harold Severson, a Minnesota newspaperman, who was paid $500 for writing services, but the final draft was written by D. Harper Simms of SCS.

At their 1952 meeting in Philadelphia, the Foundation Directors established the non-salaried office of Executive Director, and elected Nolen Fuqua to the new office. For several years, it was the custom to elect the Immediate Past President to this position, until the practice was discontinued in the 1970's. Today, the Foundation continues its educational program, and stands ready to handle any role that is strictly educational and non-political. Its value as a financial bulwark, never realized, has been assumed by the NACD Endowment Fund, which will be discussed in a later chapter.

The Davis Conservation Library

A major project of the Conservation Districts Foundation is the

Waters S. Davis Conservation Library, which had its beginning in 1958 when the Alabama Association of Soil Conservation Districts contributed $1,000 to initiate the project. The action was reported to the NASCD Directors in March, 1959, and the money placed in a trust fund under the trusteeship of Nolen Fuqua. A. D. Holmes of Alabama told the Board the Alabama district supervisors hoped the library would serve not only as a memorial to Davis but as an outstanding national repository for soil and water conservation literature and documents, including those pertaining to NASCD and the district movement.

There was some talk of locating the library at the Agricultural Hall of Fame, then being established, and when Fuqua, also a Director of the Hall of Fame, was asked for a progress report by Holmes at the NASCD Board meeting in October, 1959, he asked patience for a few more months until the Hall of Fame proposal either developed or failed to materialize.

Action to establish the library and an office for the Foundation in the NASCD building at League City was taken at a Board meeting in October, 1960, at Amarillo, Texas, when the Directors authorized funds to equip an office and the library. First gifts to the library were by Fuqua -- bound volumes of the *Tuesday Letters*, issued during the Davis and Fuqua presidencies. In 1962, the library received a gift of $1,000 from Mrs. Mary Elizabeth Flynn of Robinson, Illinois, long active in the NASCD Ladies Auxiliary, in memory of her husband, William E. Flynn.

The library began to grow and to function on a broadening basis year by year. By 1972, the library had catalogued well over 2,000 books, periodicals, and reports. About 160 additions are made yearly through donations and purchases. Several donations have been made as memorials to conservationists and members of their families. A shelf containing Soil Stewardship materials was started in 1971, for example, as a memorial to Mrs. Helen Zimmerman whose sudden death occurred at the NACD annual meeting in San Francisco in February, 1970. The library's collection of the histories of state associations of conservation districts has been growing steadily, as well as its collection of state enabling acts and conservation laws, appropriation acts, and state association constitutions and by-laws.

Since March, 1970, requests to NACD for free materials on soil and water conservation have all been handled by the library. Each request is answered and a packet of free material sent. In the first year the library handled nearly 2,000 individual requests and distributed a total of 35,587 publications. SCS, the Forest Service, and industrial concerns provide many of the materials for this purpose. The library also distributes the annual Conservation District Workbook.

Soil Stewardship

At the Board meeting in Galveston, October 18-21, 1954, Waters Davis presented a guest who had a proposition. The guest, H. L. Gantz, of *Farm and Ranch Magazine*, Dallas, announced that his company was discontinuing sponsorship of "Soil Stewardship Sunday," originally called "Soil and Soul Sunday," which the magazine had supported since 1946. Gantz confirmed what he had previously told Davis; the magazine would be agreeable to having NASCD take over the program. After a short discussion, the Board approved, and started one of NASCD's most successful and rewarding activities.

David Doneen, a Director from Washington state, and William Southworth took the job of getting the project started. At the Board meeting March 28-31, 1955, they reported they had met with church leaders in Chicago and New York. They said that most of the national church organizations bought copies of the first soil stewardship booklet and volunteered to call attention to the program. The Board decided to invite church leaders to serve in an advisory capacity to the program, on Doneen's recommendation.

At the Board meeting Nov. 14-17, 1955, Doneen reported that he, Nolen Fuqua, Otis Tossett, Everett Barr, William Richards, and William Southworth had met with an Advisory Committee on Soil Stewardship in Kansas City to discuss plans for 1956. The advisors were Michael P. Dineen, National Catholic Rural Life Conference; Rev. E. W. Mueller, National Lutheran Council; Dr. Henry S. Randolph, National Council of Churches; and Rev. Leslie Templin, in charge of town and county work for the Methodist Church in Kansas. The church leaders agreed to write most of the text for the 1956 booklet.

Doneen expressed the high ideals and aims of the activity when he said to the Board: "The purpose of the Soil Stewardship Program is to further awaken in the hearts and minds of men their responsibilities to God through their stewardship of soil and water. This is not, and I hope never will become, a publicity stunt nor should we ever be put in the position of using this to further our organization as such. It should be simply an honest effort based on basic principles of good soil conservation in our responsibilities to God. We should always make it sound and resist every effort to consume it by outside interests, either commercial firms or government agencies."

Doneen told the Board that NASCD could enlist the support of national church leaders, and provide tools for use in the observance, but the success of the program would depend entirely on what was done in local conservation districts.

The first Soil Stewardship Sunday under NASCD was observed May

15, 1955. Nolen Fuqua, who had been elected President at the February annual meeting that year, spoke of the event over the NBC network on the National Farm and Home Hour. Secretary of Agriculture, Ezra Taft Benson, also issued a statement on the observance.

Each year, NASCD and districts distribute material to be used by church leaders and their congregations for the observance of Soil Stewardship Week, which begins on the fifth Sunday following Easter and ends on the subsequent Sunday. In recent years, over seven million pieces of material such as placemats, posters, church bulletin covers, program inserts, and public service announcements to be used on radio and television have been distributed each year.

The key publication is the annual Soil Stewardship booklet. The first one was titled simply, "Soil Stewardship Sunday," and those for 1956, 1957 and 1958 were titled "Soil Stewardship Week." Beginning in 1959, each booklet has had a specific title, and they began to attract attention both as to text and layout. From 1960 until 1979, the texts were written by Gordon Zimmerman. Those in recent years have been written by Leland DuVall, Associate Editor of the *Arkansas Gazette*.

The titles of the booklets reflected themes selected each year by the committee: "The Earth is the Lord's"; "The Spirit of the People"; "Crisis in the Countryside"; "A Time for Initiative"; "Confronting the Issues"; "Resources and Renewal"; "Creative Conservation." The booklets have

---

Consider this Soil

It lies as far as the eye can see. It covers millions on millions of acres around the globe, yet it is a rare thing and cannot be replaced.

This soil is a living thing. Yet it can be destroyed.

This soil is a fruitful thing. Yet it can become sterile.

This soil is God's gift to mankind, given unto our stewardship. Yet it can be despoiled and wasted.

The soil produces crops and verdant grass and trees. It cannot be duplicated by chemistry or physics.

This soil is an intricate house of myriad elements. Yet it is so commonplace as to be known as dirt.

It fills the flower pot in Manhattan, serves as a garden in Minnesota, and produces an orchard in California -- this thing called soil.

It is the spectacle of the Grand Canyon, the flatness of the Plains, and the rolling convolutions of the Shenandoah Valley -- this thing called soil.

It is the source of our nourishment; it provides the means of our protection.

God has willed we can live with it; we cannot live without it.

Consider this soil. Consider it well.

1960 Soil Stewardship Brochure

been recognized for their high literary quality and modern design and for the comprehensive and timely information they convey on resource issues. Five Presidents -- Eisenhower, Johnson, Nixon, Carter and Reagan -- have authorized statements over their signatures in the booklets.

District Newsletter Contest

In February of 1957, at a Board meeting in St. Louis, Waters Davis told the Directors that the Farm Equipment Institute had proposed to provide $2,500 annually to support a newsletter contest among the conservation districts. The goal of the contest would be to provide incentives to districts to publish a regular newsletter, and continue to improve the quality of those that were already being published. The Board immediately accepted the offer and authorized Davis to work out the details with the FEI. That did not take long, and the contest got under way early in 1957.

The first winners were recognized at the Minneapolis annual meeting in 1958. Winning the $500 grand prize was the Harris SCD of Texas. The Todd County SCD, South Dakota, and the Cotton County SCD, Oklahoma, took home the second and third prizes, and an additional 25 honorable mentions were awarded.

Over the years, the contest has been broadened and the prize money increased, but the basics remain the same. The sponsor is now called the Farm and Industrial Equipment Institute. District newsletters are judged on the basis of readability, content, regularity of publication, and circulation. The judges are three professionals selected by NACD from other national conservation organizations, federal agencies, or national magazines. A publication entitled "Notes About Newsletters" is available from the Service Department to assist districts in developing a good letter, and the details of the contest are distributed to each district every year.

Districts are judged by the seven NACD regions, then national winners are picked out of the seven regional winners. For several years, a contest category for state association letters was included, but it has been dropped because too few state associations were publishing a regular letter. Until 1983, in addition to the regular winners, the best "new" newsletter was also recognized.

In 1957, when the first contest was held, about 50 districts were publishing regular newsletters. The number rose to 300 within two years and to 750, with an estimated total readership of over 750,000, by 1972. The combination of a reasonable, reliable printing and mailing service at

League City, a constant barrage of encouragement from NACD to tell their story to the public, and the lure of contest prizes has proven highly effective in encouraging the growth of these local communications efforts.

NACD has always strongly promoted the publication of a local newsletter as the cornerstone of a district's communications program. President John Wilder did a good job of explaining why when he announced the newsletter contest in 1972:

"First, as a subdivision of state government, you have a responsibility to report to your constituents about the work you are doing in their behalf," Wilder told the districts. "Second, conservation work often needs to be interpreted to be recognized. How many people in our urbanizing society know a diversion terrace when they see one? How many understand how vegetation, water management structures, and other conservation measures control erosion, prevent pollution, and restore the soil? A newsletter can help explain these kinds of vital environmental actions by district cooperators that seldom make headlines.

"Third, a newsletter can aid in stimulating new interest in conservation. Every district needs a hot-line of communications with its cooperators, legislators, businessmen, local officials, schools, civic clubs, and the general public."

Expanding Offices and Services

A permanent headquarters for NASCD had been a controversial topic beginning in the early 1950's. During the tenure of Waters Davis as President, his hometown, League City, Texas, had become established as NASCD headquarters. A significant service facility had grown up, and the organization had an experienced and trained staff who understood NASCD, conservation districts, and the work needed to serve them. The past practice of moving NASCD's office to the hometown of each new President was beginning to look less feasible.

It was Davis himself who first saw the need for a location near the scene of national action. At the Board meeting October 29-31, 1951, in Omaha, Davis proposed establishment of a Washington office with a permanent resident representative. He recommended Don Daily, who had been Executive Secretary since mid-1950, having succeeded Robert Calkins. The Board adopted a motion that the President had authority over all paid personnel and gave him authority to employ an "educational director." Daily was told he could headquarter at Boulder, Colorado (his home), get assignments from the President, and work on "representation" jobs in the nation's capital. Daily served until May 1, 1952, when his resignation became effective.

Talk of a "more central office" for the NASCD continued. Kent Leavitt, in a Board meeting at Omaha on February 6, 1953, proposed establishment of a central office with an Executive Secretary. The Board deferred action. The next move came during the Board meeting at Galveston when it was apparent that the tenure of Davis was nearing the close. (At the February, 1954, meeting the Council had voted to limit the term of NASCD Officers to five years, by a vote of 35-14.) On October 19, 1954, the Directors took the unusual step of an "advisory action" for the new Board that would be elected at the February, 1955, annual meeting by adopting the following resolution:

"It is the unanimous opinion of the Board that the new President shall move the executive part of the office at his discretion; that he leave the printing part in League City, both provided that in the near future, at the first opportune moment, that the entire office be moved to a new permanent location. Also that the staff, whose services are very much appreciated, will be kept fully informed as to all intentions, and be given all consideration."

New Leadership — Nolen Fuqua Elected

At the conclusion of the 1955 Convention in San Diego, Nolen J. Fuqua, Jr., of Duncan, Oklahoma, was elected as the fourth President of NASCD. William E. Richards of Orleans, Nebraska, was elected Vice President and Waters Davis was appointed Treasurer.

Fuqua was no newcomer to the ranks. He had helped organize his own conservation district some 18 years earlier and had served it ever since; he had helped organize the Oklahoma Association of SCD's and served nine years as its President; and he had been involved in the very early meetings, dating back to 1941, that had led to the formation of NASCD.

Fuqua faced major problems when he took over the reins in 1955. The reorganization of SCS (to which we shall come in another chapter) was still smouldering, and it fell on Fuqua to reestablish communications between the participants in that fray. Drought gripped the Great Plains, and something had to be done to get the Small Watershed Program off the ground. And, clearly, not the least of his problems was the continuing controversy over what to do with the NASCD office.

At the March, 1955, meeting, the Directors asked the President to appoint a committee to investigate possible locations for a national office

Nolen J. Fuqua, Jr., was born in Duncan, Oklahoma, March 25, 1894, and has lived there all his life. After becoming involved with soil conservation work by cooperating with a demonstration project on some of his farm property, Fuqua became an original supervisor of the Stephens County Soil Conservation District. He was active in organizing the Oklahoma Soil Conservation Districts Association and in working to get the Oklahoma soil conservation districts law both enacted, then amended to be more responsive to district needs. His work with the state association led to efforts to form a multi-state group of SCD supervisors which was a direct forerunner to the National Association of Soil Conservation Districts.

He was active in the National Association from its formative years, and served as President from 1955 to 1958. He was deeply involved in the Small Watershed Program, both at home, where he is given credit for "taming" the Wildhorse watershed, and at the national level. He negotiated with SCS to get the first multiple-purpose reservoir that contained municipal water, and has a lake in the Wildhorse project named for him as recognition of his contributions.

He has received the Silver Beaver Award from the Boy Scouts of America for distinguished service, the Oklahoma Bankers Conservation Award, the Governor's Soil and Water Conservation Award, and honorary life membership in the Soil Conservation Society of America. In addition to his farming interests, Fuqua was active in various business enterprises prior to his retirement in 1945.

and report at the fall meeting of the Board. President Fuqua appointed Marion Monk of Louisiana as Chairman, with Dave Doneen of Washington and Hugh Tuttle of New Hampshire rounding out the committee. With this geographic spread, Fuqua reasoned, the committee would have a hard time showing any regional bias.

It was a proud day for NASCD when Waters Davis and Nolen Fuqua (top) raised the flag at the dedication of the new NASCD Service Department building (bottom) in League City, Texas.

Monk and his committee reported at the November, 1955, meeting of the Board in Galveston, Texas. The committee recommended: (1) that a national "business" office be established; (2) that the executive office move with the President at his discretion, thus "giving a better opportunity for any qualified member to become President"; and (3) that League City be the location of the national "business" office.

In presenting the recommendation, Monk told the Board that the committee had no trouble at all in reaching unanimous agreement once "we sat back and realized that we were directors of a national and not of a state or area group." He pointed out that the committee studied comparative costs of moving to a new location, including replacing and training personnel, remodeling a new space, and probably higher rentals with the cost of operations at the present location. The conclusion was that the disadvantages of a move far outweighed any advantages.

Hugh Tuttle pointed out that in the New England area there had been pressure to move the office from League City, but in reviewing the facts he could see no valid reason for such a move and he was sure the people of his area would agree under the circumstances. He added that it had been a privilege "to sit on this committee with a man from the deep south and the far west and find out how closely we could agree on major points after we put ourselves in the proper frame of mind and began to think in the proper way as representatives of the national association."

Vice President Richards said the committee report reflected clearly that "this is a national rather than a state, regional, or local organization, and I'm glad to see that we grow as we work together."

When the Board's decision was reached, Marion Monk revealed what up to then had been a fairly well-kept secret -- the gift to the Association of a new building, then under construction at League City, by Mr. and Mrs. Waters Davis. Commenting on the gift, Monk said: "You've given away a helluva lot of money here tonight." Davis replied: "After giving 12 years of my life to this outfit, what difference does a building make?"

Davis had been adamant that the proposed gift not be used as an inducement to select League City as the site for a national business office. President Fuqua knew about it, of course. So did Monk. How many others knew is a matter of conjecture. The importance of the decision was that the Directors, after considerable effort and careful groundwork by Fuqua, cast aside their parochial differences in favor of the merits of the proposal.

In June of 1957, Robert S. McClelland, formerly Executive Secretary of the Missouri State Soil Districts Commission, became a special assistant to President Fuqua, with offices in Duncan, Oklahoma.

Locating the National Office

The next move in the "office" story took place at the Board meeting in Washington, D.C., in March of 1958.   President Fuqua recommended that an executive office be established in the central part of the country. He said it would involve employing an additional man to work with present staff members, selecting the proper location, employing an additional man in the Service Department at League City, and raising additional funds of $40,000 to $50,000 a year to finance the expanded operation.

Board members expressed no opposition to the proposal, and were genuinely enthusiastic and optimistic that the needed funds could be raised. Of the 14 Directors then serving, only Hugh Tuttle and Marion Monk had participated in previous office site decisions. Fuqua appointed a committee on central office location composed of Vice President Richards of Nebraska, Chairman, Gilbert Cox of Virginia, and Roger Lemon of Kansas. During the next four months the committee met three times, made several on-site inspections as a committee or as individual members, and reported to the Board at a special meeting in Omaha July 21, 1958.

It was then that the long controversy over the headquarters location came to a head. Richards presented the committee's recommendation that Omaha be selected as the permanent site of the Association's national headquarters, and the argument started. Feelings were running so high that when Cox and Lemon moved to accept the report, a motion to table their motion was offered by Fred Pace of Kentucky and Sloan Rainwater of Arkansas. After some barbed debate, the motion to table was withdrawn and Cox's motion prevailed. President Fuqua thanked the committee for its "excellent" report and the Board adjourned for lunch.

When the matter was reopened after the noon recess, Richards revealed that Des Moines, St. Louis, Kansas City, Wichita, Oklahoma City, Denver, Omaha, and Louisville were studied by the survey committee and that Omaha, in the committee's judgment, most nearly met all the requirements. After Richards had summarized the committee's points in favor of Omaha, Marion Monk and Orr Garber of Wyoming proposed that the executive office be located in Washington, D.C., and that a branch office be set up as soon as possible in the western part of the country. The discussion was long and heated, but the motion finally carried, 11 votes to 9.

Monk and Gilbert Cox then proposed that the President be authorized to negotiate with Gordon K. Zimmerman for the position of Executive Secretary, and the Board adopted that motion as well.

On a further motion by Monk and Garber, the Association decided to establish field offices as rapidly as finances would permit, with highest priority to the West and Midwest sections of the country. (The first such office, with Bob McClelland as the Western Program Advisor, was opened in Denver in 1959.)

But the stormy session still wasn't over. Richards, after outlining his efforts as chairman of the survey committee, which had not listed Washington, D.C. as a possible site, said he considered it best to resign as national Vice President and left the meeting. After a long discussion, the Board rejected his resignation and convinced him to come back into the meeting.

Many of the top leaders had long felt that a Washington, D.C. headquarters was essential if the association was to establish and maintain a national position in natural resource circles, and to serve its member districts across the nation as a national association should serve them. Their reasons, or their debating skills, apparently carried the day. In retrospect, when asked if locating in Washington was the right decision, Nolen Fuqua told interviewer Douglas Helms, "It proved to be our lifesaver."[2]

Of the eight applicants for the position of Executive Director which Fuqua had been advertising, only Zimmerman had made his application contingent on location of the headquarters in Washington. Zimmerman was considered by many association leaders, in office and out, to be the outstanding choice for the top executive job, and he had been asked to apply for the position. He was informed, articulate, perhaps the ablest writer on current conservation affairs in the nation, and a person who knew the national conservation and political scene and its key practitioners on a first-name basis. He had begun helping Kent Leavitt within six weeks after Leavitt became President, and had maintained a close association with the NASCD through the early part of the Waters Davis regime.

A native of Spokane, Washington, Zimmerman was working on the staff of the *Washington Daily News* when Hugh Bennett tapped him in 1935 as his No. 2 information man on the new Soil Conservation Service staff. From 1941 until he resigned in 1951 as Bennett's mandatory retirement loomed, Zimmerman was known as the Chief's right-hand man -- a position attained by few government information people. He was a key participant in top level policy meetings, and built and directed an information staff that was the envy of administrators and information experts throughout the federal structure. At the time of his selection by NASCD, he was Research Director of the National Grange in Washington, D.C.

In retrospect, the action of the Directors at that stormy session on July 21, 1958, when they selected Washington, D.C. as the locale of their national headquarters and approved Zimmerman as chief executive officer, may well have ranked in importance with the actual launching of the organization 11 years earlier -- for at long last the association was geared for action and in position to take its place as a truly national force in conservation affairs.

Districts Fight to Survive 5

Conservation districts were affected considerably by the bickerings among the agencies in the USDA during the decade of the 1950's. The conflicts began, of course, when the Soil Conservation Service was established in 1935, and intensified in 1936 when Secretary Wallace determined that subsidies for conservation would be handled by the Agricultural Adjustment Administration and technical services by SCS.

Conservation cost-sharing, under the Agricultural Conservation Program (ACP), has been administered by the AAA's successor agencies --Production & Marketing Administration (PMA) and the Agricultural Stabilization & Conservation Service (ASCS) except during the Benson years when an independent agency, Agricultural Conservation Program Service (ACPS) was created to manage the program.

Those administering the cost-sharing program and SCS have been rivals since 1936. Also involved in these conflicts have been the Forest Service, oldest of all conservation agencies, and the Federal Extension Service and the state extension services. On any given issue, the lineup sometimes was two agencies against the other two, sometimes three versus one. Conservation districts were seldom unaffected by these changing rivalries.

The conservation cost-sharing group considered the whole-farm conservation plan as unnecessary SCS technical hocus pocus, and most of the extension people agreed with them. The main interest of the Forest Service was to keep the SCS out of the farm woodlot, insisting that this was the exclusive domain of the professional forester. Some SCS technicians, on the other hand, criticized the "narrow-minded" and "non-technical" agencies whose contributions to conservation they referred to as check-writing or "merely" educational work.

The foregoing was not a general pattern, but enough of it was going on to create considerable ill will. Farmers and the public in general probably didn't care much about any of this. All the programs were popular, and what the farmers desired -- and the public expected -- was effective administration. Just who did it, and how it was done, was a matter that raised heated emotions mainly in the participants themselves.

But the districts could not escape the fray. Since they had been created as a special organization to further the soil conservation work of the SCS, and since SCS was the leading provider of assistance to districts, those who sought to limit, or eliminate, the SCS often felt that the way to do that job was to prevent districts from being formed or, if they were formed, to keep them from working effectively.

Battleground in Missouri

Although there were over 2,300 conservation districts in the early 1950's, covering about three-fourths of the contiguous 48 states, there were some states where districts had hardly gained any acceptance. One of these was Missouri, where the battles were long and bitter.

Missouri had passed a soil conservation district law in 1943, after unsuccessful attempts dating back to 1939. In passing the bill, the state legislature (as did many others) removed the provisions in the USDA-proposed model law that would have given the districts regulatory authority. Formation of districts proceeded slowly, however. By 1952, only 28 out of a potential 114 districts had been formed. [1]

In addition to a strong feeling in Missouri that the SCS approach, bringing federal technicians into direct contact with farmers, was an unwarranted infringement into areas previously considered the responsibility of state and local governments, there was also a more organized competitive program to assist farmers under way.

Missouri's Extension Service provided a service called a "balanced farming plan," that they felt strongly was superior to the conservation plans provided by SCS. It involved all aspects of the family farm, with a goal of tying all the individual farm enterprises into a "balanced" whole. In 1946, in an attempt to extend the concept, the formation of Balanced Farming Associations was encouraged. These associations were to consist of 50 farmers, paying $50 each. The idea was then to raise an additional $1,250 in the community, take $1,250 from the Extension budget, and thus have $5,000 which could be used to hire an associate county agent to help the member farmers develop their plans. [2]

But the balanced farming approach had its critics, too, who charged that it resulted in extension services being provided mainly to farmers who could afford the $50 fee. In addition, Extension found it difficult to coordinate the assistance of different subject matter specialists in the preparation of a plan for a farm. Each specialist was too anxious to push his or her own specialty.[3] At any rate, the balanced farming movement failed to spread to other states.

The existence of the "alternative" to SCS assistance, however, was no doubt a factor in the slow formation of districts. So, too, was the bitterness that permeated the debates at the local level. SCS was accused of "promoting" district formation, and there is little doubt that they did just that. On the other hand, Extension was accused of distributing critical flyers in the middle of the night prior to a district referendum.[4] One such flyer was unearthed and reprinted by investigators for the House Subcommittee on Agricultural Appropriations in 1951.

"In most of the States visited," the House report said, "the Extension Service, as a matter of policy, is strongly opposing not only the work being done by the Soil Conservation Service, but also is in active opposition to the formation of additional soil conservation districts. This policy was confirmed in conversation with the deans of the State colleges of agriculture and the directors of extension services.

"A typical propaganda handbill which was placed under the mail box of each farmer in one county on the night preceding a referendum (to determine whether farmers desired a district to be established) is . . . ." The report then proceeded to reprint the text of the handbill, an original of which is reproduced at right.

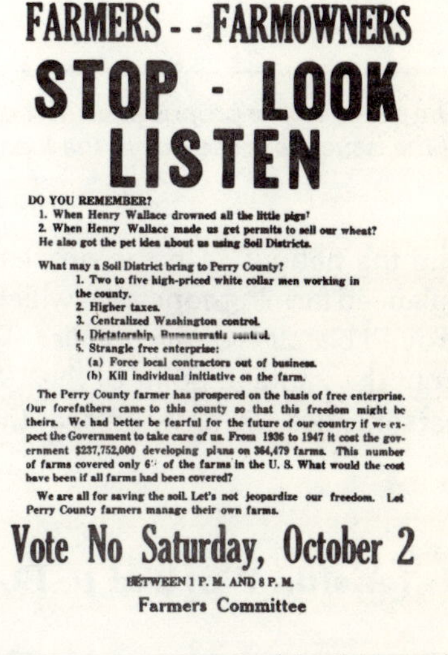

The House investigators went further, and asked the State Director of Extension about this situation. He admitted that "the county extension agent in Perry County 'probably' participated in the authorship of this handbill and that members of the Extension Service sponsored State Conservation Contractors Association 'probably' paid for its publication and were responsible for its distribution."[5]

The result of such acrimonious conflict, of course, was that conservation district formation -- and conservation work -- in Missouri lagged behind much of the rest of the nation. A recent assessment by Michael Childs and J. C. Headley is that "the real loser was the public, in Missouri

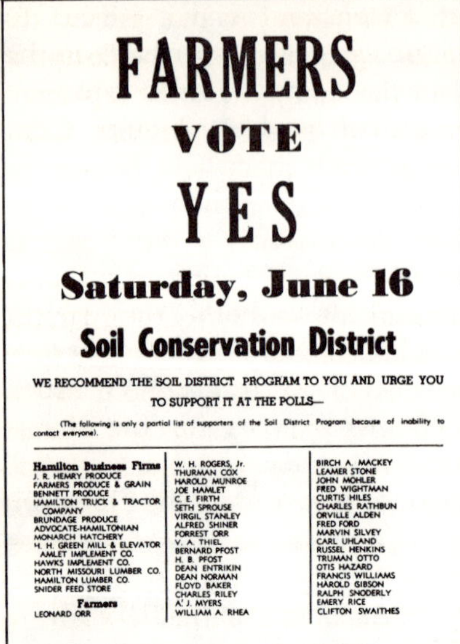

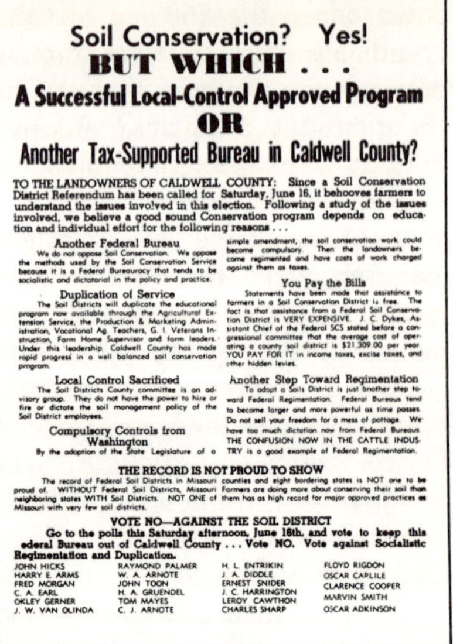

The public in one proposed district was bombarded by information on both sides of the issue, as these ads in the local newspaper illustrate.

and the nation."[6] In the process, both soil conservation work and the balanced farming concept -- which has much to offer if done properly -- lost ground because of the conflict. That is fairly easy to say, in hindsight, but from the vantage point of the 1950's, the issues were too polarized; the personalities too antagonistic; the "turf" too important.

Extension Worked to Form Districts

Lest one think that the relationships between conservation districts and the Extension Service were always marked with antagonism, it is well to relate one of the many instances where the work of the county agent was instrumental in district formation. (Just how the balance tipped is not known; but a review of the evidence suggests that there were far more states and counties where county agents were helpful than where they were antagonistic. The areas of antagonism made the most headlines, however, so the record is hard to evaluate.)

In Switzerland County, Indiana, a district referendum brought out almost 3/4 of all eligible voters, with 1,357 voting for the district and 52 voting against it. Instead of fighting the formation of the district, the county agent and the home demonstration agent discussed the district in every group meeting that they held in the county. Cards explaining the district and the referendum were sent to every landowner. Committees were formed, and followup calls were made just before the election.[7]

In many states, the Extension Service provided a great deal of leadership and educational support in the formation and operation of districts. In some, they served by law or appointment as secretary to the district board. In many, they were instrumental in identifying farm community leaders as candidates for election or appointment to the board. It was a Galveston County agricultural agent that caught Waters Davis in the spring of 1944 and talked him into being a candidate for the job of supervisor in the newly-created Brazoria-Galveston SCD. That one accomplishment may have had as much effect on the soil conservation district movement as any other single event.

Many states assigned a soil conservation specialist at the state level to provide statewide leadership.[8] It was in those states where the formation of districts proceeded rapidly. Unfortunately, it was in the others where the headlines were made and the animosities created that caused lasting scars.

The F.A.R.M. Fracas

One of the more bitter fights of the 1950's centered in South Dakota, where a group of 17 farmers incorporated an organization called Farmers Association for Resource Management (F.A.R.M.) in the spring of 1958, with the stated purpose of seeking a greater voice for the farmer in developing and administering his own farm program. All 17, according to Nolen Fuqua, had served as ASC committeemen or were then active.[9]

The major concerns behind the organization were apparently two-fold: the Great Plains Conservation Program had put SCS in the position of offering cost-sharing as well as technical assistance, and there were rumors out of Washington that Secretary Benson was about to transfer the whole cost-sharing program to SCS.

The F.A.R.M. leaders sponsored meetings throughout South Dakota that spring, urging ASC committeemen and staff to join. A letter sent to ASC committeemen in many counties contained the following paragraph:

"This organization believes that a Farm Program is necessary and that the county and community committees who are farmers and farmer elected are the ones to administer it. The ASC can furnish all the benefits necessary to carry out all conservation practices. All payments are made through ASC anyway. With SCS in the picture it creates an unnecessary overlapping of Federal agencies which certainly creates taxes, expenses, and headaches."

F.A.R.M. was highly critical of soil conservation districts, arguing that the SCS services were too expensive, that the district was not needed, and that the benefits received by landowners no longer justified the district's operation. They were successful in getting recall petitions started for the dissolution of two districts, East Corson and Davison County.

As the battle heated up, Nolen Fuqua continued to cover the subject almost weekly in *Tuesday Letter,* taking care to note that the issue was not between NASCD and ASC. "NASCD has not and will not propose to remove the administration of ACP from the ASC committee system," he wrote. *"We want no quarrel with ASC committeemen* (emphasis in original) because they are a part of the soil and water conservation team and have an important job to do for American agriculture."[10]

Fuqua received immediate support from farm leaders such as Herschel D. Newsom, Master of the National Grange, and Jim Patton, President of the National Farmers Union. Senator Hubert Humphrey of Minnesota wrote Fuqua a letter in May of 1958, saying that he had asked Secretary Benson to investigate the F.A.R.M. situation and calling the attack on soil conservation districts "unfair and unwarranted." "Rest assured that I shall keep an alert and watchful eye on all developments," Humphrey concluded.

In May, the Department of Agriculture became concerned, and Secretary Benson sent his Director of Personnel, Ernest C. Betts, Jr., to South Dakota to investigate the situation. Upon receiving Betts' report, Benson issued a policy statement saying that, although ASC committees were important to USDA efforts and USDA had tried to give committee members a minimum of restraint, "the Department cannot permit them to subordinate or prejudice their official work on account of affiliation with any private organization, or for any other reason, to the real detriment of the programs which it is their responsibility to support and carry out."

"The Soil Conservation Districts are one of the principal subdivisions of State Government which this Department must support," the Secretary continued. "The Memoranda of Understanding which the Secretary has entered into with these Districts commit this Department to cooperate with them in every proper way and to recognize and assist them in carrying out the important responsibility which they have with respect to those phases of soil conservation work contemplated by the Memoranda. All persons engaged in carrying out official duties for this Department are expected to refrain from action tending to abrogate those Memoranda."

Benson's statement was clearly aimed at the ASC committeemen and staff in South Dakota, but the evidence is fairly clear that part of the problem was a lot closer to home, in the South Building of USDA itself. And, in typical fashion, the Secretary's statement did not immediately turn the situation around. In July, Nolen Fuqua would report that he had in his possession three anti-district letters received by a farmer in Davison County before the referendum. One was from F.A.R.M. President Loyd G. Knudson, postmarked McLaughlin, SD; one was from F.A.R.M. Vice President John L. Hofer, postmarked Freeman, SD; and one was from Robert M. Koch, President of the Agricultural Limestone Institute, postmarked Washington, D.C. All had been addressed on the same addressograph machine (there was a typographical error that gave them away), and the letter contained ACP statistical data that Fuqua said "could have come only from USDA."[11]

Koch, a former ASC employee in Massachussets and Washington, D.C., allied the Limestone Institute solidly with the F.A.R.M. movement and put out reams of mimeographed material to South Dakota farmers, ASC committees, and members of Congress. In an editorial, *The Mobridge Tribune* in Corson County, SD, said it was "obvious" why the Limestone Institute entered the squabble. "It is a special interest group attempting to further the use of lime in farming. We South Dakotans are not interested in the use of lime in our farming operations but in the East it is a necessity because of the acidity of their soil. The Lime Institute has no interest in South Dakota other than its fight with the National Association of Soil Conservation Districts, who advocated the dropping of the cost-share for liming from the Agricultural Conservation Program (ACP)."

So the fight became more bitter and more national in scope. Meanwhile, at the local level, the East Corson District was abolished by the voters on a vote of 329 to 166, leaving the South Dakota Soil Conservation Committee the task of liquidating the district and disposing of its equipment and resources. SCS Administrator Don Williams announced that the SCS office in McLaughlin would be closed and the technicians assigned elsewhere.

In the next election, Davison County, the vote was close: 454 to abolish the district; 450 to continue it. A group of landowners took the case to court, contending that the referendum contained irregularities and should be declared invalid. On August 1, 1958, Circuit Judge O.K. Whitney ruled that the referendum was null and void, on the grounds that the election was by mail ballot without identification of the voter on the ballot. Persons who were not landowners were allowed to vote and there was no guarantee that some people did not vote more than once. Thus, the Davison County District was retained.

The third election, in Walworth County, was "won hands down" by the pro-district forces, according to Norman A. Berg, who was an SCS

Assistant State Conservationist in South Dakota at the time. "The South Dakota Commission had some 17 other petitions to abolish districts on hand at the time, but the supporters of the anti-district drive realized that there was no real support for continuing, and dropped the effort," Berg recalls.

The F.A.R.M. movement attempted to go national, but soon faded from the scene. What did not fade, until Koch's retirement in the early 1980's, was the rancor that had developed between NASCD and the National Limestone Institute. Periodic bombasts from the Institute's newsletter kept the ASC-SCS fight boiling for a quarter-century, both at the local level and in Washington.

Out in South Dakota, after the bitterness died down to some degree, the soil conservation district was gradually re-established in Corson County as townships from the old East Corson District began requesting that they be annexed into the West Corson SCD. This started in 1965 and in 1979, the entire county was once again within the boundaries of the Corson Conservation District.[12]

Districts Continue to Grow

Despite the battles that captured the headlines and newsletters of the 1950's, conservation districts emerged from the decade growing in both numbers and prestige. At the close of the decade, NASCD President Bill Richards reported that there were 2,865 SCD's, covering some 90 percent of the land in farms and about 95 percent of all the farms and ranches in the country. Twenty-one states were completely covered by districts and only four states had less than 70 percent coverage.

The reasons for this rapid expansion are open to interpretation, but what seems clear is that the farmers of America found the conservation districts to serve a useful purpose. To many observers, that purpose was mainly the fact that forming and operating a district was the key to gaining the services and programs of the Soil Conservation Service in the community. What that often overlooked, however, were the real services that the district officials themselves performed, and that the district as a local entity was able to provide.

District boards, with their local understanding of people and attitudes, were a sympathetic buffer between farmers and the federal technicians. When the local SCS technician was pushed too hard by the engineers or other scientists for rigid technical specifications in their work, they would often come up against a district board that wanted to see more flexibility

District supervisors spent many hours studying maps and photographs of the district, thinking about the resource problems that needed to be addressed (top - Gage Co., Nebraska, 1957). The goal, of course, was to get conservation practices on the land, as this 1941 photo (bottom) in Frederick Co., MD, shows. (SCS Photos)

and moderation. The resulting negotiations were generally concluded to the best interests of everyone involved, and farmers felt assured that their voice was able to be heard in those kinds of considerations.

In addition to working with local landowners and helping to see that they got the kind of coordinated help from various agencies that might not otherwise have been available, the districts were instrumental in assuring that many aspects of the local conservation program were carried out. Educational programs, for example, often got into schools because district officials carried them there in person, or helped ease through some of the barriers so that an SCS technician could be invited in to present a program proposal.

District officials felt, in the vast majority of cases, that their position on the district board meant that they should be exemplary conservation farmers themselves, and that often meant testing new conservation practices on their own land. This spawned interest in research, because virtually every conservation challenge raised unanswered questions, so district officials became heavily involved in lobbying for additional soil and water research efforts, and in advising research scientists as to priorities and research needs. This developed into close working relationships with land grant colleges, state experiment stations, and the federal research agencies, so district officials could often be the catalyst that brought together and helped these agencies work together, and with SCS, to address conservation problems.

At the local level, districts were the only unit of government in most communities that was specifically chartered to deal with natural resource topics. As a result, they began looking at flooding problems, agricultural, industrial and municipal water needs, water-based recreational opportunities, and a host of similar issues with other elements in their local community, and joining in the search for solutions.

Because they had developed a familiarity with the agencies of USDA, and were developing leadership and communications skills in their work with the district and, often, the state association, these leaders could work effectively with USDA all the way to Washington. As a direct result of their district experience, many of these officials found themselves leading major efforts to attract a watershed project or other federal program to assist their communities. In the next chapter, the story of the Small Watershed Program unfolds, and in thousands of communities, that program was a success because of the dedicated leadership of conservation district supervisors, most of whom will never have their names known beyond their hometown.

Conservation progress on the land was significant as well, and that was one of the best testimonies to the success of the district approach. Over a million miles of terraces, and more than 900,000 farm ponds were reported to have been built by the end of the 1950's. Millions of acres were being operated in accordance with a conservation plan based on soil capabilities. More than 100 watershed projects reached the construction phase and nearly 3,500 Great Plains farmers and ranchers were operating under a complete conservation system, based on a contract with the federal government.

Former foes such as the American Farm Bureau Federation now supported conservation districts and their activities. The 1960 policy position of the Farm Bureau said: "Every effort should be made to further soil and water conservation through soil conservation districts where this is the desire of local people."

But the gains reported by Richards had not come easily. At the national level, NASCD leaders of the 1950's, starting with Waters Davis and continuing through Nolen Fuqua and Richards himself, had worked tirelessly to keep the foes of SCS and districts from damaging or destroying the district program. Those national battles would not only establish NASCD as a national organizational power, but would also end with the national soil conservation program much stronger and more comprehensive as a result.

National Issues Heat Up

6

The early years of the soil conservation movement were fraught with political and technical conflict over the new approaches developed to deal with farmers and their soil conservation problems. Conservation districts had strong critics and equally strong supporters, and a national association that was beginning to make its voice heard in their behalf.

When legislative attempts to redefine the roles of the various conservation agencies and programs failed in the late 1940's, the stage was set for intensified competition at the national level. Soil conservation districts had become a major actor in rural America, with over 2,300 districts embracing about 75 percent of the nation's agricultural land.[1] The state, county and community committee system of the Production and Marketing Administration (PMA) was in full operation and the Agricultural Conservation Program's ability to share in the cost of installing soil conservation practices was a key factor in the national effort.

The Soil Conservation Service had a staff of around 14,500 full and part-time technicians, 90 percent of whom were stationed (according to Hugh Bennett) "in the field -- visiting farmers day in and day out, going over their soil and water problems with them field by field, figuring out the answers farm by farm."[2]

One major contest between Extension, SCS and PMA over who would provide technical assistance to farmers on the permanent practices installed with ACP cost-sharing had been settled in 1949. The House Agricultural Appropriations Subcommittee, under the leadership of Jamie Whitten of Mississippi, had negotiated a settlement designed to force the agencies to work together, without either agency having clear control. The 1950 Appropriations Act (and every Agricultural Appropriations Act since) carried language to the effect that five percent of the ACP cost-sharing money could be transferred to the SCS to pay for the cost of doing the technical work on permanent practices. SCS would, in turn, provide

116

this technical service no matter whether or not the recipient was a cooperator with the local conservation district.

This settled several questions, but to virtually no one's satisfaction. It kept the PMA (and its successor agencies) from establishing a technical service force of its own that would duplicate the SCS capabilities. This pleased SCS. But it also told SCS that it would no longer serve only district cooperators or, for that matter, only work on the priorities established by the conservation districts, as it had done in the past. In insisting that SCS serve an ACP participant whether or not that person was a cooperator within the district (or even whether or not they resided in an established district), Congress told SCS that they were, in fact, a federally-funded agency that would, from time to time, need to respond to federal program mandates irregardless of whether or not the conservation districts approved.

For Extension Service -- who had previously felt in some states that if conservation district formation could be prevented, the competition from SCS at the local level would be averted -- the idea of SCS serving ACP participants whether or not a district was involved was not particularly gratifying, either.

But the basic question as to whether or not USDA agencies would have an "action" ability to reach out and directly contact farmers had still not been settled, at least not to the satisfaction of those who deeply feared direct federal intervention in private matters, or to those who had a personal or professional stake in seeing that the decentralized system characterized by the Extension Services remained the central delivery mechanism employed by the Department.

The Farm Bureau and NASCD held another special session on policies at the Baker Hotel in Dallas, December 7, 1950. Present for the American Farm Bureau Federation were R. E. Short, Vice-President, Arkansas; Delmar Roberts, New Mexico; Warren Hawley, New York; Walter Randolph, Alabama; Roger Fleming, Executive Secretary; Hassil E. Schenck, Indiana; and Allen Kline, President. NASCD was represented by Waters Davis, President; George Heidrich, West Virginia; R. M. Boswell, Texas; Nolen Fuqua, Oklahoma; and Don Daily, Executive Secretary.

The two groups got a little closer to agreement on most issues, but there was no softening on either side concerning Farm Bureau insistence that, to prevent federal domination, a break in the direct SCS line from Washington to the farmer was essential, and that the break should be at the state level. NASCD agreed in principle, but insisted that the break was already established at the conservation district level, a break sufficient to prevent federal domination.

Farm Bureau accused the districts and NASCD of being wed to SCS, and NASCD accused Farm Bureau of wanting to give the popular soil conservation work to Extension in order to strengthen its own organization's ties to the Land-Grant College system.

As a result, the situation was described by field investigators for the House Appropriations Committee as a "civil war." In a 1951 report filed in connection with the Fiscal 1952 Appropriations hearings, they made the following assessment:

"The national soil conservation program as currently administered by the U.S. Department of Agriculture is permeated with duplication, overlap, conflict, and lack of coordination, and what has been aptly decribed as a state of 'civil war' exists in many areas between the Extension Service, the Agricultural Conservation Program Branch of the Production and Marketing Administration, Soil Conservation Service, and Farmers Home Administration."[3]

Clearly, something had to be done, and it fell on the shoulders of Secretary of Agriculture Charles F. Brannan to do it. The result was Memorandum 1278, issued in February, 1951, which set forth in no uncertain terms what each agency would do. It was a bold and necessary step, but not one that Brannan (or any other political leader) could take without reservation. After the memorandum was issued (Brannan somewhat uncomfortably referred to it as an "Order"), he gave the following account to the 1951 NASCD Convention:

"You know there were a lot of things I would rather have done than try to work out this Order. Sometimes I just wish the matter hadn't come up, but it did, and it is my obligation as a public servant to do my best to solve the problems as they do come up . . . . I am sure there are a lot of people in this room that would have worked it out in a smarter fashion than I did, but I assure you there is no one in the room that would have worked any more conscientiously to find an equitable and proper and appropriate way out within the authorities the Secretary had."[4]

Hugh Bennett, SCS Chief, and Secretary of Agriculture Charles F. Brannan were the major forces behind Memorandum 1278, which tried to smooth out USDA conservation agency relations in 1951.

Memorandum 1278

Memorandum 1278 directed closer coordination of the functions and activities of the Soil Conservation Service, the Agricultural Conservation Program and the conservation programs of the Forest Service under supervision of the Assistant Secretary of Agriculture. The memorandum directed the PMA County Committee and the local SCS representatives, "working with the governing body of the conservation district," to jointly develop the soil conservation policies and programs for the county.

The policy of the unified program was stated as follows: "The basic physical objective of soil conservation activities by the Department agencies shall be the use of each acre of agricultural land within its capabilities and the treatment of each acre of agricultural land in accordance with its needs for protection and improvement." The SCS was made responsible for all technical phases of the "permanent" type practices that were cost-shared by the ACP.

NASCD Officers were deeply involved in the development of Memorandum 1278. On January 15, 1952, Waters Davis wrote: "Early in 1951 we were active in the extreme in helping the Secretary of Agriculture with his famous Memorandum 1278. We can safely say that without our efforts and the Secretary's generosity in taking our advice, the soil conservation district movement as we have it today would have been a thing of the past."

Among the items said to have been considered by the Secretary and his advisors before Memorandum 1278 was issued were consolidating SCS with Extension; consolidating SCS with PMA; and transferring conservation cost-sharing from PMA to SCS.

Memorandum 1278 did not make the state extension services and the land grant colleges happy, because it established SCS principles as departmental policy, and made SCS responsible for technical aspects of ACP work in counties where there were no conservation districts, about 600 at that time, an area then served by Extension workers.

To clarify misinterpretations that apparently were being placed on Memorandum 1278, Secretary Brannan issued another memorandum dated April 9, 1952, which he addressed to Gus Geissler, PMA Administrator, and Robert N. Salter, Chief of SCS:

"The purpose of this memorandum is to clarify any confusion within your agencies, and with others concerned, about Department of Agriculture policy in regard to soil conservation districts.

"The national interest demands that measures for soil and water conservation be applied on all farms and ranches in the United States as rapidly as possible in order to protect and build up soil productivity to sustain higher crop yields. It is our ultimate objective that each farmer and rancher have a scientifically developed, technically sound conservation plan related specifically to the pattern of soil and water resources of the land he operates and to his aptitudes and personal resources, and that he be furnished the technical and financial assistance needed to put that plan into use on the land.

"Soil conservation districts play a key role in helping farmers to get well-rounded conservation systems developed and applied. I believe that it is in the national interest for every farmer and every acre of farmland in the country to be in soil conservation districts. For this reason in Memorandum No. 1278 I directed the PMA State Committee and the State Conservationist of the Soil Conservation Service to jointly encourage the creation and development of soil conservation districts.

"I feel strongly about the importance of local democratic leadership in farm programs. We are continually striving to put more responsibility for carrying out programs in the hands of farmers themselves. Therefore, in Memorandum No. 1278 I directed the PMA County Committee and the local technicians of the SCS, working with the governing body of the soil conservation district, to jointly formulate and determine the soil conservation policies and programs for the county within the state-wide framework established by the Department of Agriculture.

"One purpose of Memorandum No. 1278 was to put a sounder technical foundation under the financial assistance phase of the conservation program. I assigned SCS the responsiblity for the technical soundness of permanent type practices applied with financial assistance from the ACP Program. Arrangements should be worked out as rapidly as possible, making use of existing provisions of law and such other arrangements as may be developed, whereby the SCS can handle this added responsibility without impairing the technical assistance that the SCS is furnishing to soil conservation districts.

"I suggest that you distribute this memorandum throughout your respective agencies and I shall furnish a copy to the President of the National Association of Soil Conservation Districts."

SCS duties in connection with the permanent type cost-sharing practices are to determine need and practicability, select site, supervise installation, and certify performance. Those who apply to their county ASC Committee for cost-sharing need not be conservation district cooperators. This ACP-related work, through the years, became a growing part of the SCS work load and has in many areas subtracted substantially from the technical assistance to conservation districts.

The "five percent" transfer authority, which Congress has continued annually, has never covered the actual cost to the SCS of providing service to the ACP participants. For many years, the transfer was permissive and many counties made no transfer of funds at all. Where this occurred, the impact on district programs was particularly severe. As a result of the growing criticism by conservation districts, on January 22, 1975, the SCS and ASCS agreed to transfer the money at the state level, thereby reducing the local inconsistencies that had existed before. SCS agreed to service all ACP referrals if the full five percent was made available.

Country Gentleman Articles

"It's high time that Government agencies quit arguing and bickering among themselves about who's going to be 'boss' of soil conservation because the truth is, none of them is going to be 'boss'."

That was the opening paragraph of an article by Waters Davis in the May, 1953, issue of *Country Gentleman*. It was the last in a series of three articles the magazine had published, the first by an anonymous county agent and the second by Dr. Firman E. Bear of Rutgers University. The three articles were published under the editorial heading, "I Believe." The county agent's article had argued for consolidation of all agricultural programs under the state extension services, citing soil conservation activities as a major disaster area. Dr. Bear's article was an analysis of conservation districts and their effectiveness. He called them "our first line of defense against national decay."

Davis fired both barrels in his article and donated the $150 check he received in payment to the NASCD. He said, in part:

"The people of America decided a long time ago that soil conservation was much too important to turn over to government 'hired hands'.

"There are 12,574 soil conservation district supervisors, commissioners, and directors scattered around the country and, believe me, no government agency, whether it be the Extension Service, the Soil Conservation Service, the Forest Service, or the Bureau of Missing Topsoil is going to dominate, intimidate, coerce, or boss these people.

"The reason I say that is because practically all these folks are working free. They are volunteers. Most of us shell out a good piece of change out of our own pockets each year to make doubly sure that our districts are kept independent.

"Early this year we sent a questionnaire to every soil conservation district supervisor, commissioner, and director. One of our questions asked specifically if they would approve a proposal to have all technical help on soil conservation handled by county agents. The vote was 4,594 to 573 against the idea.

"Personally, I don't interpret that vote as any lack of confidence in our county agents. They are doing, and have done for many years, a magnificent job in a specialized field -- education. In most states, they have done a good job of helping soil conservation districts with educational work. But the fact that our county agents are conscientious, hardworking members of our soil-conservation team, is no reason to believe they would make good (bosses) of all the many other government (hired hands) who are helping too.

"On the contrary, I don't believe our land grant colleges and extension services can successfully administer the soil conservation program. The Soil Conservation Service is an action agency whose technicians spend their time in the fields and pastures planning with the land operator how best to use every acre.

"Another thing we in districts like about the SCS is its policy of helping build local leadership and its willingness to be bossed by local people. That's a policy unique in all history.

"And let's not kid ourselves about state bureaucracies being any less domineering or dangerous than the federal breed. It's no secret that soil conservation districts have their greatest difficulties where local state bureaucracies are most firmly entrenched.

". . . And that's why I say it's high time government agencies quit bickering and recognize that soil conservation is the people's problem and that the people are going to be boss in their soil conservation districts."

It might have been "high time to quit bickering," as Davis suggested in his article, but the controversy over soil conservation was to heat up more than ever as a new Administration came to power in the Department of Agriculture.

The Brawl with Benson

Shortly after Dwight D. Eisenhower became President, he named Ezra Taft Benson of Utah as Secretary of Agriculture. Benson was known to have strong Extension Service ties as a former employee, and he was believed to have been appointed through the efforts of the President's brother, Dr. Milton S. Eisenhower, then President of the Pennsylvania State University, and of Dean W. I. Myers of the State College of Agriculture at Cornell University. Suspicion was not softened by Benson's appointment of J. Earl Coke, California's State Extension Director, as Assistant Secretary in charge of the Department's research, extension and land use activities.

When Secretary Benson and Assistant Secretary Coke took office, rumblings of a pending reorganization of the SCS and the gradual elimination of conservation districts began to spread. Some of the concern stemmed from a speech made a year earlier by Milton Eisenhower at a meeting of the Agricultural Division of the Land Grant Colleges in Houston on November 13, 1951. Copies of this speech were circulated across the country and, in the minds of some NASCD leaders, especially the fiery Waters Davis, it represented the thinking of the new administration.

In the speech, Dr. Eisenhower, who had been Director of Information and Land Use Coordinator of the USDA when SCS was transferred to Agriculture in 1935 and had much to do with developing early policies and procedures pertaining to the new agency, advocated consolidation of SCS with Extension.

He said: "I have felt for some years that the Soil Conservation Service should be consolidated with Extension. This should be done at the federal, state, and local levels. Specifically, I believe that the federal SCS staff should become a special though small division of the office of the federal director of extension work; the state SCS staff should become a special unit in the office of the state director of extension, serving as subject-matter specialists for the state-wide conservation efforts, just as specialists in livestock, dairy, poultry, and other areas so serve in their fields of competence; at the local level, the conservation technicians should become assistant county agents."

Dr. Eisenhower said he believed such a consolidation would not only improve "educational" services to farmers, but might well result in a reduction in total cost of the two programs of $25 million a year. He acknowledged that the consolidation would require federal and state legislation and that he doubted if such a measure would get "50 votes today" in the Congress.

Near the end of the Houston speech, Dr. Eisenhower startled the NASCD leaders and their members by stating that the reasons for soil conservation districts would no longer be valid if SCS were consolidated with the Extension Service. "Extension now cooperates with a local organization in each county; two separate local organizations would not be needed if the two agencies were combined," he said.

On December 2, 1952, Waters Davis reported on a conversation with Dr. Eisenhower and quoted him as saying that he did not think SCS and Extension should be put together *at this time* but he was not giving up on the long range principles of his speech at Houston.

On March 25, 1953, President Eisenhower submitted to Congress Reorganization Plan No. 2 of 1953, transferring to the Secretary of Agriculture personnel, functions and authorities of all USDA agencies, adding two Assistant Secretaries and an Administrative Assistant Secretary, and giving the Secretary unlimited power to consolidate or transfer agencies within USDA after giving advance public notice.

Disagreements with USDA did not prevent a jovial discussion between Waters Davis of NASCD and President Dwight D. Eisenhower.

Benson's views on USDA's major responsibilities presumably were outlined in the first major publication issued after he took office. Titled "Strengthening American Agriculture Through Research and Education," the publication ignored soil and water conservation as major agricultural problems. It cited the basic long-range need of agriculture as reducing costs, improving quality, and expanding markets, with the sound approach to these needs being through research and education. Further, the publication said that "the spearhead of an enlarged extension program should be an expanding farm advisory service in each county that will work directly with farm people, helping them to take research findings and fit them together so that they will work profitably on a particular farm. Through direct contacts, this advisory staff would become the channel for bringing to farm people technical and economic information needed to develop sound long-range plans for their farms."

Waters Davis labeled this publication the "Blue Book" and told *Tuesday Letter* readers, "It scared me to death." Davis and NASCD Program Advisor William L. Southworth saw the "Blue Book," coupled with Milton Eisenhower's speech and the new reorganization authority, as "handwriting on the wall."

Davis hot-footed it to Washington, consulted with Benson and Undersecretary True Morse, and reported that they had assured him the

"Blue Book" was not a preview of USDA's reorganization plans. "Though Secretary Benson promised to seek our views on reorganization as it affects soil conservation and soil conservation districts *before it is made public,* I'm still scared," Davis wrote. (emphasis in original)

The running fight over Benson's reorganization plans continued for several months, and a blow-by-blow account would in itself require a small book to report in full. Davis and Southworth blasted away with a series of questions labeled "Why?" in the NASCD *Tuesday Letter* on September 29, 1953:

"Why, for 10 frustrating months, has the Secretary of Agriculture and every member of his top staff shunned the outstretched hand of friendship and help offered over and over again by America's 2,500 soil conservation districts and their 1,300,000 farmer-cooperators?

"Why, the moment Congress gave them 'blank check' powers to reorganize the Department of Agriculture, did the Secretary of Agriculture and his staff launch an all-out campaign to discredit and belittle soil conservation and try to convince the American public that soil conservation is just another part of EDUCATION?

"Why has Secretary Benson been seeking the advice of all those interested in agriculture EXCEPT the grass roots soil conservation district officials?

"Why, in spite of the most cordial invitations, were Secretary Benson and every member of his top staff 'too busy' to attend even one of our six area meetings during June, July, August, and September? Why was the Secretary too busy to even send a representative to our national convention? Why, with any time during a three-week period from which to choose, was the Secretary 'too busy' to sit down with our national officers in Washington last March to talk over the most important single problem of Agriculture?"

The key to the confrontation apparently was the exposure by Davis of a supposedly secret reorganization plan that would abolish SCS regional offices, reduce or eliminate the agency's technical staffs in agronomy, biology, range, and forestry, and transfer SCS research work to other agencies.

The NASCD Board's first opportunity to discuss Benson's reorganization plans as a group came at a meeting in Houston, October 19-22, 1953. There was general agreement on the overall objective to oppose the plan, but a few fireworks exploded when one or two raised questions concerning parts of the proposal and NASCD's tactics. Clarence Svedman of Colorado said he was 100 percent behind the objectives but was not completely convinced that NASCD was using the best strategy. "Until we had the facts," he said, "some people didn't think we knew what we were talking about and we undoubtedly antagonized some good friends."

Kent Leavitt said he felt the group must prove to its friends that the proposal would seriously damage conservation districts. He said SCS regional offices had been made more and more independent and this had caused friction both inside and outside the conservation movement. "I had a chance to discuss this entire thing with J. Earl Coke a week ago in Washington and explained that the regional offices had gotten out of control," Leavitt said.

Nolen Fuqua asked Leavitt if he had made any other statements to Coke that would be of interest to NASCD officers. Leavitt replied that he had seen Coke at the urging of Herschel Newsom, Master of the National Grange, and Homer Brinkley, Executive Vice President of the National Council of Farmer Cooperatives. He said: "I reviewed this thing from every angle with Coke. When I got back home I called Herschel and asked him to call Coke and see what impression Coke got from my visit with him. He gave me the very definite impression that the door was still open."

Fuqua then asked Leavitt if he had not told Coke that a committee of NASCD leaders scheduled to meet with Coke the next day was not truly representative of the organization and had been hand-picked by Waters Davis. Leavitt denied saying this to Coke. Houser Davidson of Georgia asked Leavitt why he did not wait to express his views to the officers rather than weaken the NASCD position by "such tactics as going down to Washington the very day before our committee arrived and creating doubt as to whether the committee truly represented districts." Leavitt retorted: "The decision as to whether to attack the Secretary should have been made by the board of directors and the executive committee." Russ Fisher of Virginia said: "We must be careful not to let personalities enter into our deliberations."

Following this tiff, the Board gave a vote of confidence to Waters Davis on a motion by Tommy Moore of Louisiana and Houser Davidson. The motion carried unanimously except Leavitt asked that the record show him "present but not voting." George Heidrich of West Virginia was authorized to prepare a statement on the reorganization, to be signed by all national officers and mailed to all names on the *Tuesday Letter* list.

The storm aroused by NASCD and the Emergency Committee on Natural Resources, organized to carry on the fight under the chairmanship of Dr. Ira N. Gabrielson, distinguished wildlife conservation leader, spread into the nation's leading newspapers and raised a clamor in the Congress. Many Republican congressmen, including Chairman Clifford R. Hope of the House Agriculture Committee, as well as leading Democrats, opposed the reorganization plans they had heard about. In a telegram, Hope urged Secretary Benson to defer the reorganization, including the elimination of SCS regional offices.

Benson's reorganization plan was announced November 2, 1953. It consisted in the main of eliminating the seven regional offices of the SCS. It is not known how much further he would have gone with the so-called original plan, or in carrying out Milton Eisenhower's recommendations, had less of a protest been aroused.

But Waters Davis made it clear in a statement on November 17, 1953, that "storms of protest from soil conservation districts from all parts of America have brought complete victory close at hand. Here is what your storm of protest has accomplished so far:

"1. In 16 short days between October 13 and October 29 the original reorganization plans for the Soil Conservation Service were completely changed. The first plan, which SCS began putting into effect on October 13, wiped out the top level 'technical brains' of the organization.

"2. The original reorganization plans dealt a crippling blow to the small watershed programs which soil conservation districts have pleaded for so earnestly all these years. This, too, is all changed in the new plan. Complete technical staffs, much like districts had before, are to be retained.

"3. The job of state director has been changed back to state conservationist. Secretary Benson has stated emphatically that this job is to be a career, civil service job as before.

"4. The Secretary has now publicly stated that he has no intention of turning the technical job of soil conservation over to land grant colleges and state extension services. This public statement is a resounding victory for soil conservation districts. There are still powerful forces working relentlessly to accomplish this goal. But with the Secretary of Agriculture now publicly on record as opposed, those forces have a most difficult obstacle in their way.

"5. The SCS has a new administrator, Don Williams, who is a tried and true friend of districts. Don literally came up through the SCS ranks. He knows the organization from top to bottom. His appointment is a real victory for districts.

"6. More changes are coming. The echoes of your storm of protest are still being heard and listened to most attentively. The new state office setup, which replaces the old regional system, is to be genuinely strengthened. Exactly how much technical help the districts in your state will receive is uncertain now. But there is no longer any question about Congress and the Secretary of Agriculture being responsive to your wishes. It's up to you to keep on letting them both know that you want a unified, effective, crusading technical service."

Healing the Wounds

On the following day, November 18, Secretary Benson spoke at a meeting of the SCS State Conservationists in Washington. He assured them that SCS would continue as the Department's technical service agency in the field of soil and water conservation and flood prevention. He stressed the importance of local responsibility in carrying out soil and water conservation work and said that SCS would continue to make its services available to farmers and ranchers through locally organized and locally directed soil conservation districts.

He also recognized the rapid growth of interest in watershed protection programs and said the SCS had been given leadership in that important phase of the Department's work. The importance of the watershed program was perhaps indicated by the fact that, in eliminating the SCS regional offices, the reorganization plan allowed SCS to retain certain functions on a regional level, including engineering and watershed planning units that assisted in administering the watershed program from a regional vantage point.

But salving the fears of the SCS did not do what needed to be done in healing the wounds between the Secretary and NASCD. The fight had been bitter, and the participants were pretty wary of each other. The peacemaker turned out to be Nolen Fuqua, who wrangled an appointment with the Secretary through one of Benson's top staff members. "The meeting started off rather cool," Fuqua recalls, "but I knew we had at least one common interest and that was the Boy Scouts of America." In response to a question from Benson as to why he was associated with the conservation districts, Fuqua said, "I've always tried to do the right things with my free work, and that is to carry forward two purposes: the preservation of our soil and water, and building character in the young men of America."[5]

After that ice-breaker, Fuqua asked Benson if he would be willing to come speak to the NASCD Convention in New Orleans. "Do you want to get me shot?" was the reply. "No, I sure don't," said Fuqua. "I just want you to make some good friends."[6]

The Secretary accepted the invitation and, in Fuqua's words, made a "canned speech" that did not receive applause or a positive reaction from the crowd. "I felt sorry for him," Fuqua recalls. "He hadn't said the right thing." But the Secretary remained on the stage, and listened to Mrs. W. L. Spears of Okmulgee, Oklahoma, give her contest-winning conservation speech. When Mrs. Spears finished, Secretary Benson asked permission to say another word or two.

"I wish every American could hear those remarks," Benson said, referring to Mrs. Spears' speech. "I want to express appreciation for the opportunity of being here and looking into your faces and having the opportunity of meeting personally the members of your board," he said. "I want to say that I have no feeling of ill-will in my heart toward any person in America, so far as I know, and certainly not in this group." After joking with the group for a few minutes, Benson announced that "high-level conferences" were under way "looking toward the establishment of a proper advisory committee on this very important subject of the conservation of our soil."[7] When he finished those remarks, Fuqua said, "the crowd gave him a standing ovation." Benson had finally "said the right thing."

After that, relationships between USDA and districts began to warm up again. J. Earl Coke, the chosen "hatchetman" for the reorganization, returned to his post as California Director of Extension in December, soon after the fires started to cool, but influential California conservationists forced him out. He became a Vice President of the Bank of America.

Coke's successor in USDA was Ervin L. Peterson, former state Secretary of Agriculture in Oregon and prominent in Grange circles. Peterson was appointed Assistant Secretary of Agriculture for Federal-State Relations by President Eisenhower on November 15, 1954. Under his supervision were the Agricultural Conservation Program Service, Agricultural Research Service, Farmer Cooperative Service, Federal Extension Service, Forest Service, and Soil Conservation Service.

Peterson's diversified background in farming and state government was reflected in his intense interest in the conservation of soil, water, timber, and wildlife, as well as his emphasis on state and local participation and leadership in conservation programs of the USDA.

He became a staunch friend of conservation districts and their national association. As new programs developed in the mid and late 1950's, Peterson constantly emphasized the role of districts in their implementation. His view of conservation and of conservation districts is capsuled in the following excerpts from an address he gave before the North Dakota State Association of Districts in November, 1957:

"Three years ago I was only generally informed regarding the work which you and your colleagues are so effectively carrying forward. During these past three years, I have visited every section of the country, met with soil conservation district supervisors, observed on the farms of cooperators the work which is being done, the accomplishments which are being achieved, and the several methods and programs in use which serve as tools for use in applying soil and water conservation practices to the land.

"Everywhere I have found soil conservation districts taking the leadership in this effort. Everywhere the districts and their programs have the respect, admiration, confidence, and support of everyone who has an interest in conservation. This support takes many forms. It comes from many places -- the private business community, banks, equipment manufacturers, fertilizer manufacturers. In fact, all who supply the farm market -- educational groups, religious organizations, the farm press, television, radio, and others -- are working with you to help achieve the proper use and treatment of the nation's land resources."

In 1958, Peterson was given the NASCD's Distinguished Service Award at its Minneapolis Convention. In accepting the award, Peterson again paid tribute to conservation districts when he said, "The nation perhaps does not recognize the debt of gratitude it owes to you and those joined with you.

"I know of no organization within my experience that represents more fully the concept of representative government than do the soil conservation districts of these United States of America. If in some small way I have been of some help to you in achieving the stature you so greatly deserve, I have been well paid for my time and efforts."

National Advisory Committee on Soil and Water Conservation

In October, 1955, Secretary Benson completed the formal appointment of a Secretary's Advisory Committee on Soil and Water Conservation, long advocated by NASCD. In announcing the committee, Benson said he wanted it to "function on a continuing basis to advise me, my staff, and Department agencies dealing with soil and water conservation problems."

In addition to NASCD Directors R. Edward Baur of Iowa and A.D. Holmes, Jr., of Alabama, district friends on the committee included Dr. Firman E. Bear, retired Chairman of the Soils Department at Rutgers University; T.R. Hedges, former Chairman of the Washington Association of Soil Conservation Districts; L. L. "Red" Males, prominent district official in Oklahoma; and Raymond A. McConnell, Editor of the *Nebraska State Journal*.

McConnell's assessment of the committee's first meeting was positive: "During the meeting we learned of a number of things in the works that should more closely coordinate the efforts of SCS with other USDA agencies as well as those in the Department of the Interior and the U.S. Army Engineer Corps. These will tremendously strengthen the whole land and water conservation program. And they are definitely in the direction that conservation organizations like NASCD have been recommending for years.

"I am convinced that the Department of Agriculture is acting in complete good faith in creating this committee. I can say that this is definitely not a phony committee and is not to be regarded as window dressing."

The Advisory Committee continued to operate under succeeding Secretaries of Agriculture until 1977, when it was disbanded by Secretary Bob Bergland as part of a government-wide cutback in advisory committees. The action to discontinue the committee met with no resistance from NACD, apparently because most realized that the Advisory Committee had served its purpose. It had prevented the dismantling of either the SCS or the district movement until those threats no longer seemed to exist. Conservation issues had, because of a variety of pressures, taken a much more prominent place on the USDA agenda, and no longer relied on an outside committee for expression. But that is getting ahead of our story.

"Surely the lessons of history teach us that a nation's ultimate strength lies not in its potential to destroy other peoples but in the simple, gentle and loving care of the soil, which is the source of vigor in the growth of the physical, moral and spiritual man. What applies to a nation applies to all its parts.

"What do you need in your county in order to make it a better place in which to work and live and raise your children? Well, I don't need to tell you, I am sure, that even just a moderate increase in the productivity of your land means better schools, better churches, better men and women, and better boys and girls -- physically, mentally, morally and spiritually."

Clifford R. Hope, "Layeth It to Your Heart,"
Hoard's Dairyman,
December 25, 1956, p. 43.

Small Watershed Program

New soil and water conservation and land use concepts and programs emerged in the 1950's and early 1960's with the help of NASCD and its member conservation districts. Most prominent in the expanding conservation concept was the new emphasis on water. This evolved into programs for flood prevention that for the first time recognized the place of private and agricultural lands in the water picture. And it expanded into multiple water use -- water for domestic and industrial supply, for agriculture, and for wildlife and recreation.

In June, 1936, Congress enacted a flood control act, usually called the Omnibus Flood Control Act, in which it recognized for the first time the importance of providing upstream watershed protection and flood prevention as a complement to the downstream flood control program of the U.S. Corps of Engineers. The Omnibus Flood Control Act authorized the Department of Agriculture to make preliminary surveys and carry out improvements for runoff and waterflow retardation and soil erosion prevention on the watersheds of rivers and other waterways.

Under this act, USDA made surveys and reports on more than 200 watersheds, but due to a disagreement between Congressional committees (Agriculture and Public Works) over the proper authorization process, only 11 of those survey reports were authorized in the Flood Control Act of 1944. Plans for upstream watershed programs were basically limited to land treatment measures and minor structures for land stabilization.

When work was started in the 11 watersheds in 1946, after a hiatus because of World War II, it became apparent, as had long been suspected, that the measures authorized by the survey reports would provide very limited flood protection benefits. There was a strong and building desire for more positive flood protection in the small tributaries.

As a result, language was included in subsequent USDA appropriation acts to authorize funds for both land treatment and complementary structural measures to achieve desired levels of prevention in the upstream watersheds. That is how floodwater retarding dams got into the picture in the first 11 watershed projects authorized by the Congress. The first upstream floodwater retarding dam in such a project was completed in 1948 in the Cloud Creek Tributary of Washita Basin in Oklahoma.

By 1950, more than 300 watershed associations and similar groups, most of them sparked by conservation districts and all of them actively supported by them, had organized and were seeking help in developing watershed projects for flood prevention and allied purposes. The watershed voice was a growing one, and it was demanding to be heard. These people believed deeply that the attack on flood prevention must begin where the rains fall and runoff begins -- in the fields and pastures and forests, and that it can end only when the runoff has safely reached the ocean.

This thinking began to affect the legislative process, but between 1944 and 1954, when P.L. 566, the Watershed Protection and Flood Prevention Act, was passed, there was continual pot shooting at each other by the proponents of the "upstream" and "downstream" concepts.

The Army Engineers began to be concerned about competition when the SCS-developed technique of combining conservation land treatment with small floodwater retarding dams became popular. Traditionally, flood control or flood prevention (as advocates of the upstream concept preferred) had been restricted to channel work levees and big dams on the major streams. Thus, rural and urban communities in the so-called small watersheds had been unable to get help. Too, people in these areas, especially farmers, preferred the small dams because they believed they inundated less land than big dams.

The controversy blossomed into a rivalry between the House Public Works Committee, which handled authorizations for the Army Engineers and generally supported their point of view, and the House Agriculture Committee, which saw great merit in the upstream concept.

In 1951, the House Agriculture Committee held hearings to obtain a basis for Small Watershed Program legislation. The following year Representative W.R. Poage of Texas introduced a bill to implement a watershed program. It was reported favorably by the committee, but did not obtain a place on the calendar prior to adjournment.

In July, 1953, through the Subcommittee on Agricultural Appropriations of the House, headed by Representative Jamie Whitten of Mississippi, supporters of the Small Watershed Program obtained a $5 million addition to the appropriation bill for 1954 that was earmarked for pilot watershed projects. This money was used to start 58 small pilot watershed projects. The objectives were to demonstrate the benefits of combining land conservation treatment with flood-prevention dams, and to find out the best ways to achieve local, state, and federal teamwork in planning and carrying out watershed protection and development.

In 1953, the House Agriculture Committee conducted hearings throughout the Midwest on the general subject of watershed programs. The hearings, in which NASCD participated at every step, were chaired by Representative Poage. Following these hearings, Representatives Hope and Poage introduced similar bills to authorize an upstream watershed program.

Senator George D. Aiken of Vermont introduced a companion bill in the Senate. President Eisenhower had expressed interest in the program and in a special message to Congress dated July 31, 1953, he said:

"It is fortunate that today there is a growing recognition on the part of land users and the public generally of the need to strengthen conservation in our upstream watersheds and to minimize flood damage. Inadequate conservation measures and unsound land use patterns vastly increase the danger of loss of valuable topsoil from wind erosion in time of subnormal rainfall and from water erosion in time of floods.

"This should be done as an integral part of our total flood-control and water-use program. In our past efforts to better utilize our water resources, to control floods and to prevent loss of life and property, we have made large investments on the major waterways of the nation. Yet we have tended to neglect the serious waste involved in the loss of topsoil from the nation's farms and the clogging of our streams and channels which results from erosion on the upper reaches of the small streams and tributaries.

"It is important, too, for groups of farmers banded together in local organizations, such as soil conservation districts and watershed associations, to take the initiative, with the technical advice and guidance of the appropriate Federal and State agencies, in developing adequate plans for proper land use and resource improvement in watersheds throughout the Nation. As these plans are prepared and local agreement and cooperation are assured I believe that we should move ahead in the construction of works of improvement and the installation of land-treatment measures as rapidly as possible consistent with a sound overall fiscal program."

The NASCD had maintained a continuing leading role in all moves to get a Small Watershed Program started. NASCD helped organize, and was well represented on a Watershed Committee headed by Ray McConnell, Editor of the *Lincoln Journal,* that met in Washington, D.C. on February 24-25, 1953.

McConnell was spokesman for the committee at a one-hour conference with President Eisenhower and made two requests: "(1) without increasing the overall budget, see that sufficient funds are made available to the Department of Agriculture to greatly accelerate the flood prevention work on the fields, pastures, and creeks where the raindrops fall, and (2) appoint a citizen committee advisory to the Secretary of Agriculture on watershed conservation and flood prevention."

Signs proclaiming community involvement in watershed improvement became common sights in many parts of rural America after implementation of the P.L. 566 Small Watershed Program.

Present at the meeting of the committee with the President were Secretary of Agriculture Ezra T. Benson, Secretary of the Interior Douglas McKay, Budget Director Joseph M. Dodge, Major General Samuel D. Sturgis, Chief of the Corps of Engineers, and Milton Eisenhower, the President's brother.

The McConnell committee later met for two hours with agency heads of the Departments of Agriculture and Interior at a session chaired by Assistant Secretary of Agriculture Coke. The discussion brought out the need for a single national policy to guide all agencies concerned with flood prevention, as well as the two requests McConnell had made to the

President. The committee had lunch on Capitol Hill with 15 Senators and later met with other Senators and members of the House. The committee attracted considerable attention and made a favorable impression on representatives of both the executive and legislative branches.

Members of the committee present were: Don Anderson, IA; John Bird, PA; Bryce C. Browning, OH; Waters Davis, TX; Clair P. Guess, SC; J. T. Graham, NC; Irving Hill, KS; Clayton M. Hoff, DE; Paul Hardin, TX; Walter C. Gumbel, WV; Roland Boyd, TX; George R. Heidrich, WV; Mrs. W. K. Jackson, NH; Otto Liebers, NE; Francis C. Lindsay, CA; Richard C. Longmire, OK; L. L. Males, OK; Bright McConnell, GA; Truette Smith, TX; Richard Searles, AZ; Hugh C. Tuttle, NH; and Col. W. B. Tuttle, TX.

In the Congress, the Hope Bill (H.R. 877) eventually prevailed and (with amendments) became law on August 4, 1954. This act (Public Law 566) was the first permanent small watershed legislation in the nation's history, and although amended several times, is still the authority under which small watershed projects are carried out.

The law broke new ground in several ways. It placed full responsibility for starting watershed projects on the local people, acting through their own organizations. It clearly labeled them as local projects with federal assistance — not federal projects. It specified that the local organization must share in the cost, and that it must maintain and operate the project when completed. It specified that the local organization must obtain all land, easements, and rights-of-way (no land could be acquired by the federal government) and that all structures would be owned by the local people.

"The coordinated watershed approach is one of people working together, utilizing all segments of a community and thereby exemplifying the true meaning and the spirit of soil conservation districts. Our watershed program is based on the principle whereby agencies must not do things for people, but aid them in accomplishing things for themselves. Such a procedure may seem slow, it may be costly, and sometimes it may be besieged with error. However, when a project is planned, executed, and owned by local people, it has a long-time vitality characteristic of the best traditional American spirit.

"If local people and local organization and community interests have carefully and intelligently worked out the details for the watershed program, it will be their watershed. This is essential. However slow it may seem, whatever details it may involve, and regardless of the great amount of local effort that may be required, after careful analysis there can be no other satisfactory way."

Nolen J. Fuqua, "A Coordinated Watershed Approach
to Soil and Water Problems,"
Speech to SCSA Annual Meeting,
Pacific Grove, CA, August 28, 1957.

P.L. 566 specified that the local organization must help develop the plan, with federal assistance, and have full right to approve or disapprove, and that it be responsible for awarding construction contracts. It specified that each project must be approved by the state government before it could receive federal help, and then on a priority basis assigned by the state. It specified new authority for continuing river basin surveys and investigations in cooperation with other federal and state agencies.

But the road was not always easy. On September 27, 1957, Fuqua wrote to General John L. Person of the Army Corps of Engineers, complaining that the Corps was failing to review proposed watershed plans in the 30-day time allotted by the law and asking for "a clear cut statement" from the General as to the "old rumors regarding your desire to take over the engineering part of our small watershed program" which Fuqua said had been recently resurfacing.

Person's reply was dated October 2, 1957. (Try getting a reply from a federal agency in 5 days today!) The General said he and other leaders were "very concerned" about the fact that the Corps reviews had been averaging 65 days instead of the mandated 30, and that steps were being taken to meet the law's requirements. In regard to the engineering work, Person said Corps position was that "the local organizations themselves should assume responsibility for the engineering of Public Law 566 projects, and that they should retain professional engineers to design the structures, prepare the specifications, and supervise construction." Apparently, while the Corps did not want to do the engineering work on the small watersheds, they did not want SCS to do it either, a position that was not gladly received by the conservation districts. The Corps did not get its way, however, and SCS continued to work closely with districts and other sponsors in the expanding program.

Over the years, the Small Watershed Program has been broadened and strengthened by Congress, enabling it to provide federal assistance for projects that include municipal and industrial water supply development, recreation, fish and wildlife, irrigation, and other phases of agricultural water management. The program has been extended to all states, Puerto Rico and the Virgin Islands. Recreation was added as a purpose eligible for cost sharing, and the limits on floodwater detention capacity in any single reservoir were raised.

Few of these amendments came easy. They had to be fought for by proponents of the Small Watershed Program, with NASCD in the forefront, and most had to overcome the continuing opposition of the Army Corps of Engineers, who opposed most of them with the same vigor that NASCD and its supporters expended in support.

In addition, federal funding for the new program was always a difficult problem. In 1959, Fuqua spoke to the American Farm Bureau's annual meeting in Chicago. After reviewing the background of the watershed program and its value to rural America, he pointed out that, for every dollar going into small watershed projects, 20 federal dollars were going into big dam projects through the Corps of Engineers and the Bureau of Reclamation. Facing a federal budget proposal for the next year that would make this gap even worse -- an 11.1 percent increase had been proposed for the Corps and a 13.9 percent cut for the USDA programs -- Fuqua called on the farm organization to "do everything you can to get the unfair and unreasonable 20 to 1 ratio adjusted."

To wage these battles and to promote the watershed concept as the most suitable basis upon which to address many conservation and development problems, a unique coalition of organizations was formed which would, for a quarter of a century, be the forge where national policies on small watersheds would be hammered out.

The National Watershed Congress

The First National Watershed Congress was held at the Hotel Statler, Washington, D.C. on December 6-7, 1954. The Congress participants were organizations dedicated to the upstream watershed management concept. The organizational spadework was done by a general committee composed of Waters Davis, NASCD; Ray McConnell, Editor, Lincoln, Nebraska; C. R. (Pink) Gutermuth, Wildlife Management Institute; and Edward R. Cotton, Gowanda, New York, and John H. Jones, Fairmont, West Virginia, both of the American Watershed Council.

Twenty-three organizations participated. For many, it was the very first time they had joined hands in common cause. Indeed, several were at sword's point on everything but the small watershed idea. The sponsors were: American Federation of Labor; American Nature Society; American Watershed Council; Congress of Industrial Organizations; the Conservation Foundation; Forest Conservation Society of America; Friends of the Land; Independent Timber Farmers of America; International Association of Game, Fish and Conservation Commissioners; Izaak Walton League of America; National Association of Manufacturers; National Association of Soil Conservation Districts; National Audubon Society; National Farmers Union; National Grange; National Parks Association; National Wildlife Federation; Nature Conservancy; Outdoor Writers Association of America; Soil Conservation Society of America; United States Chamber of Commerce; Wilderness Society; Wildlife Management Institute.

Three hundred persons from 40 states attended the first Watershed

Congress. Highlights of the program included the reports of the committees and discussions pro and con from the floor at sessions presided over by Fairfield Osborn, Conservation Foundation; Dr. Jonathan Forman, Friends of the Land; Lloyd E. Partain, *Country Gentleman;* Herbert Eagon, an Ohio farmer; Gordon K. Zimmerman, National Grange; Dr. Ira N. Gabrielson, Wildlife Management Institute; and John H. Baker, National Audubon Society. Ray McConnell was banquet toastmaster. Speakers were Secretary of the Interior Douglas McKay; Secretary of Agriculture Ezra Taft Benson; and Secretary of the Army Robert Stevens. Others at the head table included Undersecretary of Interior Clarence Davis; Assistant Secretaries of Interior Orme Lewis and Fred Aandahl; Undersecretary of Agriculture True D. Morse; Assistant Secretaries of Agriculture Peterson and Earl Butz; Assistant Secretary of Defense (later Secretary of Interior) Fred A. Seaton; Senators Hazel Abeil, Nebraska, and Guy Cordon, Oregon; and Representatives Roman Hruska, Nebraska; Cleveland Bailey, West Virginia; Howard Miller, Kansas; and Clair Engle, California.

The National Watershed Congress grew into a unique annual affair. It was not a membership organization. The participating organizations selected and directed a Steering Committee that planned and conducted the annual meetings, which were financed by a registration fee and voluntary contributions. The Congress did not adopt resolutions, promote projects, or take any action. It was a forum for discussing ways and means of expediting, broadening, and improving local watershed programs.

The National Watershed Congress exerted a tremendous influence on the Small Watershed Program because of the broad cross-section of America it represented, the views and opinions expressed at its meetings, and the caliber of the participating organizations. The fact that the organizations held diverse views on other issues (and on many of the issues involved in the watershed approach) generally favored the development of more balanced upstream watershed programs, helped deter some opposition, and created favorable congressional and public reactions.

NASCD had a prominent role in the National Watershed Congress from the beginning, starting with Waters Davis and Gordon Zimmerman, who chaired one of the sessions of the first Congress in 1954 before he became Executive Secretary of NASCD. For several years, Zimmerman was Chairman of the Steering Committee and David Unger, NASCD Assistant Executive Secretary, was Secretary-Treasurer. Other key members of the Steering Committee were James B. Craig, American Forestry Association; C. R. (Pink) Gutermuth, Wildlife Management Institute; Carl J. Johnson, Soil Conservation Society of America; and Clifford G. McIntire, American Farm Bureau Federation.

Great Plains Conservation Program

Bounded on the west by the Rockies and on the east by an imaginary line where rainfall averages 20 inches a year, lie parts of ten states known as the Great Plains. Here drought is a continuing threat, and it usually comes in cycles. Winters are usually bitterly cold and summers blazing hot and dry. Wind velocities are high, often in the winter and early spring when they can do the most damage to soils that are uncovered and dry.

The Great Plains represents about 37 percent of the nation's land and up to 40 percent of its cropland. In good years the region has produced about 60 percent of the nation's wheat and some 40 percent of its cattle. But it is a hard land, and crop failures can happen year upon year in a dry cycle.

A major problem, aside from natural climatic and physical hazards, is the use of marginal soil for crops, mainly wheat. Much of this land should not be plowed. It is natural grassland, the remnants of what was perhaps the greatest grassland empire the world has ever known. The national soil conservation program, as we have seen, had its impetus in the dust storms and economic distress that resulted from plowing these soils in the 1920's.

A long drought in the 1950's again focused attention on the Plains area, and in August, 1956, Congress enacted the Great Plains Conservation Program (P.L. 1021), which was tailored to the needs of that vast area. Secretary of Agriculture Benson assigned the Soil Conservation Service leadership in administering the new program, which was rather startling in its concept and entirely different from any before attempted.

The concept had been building for several years. It grew out of recommendations of NASCD, conservation districts in the Plains states, land grant colleges and universities, and the general farm organizations. Although their viewpoint differed, there was unanimity that a *specialized* program was essential to cope with conservation problems in the region.

Although many aided materially in developing the concept of the Great Plains Conservation Program, the unsung architect was Jefferson C. (Fats) Dykes, Deputy Administrator of SCS and former SCS Assistant Regional Conservator at Fort Worth. A native Texan who had lived through the "dirty thirties," Dykes knew the peculiar problems of the region as well as any plainsman. His long years of study brought forth a creative concept that eventually was incorporated in P.L. 1021.

The action began when Dykes met with conservation district leaders from the wind erosion areas of New Mexico, Colorado, Nebraska, Kansas, Oklahoma, and Texas at Amarillo in June, 1954. Dykes explained his ideas, and they were received enthusiastically. NASCD leaders met with the Great Plains Agricultural Council, in July, 1956. NASCD President Nolen Fuqua was one of the agricultural leaders who met with

President Eisenhower to present proposals for a long-range Plains program.

NASCD set up a "Great Plains Action Group" consisting of one member selected from each state association of district supervisors in the ten-state area at a special meeting held in Denver, January 11, 1957. The meeting, which was attended by Assistant Secretary of Agriculture Ervin L. Peterson and SCS Administrator Don Williams, spent much of the day talking about the soil conservation practices needed in the special conditions facing Plains farmers and ranchers, and working on ideas for organizing district supervisors so that they might more effectively cooperate in the new program.

The "action group" soon became a standing committee of NASCD and began publication of a monthly Great Plains newsletter to air its views, generate support, and report developments. A. P. (Red) Atkins of Oklahoma was named as the first Chairman of the NASCD Great Plains Action Committee. Other NASCD leaders especially active in helping to develop the legislation and nurse the program into action were L. L. (Red) Males of Oklahoma, Otis Tossett of North Dakota, Tony Krebs of South Dakota, and Everett Barr and William E. Richards of Nebraska.

P.L. 1021 authorized a 15-year program, an appropriations limit of $150 million per year, and priority help to landowners seeking to participate. Most funds were to be used for cost-sharing, to enable

---

"We see in this program an opportunity for all federal and state agencies which are in the field of soil and water conservation to coordinate their activities through local agencies of state government, such as Soil Conservation Districts, in the implementation of all of their programs into a coordinated program in the Great Plains. We, as representatives of the Soil Conservation Districts, are appreciative of the opportunity and certainly accept the challenge that is thrown to us to do this job."

Motion by William E. Richards,
adopted unanimously by NASCD Great Plains meeting,
Denver, CO, January 11, 1957.

---

farmers and ranchers to do their conservation work on a planned, long-range basis and much more rapidly than their own resources would permit. The law provided that a participant develop a satisfactory conservation plan, a timetable for applying it, and enter into an agreement with the Secretary of Agriculture. Because of the complexities of the legislation, and the need to work out detailed regulations, the first GPCP agreement was not signed until December, 1957.

The Great Plains Conservation Program differs from other programs directed at conserving soil and water in several ways. It requires the participant to develop a complete long-range plan for making needed land use or cropping system changes. It requires the participant to sign an agreement with the Secretary of Agriculture to carry out the plan according to an agreed upon schedule and to complete the work within ten years.

All cost-sharing for the entire job, ranging from 50 percent to 80 percent of the cost, is earmarked for the participant when the agreement is signed, and payments are made as the participant completes each step of his plan. SCS technical assistance in planning and installing the measures in the plan is available at an accelerated rate. Other services of the USDA for conservation are also available to the participants.

During the interval while regulations for the new program were being threshed out in the Department of Agriculture, inter-agency squabbling broke out anew. ASCS thought the Great Plains Conservation Program conflicted with their cost-sharing program, which applied throughout the nation, including the Great Plains, and fought against regulations that would provide more favorable cost-sharing under P.L. 1021 for any conservation practice than under the program they administered. SCS, which had never handled cost-sharing payments, wanted ASCS to assume the bookkeeping and payment aspects of the new law. ASCS refused. It wanted to handle the entire program or none of it. And so, SCS was left with the whole program, including the cost-sharing.

The Agricultural Conservation Program Group and its supporters feared the new program, not only because of possible conflicts in the Plains states on cost-sharing rates, but because P.L. 1021 required a basic conservation plan before a participant could be eligible for federal help, including cost-sharing. ACP considered the conservation plan unnecessary. It was geared to single-practice cost-sharing on an annual basis, no strings attached. A program that guaranteed cost-sharing over a period of several years, tied to a conservation plan, seemed to threaten the existence of their program.

Out of this concern came charges that SCS and conservation districts meant to take over the ACP, lock, stock, and barrel. This evolved into the abortive campaign by the organization called F.A.R.M., with the support of the limestone lobby, and of the ACP itself, to wipe out conservation districts.

The first report on the Great Plains Program to the NASCD Directors was made at the Board meeting October 21-24, 1957, at League City by "Red" Atkins of Oklahoma, the NASCD Great Plains Committee Chairman. He reported the special Plains newsletter was being well received and that the program was now authorized in 232 counties in the ten states. He said the program was significant because "it is the first time in our history we've had an agricultural program designed to do a complete job in a large area through the basic conservation farm plan with government cost-sharing."

NASCD published a leaflet entitled "A Job to be Done by Soil Conservation District Officials in the Great Plains Program," in which it explained the basic policies of the program, and, under the byline of Chairman Atkins, urged districts in the Plains states to make the program work.

The leaflet quoted Assistant Secretary of Agriculture Ervin Peterson as saying: "I view the soil conservation districts as being the catalyst or the magnet that can bring together within the local communities interests that stand to benefit and that have an interest in the success of this operation."

The Great Plains Conservation Program, with its new approach to implementing the SCS-district-landowner voluntary partnership approach through long-term contracting, has not only succeeded over the years, but been the basis of many new program proposals, as will be seen in coming chapters. It was amended in 1969 to specify that GPCP conservation plans would be approved by the local conservation district, thus becoming the first federal statute to codify the relationship between SCS and districts. Proposals to extend the program, or its methods, into other areas have regularly arisen, and in the Plains states, farmers and ranchers wanting to take part in the program have always outnumbered the available funds, creating a backlog of up to 5,000 whose requests could not be served.

The Broadening Perspective

The perspective of conservation districts began to broaden in the mid-1950's and early 1960's. The changing outlook was attributed in part to the additional responsibilities of districts in the new national conservation programs. But it was even more attributable to unprecedented technological advances, accelerating population growth, and rapid urbanization.

Urbanization, an end product of advancing technology and population growth, became a major conservation district concern when Don Williams, SCS Administrator, spoke of its toll of productive land and the new conservation problems it was creating, at the February, 1956, annual NASCD meeting in Boston.

Williams was the first to call attention to the national aspects of the effect on productive land of the rapid spread of housing, airports, factories, highways, and shopping centers to the countryside adjacent to the great metropolitan centers. He observed the shift of good agricultural land to urban uses as he travelled across the country, and noted that the process was recognized as a problem only in the areas where it was acute and not as one having national consequences. His main concern was not that open land on the urban fringe was being gobbled up for urban-type uses, but the kind of land that was being gobbled up. He directed John W. Barnard of the SCS planning staff to make a study, and Barnard's report in 1955 confirmed Williams' observation.

In his talk at the Boston NASCD Convention Williams said in part:

"We knew that a lot of land was going into housing developments, airports, and similar non-agricultural uses. But until a recent study we didn't know how much of it was our best agriculture production land. We estimate that during the last 15 years, about 17 million acres of cultivable land in Classes I, II, III, and IV have been diverted from cultivation.

"This is a rate of more than a million acres a year. Our nation is currently distressed by surpluses in some crops and we must act to protect farmers from the ill effects of those surpluses. But we must not let that cloud the fact that some day we may need every acre of cultivable land to produce food and fiber.

"Once buried under steel and concrete, productive cropland, for all practical purposes, is never again available for agricultural production. And the conservation implications of this trend are clear, too. As non-agricultural users seek out and take up the better, level lands where construction is cheaper and easier, food production tends to shift to lands less suitable for cultivation. This not only increases the cost of production, but raises problems of accelerated erosion, water waste, and similar difficulties."

The *New York Times* published a series of comprehensive articles on urbanization in its issues of January 27 to February 3, 1957, probably the first major treatment of the subject. But the series did not touch on the thesis Williams was expounding at every opportunity. A letter he wrote to the editor, which the *Times* published in full, said, "A footnote I would add to your series pertains to the estimated one million acres of productive land that are converted to non-agricultural uses each year, and what a continuance of this trend might mean to future generations.

"Projection of the present rate indicates that an additional 27 million acres of productive land will be withdrawn from agriculture by 1975. If both the rate of population increase and the rate of annual withdrawal of productive land remain stable, we estimate the curve of increased consumption of food will cross that of total food production sometime before the year 2000.

". . . The real concern is not to curb urbanization; it is where urbanization should take place. Where reasonable alternatives exist, the growth of our cities, our highways, and our industries should be directed away from our most productive lands. Failure to both prevent undue conversion of good lands to other purposes and to protect and improve our remaining productive soils, might have serious repercussions upon future Americans."

The nation's first "National Inventory of Soil and Water Conservation Needs," undertaken in 1958 by the USDA under SCS leadership with the help of state and local agencies and conservation districts, was published in 1960. It showed that the annual rate of conversion of productive land into non-agricultural uses was about 1 1/3 million acres. A new inventory in 1967, published in 1971, showed that there had been a net shift of 15 million acres to non-farming uses during the nine years since the previous inventory.

Aside from its consumption of vast amounts of productive agricultural land, the sprawling march of homes, buildings and pavements on the urban fringe was creating a whole new set of land use and soil and water conservation problems. Urbanization had been chaotic in most areas, with little regard being given to the suitability of sites for non-agricultural purposes—and the consequences for the land, water, and other natural resources involved were often serious.

Involvement of Districts

Conservation districts were agriculturally oriented and for the most part operated by farmers and ranchers for farmers and ranchers, since most of them had been organized at a time when the major problem was soil erosion by wind and water on privately owned agricultural lands.

Urbanization changed the picture, and changed it quite rapidly. All of a sudden the transplanted urbanites were part of the problem. Homeowners and developers began to learn that soil erosion could and did happen to them. So did problems of water supply, poor drainage, flooding, water pollution, siltation, and waste disposal. Many of them discovered that the suitability of soil must be matched with the proposed use -- that not all soils would absorb septic tank effluent; that not all soils would support houses or schools or other buildings; that streets and roads and shopping centers could not be located safely without a soil survey interpreted by competent scientists.

They discovered, too, that many of their communities were within conservation districts, and that methods developed to solve the same problems on farms could be used, sometimes with adaptations, of course, on lands in other uses. They discovered that the conservation districts and the agricultural landowners received technical assistance from SCS and other help from state, local, and federal agencies. They began to demand their share of this help.

Conservation districts in the expanding metropolitan areas began to feel the heat. At the NASCD Council meeting during the Annual Convention at Minneapolis in February, 1958, Hans Van Leer of Massachusetts called attention to the "increasingly acute" urban problems in the Northeast. He said the duties and responsibilities of conservation districts "are changing" as the result of rapid urban encroachment of rural lands. He suggested that a committee be appointed to work with SCS in an effort to establish policies and procedures on technical assistance to non-farm occupiers.

Hugh Tuttle of New Hampshire was named Chairman of a Rural-Urban Committee, which did considerable preliminary work before it met during the NASCD Annual Convention at Houston in February, 1959. At that time, E. A. "Bones" Norton of SCS explained that SCS policy would be to give technical information and assistance in urban areas where requested, but only in the amounts and according to the priorities established by the governing bodies of conservation districts. This clearly put the decisions in the hands of the districts.

Committee discussion revealed that the urban problem was a major one in more than 500 conservation districts and was being felt to a lesser degree in many more. It was most serious in southern New England, southeastern New York, central California, and in areas surrounding most of the nation's largest cities. The committee adopted a seven-point policy that was approved by the NASCD Directors at the Houston Convention. In recommending the following policies, the committee said it recognized that no specific set of precedures would fit every situation and that policies should be considered as a framework within which to work:

1. Conservation districts will accept responsibility for soil and water conservation in rurban (a word coined to suggest the intermingled rural-urban zone) areas within their boundaries upon request.

2. Districts should develop an application form especially designed for rurban cooperators that will be different from the usual farmer-rancher cooperative agreement.

3. The two types of cooperators -- farmer -- rancher and rurban --should be distinguished between, and separate priorities of work should be set up for each.

4. Districts should provide planning consultation to rurban land occupiers but not technical layout or application unless it cannot be obtained locally from private sources.

5. All local and state agencies should be called upon to give assistance

on rurban problems.

6. Districts should recognize that any procedure used must be in accordance with the state law under which they are operating.

7. Every district affected by the rurban problem should sponsor an intensive informational and educational program designed to hold good farmland as long as possible for agricultural use. Close working relationships with planning and zoning boards, industrial development groups, housing commissions and other local groups should be established and fostered.

With this policy, NASCD was poised to enter a decade of broadening interests and issues.

Broadening the Base

7

Conservation districts and their national association moved into the decade of the 1960's strong and growing, but facing new and challenging demands. The F.A.R.M. movement, which had threatened to wipe out conservation districts, had itself fallen by the wayside. Districts were being given more recognition in some states, with both additional responsibilities and added resources. In Kentucky, for example, a 1958 law authorized county courts to levy up to two cents an acre on all lands for use by conservation districts.

The national association had greatly expanded its ability to serve, as well. The establishment of the Washington office in September of 1958 had given the organization a voice in Washington, and many of the details that had formerly fallen on the President could now be handled by Executive Secretary Gordon Zimmerman. In March of 1959, a Denver field office had opened, with Robert S. McClelland as the Program Advisor, serving the state associations, state soil conservation agencies and conservation districts of the three westernmost NASCD regions.

Changing the Structure

In 1959, the thirteenth annual meeting of NASCD drew 1,647 to Houston, Texas. This meeting, second largest in the history of the association, resulted in several significant changes.

The Council changed the term of the national President, effective in 1960, to a two-year term to reduce the uncertainty and instability associated with annual elections. The Executive Secretary was placed in charge of supervision of all employees and offices.

A huge crowd turned out at Houston in 1959 for the thirteenth annual meeting of the NASCD.

The Board and Officers at the 1954 New Orleans NASCD meeting. Seated (l. to r.) Alf Larson, MN; Francis Lindsay, CA; Nolen J. Fuqua, OK; Waters S. Davis, Jr., TX; W.F. Hall, GA; George Heidrich, WV; Ed Baur, IA and L.E. Thorderson, UT. Standing (l. to r.) William E. Richards, NE; Red Atkins, OK; E.O. Moore, NM; Hugh C. Tuttle, NH; John Faught, TX; Otis Tossett, ND; Herb Van Aken, MI; Harry Reich, MD; Tom P. Moore, Jr., LA; A.D. Holmes, Jr., AL; Clarence Svedman, CO; Ed Fisher, VA; Gordon McGowan, MT; and Dave J. Doneen, WA.

Nolen Fuqua, bowing to the wishes of his family, announced that he would be unavailable for a fifth term in office, and the Board elected William E. Richards of Holdredge, Nebraska, as President. Richards had been active in district affairs for over a decade, and had been active in NASCD since 1952.

Richards faced the task of guiding the association as it expanded. When Waters Davis had been President, he had done virtually all the work of managing the association, in addition to carrying on a heavy travel and speaking schedule. Nolen Fuqua, in attempting to continue this tradition, faced the burden of being in Duncan, Oklahoma, while the main NASCD office was in League City, Texas, and the main focus of action needing his attention was in Washington, D.C. In 1958, after saying that he would not be a candidate for President for another year, Fuqua had agreed to serve again on the condition that he be allowed to hire a full-time assistant to help ease the load.

But Richards really established a new operating style for the organization. With an Executive Secretary to cover the scene in Washington and assist the districts in the eastern part of the country, a paid Manager to run the Service Department in League City, and a field office in Denver to assist the western districts, Richards could concentrate more on the task of establishing relationships and communicating with other organizations, with state association leadership, and with political leaders.

As a result of these additional capabilities, the conservation district movement, as well as the NASCD, gained additional stature and made many new allies and friends.

Industry leaders, who had long supported NASCD and its goals, formalized their efforts with the formation of a Business Advisory Committee to NASCD. The nucleus of the committee had been meeting and working together for two years under the leadership of Nolen Fuqua, Past President of NASCD. In 1961, however, the committee officially formed itself and elected its own leaders. The first Chairman was Stanley Learned, Chairman of the Executive Committee and Assistant to the President of Phillips Petroleum Company. William E. Klein, Vice President of Allis-Chalmers Company, was the Vice-Chairman.

The Business Advisory Committee dedicated itself to helping NASCD with the task of educating the American public, especially non-farm people and school children, about the soil and water conservation situation and the role of conservation districts in addressing resource needs. Through support of NASCD's educational programs, through the Goodyear Conservation Awards Program, the annual FIEI Newsletter Contest, and by helping support the organization's annual programs, the committee brought the considerable power of American industry to the assistance of the conservation district movement.

Suffering Some Losses

The conservation movement lost some friends, as well, in this period. Waters Davis died in November of 1958, and left a tremendous void in the

William E. Richards was elected supervisor of the Harlan County Soil Conservation District in 1947 and soon became a Director of the Nebraska Association of Soil and Water Conservation Districts. He was the President of the Nebraska Association in 1956 and 1957, and served as Chairman of the Nebraska Soil and Water Conservation Commission during his 11-year tenure on that board. In 1952, he was elected Director of the National Association of Soil Conservation Districts and three years later, became the Vice President. He was elected to the Presidency in 1959.

He has always been active in civic affairs, serving as a Director of the Holdredge Chamber of Commerce, a member of the executive committee or officer of the Tri-Trails Boy Scouts of America, the Nebraska Association of Commerce and Industry, the Independent Bankers Association of Nebraska and the Kearney State College Foundation Board.

He has received many citations for his public service including the AK-SAR-BEN Agricultural Achievement Award, the Distinguished Service Award from the Nebraska Association of Soil and Water Conservation Districts, and the Special Service Award from NACD.

Richards graduated from Kearney State College and attended the University of Nebraska College of Law. He has been, for many years, Chairman and President of the First Security Bank of Holdredge, Nebraska.

NASCD organization. In addition to serving as Treasurer, Davis had also served, essentially, as a full-time staff director for the Service Department at League City. He was the essence of the "$1 a year man," giving his full time and energy to the operation of NASCD and the improvement of its programs.

His inspirational leadership had provided many in NASCD with a sense of pride and purpose, as well. R. Sloan Rainwater of Arkansas, in a tribute to Davis at the 1959 Annual Meeting, said, "He was a man of unusual talents and constructive leadership. He not only loved the soil and dedicated much of his life to the preservation of its fertility, but he believed deeply that the strength of our country -- the American way -- is built on the liberty and freedom of the individual. It was he who put together the words that appear on the seal of our Association, 'Conservation - Development - Self-Government'."

The legacy Davis left behind was both inspirational and substantive. In addition to the building he had built and given NASCD, his will bequeathed additional adjoining property to the organization -- property which would allow the Service Department to have room for future expansion and growth.

After the death of Waters Davis, Clair P. Guess, Jr., who had been serving as Program Advisor and staff assistant at League City, was named to the position of Service Department Manager, and the operation was required to turn a profit sizeable enough to support a paid director. This was accomplished, according to President Richards, by the hard work and dedication of the League City staff, who continued to turn out great quantities of high quality work that resulted in a steadily growing business for the service facility.

In May of 1960, NASCD sponsored a dinner at the National Press Club in Washington, honoring the 25th anniversary of the formation of the Soil Conservation Service. Many speakers, including Congressional leaders, reviewed the history of the SCS and its work. President Richards called it "a heart-warming occasion, with friends from Congress, the press, all the major farm organizations, the business community, agencies of government, and other cooperating conservation organizations on hand to pay their respects."

"Naturally the occasion wouldn't have been complete without Dr. Hugh H. Bennett, the first Chief of SCS," Richards said in the *Tuesday Letter*. "His review of the formative years was a delight." Bennett's remarks, which were done without notes or written materials, cannot be found today, but apparently he told many of the stories of early battles that the SCS fought to stay in business in the Department of Agriculture.

It was to be Bennett's last appearance on the national stage. He died on July 7, 1960, at his home in Burlington, North Carolina, and was buried with full honors in Arlington National Cemetary. In eulogizing him, Richards said, "Bennett was responsible, as nearly as one man can be, for launching the modern soil conservation program which is changing the landscape of the nation. He built and inspired a far-flung organization of conservation technician-salesmen. He transformed principles of wise land use from excessive scientific detail to understandable workaday practice. Farmers respected him, believed in him, and loved him."

*Donald A. Williams, SCS Administrator, and Gordon Zimmerman, NASCD
Executive Secretary, admire the plaque presented by NASCD to SCS in honor of
the agency's 25 years of service to the American people.*

New Problems for Conservation

As the nation entered the decade of the 1960's, "soil conservation," as
such, was not a high priority with agricultural policymakers. After years of
fighting burdensome surpluses which continued to keep farm prices down
and drive millions of farmers off the land, the last thing most farm leaders
were concerned about was the loss of farmland or topsoil.

Thus, the federal department charged with administering the programs
to conserve America's agricultural productivity was, at the same time,
charged with controlling and throttling production back. Soil conservation
measures, in addition to being generally viewed as not too important,
could even be castigated for causing part of the surplus problem. It was a
well-touted fact that farmers who undertook conservation management of
their abused lands could often realize higher production and profits. SCS
technicians and others used this fact with farmers to get them interested in
switching to conservation methods; without this inviting appeal, voluntary
cooperation lagged badly.

But the fundamental policy inconsistency was not lost on the policy
analysts in Washington. Speaking for this point of view, economists
Bernard Held and Marion Clawson of Resources for the Future pointed

out that, since it was clear that there was not then, nor would there be in the foreseeable future, any hint of a resource shortage in agriculture, and since the major problem for farm policy was to slow down production, it made little sense for the federal government to fund soil and water conservation efforts. It was, they said, "stepping on the gas and stepping on the brake simultaneously."[1]

Increasingly, however, it was recognized that *soil conservation* did not necessarily have to mean simply *conserving farm soils for more profitable production.* In fact, given the situation that existed, it was prudent of soil conservation leaders to find other rationales for a continued soil conservation effort. That rationale came when leaders in NASCD, USDA, and SCS decided to take a hard look at where the country was going, where the conservation movement was going, and where conservation districts fit into that whole pattern.

What they decided was that the soil conservation movement needed to be broader than the protection of farm soils from erosion: it had to consider water, both in terms of quantity and quality, as an interrelated resource. (That had been seen in the 1930's, but not really taken to heart until the mid-1950's.) In addition, there was new realization that lands in other uses -- even urban uses -- could suffer serious damage from improper care, and that much of the standard soil conservation technology developed on farms could be adapted to other land uses fairly easily.

This adaptation was most effective when soil management practices were made an integral part of the land development process. Districts began to look closely at the lands undergoing transition from undeveloped to developed uses, and finding ways to assist private landowners, developers, and local governments so that the resulting land uses were in keeping with sound soil and water management principles.

There was also growing public recognition and concern over the fact that vast rural areas were drying up economically as farm people fled to find a better future in urban areas. Could widespread and growing rural poverty be addressed by wiser resource development and use? Many thought not only that it could be done, but that it must be, to keep rural America from becoming an economic disaster area.

The result was a realization that the soil conservation movement needed to become a natural resource conservation and development movement, concerned with all non-federal lands, all land uses, and all inter-related resource concerns. But, it was generally conceded, soil conservation districts had not been fully operating in that vein, and might have a difficult time enlarging their scope far enough, fast enough. The question, then, was could districts modernize and become relevant to the needs of the new decade, or would they gradually fade away as a relic of the Dust Bowl?

Freeman's Challenge

Secretary of Agriculture Orville L. Freeman laid the challenge squarely in front of conservation district leaders when he addressed the NASCD Annual Convention at Philadelphia in February, 1962.

Freeman told the NASCD that the farm problem and the conservation problem are "intrinsically and inseparably linked, and our agricultural policy must come to grips with the physical problems of land use, the economics of production and adjustment and farm income, and the social necessities of rural rehabilitation, as a totality." He said agricultural policy and conservation policy "must merge in programs designed to relieve or eliminate rural areas of chronic distress, to enlarge and improve facilities for recreation, to harness our rivers against floods, and to provide for orderly urban and industrial expansion."

Secretary Freeman cited three new areas for land use action -- creating new facilities for recreation, combatting urban sprawl, and driving toward rural renewal -- areas in which "conservation districts have an unprecedented opportunity for constructive service to their communities and the country."

To gird themselves for action in the new areas of opportunity, the Secretary challenged conservation districts to modernize their activities by updating their work programs, and he offered a new memorandum of understanding between individual districts and the USDA that would reflect the broadened concept of conservation and land use.

New Leaders, New Name

At the Philadelphia Convention in 1962, Marion S. Monk, Jr., of Batchelor, LA, was elected President; Sam Studebaker of Tipp City, OH, Vice President; and Max Wilson, Lompoc, CA, was appointed Treasurer. The name of the organization was lengthened to The National Association of Soil and Water Conservation Districts to recognize the broadening mandate falling to districts, but the official abbreviation was shortened to NACD to prevent the use of the unwieldy NASWCD.

Monk had been a district supervisor for many years, and an NASCD Director since 1955. A noted public speaker, he had delivered the keynote address at the 1959 NASCD Convention, and had been appointed NASCD Treasurer upon the death of Waters Davis.

As Monk took over the reins of NACD, the *Tuesday Letter* contained an almost continuous running account of conservation activity in

> "Back in 1951, NASCD was an infant organization struggling for recognition, beset with a multitude of problems, all of which were critical to our continued existence. Our total budget was about $20,000. Our national headquarters was a 20x30 abandoned warehouse in a small village outside of Houston, Texas.
>
> "Our greatest asset was a burning desire on the part of 23 men that the basic physical resources of this nation, water and soil, should be conserved, developed and utilized by a free people acting on their own initiative and through their own local organization — dedicated to the principle of local self-government.
>
> "From that unpretentious beginning, NASCD has progressed steadily until today it stands as one of the most influential voices in the nation in the area of resource development. You command the respect and admiration of the entire nation."
>
> Outgoing NASCD President William E. Richards,
> Philadelphia Convention, 1962.

Washington. One issue, for example, was totally given to President John F. Kennedy's special message on conservation to the Congress in March of 1962, in which he recognized the leadership of the nation's 2,900 conservation districts in directing the nation's soil and water conservation program.[2]

Kennedy also called for an accelerated pace in the P.L. 566 watershed program, intensified forestry assistance for small private woodland owners, a comprehensive resource inventory on the public lands, establishment of water research institutes, a National Wilderness System, a Youth Conservation Corps, establishment of the Bureau of Outdoor Recreation in the Department of the Interior, and creation of the Land and Water Conservation Fund. Clearly, a strong pro-conservation mood prevailed in the Administration, and conservation districts needed to be a part of the new action.

In March of 1962 the Natural Resources Council of America paid tribute to the fact that conservation districts were 25 years old. C.R. "Pink" Gutermuth, Vice President of the Wildlife Management Institute and long-time friend and supporter of NACD, presented plaques to the Brown Creek SCD of North Carolina, the nation's first district, and the State of Arkansas, the first state passing district legislation in 1937.

In his remarks at the anniversary tribute, Secretary of Agriculture Orville Freeman praised the role of districts and their governing bodies in reaffirming the effectiveness of local self-government, but pointedly challenged district leaders that they would have to accept wider responsibilities in land-use planning and management.

Marion S. Monk, Jr., started his career as a stock broker and investment banker. For several years following graduation from Tulane University's School of Business Administration, he was with various firms, as an associate member of the Chicago Board of Trade, the New York Stock Exchange, and the New York Curb Exchange.

Late in 1940, Monk and his wife, Betty, purchased the property on which they now reside, in Batchelor, Louisiana. At the time of the purchase, the property had been in absentee ownership for some 30 years and was badly run down and overgrown. The Monks restored the antebellum French Colonial home that had been originally built in 1830 and established conservation practices such as drainage, pasture planting, and conservation cropping systems on the 3,480 acres of Lakeside Plantation.

In addition to his farming interests, Monk carried on an active business career, operating a general store on Lakeside Plantation, the Guaranty Bank and Trust Company of New Roads, Louisiana, and various investments in New Orleans.

Monk was active in the organization of the Upper Delta Soil Conservation District and was elected one of the original members of the Board. He was President of the Louisiana Association of Soil Conservation District Supervisors from 1953 until 1959 and Chairman of the Louisiana State Soil Conservation Committee for many years. He was elected a Director of NASCD in 1954 and served as Treasurer from 1959 until 1962.

Monk has been active in such diverse organizations as the Pointe Coupee Parish School Board, the Louisiana Bankers Association, the Rural Development Committee, and the Louisiana Cattlemen's Association.

In May, Congress recognized the 25th anniversary, with the passage of Senate Concurrent Resolution 62. The resolution said, in part: "Congress hereby acknowledges the debt owed the soil conservation districts, expresses its appreciation of, its gratitude to, and its pride in these districts which are the custodians of the Nation's agricultural lands . . . ."[3]

Recognizing what was happening, Monk wrote in *Tuesday Letter* that, "A significant change has been taking place in Districts across the country. The interests of District Supervisors are broadening -- and this is being reflected in a widening range of District activities and programs.

"Whether the broader scale approach was initiated by District Supervisors themselves, or whether they are simply responding to the evident demands of our time, is not too important. The facts are that more and more Districts are usefully and effectively concerning themselves with the development of watershed projects, farm forestry, recreational areas and facilities, water supply and flood prevention, rural area development, public land conservation, local land-use planning, and other undertakings associated with the operation of District programs."[4]

NACD Officers, Directors and Staff at the New Orleans fall meeting in 1963. Back row (l. to r.) are David Stewart (staff), Bill Williams (NM), John Olson (AZ), Osborne Galde (ND), Leo Harvey (UT), Wally Petersen (MI), Oscar Hippe (MT), Ancel Webb (MO), Oscar Laper (WI), Robert Graf (VT), A. D. Holmes (AL), John Wilder (TN), Charles Ladd (NC), Nolen Fuqua (OK), Monroe Samuel (AR), Ralph Saylor (OR), John Wells (TX), and Cashar Evans (DE). Front row (l. to r.) are Robert McClelland (staff), Clair P. Guess, Jr. (staff), Raymond Shaffer (PA), Treasurer J. M. Wilson (CA), Philip Glick (Counsel), Vice President Sam Studebaker (OH), President Marion S. Monk (LA), Auxiliary President Gladys Hippe (MT), Gordon K. Zimmerman (staff), Milton Fricke (NE), Richard Thompson (LA) and Lee Conahan (staff).

Budget Problems Grow Worse

But a new problem was making itself dramatically felt; one that would plague the conservation district program for the next quarter-century: new programs and new demands were not being matched by new resources, and the district programs were suffering as a result. In outlining the problem, Monk noted that in the past decade, U.S. landowners had established 500 new conservation districts while the technical assistance available to districts from the SCS had declined. Instead of one technician for ever 80 district cooperators, as had existed in 1951, there were now 170 cooperators for each technician to serve.

The answer, Monk argued, was for districts to seek more assistance from county, state and federal sources. "The time has come," Monk said, "to recognize we're in a race here in America -- a race to plan and get moving toward a more beneficial, intelligent use of our land and water resources before the massive pressures of a fast-growing nation push us sprawling and unprepared along a tragic course of waste."[5]

By 1964, the situation had tightened considerably. Early budget proposals for Fiscal Year 1965 would force SCS to close as many as 50 offices serving districts, along with 10 of the area offices which oversee the work of 10-15 of the local units. Conservation cost-sharing would be cut 40 percent. "Putting the brakes on district programs at this stage, when Secretary of Agriculture Orville Freeman and Secretary of the Interior Stewart Udall have been calling for increased resource conservation efforts from the nation, indicates a serious mix-up somewhere in national goals," Monk told his *Tuesday Letter* readers.

The situation that year was remedied fairly simply by the House Agriculture Appropriations Subcommittee, under the leadership of Jamie Whitten of Mississippi. Technical assistance, watershed planning and ACP cost-sharing funds were all restored to the 1964 level, and there were new funds to staff the 28 new conservation districts envisioned in the coming year.

But the following year, a similar (20 percent) cut was proposed, along with a new wrinkle -- a proposal that farmers and ranchers begin paying for the technical assistance they were receiving from SCS through the conservation district program.

This proposal, it was reported, stemmed from President Lyndon B. Johnson himself. Johnson was a cooperator with several Texas soil conservation districts and insisted, after he became President, that he should have paid for the abundant and effective technical service he received from the SCS through the conservation districts. The service was great, he said, and he would have gladly paid for it.

Johnson attempted, through the Budget Bureau, headed by Kermit Gordon, to require districts and cooperators to pay a "user fee" for their SCS planning help and for their land capability maps, at a rate which would build a "revolving fund" of $20 million a year. This money could then be cut from the SCS budget. The uproar in Congress and among conservationists, largely due to vigorous NACD information efforts, caused the proposal to die within a matter of a few months, but emotions ran high in the conservation community while it was being debated.

One Congressional leader, Senator George McGovern of South Dakota attacked the proposal in a fighting speech at the NACD annual meeting at Portland, Oregon, in 1965, and laid the blame on the Budget Bureau. "There is every indication that this is another example of callous Budget Bureau policy making," McGovern said. "I could be wrong," he continued, "but I am convinced we are up against a serious fight because somebody who obviously lacked a substantive understanding of the tremendous importance of soil conservation to this nation, who did not comprehend the significance of the program, pushed the button that started this conflict."[6]

As any who have been involved in conservation since can testify, the "user fee" idea may have gone away -- or at least faded into the background for a while -- but the problem of attracting national priority to the budgets of resource conservation agencies and programs has turned into a chronic battle; one which has too often captured the full attention of conservation policymakers and deflected debate away from far more critical studies on how to improve the effectiveness of the federal programs.

Each year, NACD was forced into the position of fighting for higher federal appropriations, often just to restore Presidential cuts so that last year's programs could be maintained. It is a position that often galls district officials, who do not like to be identified as proponents of "big federal spending." But there is little choice; without such battles each year, the federal budget process would have completely killed all resource programs that assist the nation's private land users. While this has not happened, the beginnings of the budget battles in Washington in the mid-60's were a sign that the balance in the federal-state-local partnership was beginning to shift. The future would see a less active role by Washington. The question: would states and districts be able to fill the gaps?

Districts Update Programs

Conservation districts accepted Secretary Freeman's challenge with enthusiasm, although admittedly there were many district officials who believed the job was still mainly what it had always been -- erosion control on farms and ranches. Some were not too keen about certain of the new conservation programs and quite a few, especially those in areas far removed from expanding urban centers, took a dim view of involvement in non-farm activities.

But more than 200 conservation districts updated their work programs during 1962, and over 1,000 had completed the task by the end of 1963. The new programs recognized conservation needs and opportunities such as watershed management and flood prevention, creation of recreational facilities on private land, rural economic development, siltation of streams and other forms of water pollution, development of wildlife habitat, farm woodland conservation, non-farm conservation, and many other items that had not been included in their original work programs, some of which dated back to the late 1930's.

This is not to say that all districts had ignored these problems in the past -- some had worked on them for years. But many had not. And few had incorporated them into their work programs. The updating program continued and accelerated. Secretary Freeman encouraged the movement by issuing press releases as new agreements were signed by him for USDA and by the supervisors of individual districts. Several district boards went to Washington for the signing ceremony and were photographed with the Secretary. Officers of several state associations conducted special ceremonies, a few of them in the Secretary's office, when all districts in the state had updated their program and signed new agreements.

In commenting on one such signing ceremony in May of 1962, Monk said in the *Tuesday Letter* that "nothing will be gained by revising words and signing new agreements unless they represent thoughtful program preparation by the governing body; and a determination to make their district program meet more of the needs of more of the people."[7]

Freeman's challenge, and the growing conservation problems of urban sprawl, were the major topics at the NACD's area meetings during 1962. NACD officers and state association leaders pushed a campaign to broaden and update conservation district work programs. By year's end, members of district governing bodies representing 43 states, had, at six area meetings, endorsed a broadened program to include rural area development, recreational development, community land use planning, and related resource activities.

In addition to working with USDA, conservation districts turned to the Department of the Interior as well, with a new thrust in the development of cooperatively-developed long range programs that could cover all lands -- public and private -- in the district. These would serve as the basis for a Memorandum of Understanding between the district and USDI, similar to the ones that were being initiated with the USDA.

Resource Conservation and Development Projects

Tucked away in the so-called omnibus farm bill, the Food and Agriculture Act of 1962, was an idea of Orville L. Freeman's that led to a new and expanded community development role for SCS and conservation districts. Freeman had preached, from the time he became President Kennedy's Secretary of Agriculture, that the Department was a "department of all the people" -- not just for farmers and ranchers -- and that more than half of its activities related directly to urban and other non-farm groups. He had often said that USDA was the chief conservation agency of government, and he advanced the idea that the name of USDA should be changed to reflect its broader scope in the area of service to consumers and in conservation.

One of his major concerns was the continued migration of people from rural areas into the cities, already too big, he said, and plagued by too much poverty, unemployment, crime, and smog. To improve the economy and the attractiveness of rural areas, and increase the job opportunities there, was a pressing national need, he believed.

He sought a new kind of federal program to help meet this need, one that would serve to meld the interests of urban and rural people. His first idea was a "Town and Country" proposal that revolved around townspeople and sportsmen working together on mutually beneficial projects. Don Williams, SCS Administrator, suggested a broader approach that was eventually incorporated in the 1962 farm legislation. The idea was to help the people in a specific area (usually multicounty in size) to work together to provide better educational, employment, cultural, and recreational opportunities, mainly through conservation and development of their natural resources.

Under the program, organizations, local governments and agencies in an area would create an umbrella organization to sponsor the project, then ask for USDA assistance in developing and carrying out a plan for the project area. Each Resource Conservation and Development (RC&D) area has its own goals, but most of them center on the development of local resources, facilities and services to improve economic and living conditions in the area.

A brief account of some of the accomplishments of one project may be helpful in illustrating the RC&D program. This case history is from the Hull-York-Lakeland RC&D area, which included 11 counties in the southern Appalachian region of middle Tennessee. It is adapted from an account prepared by the Project Coordinator, A.K. Booher, SCS, Cookeville, Tennessee.[8]

"Farming had become mechanized to the point that some farmers could no longer compete, coal mines were being worked out or mechanized, and decades of exploitation had left the woodlands in poor condition. This mechanization and resource depletion had left an indelible imprint on the region's population in the decade of the fifties. Outmigration had robbed the area of much of its youth. One county lost a third of its population during the period.

"More than 3,000 people attended grass-roots meetings to help develop the RC&D plan. The sponsors were all the region's soil conservation districts, watershed districts, county courts, and municipalities. In October, 1966, the project was authorized for operations and implementation of project measures began almost immediately.

"During the early stages of development the sponsors realized that recreation and tourism, woodland development, and industrial growth held the greatest promise for economic development. One hundred thousand copies of a color booklet extolling the recreation and scenic attractions of the region were printed and distributed. Fifty thousand bumper stickers and one hundred thousand place mats were printed, all financed with local contributions that exceeded $11,000.

"Private developers and government agencies have established 26 recreational project measures encompassing more than 75,000 acres. RC&D loans for $495,000 have helped four non-profit corporations develop urgently needed recreational facilities in their communities. Project sponsors helped organize and staff an 11-county tourist association in 1968.

"Since 63 percent of the project area is woodland, project sponsors arranged for organizing and staffing the Appalachian Forest Improvement Association in 1969. Seven libraries, eight health centers, three community facilities buildings, and additions to several hospitals have been built.

"In 1967, the RC&D Association joined with the Economic Development Center to sponsor an arts and crafts cooperative and to develop a unified market place for these mountain crafts. Today the Upper Cumberland Crafts Association has nearly 400 members. A warehouse and showroom have been built with help of a loan from the Farmers Home Administration. The association recently opened a retail store in a Nashville shopping center.

"Of the four watershed projects in the area one has been completed and another is nearing completion. Four others are organized, and five watershed studies authorized by the Appalachia Act have been completed.

"Support for the area's continuous environmental and beautification campaign is growing. Thousands of flowering plants now beautify homes, public facilities and roadsides. Trees screen unsightly areas, and cleanup drives have been promoted to remove litter. Twelve sanitary landfills have been established. Ten water utility districts now have modern water systems, and three other districts currently are installing systems. Some municipalities have water and sewage systems installed for the first time in history."

Much the same story could be told in many other RC&D areas. All they needed to get off dead center was a set of objectives or goals, an organization to work through and coordinate activities, help of various local, state, and federal agencies, and above all, the willingness of citizens to work together to improve their region. Operation bootstrap still works as it did in pioneer days, given a chance.

In reaching out through their sponsorship of the RC&D program, as in the watershed programs, conservation districts found themselves working more and more with county and city governments, as well as a variety of state and local agencies that had been largely uninvolved in the fight against soil erosion on farms. As will be told in later chapters, these associations developed a broader political constituency for many phases of the conservation district program -- a constituency that made itself felt when policy changes and budget cuts threatened the continuation of the RC&D program, among others.

Additional Federal Program Changes

Although the RC&D program had the most significant effect on conservation district programs of any portion of the 1962 Farm Bill, it was not the only conservation section contained in the law. Also included, for example, were six amendments to the P.L. 566 watershed program, broadening the authorizations for USDA to cost-share for land, easements and rights-of-way; cost-sharing for agricultural water management; and allowing USDA to make loans to assist local watershed sponsors.

Another section of the bill authorized a "Cropland Conversion Program," aimed at assisting farmers with the transition of excess cropland to other uses such as trees, grass, water storage, recreational facilities or wildlife habitat. The program, which was tested in 41 counties in 13 states, featured 5-10 year contracts between the farmers and the USDA, based on a farm conservation plan developed between the farmer and SCS in cooperation with the conservation district.

NACD leaders supported the concepts in the Cropland Conversion Program enthusiastically, and urged Congress and the Administration (in vain, as it turned out) to keep the procedures whereby any conservation reserve or cropland set-aside program would be based on a farm-wide conservation plan "in force in any future land use adjustment program."[9]

> The partnership nature of the conservation district program is underscored by the growth in contributions of funds and services from non-federal sources. The latest estimates place this amount at $114.1 million per year -- nearly triple that provided eight years ago. Included in the estimate are all appropriations of funds and contributions of services by state governments, county and other local governments, and private individuals and organizations. Of the total, $36.9 million was provided by the states, $40.1 million by local governments, and $37.1 million by private sources. About 40 percent of the money was used for watershed protection and flood prevention projects. Other uses were for conservation practice design and layout, program direction and information, soil surveys, and conservation planning. Federal funds are vital to our conservation district programs. But the states, counties, cities, and private citizens are helping with their share!
>
> —NACD *Tuesday Letter,* March 21, 1972.

Ex-President Harry S. Truman entertained the luncheon guests at the 1964 NACD annual meeting in Kansas City. Looking on are Orville L. Freeman, Secretary of Agriculture, John S. Wilder, NACD Treasurer, and Betty Johnson, Miss Rodeo Missouri.

A major crisis in the Small Watershed Program came during the last three years of the Johnson Administration -- a jurisdictional dispute between the Executive and Legislative Branches that was not settled until the Nixon Administration took over.

The Johnson Administration notified Congress in July, 1966, that the provision of P.L. 566 authorizing Congressional committees (Agriculture or Public Works) to approve certain watershed project plans was an encroachment on the authority of the Executive Branch and that no funds would be allocated for such projects unless they were approved by the White House or by the entire membership of Congress via the regular authorization process.

This was a case of the irresistible force meeting the immovable object. Neither President Johnson nor the Congressional committees would back down. No Member of Congress would introduce the amendment wanted by the White House. Stalemated watershed projects piled up after being approved by the appropriate Congressional committee because the White House refused to release funds. NACD tried, in vain, to have the "blockade" lifted.

Early in the Nixon Administration, NACD President Sam Studebaker sought to end the stalemate by writing directly to the President. In the letter, he reviewed the history of the controversy and said: "The program is at a deplorable impasse and we respectfully urge your intervention to rescue it." Many members of Congress issued public statements and wrote to the White House, and so did many supporters of the program, including Charles B. Shuman, President of the American Farm Bureau Federation.

President Nixon notified the Secretary of Agriculture on March 27, 1969, that he did not object to the original approval procedure by Congressional committees and thus released 96 watershed projects that had been caught in the jam for nearly three years.

The winds of change were blowing elsewhere, as well. Some of the states were beginning to re-think their soil conservation district laws and many districts were moving out to do, in fact, what Secretary Freeman had challenged them to do in concept. Whether or not they could move far enough, fast enough, was still debated, however, and the national association needed a better way to assist that process. The chosen vehicle was an "outlook" committee, charged with the task of looking into the future and helping districts and NACD guide their course toward what that future demanded.

District Outlook Committee

At the October, 1963, Board meeting in New Orleans, on a motion from Treasurer Max Wilson, President Monk was authorized to appoint a special task force "to work with organizations and agencies in developing a policy concerning the expanding role conservation districts may take in the future in assuming new and added responsibilities for the orderly development of the nation's land, water, timber, wildlife, recreational facilities, and all basic resources."

In 1964, President Monk appointed John Wilder of Tennessee, newly named Treasurer, as Chairman of the Special Committee on District Outlook, and, as members, R. Wally Peterson of Michigan and Raymond D. Shaffer of Pennsylvania. Later he added George R. Bagley of Louisiana, Earl McClellan of Idaho, and Philip Glick, General Counsel.

Consultants to the committee named as the work progressed were Grant Walton, New Jersey, and Arthur Darsey, California, then Executive Secretaries of their respective State Soil Conservation Committees; William H. Greiner, Executive Secretary of the Iowa State Committee; and Ewing W. Kinkead, then Executive Director of the Arkansas State Committee. The committee held its first meeting in January, 1964. At President Monk's request, SCS Administrator Don Williams named a committee comprised of Norman A. Berg, Chairman, Hollis R. Williams, Val Silkett, Darnell Whitt, and D. Harper Simms to work with the NACD group.

Monk spoke of the new project in his presidential address at the February, 1964, national convention in Kansas City, citing the activation of the Outlook Committee and the fact that it had held its first meeting the previous month.

"The trend toward broader district programs and interest continues," Monk said. "In varying localities, according to the circumstances, they encompass suburban expansion, highway development, water pollution controls, public land development, protection of open spaces, and other considerations which may be of greater service to the community as a whole than to agriculture.

"How can the NACD now help districts adjust to new and changing conditions and changing needs and thereby serve the citizens, the resources, and the country even better in the years ahead?

"The Special Committee on District Outlook, so wisely authorized by our directors, has a big job and one that will take time as well as vision and conscientious work."

Wilder reported on three committee sessions at the Board meeting in October, 1964, at Asheville, North Carolina. He said the committee had decided on the following objectives:

(1) Appraise coming national needs for conservation districts;

(2) Appraise coming national needs for SCS;

(3) Appraise current and oncoming problems affecting conservation districts;

(4) Appraise the adequacy of existing resources and district laws;

(5) Recommend additions and changes in federal laws;

(6) Recommend additions and changes in state laws;

(7) Draft a statement on recommended role of conservation districts in the future;

(8) Develop a timetable of needed changes, by regions, to include:

(a) Short-range objectives (1965-1968) -- a period for education, consultation, and negotiations;

(b) Middle-range objectives (1968-1980) -- a period for legislative enactments and initial implementation of new authorities;

(c) Long-range objectives (1980-2000) -- a period for reappraisal of resource situation and modernization of planning for conservation district movement;

(9) Develop recommended methods and procedures for obtaining short-range and middle-range objectives.

The committee worked long hours in meeting after meeting. They debated frankly and vigorously, and between meetings subcommittees reviewed study materials and prepared recommendations. Members consulted experts in many fields at federal and state levels and the staffs of private organizations. Guest experts met with the committee often. David G. Unger, Assistant NACD Executive Secretary, became the committee's Secretary and draftsman in mid-1964. Gradually, a file of material and a record of work began to bulge between the covers of the committee's minutes. Several preliminary reports were drafted and revised.

The District Outlook Committee submitted a report in two parts at the NACD Board meeting in October, 1965, at Nassau Bay, Texas. The first part, "Coming Resource Requirements and the Need for Local Action to Meet Them," was accepted almost 100 percent. The second part, "Report and Suggested Alternatives of the NACD Special Committee on District Outlook," included many specific suggestions and recommendations for legislation that created a great deal of discussion and some disagreement on details. The Board approved the first part of the report, and approved the second part in principle, but voted that it be further edited by a subcommittee composed of Chairman Wilder, Executive Secretary Zimmerman, and General Counsel Glick, and that model legislation be drafted for the use of state associations.

The revised second part of the committee report later was titled "Guidelines for Strengthening Conservation Districts" and it became the main reference document at a series of seminars NACD held throughout the country.

The NACD Council ratified the District Outlook report at the February, 1966, annual meeting in New Orleans and authorized the NACD to assist districts and state associations, on request, in its implementation.

The first part of the committee report, a thoughtful and highly readable document that should rate high on any national list of significant conservation literature, was printed as a brochure titled "The Future of Districts -- Strengthening Local Self-Government in Conservation and Resource Development." It was widely distributed.

In the report, the committee referred to an "erosion of influence in resource affairs" on the part of conservation districts in these words: "In the early days of the program the genuine desire to create a new, voluntary, and democratic movement resulted in districts that conceived their policies and tasks narrowly and found themselves relying on others to make many major decisions. The watershed protection and flood prevention program of today -- at the very moment that it advances the concept and usefulness of conservation efforts -- may paradoxically reduce the influence of district officials in many parts of the country and thereby diminish to some extent their role of local leadership.

"It is significant that when this program appeared, and state laws did not appear to give districts adequate powers of sponsorship of watershed projects, district officials in many states chose not to accept the new responsibilities of this program (or to exercise authorities they already had). The result was the creation of more than 700 new local organizations which either have duplicated district authorities or have exercised new powers which might have been granted to districts.

"The relationship of districts with their oldest and closest working partner -- the SCS -- reflects this growing problem. There has been a steady diminution of district influence over the directions and kinds of conservation work carried out by the SCS. The directive from the Secretary of Agriculture requiring SCS to service applications for ACP practices; the passage of the watershed protection act giving SCS an entirely new "clientele" group; and the birth of the project-type programs administered directly by SCS -- all these have resulted in moving greater shares of SCS time away from the effective guidance, direction, and control of district officials.

"When district officials try to function with too few resources, professional conservationists make too many decisions. Because so many officials are farmers, urban and other values are often ignored. Without staff and funds, the trend of conservation needs and programs may not be assessed rationally and adequately. The end result can be a district official who feels that his role is to facilitate and promote a governmental program established at the state or national capital. He is not, under these conditions, an able representative of the public and maker of decisions reflecting local judgment -- but a salesman."

The committee concluded that if districts were to grow and make their most effective contribution to society in the future, they must expand their programs to embrace new phases of conservation and resource development. "If our analysis of potential resource requirements and the prospective limitations of districts in meeting them is correct," the report said, "there exists in America a need for organized bodies to --

"1. Represent all the people and all community interests in ascertaining conservation needs and responding to their desires. To accomplish this, these bodies would need broad and diverse leadership, representative of agriculture, business, industry, recreation, and community interests.

"2. Develop conservation and resource development programs for all of the people.

"3. Involve all the people through appropriate representation in the decision-making process relating to natural resource conservation and development.

"4. Accept and carry out responsibilities, including the expenditures of local, state, and federal financial allocations on behalf of all the people, in connection with resource programs and projects.

"In the opinion of this committee, soil and water conservation districts should become these bodies. Such a policy, we believe, holds the most promise for organizing an effective and enlightened natural resource conservation and development program for America, a program in which local self-government is realized to the highest possible degree.

"If it is agreed that this is the direction in which we are to move, some changes will need to be made. These will not be easy nor will they come about overnight. They will not, and should not, be undertaken in every state and district at the same time. The committee recognizes that no single pattern of organization and operations can serve the needs of every state or region of the country. There are basic diversities in interest, capacities, problems, and convictions that must be recognized and accommodated.

"The changes needed will require that district officials assess their strengths and weaknesses carefully and objectively. They will require due regard for the programs and policies of other groups. And, most important of all, they will require the dedication of informed, intelligent, active, and effective district officials -- the best that can be found -- to the tasks that lie ahead."

In the second part of the report, "Guidelines for Strengthening Conservation Districts," the committee got down to details. It spelled out a series of specific legislative needs to be considered in the development of long-range action programs to meet changing conditions. In summary, "Guidelines" proposed that conservation district work programs and state enabling acts be systematically amended to make districts responsible for the conservation of all renewable natural resources (rather than for soil and water alone) and for multiple purposes, and to broaden representation on district boards so as to include people from cities, suburban areas, and industry as well as farmers and ranchers.

Thus, the change in name from *soil conservation districts* to *conservation districts* or *natural resource districts,* as was done in many states, was intended to indicate an important change in direction and focus.

"Guidelines" proposed broader legal powers for districts including (1) the power of eminent domain to acquire title to lands and interest in lands; (2) the power to derive revenue for administrative and program purposes (within defined limits) from local real property taxation; and (3) the power to serve as the local operating agency (by contracts similar to the agreements with SCS) of any federal or state department or bureau that carries national or state responsibility for the conservation of any renewable natural resource.

The report proposed strengthening the mandate of the state committees administering conservation district laws by changing the name to State Conservation Commission, broadening their membership, making them independent instrumentalities of the state reporting directly to the Governor, and enlarging their duties and responsibilities.

Implementing the Report

Although Marion Monk and NACD's leaders gave the Outlook Committee their unstinting support, it was a series of educational seminars NACD conducted across the country under the committee's leadership that really spread the word and created action. "All along, Marion made sure that we didn't move too fast, and adequately prepared everybody for the next step," Dave Unger recalls.

Three rounds of seminars, titled "District Leadership Seminars," each with a specific theme, were held, the final series in 1971. Representatives of all the states participated in the seminars in their area.

Sam Studebaker, who had succeeded Monk as NACD President in 1966, took over personal leadership of the movement by spearheading the seminars and giving himself the assignment of explaining the committee recommendations. Wilder presided at most of the seminars before he became President. Other regular seminar participants included Norm Berg of SCS and Mary Garner of the USDA's Office of General Counsel.

A typical early seminar saw Wilder opening the discussion by explaining the committee's charge and how it went about the job. Studebaker then took over and went into detail concerning the reasons behind the committee's recommendations and why conservation districts had to adjust to new problems and adopt new ways no matter how much they might be wedded to past procedures.

Many of the seminar participants were shocked at some of the committee's proposals at first hearing. Eminent domain, revenue raising authority through local taxation and bond selling, and authority to handle all state and federal programs dealing with renewable natural resources -- these were radical departures from the long-held concepts of conservation districts.

The first series of seminars was devoted largely to presenting and discussing the committee's report, explaining the needs, as the committee saw them, and giving background information on the material studied and the opinions gathered by the committee. There were questions galore, and many objections.

Studebaker, Wilder and the others kept their presentations low key. They emphasized the fact that every major recommendation of the committee was already in effect some place in the country; every idea was based on something that some district, somewhere, had put in place. They made no effort to force a showdown. They tried mainly to plant the idea that a time for change had come, and unless changes were made, the conservation district movement would eventually come to a dead end. In this they were successful, for the second series of seminars saw growing support for the committee viewpoint. "I've done a lot of thinking, and have decided that you are on the right track," was a common remark by previous protesters. Legislative accomplishments along the lines recommended by the Outlook Committee began to be reported during the second series of seminars, and the number of such reports increased considerably during the third series.

The Special Committee on District Outlook received a mandate at the NACD annual meeting in Chicago in 1971 when the Board adopted a long-range program entitled "NACD in the Seventies - Goals and Objectives," a report presented by Vice President Bagley and later published. This document listed the Outlook Committee's work as Number 1 in a list of goals and objectives, in the words:

"The work initiated under the auspices of the Special Committee on District Outlook should be continued and expanded. The emphasis should be on equipping districts with the authorities, powers, funds, and staff that will enable them to serve as representative, effective units of government."

State Legislatures Respond

Massachusetts led the nation by making the first complete overhaul of state legislation concerning districts in 1963. The new law broadened the

Samuel S. Studebaker was born in Bethel Township, Miami County, Ohio, on July 25, 1897. He received his B.S. in Agriculture from Ohio State University and completed a year of graduate study in Educational Administration at that institution. From 1921 until 1932, he was a high school principal and superintendent of schools, then served on the Miami County School Board from 1932 until 1960.

Following his work as a school administrator, Studebaker operated a 450-acre dairy farm near Tipp City, Ohio. He was a supervisor of the Miami County Soil and Water Conservation District for more than 2 decades, and was elected President of the Ohio Federation of Soil and Water Conservation Districts in 1959. He served as NASCD Director in 1960-61, Vice President from 1962 to 1966 and President from 1966 to 1970.

A member of the Church of the Brethren, American Farm Bureau Federation, and the Grange, he was an incorporator of the Miami Valley Production Credit Association and served as its manager for 11 years. He was a member of the Miami Valley Milk Producers Association and the Farm Credit Board of the Louisville District, as well as Chairman of the Miami County Planning Commission.

A tireless traveler and an excellent "explainer," he inspired a new spirit of cooperation among district leaders, state associations, and the NACD. He was credited with bringing a new sense of unity and common purpose to the district movement during a period when diverse objectives and geographical differences had threatened NACD. Studebaker died of a heart attack at age 80, in October of 1977.

jurisdiction and responsibilities of districts by empowering them to deal with the conservation and development of *natural resources* and serve *all citizens* of the commonwealth -- both town and country. It removed the word "soil" from the districts' name, making them "conservation districts."

When the Act was passed, Governor Endicott Peabody said with justifiable pride, "Someday it may be said of Massachusetts, where this nation began, that here also was the first practical step taken to place the fruits of natural resource conservation within the grasp of everyone."

From 1966 through 1971, state legislative activity relating to updating conservation district work resulted in 140 separate actions, stemming directly from the work of the Outlook Committee, the NACD seminars, and the resultant geared-up activities by state associations and their own outlook committees.

A report prepared by Mary Garner showed that 82 laws strengthening the role of conservation districts were enacted by the state legislatures from 1966 through 1969. The laws included broadening district responsibilities and powers, extending representation to urban areas, providing for cooperation with local governments, removing agricultural qualifications for district officials, and establishing project improvement areas for resource work.

Many of the new state laws provided for new financing for conservation districts, either through taxation or matching county-state appropriations. Many expanded the powers and functions of the state soil and water conservation agencies. Election provisions or the membership make-up of district boards were changed in 16 states, and there were many changes in name, organization, status within state government, and representation of various interests.

One of the most significant laws, the most far-reaching since the Massachusetts law, was enacted by Nebraska. It followed the recommendations of the District Outlook Committee and, in some cases, went beyond them.

In 1969, the unicameral legislature of Nebraska, by a vote of 29 to 9, enacted legislation that resulted in the consolidation of the state's proliferation of 150 soil and water conservation districts, watershed conservancy districts, watershed districts, watershed advisory boards, watershed planning boards, and mosquito abatement districts into 28 "Natural Resource Districts."

The bill called for the new districts to be organized on the basis of "common problem areas" and to begin operations in 1972. Boundaries of the new districts were determined by the Soil and Water Conservation Commission. Other special-purpose districts, such as those dealing with rural water, ground water conservation, drainage, reclamation, and irrigation districts were encouraged in the new law to merge with the new natural resource districts. Further organization of new special-purpose resource districts was prohibited.

In 1971, the Oklahoma legislature enacted legislation establishing conservation districts as the "primary local unit of government responsible for the conservation of the renewable natural resources of the state" which the law defines as "land, soil, excess surface water, vegetation, trees, natural beauty, scenery, and open space."

Districts received new status and authority in a section of the act requiring each district to develop and keep current a long-range plan that inventories resource needs, projects future requirements and sets priorities for resource activities from among available alternatives. Districts were directed to consult with counties, municipalities, and other special-purpose districts in preparing the long-range plans and to hold public hearings to gather views on needed projects and practices.

In Iowa, effective in July, 1971, the state legislature gave conservation districts authorities far more significant than any then granted in any other state. A major provision of the Soil Conservancy District Act required Iowa's 100 soil conservation districts to establish and enforce sediment control regulations. The law said that soil erosion is a nuisance when it results in "damage by siltation to any internal improvement of a conservancy district or . . . to property not owned by the owner or occupant of the land on which such erosion is occurring." The offending landowner can be required to "take such measures as are necessary to comply" with the regulations of the soil conservation districts in which the land is located.

The districts were also given authority to establish "soil loss limits." This means "the maximum amount of soil loss due to erosion by water or wind, expressed in terms of tons per acre per year, which the commissioners of the respective soil conservation districts shall determine to be acceptable" in order to meet the objectives of the act.

South Carolina authorized county sediment control programs based on conservation plans approved by local conservation districts. County governments enforce the ordinances, which carry penalties of $5,000 for each violation. Mining and construction activities of all kinds (except for single-family residences and agricultural buildings) are covered.

South Dakota transferred jurisdiction over all surface mining of coal, clay, stone, sand, gravel, and other minerals from the former Surface Mining Commission to the State Soil Conservation Commission, which assists conservation districts in that state. The Commission issues mining permits and establishes rules and regulations for reclamation. Conservation districts are closely involved in the program.

In several states, including Louisiana, Michigan and Wyoming, incorporated cities and villages were added to districts, people in those municipalities were given the same rights to district services as rural landowners. In Virginia, the districts were extended to all incorporated towns within the existing district boundaries and the election of district officials was placed on the general ballot.

Ohio, late in 1971, enacted legislation giving conservation districts and the Ohio Division of Soil and Water Districts new responsibilities in solving agricultural pollution and urban sediment problems. Minnesota, in a 1972 law, put all cities, towns and villages within conservation district boundaries; provided for supervisors to be elected at the time of general elections; and included the State Soil and Water Commission as an agency of the Department of Natural Resources.

Thus conservation districts emerged from the decade of the 1960's in a much stronger position to deal with natural resource problems of all kinds. That was absolutely essential, for as we shall see, the next decade, the "Decade of the Environment," would bring challenges far more difficult than had characterized the previous decades.

New Agreement with SCS

The partnership of the SCS in the district outlook effort began to be seen, as well. In April, 1967, President Studebaker, in a letter to state association presidents and chairmen and executive officers of state soil and water conservation agencies, transmitted a new supplemental Memorandum of Understanding that he said would reflect the new long-range programs that conservation districts had adopted since 1962.

The new supplemental memorandum, which is the working agreement between SCS and individual districts, was to replace the one that had been revised in 1953, nearly 15 years before. In his letter, Studebaker said the new agreement form had been drafted by the NACD's District Operations Committee, under the leadership of Earl McClellan of Idaho and Edward Felton of Virginia, working with a task force of SCS personnel appointed by SCS Administrator Williams. Studebaker also enclosed a copy of a revision of "Working Together," a brochure which had been jointly prepared several years before by NACD and SCS, which he referred to as "explaining in popular language what the Memorandums of Understanding say in more formal language."

1967 Survey of Districts

To see just what was happening in the conservation districts themselves during this time of change, the Conservation Districts Foundation, under the leadership of Executive Director Marion Monk, conducted an intensive survey of districts and their officials. The results, announced in November, 1967, by NACD President Sam Studebaker, covered about 10,000 conservation district governing body members and some 73,000 district cooperators. They revealed that many of the trends promoted by the NACD Committee on District Outlook were, in fact, beginning to be realized in the operations of the districts. The changes were not complete, of course, but the trends were in evidence.

Almost half of the district officials, 48 percent, were 50 years of age or older, but new blood was coming on; almost 44 percent of all district officials had completed less than five years of service and only 28 percent had served over ten years. Geography affected the age and service of conservation district officials. The youngest officials were in the Pacific, Southwestern, and Upper Mississippi areas. States in these areas also had the largest number of officials who were new to district work. The Southwestern and South Central areas tended to have older district officials and those who had held office longer.

Farm and ranch sizes reflected the current trends in agriculture generally. Properties of 200-300 acres were reported for 36 percent of district officials and 41 percent of cooperators. For 300-1,000 acres holdings, the proportions of officials and cooperators were 35 percent and 30 percent. Twenty percent of district officials and 13 percent of the cooperators had 1,000 acres or more. The conclusion was fairly clear that district officials were, on the average, operating some of the larger farms. With the demands for unpaid service attached to district activities, that is not too surprising.

Although 90 percent of district officials reported they were farmers or ranchers, they had a wide range of other interests. More than half, for example, had business interests such as banking, retail businesses, real estate, and professional work.

District officials were active in their communities. About a quarter of them held public office, 23 percent belonged to school organizations, 28 percent were members of service clubs, and 11 percent were associated with professional groups. More than 70 percent participated in farm organization activities.

Districts were reaching out to a broader range of cooperators, as well, with 30 percent of the cooperators surveyed reporting they had business or industrial connections. Seven percent were public agencies. Again, the District Outlook Committee had either encouraged districts to broaden their programs and services, or they had correctly guessed what the demands of the time would mean to the district program. If there were doubts before, the survey put them to rest: the district program was definitely changing, and the changes were coming fairly rapidly.

A follow-up to this study was conducted in 1984 by the NACD District Outlook Committee, but results were not final in time for inclusion here. Results from 48 of the states and territories indicated that, of 14,846 district officials, 370 were women. About 80 percent were elected, 20 percent appointed to their district role. Full information on district officials, district programs, state programs, and the major conservation objectives of districts will be obtained before the study is complete. That information should be available from NACD's Washington office by late 1984.

Finding a New Leadership Role 

A whole new public focus on conservation issues buffeted NACD and conservation districts during the decade of the 1970's. Many of the people involved in environmental matters knew nothing of the history of the soil and water conservation movement; most had little, if anything, to do with agriculture. The array of new issues, and new people, coupled with a strong sentiment in much of the country that favored the use of federal authorities and powers to solve environmental problems, led some people to question the need for conservation districts. Were districts a necessary part of the conservation scene in America, or were they an anachronism of the past? The District Outlook Committee had decided, in the 1960's, that the answer to that question lay with the districts themselves.

NACD's leaders, immersed in the District Outlook process from the beginning, also felt strongly that the national association could do a great deal to help its member districts establish a new credibility. The first challenge, they thought, was to define which of the ever-changing array of conservation and environmental issues that was being brought to the attention of the public were really of critical importance for district and national attention.

As the decade of the 1970's opened, a new set of NACD leaders developed a fresh strategy, aimed at managing the conservation agenda rather than simply reacting to other people's definition of what needed to be done. First, NACD would define the soil and water conservation issues that should receive top national priority in the coming years. This would give them the opportunity to take national leadership. Secondly, they would devise a strategy to strengthen the association's outreach to its member districts, and work to build the capability of the district movement from the ground up.

A Training Ground

NACD President Sam Studebaker had been involved in the activities of the District Outlook Committee since its inception, and, beginning in 1970, NACD was to be led by three Presidents who had been active in the committee's work from the outset.

In 1970, John Wilder of Tennessee was elected President of NACD. Wilder, who had been the District Outlook Committee's first Chairman, headed a family firm and cotton gin, as well as a farm of some 4,000 acres near Memphis. He is a lawyer and State Senator, who has served many years as the Speaker of the Senate and Lieutenant Governor of Tennessee. He had served NACD as Treasurer and Vice President before being elected President.

Wilder's Vice President in 1970 was George Bagley of Louisiana, a cotton planter and banker. The Treasurer was Lyle Bauer, a wheat farmer and businessman from Harper, Kansas. Both Bagley and Bauer were deeply involved in the work of the District Outlook Committee, and both, in turn, would serve a 4-year term as NACD's President. Thus, from 1966 until 1982, NACD's leadership was firmly rooted in the efforts during the 1960's to pioneer new roles and responsibilities for conservation districts and NACD.

NACD's staff was affected, as well. Of the State Soil Conservation Administrative Officers that were members and advisors on the District Outlook Committee, two (Malcolm Crooks of New Jersey and Robert Baum of Oregon) were to become NACD Regional Representatives in the staff expansions of the 1970's, and a third, Charles Boothby of Maine, would become Executive Secretary in the Washington office in 1977 and, in 1984, Executive Vice President.

On the SCS side, Norm Berg, who led the SCS contingent that advised the committee, was the number two man in the agency from 1969 until 1979, when he was named Administrator, a post he held until 1982. With Berg as one of the key actors, a "Framework Plan" was developed by SCS in 1972. Entitled "Soil and Water Conservation for a Better America," the plan established as SCS's objectives the search for "quality in the natural resource base for sustained use, quality in the environment, and quality in the standard of living for all Americans."

Commenting on the Framework Plan, John Wilder called it "a fundamental document, prepared partly in response to the ideas and objectives outlined in NACD's report on the 'Future of Districts.' It sets forth a modern approach to soil and water conservation, envisioning the use of computers and the latest management techniques to help build a better America for all her citizens."[1]

Thus the ideas that prevailed in the District Outlook Committee -- that districts would have to become more comprehensive and more active in their program approaches; that conservation would need to involve all the people, not just farmers; and that national programs and budgets should be based on a plan that stemmed from an assessment of the resource needs of the nation -- were to dominate the NACD and conservation district policy scene for many years. They shaped the attitudes of the federal government as well, both within SCS and in the Departmental and Congressional initiatives that NACD and SCS were able to initiate.

When Wilder took over as NACD President, he named Sam Studebaker as the Chairman of the District Outlook Committee, a post Studebaker held until 1973. Bagley and Bauer continued as members of the committee. In 1974, when Bagley was elected President, he named Bauer as District Outlook Chairman. In 1978, as Bauer took over the NACD reins, Bagley was the choice to chair the Outlook Committee. Thus, throughout the 1970's, as the District Outlook Committee continued to develop additional studies and reports that would assist NACD's leaders in charting their course, a tightly-knit leadership "team" continued to work together to investigate new ways for the organization to direct its efforts.

A Resources Agenda for the 70's

In 1968 the Committee on District Outlook began to outline the ideas that would need to be considered in the decade ahead. The result was "A Resources Agenda for the 70's," NACD's listing of what still needed doing in the resource conservation effort.

The policy statement, adopted by the NACD Council in 1969, began by pointing out that the nation was directing a great deal of attention to the problems of the cities, but argued that there were urgent needs for conservation and wise development of natural resources that should not be overlooked in the process.

"We live by and with these resources," NACD said. "We cannot live without them. They are limited in extent and highly vulnerable to damage and waste. Today they are under pressures that are unprecedented. A growing economy, a broadening technology, and an increasing population are demanding more and more from resources -- more uses, more products, and on all sides a better environment for living."

"For our own generation," the statement continued, "as well as for those of the future, we need to pursue the work of conservation and wise development of resources as a matter of high national priority. Solving all

John S. Wilder was born on a farm in Fayette County, Tennessee, attended public schools there, and then attended the College of Agriculture at the University of Tennessee until his enlistment in the U.S. Army during World War II. After the war, he returned to Fayette County, while directing his family's commercial and farming enterprises there, attended and graduated from the University of Memphis Law School.

He was prominent in the organization of the soil conservation district in his home county, and served on its board from 1950 to 1975. He served as President of the Tennessee Association of Soil Conservation Districts for five years and was elected to the NACD Board of Directors in 1962. He served as Area Vice President, Treasurer, and Vice President until his election to NACD's Presidency in 1970.

Wilder manages the Longtown Supply Company, a family firm founded in 1887, which owns and operates a 4,000-acre cotton and cattle farm and a cotton gin and also engages in financing farm loans. He was admitted to the Tennessee Bar in 1957, and practices law in Somerville.

Elected to the Tennessee State Senate in 1959, he has served there since that time and is currently Lieutenant Governor and Speaker of the Senate in Tennessee. He has also served as President of the Tennessee Cotton Ginners Association and the Tennessee Agricultural Council, and as a Director of the Oakland Deposit Bank and the Somerville Bank and Trust Company.

the problems of the central cities would surely produce a hollow victory if, in the process, we turned our backs on the resources which sustain us all."

The policy statement went on to propose 11 "key elements" that should be part of a new "natural resources agenda" to "give positive direction to our efforts . . . ."

1. Establishment of a national land use policy that would relate the

privately-owned land resource activities in the United States to the national interest.

2. Completion of the National Cooperative Soil Survey within a decade.

3. Progress in the comprehensive survey and planning of the country's major river basins.

4. Acceleration of the Small Watershed Program, to double the rate of its implementation.

5. Integration of environmental education into the school curriculums of the country.

6. A nationwide program to reduce and control sedimentation damages to water bodies.

7. Support for local efforts to develop natural resource inventories at the county or multi-county level.

8. Federal funding for resource programs based on forecasts of what is needed to produce the quantity and quality of resource conditions people need and desire, rather than annual budgets based largely on last year's budget.

9. Reinvigoration of the countryside through programs to improve the economic health and physical environment of rural America.

10. Strengthening state and local government involvement in resource management affairs.

11. Recognition that the conservation and resource development

(l. to r.) Lyle Bauer of Kansas, John Wilder of Tennessee, Sam Studebaker of Ohio and George Bagley of Louisiana. These four men held the NACD Presidency from 1966 until 1982.

programs of USDA have broad national purposes and should not be administered as adjuncts to the government's farm and commodity programs.

While many of the specifics in the Agenda were not accomplished in the 1970's, it is interesting to look at how many of the concerns were, in fact, central to the resource debates that occupied the nation's attention during the period. National land use legislation dominated much of the legislative agenda for years, while water pollution control efforts became a central issue for conservationists. Realigning the federal budget process was the goal of the Forest and Rangeland Resources Planning Act of 1974 and the Soil and Water Resources Conservation Act of 1977.

State and local governments did, in fact, become much more involved in natural resource management. Again, whether the work of the District Outlook Committee encouraged district officials and political leaders to take a role in these issues, or whether the committee was simply skilled in identifying the issues that were coming at American policymakers, matters little. What is certain is that NACD, through the District Outlook Committee, was in tune with the resource questions of the time, and its leading thinkers were at the cutting edge of the policy debates.

How Do We Reach the Districts?

Shortly after taking office in 1970, John Wilder initiated a series of leadership meetings in Memphis. A small group, usually consisting of Wilder, Vice President George Bagley, Treasurer Lyle Bauer, Executive Secretary Gordon Zimmerman and Assistant Executive Secretary David Unger met to try and define a leadership role for the NACD that would be appropriate to the challenges foreseen by the District Outlook Committee's reports and NACD's "Resources Agenda." "The major challenge," Wilder told the group, "is to find a way to reach individual conservation district officials and help improve the effectiveness of the daily work of each conservation district."[2]

At the San Francisco Convention, the NACD Council directed that a third series of leadership seminars for state association and state commission leaders be held in 1970. The prime objective of this series of meetings was to discuss progress in strengthening district programs through legislative action, district participation in comprehensive planning, and potential district contributions to environmental control.[3]

In addition, district officials were being asked to examine the implications of the new "clearinghouse" functions being established in each state as a result of the federal policy requiring states to "clear" each proposed federal project. These "A-95" clearinghouses (named after the Bureau of the Budget circular that established the process at the federal level), were seen to have great potential significance to district operations.

At these seminars, and at meetings throughout the country, Wilder, Bagley, and Bauer challenged district officials to become more active and involved in local resource issues. Their message: "Districts need to orient their programs toward people and the quality of life," as John Wilder explained it. Wilder pointed out in the *Tuesday Letter* that Lyle Bauer had been carrying this message to district leaders around the country, and that every district leader should hear it.[4]

"The new dimension in district affairs is the human dimension," Bauer was telling his audiences. "It means acting with the well-being of people in mind instead of operating primarily for the protection of resources. It means thinking in terms of the long-range needs and benefits of the whole community rather than in terms of individual farms and watersheds."[5]

But this was not just Lyle Bauer talking. John Wilder used almost exactly the same words in his presidential message at the 1971 Annual Meeting, and George Bagley was carrying the same message wherever he went. Wilder had instituted team leadership at NACD, and the whole team worked to reach out with a consistent message.

In addition, Wilder instituted a news service, called "Spreading the Word," which was designed to help keep state association officials informed of new developments in district work, such as sediment control programs, cooperative arrangements that districts had made with other agencies, and similar success stories from around the nation.

The stakes were high, in Wilder's opinion. "I firmly believe that if districts respond to today's needs," he said in the *Tuesday Letter*, they will have a reason to be; if not, they won't have a reason to exist."[6]

But it was not just districts that needed to change to meet the times. "As America's conservation districts change to meet the resource challenges of the times, so must their national association," Wilder told his *Tuesday Letter* readers. This was the basis for the actions of the NACD Board, taken in a historic meeting at Christiansted, St. Croix, Virgin Islands, in October of 1970.

At the St. Croix meeting, the Board studied the details of a long-range plan for NACD, largely drafted by David Unger as a product of the officers meetings in Memphis. Entitled "NACD in the Seventies - Goals and Objectives," the proposal aroused a great deal of controversy on the Board. It would cost a great deal of money, and it would enlarge NACD's activities into new areas. A motion by Lorin Trubschenck of California to put off action until the spring meeting in March of 1971 was debated heatedly, then defeated. The Board decided, instead, to study the proposal for two days, then vote on it.

After studying the proposal from Monday until Wednesday, the conflicts were still not resolved. The Board was split, and the motion to adopt the proposal resulted in a 10-10 tie, leaving it to President Wilder to cast the tie-breaking ballot. "But John Wilder wouldn't accept that decision," Lyle Bauer remembers. "He wanted people to really study and understand this plan, so he asked that the Internal Affairs Subcommittee, chaired by Trubschenck, study the proposal and re-write it if needed, and bring it back in a form more acceptable to the Board."

The result was an evening session of the subcommittee, followed by an 8:30 p.m. Board session called by Wilder to make a decision on the proposal. The Internal Affairs Subcommittee had made minor revisions, and the long-range plan was unanimously adopted. "The St. Croix meeting, and John Wilder's handling of the divided Board, was a watershed in NACD's history," Lyle Bauer says today. "With that action, the Board healed some long-standing regional divisions, and the organization began to really focus its efforts on the challenges facing all of us."[7]

A Long Range Plan of Action

The plan which was adopted was relatively straightforward in concept, but demanded an almost revolutionary change in NACD capabilities. Its main points were:

1. NACD must continue to further the concepts of District Outlook, helping equip districts with the authorities, powers, funds, and staff that would enable them to serve as representative, effective units of government;

2. NACD would work more closely with state associations and the state soil conservation agencies to help them strengthen their programs and abilities to secure funds and services needed by the districts;

3. NACD would work to ensure that the federal and state governments looked to districts as useful vehicles for local planning and action in resource management, and that federal and state laws and policies recognized the role of districts in resource work;

4. NACD would help districts achieve more effective action in cooperation with county and municipal governments, Councils of Government, economic development districts and planning commissions;

5. NACD would improve communications with its member districts

through better publications, meetings, and conventions;

6. A vigorous, comprehensive, professional public relations program would be established to extend the knowledge of the public about conservation districts, through the use of new emblems, motion pictures, radio and television materials, and other means;

7. A more effective NACD public affairs program to foster support of its activities by others such as Congress, other conservation organizations, trade associations, the business community, and others who could help;

8. To accomplish these goals, NACD would need to employ sufficient personnel of the highest caliber to provide these services, to work with state associations, assist affiliated organizations such as the Auxiliary, and to serve the standing committees; and,

9. All these would demand a vigorous program to secure necessary funding through membership quotas, non-voting memberships, industry contributions, and grants from foundations and the government for special projects.[8]

The Board's adoption of the Plan was accompanied by many other significant and supporting decisions. The most difficult decision was the one to raise the annual quotas of the districts to $150 per district, a change from the previous method of basing each district's quota on the number of cooperators it served. "This criterion is no longer truly meaningful as a measure of district activity," John Wilder said. "Today's districts sponsor many types of water and economic development programs, assist towns and cities, provide services to a wide range of landowners and businesses,

The NACD Officers and Directors at Chicago, 1971. Shown standing (l. to r.) are Thaine Taylor (UT), Elmer Peterson (OR), Conrad Hougen (WA), Randel Burson (MI), Don Fraker (WY), Peter Jackson (MT), Hans Lawaetz (VI), William Bosse (ND), Silas Eakins (NY), Donald Stephens (PA), George Hartley (MA), Monroe Samuel (AR), Doyle Hutcheson (TX), and Lewis Merritt (NM). Seated are Joe Hawkins (GA), Lyle Bauer (KS), George Bagley (LA), Sam Studebaker (OH), Del Krenik (MN), and Thomas Ford (FL). Missing are John Wilder (TN), Harley Bogue (MO), Richard Longmire (OK), T L Meredith (AZ) and Lorin Trubschenck (CA).

and conduct other programs that are not measured by the number of cooperators who have requested conservation plans. The new system regards every district as an equal -- as a responsible entity of local government."[9]

But this new idea had to be sold to district officials all over the country, and accepted, or NACD's whole plan would fail.

Building a Field Staff

For many years, NACD's limited office and staff capability had been located with the President. After Waters Davis began building a Service Department in League City, however, it became apparent that a more permanent arrangement would be necessary. First the decision was made to establish a facility in League City to handle all services and financial affairs. Then came the establishment of the office in Washington, largely to represent the organization in the nation's capital. A Western field office was established in Denver in 1959 to serve the districts in the Northern Plains, Southwestern and Pacific Areas, with Bob McClelland as Western Program Advisor.

The Washington office handled the Eastern districts and the Service Department handled those in the South Central Area, with Clair P. Guess, Jr. in the dual role of Service Department Manager and Program Advisor. In 1962, Guess was transferred to Washington to serve as Eastern Program Advisor, and T. David Stewart, Jr. moved from Assistant Service Department Manager into the dual role in League City.

In 1964, David G. Unger, Soil Conservation Director of the Pennsylvania Department of Agriculture, joined the Washington office staff as Assistant Executive Secretary. In 1967, Guess resigned to return to South Carolina. He was replaced in 1968 by Malcolm P. Crooks, who moved from his role as Executive Secretary of the New Jersey State Soil Conservation Committee to establish an NACD Eastern program office in New Hope, PA.

Thus, in 1970, NACD had three Program Advisors (McClelland in the West, Crooks in the East, and Stewart in the South Central) to assist states and districts. They were, as John Wilder put it, "greatly over-extended." When the Board made the decision at St. Croix to greatly expand NACD's services to districts, many new changes needed to be set in motion.

First, the money had to be found, and the only place to find it was in the member districts. Treasurer Lyle Bauer presented the facts to the Board in a compelling way and, under Wilder's skillful hand, the Board made the difficult decision. Effective January 1, 1971, NACD changed its quota system so that each district paid $150 per year and each state association $200. Prior to that time, quotas had been on a sliding scale based on the number of cooperators in each district, with the quotas ranging from $60.50 to $302.50 per year. As with any such change, there was some grumbling, but at the same time, the district response was little short of spectacular. Overall, 2,094 districts paid the full $150 in 1971 and another 460 paid a substantial portion. Thus, 2,554 districts supported the NACD in 1971, down only 34 from the previous year's final total.

In addition, non-voting memberships were promoted and many SCS employees, eager to see NACD succeed in its bold effort, contributed by joining as non-voting members of the association. The Business Advisory Committee, anchored by such historic supporters as Goodyear, Allis-Chalmers, International Harvester, Phillips Petroleum, John Deere, Caterpillar, and many others, contributed as well, with each company providing an annual contribution in the range of $500 to $5,000 to assist NACD's program expansion efforts.

With the support of the districts evidenced in the quota response, as well as the support of so many individuals and businesses, NACD began to fill the new area slots. Robert C. Baum, former Director of the Oregon State Soil and Water Conservation Commission, became Program Advisor for the Pacific Area in July of 1971, with offices in Salem, Oregon. This reduced the workload on the Denver office to just two areas, the Northern Plains and Southwestern.

In October of 1971, David L. Firor, President of the Georgia Association of Soil Conservation Districts, was hired as the Southern Program Advisor, covering the Southeastern and South Central Areas. This reduced the workload in the Eastern program office to serving the states in the Northeast and Upper Mississippi Areas, and freed the Service Department Manager of his Program Advisor duties in the South Central Area.

In 1972, the area office expansion was completed with the establishment of an office in the Upper Mississippi (now called North Central) Area at Stevens Point, Wisconsin. The Program Advisor named to that position was William J. Horvath, who had served as Administrative Officer for the State Soil Conservation Agencies in Wisconsin and Maryland.

That office and staffing arrangement remains the same today, having served the organization well. In fact, the only personnel changes have been in the Denver office. McClelland retired in 1972, to be replaced by Marvin Cronberg, who had been the Executive Secretary of the Wyoming Conservation Commission. In 1976, Cronberg resigned to enter private business and was replaced by Robert E. Raschke, formerly District

Manager for the Oahe Water District in South Dakota.

The Regional Representatives (as they are now called) serve both as regional liaison and technical staff. Each has a professional background in conservation, with different areas of expertise and interest. Thus, each serves as staff advisor to two or more of NACD's standing committees, assisting the Chairman with meeting arrangements, program details, and helping develop issue papers, resolutions, and follow-up correspondence. NACD's standing committees, being made up of volunteers from far-flung corners of the country, are made far more effective by having a permanent staff person who can help keep track of details and issues.

Showing New Strength

By 1972, as the new arrangement was beginning to take shape, NACD showed its new strength at its annual meeting. Held in Washington, D.C., the 1972 meeting drew 2,275, the largest registration in the organization's history up to that time. At an overflow banquet held in the Washington Hilton's massive ballroom, Congressman Jamie Whitten of Mississippi, long-time Chairman of the House Appropriations Subcommittee on Agriculture, was the main speaker.

Whitten told the district officials and their many guests from Congress and the Administration that the efforts of districts, with the help of SCS and others, had resulted in "real progress toward environmental restoration." But this progress was threatened, Whitten warned, by "a rather small group of environmental extremists" who "do not understand" the practical conservation work going on as a result of district efforts and that "to delay is to damage or destroy your efforts."[10]

Whitten's warning did little to dampen the spirits of the NACD delegates, however. With over 1,200 of the women at the convention spending a morning at the White House as the guest of Julie Nixon Eisenhower, the President's daughter, and a convention program that attracted leaders in virtually every phase of the national government, the mood was one of unbounded optimism as the delegates re-elected John Wilder, George Bagley, and Lyle Bauer for a second term in office.

Over the next two years, as succeeding chapters will show, the national issues continued to heat up and demand more and more time from NACD's leaders. Whether it was national land use legislation, efforts to control water pollution, or the constant fight to see that federal budget cuts did not unduly damage the federal conservation programs, NACD and its leaders were increasingly called upon to articulate the views of the organization and the district officials that it represented.

George Bagley

In 1974, George Bagley of Louisiana succeeded John Wilder as NACD President, with Lyle Bauer moving to Vice President and TL Meredith of Arizona elected as Treasurer. A cotton planter whose land is protected from the Mississippi by levees that sometimes hold flood waters at levels 40 feet above the farm fields, Bagley has been a longtime participant in watershed, drainage and flood protection issues.

But the major issues in the mid-70's had more to do with environmental protection, pollution control, and federal regulation of land use and land management practices than with resource development. As the spokesman for NACD, Bagley walked a political minefield of issues for four years.

The Farm "Problem" Reverses

The decades of farm surpluses that had plagued farm policymakers came to an abrupt end in 1973, when a combination of production factors and foreign grain purchases suddenly depleted American grain stocks. Both USDA and farmers reacted immediately. Agriculture Secretary Earl Butz encouraged farmers to expand production to meet the new export markets, and U.S. farmers began to dramatically expand the acreage planted to wheat, corn and soybeans, the principal export crops.

Conservationists immediately sounded the alarm. In August of 1973, John Wilder warned readers of the *Tuesday Letter* that "the nation faces new and grave risks of widespread, accelerated soil erosion by wind and water." Noting that some 60 million acres, formerly set aside under the Soil Bank and other government programs, were likely to come back into cultivation in one year, he pointed out that much of this land was marginal, and that extra conservation care would be needed if it came back into production.[11]

USDA officials sounded the same warning. "This is no time to have a Great Plow-Up followed by a Great Wash-Away," Assistant Secretary

George R. Bagley is a native of Anderson, Indiana, where he is still a cooperator with the local conservation district on his great grandfather's original land grant made there in 1833. A graduate of Ball State University in Muncie, Indiana, he did graduate work in accounting before moving to Louisiana in 1947.

Starting a career in farming and banking in Louisiana, George and his wife Barbara built up a 2,300 acre cotton, cattle and soybean plantation near St. Joseph. They also operate Lake Bruin, a recreational real estate development they planned and built on the plantation.

Bagley has been a supervisor of the Tensas-Concordia Conservation District since 1956, and was President of the Louisiana Association of SWCD Supervisors prior to his election to NACD office in 1965. He served NACD as Treasurer from 1966 until 1970, Vice President from 1970-74 and President from 1974 to 1978.

He is a member of the Louisiana Water Resources Commission, the Soil Conservation Society of America, the Conservation Education Association, the Louisiana Public Affairs Research Council, and the Louisiana Farm Council. He is an advisor to the Agricultural Committee of the Louisiana Bankers Association and serves on the Citizen's Advisory Board to the Governor's Council on Environmental Quality.

Winner of the National Soil Conservation Achievement Award in 1969 from the National Wildlife Federation, and the Hugh Hammond Bennett Award from the Soil Conservation Society of America in 1982, Bagley has won many other local, state and regional awards for his leadership in the conservation program.

Robert W. Long told the Iowa Association of Soil Conservation District Commissioners. He noted that drought cycles in the Great Plains had historically been every 20 years, and with the two most recent droughts having been in the 1930's and the 1950's, "its about time for another series of dry years when soil erosion hazards are great." He warned that the nation would have to both "produce and protect" if it was to escape serious resource damage during the expanded production cycle.[12]

John Wilder hailed the Department's focus on conservation, but could not refrain from noting that the new conservation demands, along with other tasks facing the conservation agencies "cannot be accomplished adequately if the funds appropriated by Congress for technical assistance to conservation districts are not made available for the employment of required manpower."[13] This was in reference to the fact that President Nixon was refusing to spend money appropriated by Congress that was in excess of the cut-back budget he had proposed for the conservation program, a policy NACD had been fighting vigorously.

An NACD study of the Great Plains area in the fall of 1973 indicated that plowing of grasslands in the Plains was on the rise, and that 12-15 percent of the land being plowed was Class VI and VII land, considered far too marginal for sustained cropping.[14] By early spring, an SCS survey had confirmed the situation: nearly half of the "new land" going into production in 1974 would be subject to severe soil erosion.[15]

As the annual wind erosion survey from the Great Plains became available, it was estimated that about 3.8 million acres had been damaged -- more than the preceding two years, but far less than the 15 million damaged at the height of the 1954-55 drought cycle.[16] But the damage continued to occur. The wind erosion survey in 1976 showed 6 million acres damaged, with another 13 million in condition to blow.[17]

In 1976 the SCS field work was done on the 1977 National Resource Inventories. Those inventories showed, not too surprisingly, that there were tremendous soil erosion problems in certain spots of the nation. Out of those inventories grew much of the analysis for the Resource Conservation Act (RCA), and the most serious erosion areas were singled out later for "targeting" of USDA program funds. Professional conservationists in SCS and NACD had warned the nation about the potential damage inherent in the 1973 USDA policies, but their warnings went unheeded. A brief era of over-expanded production inflicted costs on the nation's land that generations will need to repay.

Reaching Out with a New Image

On the national scene, as the next two chapters will show, NACD and its leaders were caught up in a major battles on national issues, but the 1970 Long Range Plan also envisioned a considerable growth in the organization's efforts to communicate the conservation story to the public. A brief review of a few of the events of the 1970's indicates the success the organization realized in this goal.

In 1971, the Auxiliary entered into a major project, in cooperation with the National Council of State Garden Clubs, to distribute conservation curriculum guides to schools. The guides, *People and Their Environment*, had been prepared with the support of leading conservationists, and were seen as a good way to help teachers incorporate conservation principles in their daily lessons. By late 1972, Thelma McClellan of Idaho, President of the Auxiliary, reported that the Auxiliary had assisted in distributing over 150,000 copies of *People and Their Environment*.

The NACD Ladies Auxiliary leaders in 1976 were (l. to r.) Mrs. Peg Jones (KY), Mrs. Glenda Bauer (KS), Mrs. Jessie Chambers (CO), Mrs. Thelma McClellan (ID), Mrs. Helen Happel (NJ), Mrs. Tiny Buzby (AK), Mrs. Martha Bosse (ND), and Mrs. Jerry Hunter (IN).

The Environmental Film Service was launched as a project of the NACD Service Department in 1971, when SCS decided to close its regional film libraries as an economy move. NACD agreed to operate the new film service as a national effort, and SCS granted over 2,000 prints of 150 of the best conservation films available, along with some film maintenance equipment, to help initiate the service.

The addition of the Film Service, along with the Davis Conservation Library and other expansion at League City, began to badly cramp the building facilities there, so in 1972, a fund-raising drive was launched to collect $100,000 for a new addition to the Service Department. This two-year effort, which raised $132,250 to build and furnish the new addition, also raised the visibility of the Service Department with district officials around the country, giving NACD the opportunity to "tell its story" in a fresh and compelling way.

Featured in the new addition is a Mall of Honor, an attractive, skylighted brick walk joining the new offices to the original structure. Centered at the entry are photos of NACD Presidents, flanked by plaques recording more than 1,000 contributors to the building fund. On the

NACD Mall of Honor, League City, Texas

The NACD Officers, Directors and Staff at the 1977 Spring Meeting in Washington. Standing (l. to r.) are David Firor, Leonard Schultz (SD), William Patton (NM), Ray Heinen, T. David Stewart, Robert E. Williams, William Horvath, Charles L. Boothby, R. E. "Bobby" Wilkinson (VA), Hillard Morris (IL), Harold Johnson (KS), George Hartley (MA), Clarence Durban (OH), David Unger, Monroe Samuel (AR), Steve Brunson (TN), Robert E. Raschke, Desmond G. Wood (AZ), Malcolm Crooks, and Robert Lott (PA). Seated are James Busch (ID), Stanley Christensen (OR), Kenneth J. Roehrich (NJ), William Bosse (ND), Sam Chinn (CA), George Bagley (LA), Glenda Bauer (KS), Lyle Bauer (KS), John Snider (WA), and Doyle Hutcheson (TX).

opposite walls are plaques listing the names of the members of the Endowment Fund's President's and Century Clubs.

In 1972, Director William Bosse of North Dakota was appointed to USDA's National Water Bank Advisory Board and Executive Secretary Gordon Zimmerman was appointed to the Secretary of State's Advisory Committee on the 1972 United Nations Conference on the Human Environment.

In 1973, a slide show "With One Voice - The Story of NACD" was produced and began to be a "stock" part of the speeches presented by NACD Officers and Program Advisors at state association and regional meetings.

In 1974, NACD and the Allis-Chalmers Company began a new Environmental Conservation Education Awards Program to recognize conservation districts and classroom teachers who were sponsoring or conducting outstanding conservation education programs.

The Phillips Petroleum Company, working through the Business Advisory Committee, prepared a new emblem or "logo" for NACD and the conservation districts. The logo, developed by Kurt Maurer, Art Director for Phillips, is a big, bold "C" for conservation, backed up by the initials "N A C D" in flowing lettering based on the idea of contour plowing.

Strengthening the Financial Base

In 1975, Treasurer T L Meredith resigned, and Sam Chinn of California was elected to the Treasurer's post. At the time, the financial situation was not good. The initial response of the districts and state associations to the 1971 quota increase had been positive, but inflation had increased operating costs far faster than income growth could be realized.

As a result, the Board voted to increase quotas in 1976 to $200 per district and $250 per state association. In addition, Chinn began anew to develop an NACD Endowment Fund, a long-sought but elusive goal. In 1976, NACD experienced its best financial year in history, with an excess of income over expenses of some $170,000. This was the result of several contributing factors, including another positive response from districts to the quota increase, the financial success of NACD-arranged travel packages to the Honolulu convention, and high net profits in the Service Department as districts purchased specialty items commemorating the bicentennial year celebration of the United States.

In January, 1977, an NACD President's Club was established to recognize substantial contributors to the Endowment Fund. By early February, 25 people, including all the NACD officers, were recognized in Atlanta as charter members who had given $1,000 or more to the Endowment. The resulting publicity and competition for recognition helped the Fund achieve a take-off, and for the next three years, the Endowment doubled each year. By 1984, when Chinn retired as the longest-serving Treasurer in NACD's history, the Endowment Fund stood at over $250,000, and was earning significant interest to assist in the organization's operating budgets each year.

The End of an Era

In 1978, at the Anaheim, California, Convention, Lyle Bauer was elected NACD President. Milton E. "Bud" Mekelburg of Colorado was elected Vice President and Sam Chinn was elected to the newly-defined office of Secretary-Treasurer. At the same time, David Unger, who had been NACD Executive Vice-President since Gordon Zimmerman's retirement in 1976, announced his resignation to take a post in the Department of Agriculture. Thus NACD faced many changes in its internal affairs.

As the last of the "team" of officers that had formed around John Wilder and the District Outlook Committee, and with a turnover in top staff, Bauer faced some new challenges. His team of officers had not spent years in NACD strategy meetings, as had been the earlier case. Mekelburg had been on the Board only a few months, having been named at the October, 1977, meeting to replace Ross Chambers of Colorado. Chinn had no ambitions for the presidency, wishing instead to make his mark as NACD's financial management leader. As a result, the work of reaching out to the public and to the district officials themselves with the challenges of meeting new issues fell more to Bauer himself.

In addition, Bauer realized there were going to be tremendous challenges on the national level. The previous years had been loaded with intense legislative maneuvering on such issues as nonpoint source pollution control, surface mine reclamation, and development of a federal resource assessment process on which conservation program budgets could be based. This had resulted in passage of three major legislative programs, the 1977 Clean Water Act, the Surface Mine Act of 1977, and the Soil and Water Resources Conservation Act of 1977.

"By 1978," Bauer told the 1979 NACD Convention, "the excitement of

Lyle Bauer is a native of Kansas, a true child of the Dust Bowl. He remembers being taken as a young boy to see people in Western Kansas. "I decided that must be how the moon looked," he recalls. "There was just nothing there."

In 1946, Bauer began farming near Harper. Eventually, he and his wife, Glenda, built up extensive holdings in south central and southwestern Kansas, raising dryland wheat, corn and milo, as well as some irrigated crops. They also held an interest in various business and manufacturing ventures over the years.

From service on his local district board, Bauer quickly moved into offices with the Kansas Association of Conservation Districts and the Kansas Conservation Commission. He was elected an NACD Director in 1965, served as Treasurer from 1970-1974, Vice President from 1974 to 1978, and President from 1978 to 1982.

A civic and community leader, Bauer helped organize the first regional planning agencies in Kansas, and was President of the Kansas Association of Regional Planning Commissions. He is a member of the Board of Governors of the National Agricultural Hall of Fame. In 1970, he was appointed to the USDA Public Advisory Committee on Soil and Water Conservation, serving until that Committee was disbanded in 1977. He is currently a member of the National Advisory Council on Rural Development.

Bauer has been a member of the Kansas Farm Management Association, Soil Conservation Society of America, Kansas Livestock Association, Farm Bureau and Farmer's Union. He has won many state, regional and national awards for his work in conservation.

legislative maneuvering had died down, and the flush of victory had passed. We were left with the hard, frustrating job of helping make those programs actually work." There were rules, regulations and policies to be written, and, of course, there was no money to fund any of them.[18]

As a result of these situations, Bauer sought an Executive Vice President who could help him raise the public visibility of NACD's work while, at the same time, work effectively in Washington for implementation of the federal programs that had resulted from the hard-fought legislative battles of the mid-70's. His selection was R. Neil Sampson, a professional conservationist whose career had been largely with SCS, but who also had experience with USDA's main offices and had worked, for brief periods, in state government and private business.

Bauer's strategy was to reach out boldly and establish NACD as a national leader in identifying the soil and water conservation issues that needed immediate attention. In the process, that would require that NACD's spokesmen surface proposals that were new and innovative -- that had not yet had full debate and acceptance within district, state association, or national association circles. There was always the risk of alienating major constituencies within NACD, but the great risk, as Bauer saw it, was to do nothing and see NACD's influence wane as others took control of the policy agenda. One of the major issues that was clearly emerging was the increasing conflict between USDA's commodity programs and the nation's soil conservation and natural resource objectives.

In 1978, he called attention to this issue in a powerful way. "The pendulum policies of USDA, swinging from tight controls on crop production to 'fence-to-fence' planting, then back to controls, have farmers reeling," Bauer charged. "Conservation farmers are most heavily penalized in this process."

The 1978 "set-aside" program offered a perfect example, and Bauer used it to explain what was happening. "A farmer who has voluntarily planted grass on his erodible land must now cut back on his best, most efficient acres," he explained. "His neighbor who has been exploiting his land, planting marginal acres, letting soil wash into public waters, can now set aside those marginal acres, and get all the program benefits. Once again, farm programs based on crop history favor the exploiter and penalize the conservation farmer."[19]

To test these ideas, and raise suggestions as to what to do in the face of the situation, Bauer called a select task force to Washington to explore the possible elements of a national policy linking natural resource conservation with food and agricultural policy.[20] The task force included former NACD Presidents John Wilder and George Bagley, as well as experts from USDA and Congressional committee staffs.

The task force met only once, then reviewed a staff paper developed as a result of the meeting. The task of developing new national policy proposals proved too ambitious to accomplish with the limited staff available to NACD, but the concepts developed by the task force formed a basis for NACD's future outlook on farm policy questions.

The conclusion was that soil conservation practices on the nation's croplands are significantly affected, if not driven, by food and agricultural policies, not soil conservation policy. Voluntary soil conservation programs, if they are to survive, must exist in an economic climate that allows soil conservation management to be a feasible alternative for farmers. NACD, which had long avoided any involvement in farm policy questions, would have to improve its capability to analyze food and agricultural issues, and speak out publicly about the conservation effects likely to result from different proposals.

With this overview of the internal changes in leadership and capability that affected NACD in the 1970's, it is useful now to turn back and review the major issues of that dynamic decade. It was a decade where NACD played a major role in shaping national issues, but it was also a decade that did much to shape the organization itself. Known as the "Decade of the Environment," the 1970's called into play the evangelistic zeal for conservation and the fighting spirit instilled by E.C. McArthur, Kent Leavitt and Waters Davis; the solid base of conservation program experience learned in the Nolen Fuqua, Bill Richards and Marion Monk years; and seriously tested the national unity within the NACD that had been nurtured by Sam Studebaker.

The Decade of the Environment 9

Concern for the environment was certainly nothing new to the people who worked with soil conservation programs. The environmental awakening in the American public during the late 1960's and early 1970's was little short of a revolution, however, and for several years districts found themselves being pushed aside as people searched for new solutions to environmental problems. Existing institutions were questioned; new laws were passed; and new activism raised once more the issue of how far, and in what ways, the federal government should intrude into the private lives of its citizens.

Many of the major environmental battles of the 1970's were about land use -- who would say how certain lands were to be used; what standards would be set; who would enforce them; which lands would be affected; and how an owner's rights would be protected. These questions deeply divided the "environmental community" from the "agricultural community." Conservation districts, as organizations guided largely by farmers who had long felt a very strong personal sense of responsibility and stewardship to the land, found themselves caught in the middle.

In looking for the "triggering event" of the Environmental Revolution, many historians point to Rachel Carson's *Silent Spring* which, in 1962, sounded the alarm about pesticide hazards. Many (particularly in agriculture) thought that Carson had overstated the case; few doubted the importance of the book in raising public consciousness.

It may be well, however, to look to 1969 for the turning point. People already sensitized by *Silent Spring* and Paul Ehrlich's *The Population Bomb* were suddenly besieged by an amazing series of events that focused attention on some of the increasingly serious environmental problems facing the country. To mention just a few:

In January, the Santa Barbara oil spill coated 13 miles of California beach with oil, and covered every newspaper front page and television

200

screen with photographs of wildlife dying as a result. In March, U.S. marshalls seized nearly 14 tons of frozen salmon from the Great Lakes because of excessive DDT residues. In June, the Cuyahoga River in Cleveland, covered by a thick scum of oil, sludge and industrial waste, caught fire. In August, Los Angeles residents were warned -- again -- not to do any outdoor exercise that required deep breathing. In September, President Nixon announced that we would go ahead and build the SST, in spite of warnings about its economic and environmental costs.[1]

In the wake of such events, the Environmental Age jumped into full swing. Earth Day 1970 was a focal point; new words like "ecology" and "environment" could be used to explain, justify, or oppose just about anything; and a new era of political militancy and confrontation over matters affecting the land was under way.

The messages were not soothing. Actor Eddie Albert, in a speech to the NACD Convention in San Francisco in 1970, shocked the delegates with his message. "Our priority today is survival," he said. "It is not Viet Nam, nor the moon. It is not Mars, nor the SST, nor racism, nor communism. It may not even be a life of quality any more. Just survival."[2]

New laws were enacted by Congress and in the states, and new federal and state agencies, boards, councils, and commissions were established to deal with environmental (mainly pollution) problems. Many industries, sensing that efforts to control air and water pollution could well wind up on their doorsteps, came forth with four-color brochures and magazine advertisements proclaiming their interest in, and efforts for, a better environment.

On January 1, 1970, President Nixon approved the National Environmental Policy Act of 1969, which created the Council on Environmental Quality. The purposes of the Act were "To declare a national policy which will encourage productive and enjoyable harmony between man and his environment; to promote efforts which will prevent or eliminate damage to the environment and biosphere and stimulate the health and welfare of man; to enrich the understanding of the ecological systems and natural resources important to the nation; and to establish the Council on Environmental Quality."

On December 2, 1970, the Environmental Protection Agency was officially born. The new agency, headed by William D. Ruckelshaus, combined the Federal Water Quality Administration, the air pollution and solid waste management programs of the Department of Health, Education and Welfare, the pesticide standards work of the Food and Drug Administration, and the radiation regulation activities of the Atomic Energy Commission.

> "Those of us who have labored in the vineyards of conservation for years on end can only be enthusiastic about the extent of interest that is being displayed in the cause of the environment. The concept of environmental quality is a new and broader interpretation of conservation needs -- and it is an interpretation that the majority of our citizens perceive as relevant.
>
> "Today conservationists are flying a new flag, the flag of the environment. It's a more sophisticated approach, an approach that recognizes that we all live on a spaceship named Earth. Just as astronauts must survive in a finite environment, an environment containing only so much air, water, and space -- so must man. We cannot poison the atmosphere, pollute drinking water, or interfere with delicate natural processes without endangering our very existence.
>
> "Where do districts fit into this battle for the environment? The answer is, everywhere. There is hardly any aspect of environmental conservation that districts are not engaged in. Sediment control, solid waste disposal, beautification, wise land use, water development, wildlife enhancement, open space planning -- these are all familiar aspects of district programs."
>
> Sam S. Studebaker, "Thirty Years to 2000,"
> NACD Convention, San Francisco, CA, February 2, 1970.

The New Tidal Wave

William E. Towell, Executive Vice-President of the American Forestry Association, the nation's oldest conservation organization, discussed the environmental thrust in a talk to the Business Advisory Committee of NACD on May 4, 1971.

"Earth Day ushered in an era of public concern for ecology and the environment," Towell said. "It signaled the awakening of people to their polluted world about them . . . . It was a dream come true to the poor biologists or foresters struggling for recognition -- or was it?

"Have we started a tidal wave of protectionism which will destroy the wise-use concept of resource use? In many areas it would appear so. Have we oversold endangered wildlife species to the point that hunting as a sport is doomed? It could be. Have we established a reverence for trees which may deny further cutting in the virgin forests? There is such a bill before Congress, even though 60 percent of the nation's available sawtimber may be affected. Frankly, I am genuinely concerned about the new preservation movement which we have created, and we must admit our part in that creation."

After predicting that he saw a continued growth of the trend toward preservation for some time to come, Towell said, "There is no way to avoid the rational or wise use of natural resources."

Holt Bodinson, writing in the *New York State Environment* published by the New York State Department of Environmental Conservation, also had a few harsh things to say about the environmental movement in a mid-summer, 1971, issue.

Under the heading, "The Land Is All We Have," Bodinson claimed that many carrying the label of "environmentalist" knew next to nothing about the natural resource base of life, "even though *every* environmental problem is ultimately a reflection of man's relationship to the land."

Bodinson concluded that "the environmental movement can be kept strong and healthy only if the basics of natural resource management are kept out in the open and in proper perspective. If your environmental education does not include a good textbook on natural resource management, it is time you put a foundation under your ecological concern."

Clearly it was not just farmers -- or conservation districts -- who found themselves uneasy about some of the extreme proposals being brought forward in the name of environmental protection. And it was not just that the movement was pro-preservation; the political ramifications were troublesome as well. Environmental groups invariably proposed that the solution to most problems was a federally-directed solution. Whether it was federally-enforced standards for water or air quality, or guidelines for state land use programs, with penalties for non-compliance, the increased use of direct federal intervention to solve environmental problems was a key feature of the environmental agenda.

Thus NACD -- along with some other old-line conservation organizations -- found themselves in a dilemma. While they did not wish to appear anti-conservation or anti-environmental (and, in fact, felt they had strong

> "We must all seek to learn. It is unfortunate, I believe, that the term 'environmentalists' has come to signify a particular interest, a particular approach, and a particular group of people. We should all be environmentalists. All people should be environmentalists, for a rational and practical environmentalism is what will ensure the survival and progress of mankind."
>
> John S. Wilder,
> "Conservation Districts in the Decade Ahead,"
> 1974 Annual Convention, Houston, TX.

pro-conservation motives), they were forced to oppose many of the proposed environmental laws on the basis that, while they agreed fully with the objectives sought, they could not agree to the means being proposed. Two examples serve to illustrate this dilemma -- the fight over national land use legislation and the search for a workable solution to the control of nonpoint sources of water pollution.

National Land Use Legislation

Comprehensive national land use legislation was first introduced in the Congress in 1970, with a proposal that the Water Resources Council be expanded to a Land and Water Resources Council that could operate a program of federal assistance to the states which could encourage a stronger state role in the planning and regulation of land use and development.

This first proposal did not attract a great deal of support, and was replaced in the next Congress by bills that were significantly different. These bills, sponsored in the Senate by Henry Jackson of Washington and in the House by Morris Udall of Arizona, were based largely on a model developed in the late 1960's by the American Law Institute (ALI). In general, they proposed to provide funds to state governments who would agree to address such concerns as "areas of critical concern," and "developments of regional impact." The theory, for which a great deal of evidence could be marshalled, was that the scale of much development had far exceeded the grasp of most local governments, and that a more significant role for the state was required. The Department of the Interior was named as the lead agency at the federal level. It would be required to establish a new agency to oversee the administration of this new program.

In 1971, the Nixon Administration joined the Congressional Democrats in the push for a national bill based on the ALI pattern. White House Coordinator for Domestic Affairs John R. Ehrlichman, a former land use lawyer in Seattle, Washington, was credited with marshalling the necessary support at the White House level. In 1972, the bill passed the Senate, but did not reach the floor of the House prior to adjournment. In 1973, the Senate passed the bill again, and the House Committee on Interior and Insular Affairs reported it favorably to the floor, but the House, when it finally received the bill in 1974, voted not to debate it.[3]

These legislative attempts left the long-time participants in the land use debate with some real problems. USDA, which had been the bastion of land use planning thought in the New Deal era of Henry Wallace, Rexford

Tugwell, and the National Resources Board, was left completely out of the legislative proposal. Members of the Soil Conservation Society of America, established by Hugh Hammond Bennett as a professional society focused on "the Science and Art of Good Land Use," were ignored, as was the Soil Conservation Service and the institutional "solution" to the land use problem of the prior era, conservation districts.

Add to this the fact that the issue was tailor-made for arguments based more on ideological grounds than fact, and the stage was set for an incredible public policy battle. SCSA declared itself a significant part of the debate in 1972 with a three-day conference on "National Land Use Policy" in Des Moines, IA, that attracted many of the leading thinkers in the land grant colleges and USDA, as well as Congressional leaders such as Wayne N. Aspinall of Colorado, Chairman of the House Committee on Interior and Insular Affairs, who had just completed his service as Chairman of the Public Land Law Review Commission.

Governor Robert D. Ray of Iowa addressed the luncheon session, calling attention to the fact that moving too fast in the name of conservation could result in a process that was unfair to the people it was designed to serve, and giving notice that he would be a significant contributor to any future conservation and land use debate. (Few there at that time, probably not even Ray himself, foresaw that he would be Governor of Iowa for 12 years, leading that state into some of the most significant soil conservation pioneering efforts in America.)

USDA, under Secretary Earl Butz, weighed into the fray in late 1973 with a "Statement on Land Use Policy," stating that private farmers and ranchers, who owned and managed 75 percent of the nation's non-federal lands, should have a major influence on how that land would be utilized. The statement called attention to the many programs administered by the Department that had direct, day-to-day impact on land use decisions. It served notice that the Department was not going to take the Interior-focused land use bill without a leadership fight. John Wilder hailed this "progressive policy statement" as a clear sign of how USDA programs could "contribute to better land use policies in the future."[4]

But it was in 1974 and 1975 that the issue really broke out into the open. In 1974, the Senate had passed a land use bill, and the House was considered very close to following suit. The vehicle in the House was H.R. 10294, sponsored by Morris Udall of Arizona. The opposition was led by Sam Steiger, also of Arizona. Hearings were held in April, and eight representatives of conservation districts, state associations and the NACD appeared before the Committee.

George Bagley, NACD President, spoke for the concerns of all: the bill was being pushed too fast, and field hearings should be held; the bill promised no intervention in private land rights, but many felt this had not been well enough established; Interior was the wrong leader, an expanded Water Resources Council or USDA would be preferable; and, the "areas of critical concern," were defined so broadly that no one could be sure that whole states would not be placed under stringent land use regulation.

At the same time, Bagley signalled the dilemma facing the NACD. "We are keenly aware of the waste, mis-use, and damage to land resources that is taking place in many parts of the nation . . . . We are faced with the threat of greater crises to come . . . . We in the NACD are not opposed to land use planning -- or the land use planning process. We believe it should be fostered and extended. At the same time, we recognize it is a difficult and complex business, because it directly affects the lives, the property, the personal investments, and the future well-being of millions of Americans and their families."

Lyle Bauer, NACD's Vice President, spoke in his capacity as Chairman of the Kansas State Conservation Commission. He gave the same outline of concerns on the bill: it was moving too fast, put the wrong federal department in control, and gave undue emphasis to natural environmental factors as compared with social and economic factors. Again, however, his own experience pointed to the need for something, even though it might be different than the bill before the Committee.

"In drawing attention to these points," Bauer said after listing the factors in H.R. 10294 that troubled him, "I would like to emphasize my personal commitment to the concept of comprehensive land use planning. I am a member of the Chikaskia and Indian Hills Regional Planning Commissions. I am the Chairman of the State Regional Planning Commissions Association. My work in these capacities, and as a supervisor of my conservation district for 18 years, has confirmed my conviction for the need of land use planning."[5]

Bagley carried the NACD Council's policy position to the Congress: not enough people in the countryside understood the proposed bill; field hearings should be held to foster wider understanding. Other conservation district leaders echoed the NACD position at the hearings. Thus NACD, although it was aligned with many of the goals of the legislation, and had a policy statement supporting establishment of a national land use policy in its "Resources Agenda for the 70's," found itself fighting the bill because of the methods being proposed.

This, coupled with the heavy opposition that was based on ideological opposition to any governmental interference in land use matters, for any reason, was too much for the proponents of the bill. Under heavy political pressure, the House Rules Committee finally voted 8-7 to clear the bill for a floor vote.[6] The House, however, refused to debate the bill on a close (211-204) vote.

Both the House and Senate had new bills in 1975 -- bills that were, in many ways, more acceptable to conservation districts. The heavily pro-federal regulatory role had been toned down, as had the focus on environmental impacts at the almost total avoidance of economic and social implications. George Bagley testified that the year's delay urged upon Congress in 1974 had "been beneficial to the country." "The new legislation," Bagley told the House Committee, "represents an important improvement over the 1974 bills. It is more balanced, gives attention to social and economic as well as environmental factors, elevates attention to be given to its food- and fiber-producing lands, recognizes rights and responsibilities of private property ownership, and promotes better collaboration and improved management of public and private lands."

But there were still problems, and a bitter debate broke out within NACD about the bill. At the Board meeting in March of 1975, the Directors agonized over their position for four days. The opening discussions on Monday were mixed, with Doyle Hutcheson of Texas, Ross Chambers of Colorado, and Lyle Bauer of Kansas speaking against H. R. 3510 (as the Udall bill was then numbered). Hugh Jones of Kentucky, Harold Johnson of Kansas, and Gordon Zimmerman spoke in favor of supporting the legislation. Peter Jackson of Montana thought NACD should support the bill, but seek amendments to gain full recognition of conservation districts. Richard Longmire of Oklahoma said that most of the NACD objections to the 1974 bill had been eliminated, and that the bill was about as good as NACD could expect to get.

After hearing a report from Norman Berg of SCS that the Administration would oppose the land use bill on budgetary grounds, the Board voted that NACD would support H.R. 3510, but seek amendments to more clearly define the role of conservation districts and have the law administered by USDA or an interagency Council rather than by the Department of the Interior.

On Tuesday and Wednesday, the Directors visited on Capitol Hill and came back to the Board meeting with the land use bill still on their mind. A move to reconsider the previous decision was put off until Thursday, at President Bagley's request, to give the Board a chance to finish its normal agenda.

On Thursday, P. T. Eubanks of Mississippi moved to reconsider the motion passed by the Board on Monday. After considerable discussion on land use policy and the political climate on Capitol Hill, the Board supported a motion by Sam Chinn of California that would direct NACD's staff and officers to "present its views on national land use legislation in accordance with Council policy and the following guidelines:

-- Administration of the law by USDA or a Council
-- Clarification of the role of conservation districts, and
-- Other useful amendments."[7]

The main problem for NACD, one that simply could not be negotiated with the House and Senate Interior Committees, was the assignment of federal leadership to Interior, a department with "a history of public land management," instead of Agriculture, "with its long and successful record of working with private landowners . . . ."[8] The House Interior Committee, frustrated and stalemated, voted 23-19 in July to not report the bill out to the House floor and the Senate, equally frustrated, halted consideration until something could emerge from the House.

Thus, after five years of intense legislative maneuvering, the outcome was that there was no federal land use bill. Governor Jimmy Carter of Georgia had testified before the House Subcommittee on the Environment in 1974 that he, the Southern Growth Policies Board, and the State of Georgia "support the approach promoted in H.R. 10294."[9] But when he was elected President in 1976, he and his Secretary of the Interior, former Idaho Governor Cecil D. Andrus, saw the political handwriting on the wall and never proposed a successor bill. The national land use planning and policy idea, as embodied in the Jackson-Udall Bills, was a dead issue.

Concern for land use, however, was far from dead. The Department of Agriculture maintained its Land Use Committee, re-wrote and strengthened its policies relating to assistance to local and state land use planning processes, and carried on an intensive campaign to gain recognition for the unnecessary loss of prime agricultural lands caught in the path of development. Congress had passed the Coastal Zone Management Act in 1972, which applied the same principles of national assistance, state leadership, and regional land use controls to coastal zones that the Jackson-Udall Bills had envisioned on a nationwide scale, and this program proceeded apace. In later years, Congress passed laws on surface mined-land reclamation, interstate pipelines, hazardous waste disposal and power plant siting that addressed many of the problems that had been at the root of the effort for comprehensive land use law.

Conservation districts retained and, in many areas, intensified their assistance to local land use planning and regulatory programs. As the political heat and rhetoric died down, it was still necessary to find peaceful solutions to the conflicts created as a growing population and an intensified economy pressed upon a limited supply of land and water resources.

One lesson of the land use fight seems clear: it is not always the substance of the issue at hand, but also the methods proposed for involving government in the solution that are of primary political importance. In the land use fight, as in the soil conservation fight of four decades earlier, keeping that delicate balance between private, local, state and federal interests turned out to be the most difficult and elusive goal of all.

Controlling Nonpoint Pollution

Virtually the same basic questions lay at the heart of the water pollution control fight. It was not the need to control pollution; there was little disagreement on that. The proper role for government was the issue, and developing the "right balance" of federal, state, and local powers and actions was the challenge. These concerns were to occupy much of the time and attention of conservation districts and NACD for the entire decade.

Sam Studebaker had predicted the emergence of the water quality battle in 1968. "One area certain to be of greater concern in the future is agricultural pollution -- including animal wastes and runoff which are said to carry undesirable amounts of fertilizers, pesticides, and other agricultural chemicals into the streams," Studebaker said. His message, however, was optimistic. "Soil and water conservation districts have responded with enthusiasm to the need for improvement of water quality," he said. "In every region of the country, there are districts that have taken steps to help make cleaner streams a reality."[10]

NACD had called for a nationwide effort to reduce and control sedimentation damages to water in its "Agenda for the 70's," and was strongly in support of including nonpoint source pollution abatement in the amendments to the Federal Water Pollution Control Act that were being considered in 1972.

In the 1972 hearings on the bill that ultimately became P.L. 92-500, the Legislative Chairman of NACD, Richard Longmire of Oklahoma, declared that "The abatement of pollution from municipal and industrial sources is clearly important, but even complete success in those two areas would not solve the nation's pollution problem. If we are to have clean air and clean water, it will also be necessary to control the overland flow of water and sharply reduce erosion by wind and water -- especially in situations that habitually produce large loads of sediment."

Longmire urged the committee to go beyond attention to pollution caused by municipal and industrial sources, and said that "legislation to deal with nonpoint source pollution from agricultural, rural, and developing areas is both timely and urgent."[11]

At the same time, the Council on Environmental Quality issued its Third Annual Report, citing sediment from soil erosion as the nation's major water pollutant by volume, one which "often carried other harmful pollutants such as nutrients and pesticides." The CEQ report cited conservation districts as the organization having "major responsibility for the prevention of soil erosion," but said that the voluntary methods historically used were falling short. It cited the "growing recognition that some form of regulatory authority is needed to control sediment," and listed the new laws in Iowa, Ohio and the Virgin Islands as examples of what the future might hold.[12]

By November, P.L. 92-500 had been passed, vetoed by President Nixon, and re-approved by Congress. P.L. 92-500 was to become a household word in the lexicon of federal, state and local government officials and one section, Section 208, was to become the driving force behind nonpoint source pollution abatement efforts for a decade.

NACD was ready for the passage of the Act. In 1969, NACD had joined with the National Association of Counties and the Soil Conservation Society of America to sponsor a National Conference on Sediment Control. The conference involved the Federal Water Pollution Control Administration (soon to become a major part of EPA), the Department of Housing and Urban Development, and USDA. The conference served to draw attention to the growing magnitude and urgency of the sediment problem, particularly among the federal agencies that needed to recognize it.

As EPA began to flex the new muscles provided by P.L. 92-500 (such as proposing "permits to plow" for individual farmers), NACD took several initiatives designed to help the new agency understand the capabilities available in USDA, conservation districts, and state soil conservation agencies. A major goal was to help EPA officials understand that a voluntary program for nonpoint pollution control was both desirable and potentially effective.

In 1971, NACD entered into an agreement with EPA to conduct a project supported in part by EPA funds -- a new experience for NACD -- that would investigate the role of conservation districts in the control of nonpoint sources of pollution. As one part of the project, a model state soil erosion and sediment control law was drafted. The model law, prepared in a cooperative effort by NACD, USDA and EPA staff, was approved by the Council of State Governments and made a part of their book of "suggested state legislation" for 1973.[13]

As a second phase of that effort, NACD planned and held "Sediment Control Institutes" in the states to discuss current sediment control problems with district officals, county and municipal officers, state legislators, and state and federal agencies. The seminars also explained the model law and explored its implications to districts, which were significant. As the *Tuesday Letter* noted at the outset, "Effective sediment control programs of this kind require additional funds and technical assistance and strengthened district administrative arrangements. If all the states follow the example of those pioneering in this area, it will be a bold, new departure for the district movement."[14]

The first state Sediment Control Institute was held in Kansas, and was called a "success" by NACD. Other sessions followed rapidly, and by

November, when the federal bill was finally enacted into law, NACD could report that three states had already held institutes, and that ten more were scheduled in the coming months. Discussing the final wording of Section 208, the *Tuesday Letter* noted that "these developments make the state Sediment Control Institutes now being sponsored by NACD . . . even more timely."[15]

By July of 1973, the *Tuesday Letter* could report that 15 state institutes had been held; a year later, 32 were complete. By 1975, a total of 40 had been held and a summary report was prepared by NACD and published by EPA.[16]

And state legislatures responded. Nine states had enacted some form of mandatory sediment controls by mid-1973, and at least ten other states had laws on the drafting board, or introduced into the legislatures. The momentum established was to carry into 20 states, the District of Columbia and the Virgin Islands by the end of the decade. The upshot, the *Tuesday Letter* reported was that "Soil erosion continues to be declared illegal throughout the U.S."[17] Many of the state laws, it should be noted, dealt with sediment from construction sites, not agricultural land.

NACD's involvement in this bold new departure for districts did not come without significant debate and controversy. Some district officials felt that having anything to do with EPA or sediment and erosion control was to get too involved with "regulatory conservation." The basic question facing NACD was whether to fight EPA's efforts, or to join them in an attempt to guide the outcome so that districts would find it acceptable. At the October, 1975, Board meeting in League City, TX, the Board listened to EPA staff, USDA staff, and their own staff advisors, then adopted a motion offered by Doyle Hutcheson of Texas and Stan Christensen of Oregon. The Board decided that "NACD will go all the way in using their influence to secure the leadership role for districts and state soil and water conservation agencies in nonpoint pollution control programs."

With this historic decision, NACD was ready (even though far from fully unanimous on the subject) to address the political problems of working so closely with a regulatory program. But the situation had practical, as well as political, dimensions. There were many who felt that the new programs could pose manpower and management problems that conservation districts might simply be unable to meet. It was the latter concern that led to still another "special project" in NACD funded by the EPA. Called the Sediment Control and Manpower Project (SCAMP), it had as its goal the assessment of the new programs and identification of the new staffing and administrative challenges they posed to districts.

The project was directed by Robert E. Williams, who had recently retired as Director of the SCS Plant Sciences Division. Mary Garner, who had retired from USDA after being active in the field of conservation district and sediment control law throughout her career in the Office of the General Counsel, served as legal counsel. An assessment of six state programs, as well as training manuals for erosion and sediment control specialists was developed and sent to all state soil conservation and water pollution control agencies.

In 1976, NACD received a grant of $140,000 from EPA to "encourage effective involvement of conservation districts in 208 water quality programs." Under the terms of the grant, NACD was to collect and publish needed information, hold educational meetings, and provide direct assistance on request to state associations of conservation districts to help them develop their skills in addressing water quality problems. Former SCS Field Representative Morrie Bolline was hired to direct the project, which was to run until September 30, 1977. Bolline worked with the project as Director until November, 1976, then continued as a consultant to the project, which was then directed out of NACD's Washington office by Bob Williams.

This project started the practice of publishing "Information Letters" containing detailed descriptions (or copies) of important federal policy documents, state laws, or state program outlines. There were thirteen of these letters in 1976-77, and they became a major source of information on nonpoint source pollution among conservation districts and state soil conservation agencies. Even 208 planning agencies found that the NACD material was often available before the federal agencies could churn out the official circulations. In later projects the name of the news notes was changed to "Nonpoint Notes," but the format and thrust remained the same.

In addition to working with conservation districts and 208 planning agencies, NACD worked with EPA, trying to convince the lawyers and bureaucrats in that agency that the voluntary-regulatory mix of programs being designed in districts needed a chance to work without being swept aside by attempts at direct federal or state regulation of land management.

But EPA had a difficult time being patient. They had relied on "areawide" planning agencies -- largely in metropolitan regions -- to do most of the planning work on nonpoint source pollution controls, but a court decision in 1975 required them to expand and accelerate the process. States were to be required, the court ruled, to make control plans for all their territory not covered by the area-wide plans. The deadline date was November 1, 1978. State programs to control agriculturally-related nonpoint sources were needed soon, whether the states and the soil conservation districts were ready or not.

NACD responded with a four-part series in *Tuesday Letter,* devoting virtually all of a month's issues to the subject. In the series, President

George Bagley said "It seems evident to me that the nation is soon going to have a program to control pollution from agriculturally-related and nonpoint sources. Whatever the nature of the program, one of its principal purposes will be to control sediment and associated pollutants. Control of erosion and sediment is the prime responsibility of conservation districts. In my view, districts must play a substantial role in this program."[18] The series went on to explain to district leaders what the process might entail, and how they might determine their role.

"There must be a recognition that passage of P.L. 92-500, or enactment of state sediment control laws, or issuance of permits and rules and regulations, will not by themselves get the job done. Most of the job will be accomplished by self-regulation; by the realization on the part of farmers, ranchers, contractors, developers, foresters, public land managers, and everybody else that action for better water quality is needed; and that there are reasonable, practical, and effective ways for accomplishing what must be done.

George Bagley, "We Begin Again,"
at the 1976 Annual Convention, Honolulu, HI.

But getting districts geared up was only one aspect of the challenge. Few water planners knew who districts were or what they could do, so in many areas, water quality plans were being developed that completely ignored the possible role of districts and USDA in dealing with agricultural problems. Most of these proposed such things as water quality permits for feedlots and irrigation return ditches, so that if pollution were present, farmers could be forced to either install treatment facilities or shut down operations. Such proposals, naturally, frightened farmers, and NACD's water quality staff spent a great deal of time behind the scenes with EPA trying to head off the most unacceptable proposals.

Improved communications was the answer, and NACD's role as communicator on pollution questions continued to grow throughout the decade. Under the leadership of Bob Williams, the project staff produced a steady flow of materials aimed at district officials, USDA technicians, water quality planners, and local government officials. One example was a 350-page book, *Conservation Districts and 208 Water Quality Management,* written by consultant William B. Davey and published in June 1977, that contained a complete outline of the policies and procedures needed as references during the process of program development. A series of 47 periodic newsletters, "Nonpoint Notes" were issued between 1977 and 1981 to keep people up to date on changing situations and policies.

James E. Lake, of Fort Wayne, Indiana, joined the NACD Special

Projects staff in 1977, and added a new dimension to the services provided. Lake had directed a highly successful special project for the Allen County SWCD, the Black Creek Project, which had used $1.8 million of EPA money to demonstrate what soil conservation practices could and could not do to improve the water quality in the Lake Erie Basin. Lake was expert in the day-to-day work of districts, and the NACD staff became valued advisors as both state agencies and districts worked to get the agricultural portions of their nonpoint source plans written, and into action.

In 1978, NACD produced the film "Non-Point 83" that built on the experiences of the districts in the Lake Erie Basin and made the point that, with effort, farmers could meet the goals of the Clean Water Act through the application of conservation practices as outlined by the conservation districts, SCS, and the nonpoint source plans being developed.

These events, and the issues surrounding them, could be the subject of a full book in themselves, marking a time when NACD's levels of staff, research and publishing activity hit an all-time high. Overall, the results were significant. By the time the series of NACD special projects on nonpoint pollution were completed in 1981, virtually every state had completed the agricultural portion of its nonpoint control plan. In 45 states, conservation districts or the state soil conservation agency were named as the implementing agency for agriculturally-related nonpoint pollution control programs. The methods proposed were a mixture of voluntary, incentive and regulatory approaches that were, in general, widely supported by the agricultural community.

Potential confrontations between those who sought improved water quality and those who farmed the land had been averted, and the subject of "nonpoint pollution control" had been moved from an impossible-sounding task to one that was difficult, but do-able, in the minds of most conservationists. The balance between "voluntary" and "regulatory" approaches had not been settled in absolute favor of either one, but by a complex set of compromises that reflected both the political and environmental character of each state and locality.

While that outcome did not (and still does not) satisfy those who feel that some kind of standard, predictable set of solutions ought to be stated in federal legislation, a great deal of evidence can be marshalled to support the argument that it was the best achievable outcome at the time. Clearly, it served to establish NACD as an organization that could develop communications between a wide variety of interests and promote constructive solutions to environmental problems.

The Channel Battle

NACD's success in bringing warring factions together over environmental issues was perhaps most sorely tested in the fight over stream channelization that broke out in the 1970's.

NACD had long supported the Small Watershed Program and felt that it was one of the conservation and resource development success stories of the century. In testimony before the Conservation and Natural Resources Subcommittee of the House Committee on Government Operations on June 10, 1971, NACD National Vice President George R. Bagley of Louisiana called P.L. 566 "one of the most dramatically successful acts ever created by Congress."

Bagley said: "It has upgraded the economic base of hundreds of communities throughout America. It has survived struggles between various Presidents and the Congress, budget cutbacks, and agency rivalries. Local and state governments are providing some $44.3 million annually in funds and services as their share of the responsibility. The backlog of applications, a sure measure of the program's usefulness and popularity, is soaring. People want water management -- big people, little people, and responsible people."

But there were others who did not share that enthusiasm for the program, particularly its proclivity to solve many drainage problems by opening up "drainage channels" through low-lying lands. At times, these channels were simply reconstruction or maintenance of previously man-made ditches, but at other times they involved the channelization of natural streams. Whatever the cause, justification or outcome, the stage was set for all-out war between the environmentalists and the conservationists.

The fight on channel work broke out in Congress in June, 1971, at hearings conducted by the Conservation and Natural Resources Subcommittee of the House Committee on Government Operations. The front man was Nathaniel P. Reed, then serving his first month as Assistant Secretary of the Interior for Fish, Wildlife and Parks, before a very sympathetic Committee Chairman, Henry S. Reuss of Wisconsin. Both Reed and Reuss condemned channel work in water resource projects.

Reed testified there is "shocking and irrefutable evidence of the severe damage to fish habitat and populations in the immediate area of channel alterations," although admitting that the specific impact of such work on wildlife and waterfowl had not been intensively studied. "The answer," he said, "is to turn the design of watershed projects over to the 'environmental agencies,' specifically the Department of the Interior and the Environmental Protection Agency." He accused the Soil Conservation Service of "paying nothing more than lip service to earnest environmental protection." He called for review of all channelization projects by the Council on Environmental Quality, the Interior Department, and the Environmental Protection Agency, and consideration of a complete moratorium on all projects.

Reed was answered by NACD Vice President George Bagley. "Channel work is neither good nor bad in itself," Bagley told the Reuss Committee. "Judgments can only be made on a project-by-project basis, by local people at the local level to meet local conditions. Channel improvements are included in watershed projects only when no other way can be found to meet certain problems."

"The key to a solution to the conflict over channel work is for all agencies and people concerned to work together in a cooperative spirit to find the best ways to resolve differences. NACD believes that participation by fish and wildlife, forestry, and environmental interests of all kinds is essential if conflicts are to be avoided. It has always been the policy of conservation districts and the SCS to encourage such participation. In 32 states, fish and game, forestry, parks and other state agencies are acting as legal sponsors of watershed projects and are investing substantial funds in them. Unfortunately, in some places, those who complain the most are those who took the least and sometimes no interest in the projects during the planning stages."

Even before completing his committee hearings, Reuss proposed an amendment to prohibit the use of funds for channel work in the 1972 Appropriation Act for P.L. 566 projects. He singled out the P.L. 566 projects for the prohibition even though the hearings by his committee presumably were to inquire into the channel work of all federal agencies, including the Corps of Engineers, the TVA, and the Bureau of Reclamation. The effort by Reuss was defeated 278 to 129, but environmental interests led by David R. Brower of Friends of the Earth vowed a continuing fight. NACD, without doubt, had a large hand in defeating the amendment.

In November of 1971, the battle moved into the courtroom as well. Five environmental groups sued the Soil Conservation Service to halt construction on the Chicod Creek Watershed in Pitt and Beauford Counties, North Carolina. The litigation, which dragged on until 1978 before it was finally settled, galvanized a great deal of action in the watershed program. Funding for SCS watershed planning activities was increased, as the need for developing environmental impact statements drove up the cost of preparation for each project. The search for options to channel work was accelerated, as well.

On Chicod Creek, by the time the project was finally advertised for bids in 1978, the original 66 miles of stream channel improvement had been reduced to seven miles of clearing and snagging to improve stream flow, and excavation was done on one side of the stream only. Almost two decades of litigation and re-planning was tremendously costly, but the project was completed and is now a showplace of conservation and resource development.

Also in 1971, the President's Council on Environmental Quality, responding to the pressure of opponents of stream modification, contracted with the A. D. Little Company, a consulting firm, to conduct studies of the work. The study covered channel work of the Corps of Engineers, Bureau of Reclamation, Tennessee Valley Authority, and Soil Conservation Service. The consulting firm concluded that extremism is no answer to the problems surrounding channel modification; "rather, effective solutions are to be found within some reasonable range where opposing views are harmonized."

"On balance, the weight of evidence is heavily against channeling of 'untouched' natural streams *in terms of environmental effects* . . . . There are other watercourses -- 1,095.5 miles in this assessment -- that were not untouched natural streams but previously altered channels, sometimes ditched two and three times. Here, the evidence is not so strongly against channeling, or more precisely federal re-channeling, in terms of environmental effects.

"We find that the economic merits of federal-agency channel modifications range from eminently sound to highly questionable . . . . On balance, the weight of evidence is marginally in favor of channeling both untouched natural streams and man-altered channels, in terms of local, state, regional, and national economic effect . . . . If a final value accounting could be made -- primary, secondary, indirect, external -- we offer the admittedly unsupported judgment that the net economic equivalent of total social gains to rural and urban communities would substantially outweigh the net economic equivalent of environmental losses and gains."

In the following year, the battle continued to rage. Chairman Reuss scheduled further hearings, and NACD Vice President George Bagley again appeared, arguing that "extremism in the debate is a disservice to reason and the cause of conservation." After reviewing the complexities of the channel issue, and the many conflicts involved, Bagley noted that "There is no easy answer to the resolution of such conflicts, but our Association is convinced that a positive approach is the only way to search for that answer."[19]

Bagley's point was lost on Mr. Reuss and the Subcommittee, however. In October of 1973, they released a report entitled *Stream Channelization: What Federally Financed Draglines and Bulldozers do to our Nation's Streams* that was highly critical of the watershed program, saying that SCS had abandoned its responsibility for allowing public involvement in the decisionmaking process on watershed projects. The agency had, the

Committee report said, turned over too many of the decisions on a project's features to the local sponsors who "generally have a financial interest in it."

The solution proposed by environmentalists was to allow the "environmental agencies" in the Department of the Interior to have the final say on watershed project plans. Proposals to achieve this were contained in legislation to amend and expand the Fish and Wildlife Coordination Act. The effect, NACD felt, would be to give fish and wildlife interests an absolute veto over projects that would bring the watershed program to a complete halt. NACD, along with the Water Resources Congress, the National Water Resources Association, and the National Environmental Development Association, vigorously (and successfully) opposed these bills.

Finally, in 1976, the Fish and Wildlife Service and the Soil Conservation Service responded favorably to a request from NACD and began the process of developing "mutually acceptable" guidelines for channel modification work. President George Bagley called a Washington meeting of the top leaders of SCS, F&WS, EPA and the Council on Environmental Quality, at which the agreement was made to proceed with the guidelines. Bagley hailed the agreement, and pointed out that it would have effects far beyond the watershed program. "Resolution of the channel issue," he said, "would enable us to improve the relationship between the soil conservation and fish and wildlife communities generally and move ahead with other urgent and mutual concerns involving the conservation and wise use of the nation's natural resources."[20]

Almost two years of work were required before the guidelines were issued in March of 1978, by which time a great deal of evolutionary change in the watershed planning process had been forced by the application of environmental impact assessments and other changes in planning methodology. In addition, efforts to avoid channel modifications, as well as construction methods that minimized damage to fish and wildlife values where channel work was unavoidable, were fairly well developed and in use. By the end of the decade, the virulent animosity between environmental organizations, SCS, and the conservation districts that had been aroused by the channelization issue was history.

Dredge and Fill: The "404" Battle

Another major and bitter battle between the conservationists and the environmentalists was waged around Section 404 of the Water Pollution

Control Act Amendments of 1972. This section was designed to create a regulatory framework to control the indiscriminate dredging of some lands and the equally indiscriminate dumping of the dredged materials elsewhere. Environmentalists and conservationists alike had been nauseated by the sight of draglines moving through mangrove swamps, lifting enough muck out of the "channel" areas to create dry berms between the channels which could then be sold to unsuspecting home buyers as lots for a retirement retreat. Some regulation seemed both necessary and prudent. But what emerged was not quite what many had envisioned.

The law authorized the Army Corps of Engineers to issue permits for the "discharge of dredged or fill material" into navigable waters. But "navigable waters" was defined by the act as "waters of the United States," and a U.S. District Court ruling held that this definition meant virtually all the waters of the nation, including their contiguous or adjacent "wetlands." This broadened the application of the law considerably, but just how far was a matter of major contention.

The extreme interpretation held that the authority of the Corps would extend to any landowner who wished to terrace, landlevel, or construct a check dam on his property. Even plowing could be interpreted as earthmoving when done on lands that met the, as yet, undefined, criteria of "wetland." "If you happen to own any lands that the Corps and others decide to classify as 'wetlands,' " George Bagley told *Tuesday Letter* readers, "the chances are you may be forced to leave them alone forevermore."[21]

USDA got into the act as well, blasting proposed Corps regulations as imposing the threat of "cumbersome, time-consuming procedures" on farmers every time they wanted to clean a ditch or build a pond. EPA, on the other hand, criticized the Corps for making the regulations unnecessarily burdensome in order to assure that they would be negated by public outcry or Congressional action.

As a result of the threat posed by the Corps regulations, NACD joined in an effort to amend Section 404 in the Congress. A bill was introduced in the House by John Breaux of Louisiana that would limit the scope of Section 404 to waters that had traditionally been defined as "navigable waters."

In a letter to Mr. Breaux, Bagley made the NACD position clear: "The prime purpose of the Federal Water Pollution Control Act Amendments, in our judgment, was to restore and preserve the quality of the nation's waters. It was not designed to be a federal land use control measure to prohibit development of that broad and varying category of lands known as 'wetlands.'

"It should be self-evident that not all 'wetlands' are equally critical and indispensable in their benefits to municipal water supplies, shellfish beds, fishery areas, wildlife, or recreation. Some undoubtedly perform extremely important functions in the public interest, and others may be of no more than marginal value."[22]

The Breaux Amendment failed, and was replaced by a compromise fashioned by Jim Wright of Texas. The Wright Amendment did not change the definition of "waters of the United States," but gave the Corps authority to exempt broad categories of activities by issuing "general" permits. It also exempted normal farming and ranching operations from the scope of the regulatory program. Bagley called the action a "reasonable compromise."[23]

The Senate rejected the Wright proposal and adopted an amendment sponsored by Senators Howard Baker of Tennessee and Jennings Randolph of West Virginia that left the definition of "waters" and the scope of the permit program virtually intact, except for the exemption of "normal farming, forestry, and ranching activities" from the permit system.

As Congress rushed to adjournment, all attempts at compromise failed, and the 94th Congress came to a close with no resolution on the "404" issue. The Corps regulations went into effect, and all sides girded for a struggle in the next Congress.

The next year found the same proposals, and the same combatants, lined up again. The House quickly passed a bill that would limit the application of Section 404 as had been proposed by NACD; then added it to a public jobs bill strongly supported by the Administration. That threw the issue squarely on a conference committee, where Senator Edmund Muskie of Maine was leading an effort to delay the 404 changes.[24] In May, the Senate was successful in detaching the 404 measure from the jobs bill, allowing the jobs measure to move forward while the Senate took up the 404 issue separately.

After hearings that summer, the Senate finished its work on the bill and it was adopted as the Clean Water Act of 1977. In that action, the definition of "navigable waters" was not changed, but normal farming activities such as plowing, seeding, cultivation, minor drainage, harvesting, and upland soil and water conservation practices were exempted. Also excluded from the need for a permit from the Corps were maintenance of currently serviceable structures such as dikes, dams, levees, riprap, breakwaters, and transportation structures; construction or maintenance of farm or stock ponds or irrigation ditches; construction of temporary sedimentation basins; and construction or maintenance of farm or forest roads.

George Bagley greeted the outcome cautiously. "The compromise will end a long and hotly-contested struggle," the *Tuesday Letter* said. "Although the compromise position extends federal power over land use far more widely through the countryside than NACD believes desirable, it does provide for sensible exemptions of normal land management activities, gives states authority to inaugurate their own programs, and calls for speedy decisions on permit applications."[25]

The Rural Clean Water Program

As Congress deliberated the Clean Water Act of 1977, one of the widely recognized needs was the creation of a program to assist with the implementation of nonpoint pollution control efforts. Section 208, dating back to 1972, had created a mechanism for developing areawide and local plans for pollution control, and most states and localities had done considerable work to fashion those plans. But how would the plans get off the paper and onto the land? The federal law held no financial incentives or assistance programs, it simply said that the states were responsible for seeing that nonpoint pollution was controlled. States and localities, looking at the program requirements posed by their own plans, were virtually unanimous in their opinion that, without federal assistance, the plans were beyond their capability.

Senator Dick Clark of Iowa was the first to introduce legislation to address this situation. His bill, S. 1280, was introduced in April of 1977. It would amend the Rural Development Act of 1972, authorizing $130 million the first year and up to $1 billion in 1983. The funds would be administered by USDA, and would provide cost-sharing for the implementation of water quality plans based on the 208 plans being developed under P.L. 92-500. George Bagley called the bill "a sorely-needed step in the search for effective implementation of water quality management on agricultural lands."[26] In July, a companion bill was introduced in the House by Ed Jones of Tennessee and James M. Jeffords of Vermont.

But Senator John Culver, also of Iowa, had a more direct approach in mind. In mid-July, Culver introduced an amendment to P.L. 92-500 that would create a new program in the Department of Agriculture for funding water pollution control. The program, which eventually came to be known as the Rural Clean Water Program (RCWP), was based in large measure on the Great Plains Conservation Program. In it, the Secretary would be authorized to enter into contracts with rural landowners for the installation of the conservation practices (usually called "best management practices" or "BMP's") contained in the water quality plans developed under Section 208.

The conservation plans would need to be approved by the local conservation district, and USDA would be authorized to enter into agreements with conservation districts, state soil conservation agencies, or state water quality agencies to administer the program within their jurisdictions. The amendment authorized $200 million for 1979 and $400 million for 1980. With the action on the Clean Water Bill on a "fast track" in the Senate, the Culver Amendment passed the Senate on August 9, 1977.

With a House bill already passed, the action shifted to a Conference Committee to resolve the differences in the two bills. George Bagley called for adoption of the Culver Amendment. "Adoption by the House conferees of Sec. 26 as enacted by the Senate would be a major step forward toward effective implementation of non-point pollution control through conservation districts," he said.[27]

At the fall meeting in Milwaukee, NACD's Officers and Directors held an executive session to talk about the politics of the Culver Amendment. As written, it would create a new program in USDA similar to the Great Plains Program, which NACD favored. The problem was that ASCS had let it be known that they were strongly opposed to the concept, particularly the part about USDA being able to contract administration of the program out to state and local units. They also feared that the new program, tied as it was to the politically potent issue of water quality, would siphon funds away from the ACP and endanger that long-standing source of cost-sharing. The NACD leaders strongly supported the Culver proposal, but realized the risk of starting another round of controversy between ASCS and districts.

Another option, which Culver was willing to accept if NACD would go along, would be to bypass USDA completely, and direct the program funds through EPA to the state water quality agencies. From there, state soil conservation agencies and districts could work in cooperation with the state water quality agency under whatever agreements they could work out. Going this route would eliminate (or greatly reduce) the opportunity for ASCS to fight the program effectively, but it would create another problem. If EPA got the program, and directed it through the states, there was no guarantee that the districts would be involved. In some states, where there had not been a good nonpoint planning program involving the districts, the effort might turn into a regulatory program, some NACD Directors feared.

At the conclusion of the closed-door discussion, the Board voted to support the Culver Amendment as it was written, and relayed that information back to Washington, where the House-Senate Conferees were meeting on the Clean Water Act. The Act, containing the Culver Amendment, was approved in late October and signed by President Jimmy Carter on December 28, 1977.

But the fighting in USDA foreseen earlier broke out with ferocity, and plans to implement the program were made more difficult as a result. USDA and EPA signed an agreement in April of 1978 that set forth a program design to be used in the RCWP. Interagency coordinating committees were to be established at both the national and state levels to see that each agency's interests were protected. M. Rupert Cutler, USDA Assistant Secretary, said the agreement established "a new era of local, state and federal cooperation."[28]

But the chance for cooperation never materialized. Supporters of ASCS convinced Chairman Jamie Whitten of the House Agriculture Appropriations Subcommittee that the new program would compete with the ACP program and duplicate the administrative capabilities of ASCS. Mr. Whitten was keenly aware of the widespread support being generated by NACD, state water quality agencies, and environmental groups for a financial assistance program on nonpoint source pollution. On the other hand, he was unwilling to do anything that might alter the ASCS-SCS power balance he had helped engineer in the 1950's. No easy political solution was in view. The 1979 budget eliminated funds for the RCWP, which only caused the pressure to mount.

Finally, in the 1980 Appropriations Bill, Whitten's committee created an "Experimental Rural Clean Water Program" to be administered by ASCS. The "experimental" program was not based on the authorities in the Clean Water Act, but was authorized solely in the Appropriations Bill. ASCS was directed, however, to run a program much as had been envisioned in the RCWP, only without allowing any state or local role in the program's administration. ASCS, with their political ability galvanized by what they had perceived as a serious threat to their programs, had won a complete political victory.

The "experimental RCWP" received $50 million in 1980, and 13 project areas were selected and funded. In 1981, the program was given another $20 million, and another seven projects were approved. No further funds have ever been appropriated, and the effort has been largely moribund since. As for the Culver Amendment itself, it is still very much a part of the law, and is now being re-examined as the Clean Water Act is again due for renewal. With the need for an implementation program still being voiced from many quarters, a new approach may be tried. Most observers feel that any new approach now will bypass USDA and go through EPA rather than stir up the interagency warfare again. With federal budget deficits looming so large over all political decisions, however, it will be difficult for any new program to emerge in the near future. The opportunity created in 1977 may have been a one-time chance that became a casualty of the historic battle for "turf" in the nation's conservation programs.

Federal Reorganization

A Department of Natural Resources has been talked about for a generation, going back to New Deal days in the 1930's when the Interior Secretary had ambitions to create such a department. This ambition has been echoed by many of his successors. At one time, legend goes, President Franklin D. Roosevelt had a ready-to-sign executive order on his desk transferring the Forest Service from Agriculture to Interior, but was persuaded not to sign it at the last moment by Secretary of Agriculture Henry A. Wallace. In the Congress, bills to combine all natural resource agencies into a single department have cropped up periodically for many years.

In his State of the Union message early in 1971, President Nixon proposed a governmental reorganization that would combine seven existing departments, including Agriculture and Interior, into four new departments. Legislation to implement this proposal was introduced and hearings on some of the proposals were held in 1971 and 1972. The four new departments would be Natural Resources, Human Resources, Economic Affairs, and Community Development. In effect, the Department of the Interior would become the Department of Natural Resources.

The Nixon plan drew fire from many sides, including Congress. In a letter to Senator Sam Ervin, Chairman of the Senate Committee on Governmental Operations, Senator Herman Talmadge spoke for the Senate Agriculture Committee: "The Department of Agriculture now has larger resource conservation authorities and responsibilities than does the Department of the Interior. In one way or another, USDA has responsibility for approximately 90 percent of our renewable natural resources. To interfere with this system which has worked successfully for more than one hundred years, establishing close relationships with state and local governments, would be disastrous."[29]

Following the Watergate debacle, President Gerald Ford still had the reorganization proposals with which to deal, and NACD had introduced a new angle. What was needed, Vice President Lyle Bauer told a group of ASCS county office employees in Omaha, was a Department of Agriculture and Natural Resources. Such a department could be created by enlarging USDA with the renewable natural resource agencies of Interior and creating a Department of Energy and Minerals from what was left in DOI.

Other urgencies, including the election campaign in 1976, pushed the reorganization issue aside, but not for long. In 1977, with sweeping reorganization authority granted by Congress, President Jimmy Carter established a President's Reorganization Project in the Office of Management and Budget to study options and bring forth recommendations for reorganization. Despite the views of USDA Secretary Bob Bergland, the recommendation that seemed to be gaining favor was, again, a transfer of the Forest Service and SCS to the Department of the Interior.

To counter the possibility of an OMB proposal unfavorable to agriculture, Senators George McGovern of South Dakota and Robert Dole of Kansas introduced S. 2515, a bill to establish a Department of Food, Agriculture and Renewable Resources. The bill would expand USDA much as NACD had earlier proposed. Its sponsors described USDA as "the only Department in Government willing and able to provide equity for rural America."

But the analysts at OMB were unmoved. The favored plan there was to move part, if not all, of SCS and all of Forest Service to Interior. OMB asked for public comments on an options paper; conservation districts provided almost 20 percent of the public response, most of which was heavily against the staff proposal.[30] Official Washington wasn't all that happy, either. Congressional leaders came out publicly against the USDA moves, and six former USDA Secretaries wrote the President a letter outlining the "very sound reasons" why similar proposals had been rejected in the past.[31]

When the Carter plan was finally made public in early 1979, there was no mention of moving SCS or any of its programs. The DNR would be formed from the Interior Department with the addition of the Forest Service and the National Oceanic and Atmospheric Administration. The concerns expressed by NACD, districts, and others had apparently had effect. In May, it was rumored that the President, recognizing the political problems with the DNR, would send legislation to Congress so that they could alter it if they desired. (A reorganization plan, if submitted, would be a "yes" or "no" vote, and all indications were that the DNR would be rejected.) Finally, on May 16, the *Washington Post* reported that the President had given up on the DNR idea entirely, and reorganization was a dead issue for the remainder of the Carter term.

Agricultural Service Centers

Efforts to streamline the USDA delivery system at the field level had been attempted for years, and NACD had a policy position encouraging the consolidation of USDA office space where practical and feasible. Secretary Butz announced in December of 1973 that he intended to consolidate some 7,800 of USDA's field offices so that they could provide "one-stop service." NACD's leaders were disturbed by the extent of the proposal.

"Among our major concerns are the maintenance of adequate service to district cooperators, the effect on district employees working in joint SWCD/SCS offices, and the effect of 'across county lines co-location' on the progress of soil and water conservation work," NACD President John Wilder said.[32]

In a meeting with top USDA officials, the NACD officers were assured that the consolidated offices would not change agency program responsibilities, and that no one agency would have jurisdiction over any other agency in the Center. Conservation districts who were hiring staff were encouraged to house them at the Service Center with the SCS staff. Plans were being drawn in each state by the USDA agency leaders, and would be thoroughly reviewed with conservation district leaders before approval, a policy statement issued by USDA said.[33]

But problems continued to crop up. In only two months, the NACD Board was discussing reports of "serious problems with district operations" emerging from the office consolidation efforts. Among those problems were growing frictions among the agency personnel at the field level, often caused by being brought together into unfamiliar "open space" office designs and placed on a single "rotary" telephone system.

In early April of 1974, USDA announced that it was slowing down the Service Center proposal, going to a pilot basis and extending the deadlines for states to develop and implement a plan. In December, the Department announced its plan to go ahead with the establishment of 1,000 Service Centers, but with greater flexibility to meet local conditions.

Not too suprisingly, the consolidation effort moved more slowly than foreseen by USDA, and by June 30, 1976, it was reported the 456 Agricultural Service Centers were in operation. But district leaders were still troubled. Directives from USDA mandating the use of rotary telephone systems and urging the removal of interior partitions in consolidated offices "may be counterproductive and costly," NACD told Department officials. Some of the problem was the result of "inadequate consultation with officials of conservation districts, many of which provide office space, clerical and technical assistance, equipment, and financial support in connection with USDA programs," NACD pointed out.[34]

In September of 1977, Secretary Bob Bergland revised the Service Center policy, giving far more authority to the state USDA administrative committees than before, and stating that "office design, type of telephone system, etc., are to be dependent upon local needs and availability." NACD applauded the Secretary's "decentralization" of the office co-location process, and the Service Center issue faded into the background.[35]

Both the federal reorganization and the USDA Service Center issues pointed up the complexities facing federal decisionmakers in dealing with the conservation programs. By gaining the degree of involvement from local citizens and units of government that is represented by the conservation district movement, USDA has greatly extended the ability of its programs to reach the land users of America. At the same time, they have created a complex interweaving of federal, state, local and private interests that makes it virtually impossible for any one of the participants to significantly "change the rules of the game."

This has proven to be a frustration to management analysts at the federal level, who look at the federal portion of the USDA programs and become convinced that there are better ways to structure them so that the federal government realizes more measurable benefits for the federal dollar spent. The theory is great, but in practice it is seldom feasible. There are too many factors involved, and too many other interests. Cooperative efforts must be changed with the full agreement of, and in the best interests of all the cooperating partners, and this is true even when those involved are as uneven in size, resources and power as the federal government and the conservation districts.

Improving the Federal Conservation Programs

Throughout the Decade of the Environment, as new public attention focused on the problems being created by people and technology, and new public programs emerged to address those problems, the old-line natural resource conservation programs were, for the most part, facing serious cutbacks. With but two exceptions in the early 1970's, when Assistant Secretary of Agriculture Robert W. Long was successful in winning budget increases that temporarily reversed the long decline in SCS technical assistance capability, every Presidential budget proposed reduced funding. In return, NACD and other conservation organizations would fight for budget increases and Congress, caught between the two forces, would usually compromise somewhere in the range of wherever the previous year's budget had been. The programs were, in a word, stalemated.

But new legislative attempts continued. In 1969, the Great Plains Conservation Program was extended for another ten years, a major victory for conservation districts and NACD. A. L. Black of Texas and Lyle Bauer worked to get the legislation through Congress, with amendments that gave conservation districts their first substantive recognition and role in federal law. (That had been a goal of the NACD long-range plan.) At the time of its extension, the program was so popular that over 7,000 farmers and ranchers were awaiting funds so they could join.

In January of 1971, President Nixon signed the Water Bank Act, long sought by NACD to help ease the conflict between farm and wildlife interests concerning the use of "pothole" lands. Under the Water Bank Program, landowners can enter into contracts with USDA for up to ten years, in which they agree to carry out a conservation plan approved by the conservation district and keep potholes set aside as wildlife areas. Without such assistance, economic pressures force farmers to drain these soils (which are often very productive) and grow crops on them.

Congress appropriated $10 million for the Water Bank Program in fiscal year 1972 and 1973, but the Administration announced in its 1974 budget that it was terminating the program. Congress disagreed, and has consistently disagreed with subsequent efforts to terminate the program, or fold its goals into the Agricultural Conservation Program where it would compete for funds from a reduced total allocation with the other conservation cost-sharing efforts.

In late 1972, in an effort to control federal spending, President Nixon "impounded" the funds appropriated for the 1973 Agricultural Conservation Program and announced that the program itself was terminated. In early 1974, a U.S. District Court ruled that the President had exceeded his authority and the funds were released, so Nixon lost that battle. In 1974, the Nixon budget proposed to merge the Great Plains Conservation Program into the ACP, with contract administration moved from SCS to ASCS.

At the same time, the great expansion of American cropland in response to the 1973 Russian wheat purchase was causing grave concern for the potential erosion consequences. A survey by SCS showed that nearly half of the "new" land going into crop production in 1974 (most of it coming from land that had been set aside in the conservation reserve of previous years) was susceptible to excessive soil erosion. NACD's position was that "it was time to move ahead," not backwards, in funding conservation programs.[36]

The response in Congress was to leave the Great Plains Program in SCS, and continue to fund it at $20 million per year. The response convinced the Administration that the merger would meet too much political opposition, so for fiscal 1976 their ploy was to leave the Great Plains Program alone, but propose the complete elimination of the Agricultural Conservation Program, the Forestry Incentives Program, and the Water Bank. Congress, again, refused to go along, establishing a pattern that has been repeated virtually every year since.

Another facet of the battle between Congress and the Administration over conservation policy centered around the 1972 Rural Development Act. NACD had hailed the bill in 1971, saying that, if enacted, it "would achieve most of the major watershed and resource development objectives adopted by NACD over the past five years."[37] The bill, sponsored by W.R. "Bob" Poage of Texas, passed the House in February of 1972 and its companion, sponsored by George Aiken of Vermont, passed the Senate later that summer. In August, President Nixon signed it into law.

SCS authorities were broadened by a host of provisions in the new law, including approval for federal cost-sharing for water quality management in P.L. 566 and RC&D projects; long-term contracting for land treatment in watershed areas; federal cost-sharing of up to 50 percent for the cost of water storage in watershed projects for municipal and industrial supplies; a nationwide program of long-term Rural Environmental Protection contracts; and a periodic (every five years) inventory of the nation's land and water resources.

Eighteen months later, however, NACD was complaining to the Senate Agriculture Committee that "The Department of Agriculture is not doing anything about many of the authorities contained in this legislation." USDA had done nothing with authorities for assistance on municipal and industrial water supplies, ground water recharge, disposal of solid wastes, control of agriculture-related pollution, rural water supply, and rural fire protection, NACD said.[38] Broadened program authorities, no matter how popular, were not in keeping with strong efforts to hold down federal spending, so delay -- or avoidance -- was the Administration's response to the new legislation.

New legislation, however, just continued to emerge. In a move labelled a "potential Magna Charta" for future progress in American forestry by George Bagley, Congress passed the Forest and Related Resources Planning Act of 1974 (to become known as the RPA). The new law provided for the preparation of a Renewable Resource Assessment by USDA in 1975, to be updated in 1979 and every decade thereafter. Also required by December 31, 1975, was a Renewable Resource Program outlining the direct and cooperative programs of the Forest Service that would be needed to meet the demands shown in the assessment. It, too, would be periodically updated. These documents were to be, Congress directed, used in framing the annual budget requests of the Forest Service. The stage was set for a budget process based on the needs of the nation for resource management and development, it was hoped.

As the Forest Service settled down to the work of preparing the documents called for in the RPA, the Senate Agriculture Committee moved again -- this time to the SCS. In a bill titled the Land and Water Conservation Act of 1975, a similiar process was proposed to be carried out on the private lands of the nation. This bill, in addition to a strong statement of pro-conservation national policy, called for a periodic appraisal of the land, water and related resources in the nation and a program for furthering the conservation, protection and enhancement of those resources. NACD's staff and officers were instrumental in drafting this bill, working with a group that contained staff members from Congress, SCS, and many other conservation, agricultural and forestry organizations.

Passed by the Senate in May of 1976, and the House in October, the bill was hailed by conservationists as a new day in establishing their programs in the framework of national priorities. That joy was short-lived, however. The Office of Management and Budget, seeing how effective the RPA was in justifying higher budgets for the Forest Service, had had enough of these "needs-based" budget efforts. They pressed the President to veto the bill and, on October 19, 1976, President Ford followed their advice.

George Bagley reacted strongly. "Objections cited by the President misinterpreted the intent of the bill and ignored its legislative history," the *Tuesday Letter* charged.[39]

Response from Congress was swift and decisive, as well. On the first day of the 95th Congress, Eligio de la Garza of Texas introduced H.R. 75 -- the Land and Water Resources Conservation Act of 1977. On the Senate side, Walter D. Huddleston (KY), James O. Eastland (MS), Dick Clark (IA), Robert Dole (KS), Hubert H. Humphrey (MN), George McGovern (SD) and Herman Talmadge (GA) joined to introduce S. 106 to replace the vetoed law. Congressional action was swift and decisive, and President Jimmy Carter signed the Soil and Water Resources Conservation Act of 1977 (to become known as the RCA) on November 17, 1977.

So SCS, too, had its "potential Magna Charta." The process, was, however, not as easy as it had been for the Forest Service. It was not just that there were a broader range of resources to consider, but also that so many additional institutional arrangements were involved. The first major project was to conduct an assessment and appraisal of the nation's land and water resources. This massive task, largely based on the 1977 National Resource Inventories, was a major accomplishment for SCS. In addition to providing a basis for the RCA program, it served to further fuel the public interest in the whole topic of soil and water conservation by showing the extent and severity of resource problems.

Moving from the appraisal to the program was a different matter, however. The facts, no matter how compelling, could not be easily translated into a feasible strategy for USDA action. Unable to meet the deadlines for an RCA program as the law established, SCS would take far longer, and the Carter Administration would come and go before a national conservation program would emerge. Even then, the program would be a captive of the federal budget process, not a driving factor in it.

In Summary: A Decade of Dilemma

The "Decade of the Environment" aroused public attention to environmental matters in a way never before seen, but the natural resource agencies, programs and organizations found it to be a mixed blessing. Natural resource management principles and proven land use philosophies were spurned as often as not, and a mood of protectionism, no-growth, and non-use swept through many of the battles of the decade.

While new programs proliferated, and new laws and regulations seemed to appear at every juncture, the old-line conservation programs and agencies were in a battle for survival. Virtually every Presidential budget proposed funding reductions, and often elimination of some programs.

Many felt the problem was in the Office of Management and Budget, where the same policy analysts tend to identify and quantify the "program of the President" no matter who sits in the Oval Office. Budget analysts at OMB have long said openly that the conservation programs, particularly those that provide incentives for conservation on private lands, deserve low federal priority. Each year's budget makes that point, without question.

Congress, tired of having to fight to get back even a hold-even budget, decided in the 1970's to devise new methods of analysis upon which a more rational budgeting process could be based. They hoped that passage of the RPA and the RCA would produce an analysis of the resource base and its needs, to be accompanied by a program of federal action to meet those needs. OMB, however, saw this as simply one more way in which the agencies could concoct better justifications for huge, and unnecessary, budget increases. As a result, OMB moved strongly to dominate the RPA and RCA processes, making sure that program proposals were aimed at the lowest possible targets, and still couching their recommendations with warnings that the funds might not be available to do even the most modest proposals.

Thus, the nation went through the Environmental Decade without developing a method of rationalizing public spending on natural resource programs. Pollution control programs did better, and significant gains were made in both water and air quality as a result, but the basic resources, soil and water, still lacked a definite national policy niche, as do the renewable resources like timber, grass and wildlife.

The nation's conservation districts, challenged by new issues and new constituencies, moved to expand their agenda so as to retain their credibility with the public. NACD, caught on the front lines of a dozen policy battles simultaneously in Washington, changed and expanded its agenda rapidly as well. As one of the few organizations that could claim to have one foot solidly planted in the environmentalist camp and the other equally firm in the farmer-rancher-forester domain, NACD faced serious challenges, but also encountered unique opportunities to provide a forum for communications and compromise between what often seemed like irreconcilable positions.

"Many people called the 1970's the "Decade of the Environment." For years we heard speeches from national leaders extolling the need for better environmental conservation . Many of you have labored long and hard to help find workable solutions for problems such as non-point water pollution. You were responding to a call from Washington.

"But what has really been happening in Washington this past ten years? Has all this public and private concern for the environment translated into political support for soil and water conservation?

"If we take federal budgets for soil and water conservation over the past decade, and convert them into constant 1970 dollars to eliminate inflation and compare the actual buying power of 1980 federal programs with those of 1970, it looks like this:

* Technical assistance to land users — down 2 percent.
* Watershed construction — down 10 percent.
* The Great Plains Conservation Program — down 14 percent.
* Watershed planning — down 23 percent.
* The Agricultural Conservation Program — down 51 percent.
* Soil and water conservation research — down 60 percent.

"All told, when we look at the entire range of USDA programs designed to help private land users solve soil and water conservation problems, we find that the federal government has steadily reduced its funding priority over the last ten years. In a decade where they all talked about the quality of the environment, our national leaders have allowed programs to help protect the most vital elements of that environment -- our productive soil and waters -- to shrink away.

Lyle Bauer, "1980: Year of Decision,"
1980 Annual Convention, Houston, TX.

Expanding the Agenda

10

In addition to the major legislative battles taking place in Washington over such monumental issues as national land use policy and and water pollution control, there were many other conservation issues that pushed onto the conservation agenda during the decade. Many had roots that went back for years and years, and few of them were neatly solved within the decade. Some, in fact, are still important issues, and serve to illustrate that most conservation concerns, even though they tend to peak in the public's attention for relatively short periods, are seldom solved in any final sense. For the most part, these issues are a little like the common cold; defying final solution and affecting generation after generation.

Many of the issues that sprang up in the 1970's had little, if anything, to do with soil erosion. Instead, their overriding characteristic was that they were natural resource-oriented. Their rise to public attention challenged the capability of both districts and NACD as the conservation movement sought to demonstrate that it was, indeed, a national natural resource conservation movement and not just a group of farmers fighting soil erosion.

Outdoor Recreation

NACD recognized in 1972 that an increasingly "recreation-conscious" public was going to place demands on the land and water resource base that conservation districts would need to recognize. In a 1972 statement to the Bureau of Outdoor Recreation, which was in the process of preparing a national outdoor recreation plan, John Wilder pointed out that there was a significant need for technical personnel to help private landowners, conservation districts, and other local governments plan and install needed facilities.[1]

In 1973, NACD took a bold step forward, deciding to conduct a nationwide inventory of private and semi-private outdoor recreation facilities. There was much talk about recreation as a potentially profitable use of land that was no longer needed for crop production, but virtually no information on what was already being done around the country, or how much success the ongoing enterprises were experiencing. The survey was to be a follow-up to a more limited effort conducted in 1963 by NACD and SCS, which, because it had covered only 65 percent of the nation, was limited in usefulness.

Under the direction of NACD's Recreation and Natural Environment Committee, the study was conducted in each district, but on a countywide basis, so that full coverage of the nation could be achieved.[2]

A national recreation plan, prepared in 1973 under the direction of James G. Watt (who would attain much more notoriety in the 1980's as Ronald Reagan's Secretary of the Interior) provided an overview of the public and private recreational facilities in the nation. It proposed to move forward in such areas as inventorying wetlands, opening "superlative" recreational areas in federal lands for public use, and "divestiture of lands and waters not of national significance." On its release, NACD President John Wilder said that the NACD inventory effort was "even more timely."

By August, 1974, 26 states had completed the inventory and forwarded the inventory data and maps to the Bureau of Outdoor Recreation for computer processing. But it was not until October of 1977 that the entire inventory was completed and published. The 155-page book that resulted showed a total of over 700,000 private recreation enterprises throughout the nation -- of which 45,000 were operated for profit. The data it contained were said to be "crucial in national and state recreation planning efforts now under way."[3]

Coastal Zone Management

The Coastal Zone Management Act of 1972 set in motion a land use planning and management process very similar to the one proposed in the Jackson and Udall land use bills. It provides federal assistance to the states in planning for "the effective protection and use of the land and water resources" of the coastal zones along the oceans and the Great Lakes. It is administered by the Commerce Department. All told, it touches about 500 counties, and over half of the nation's population, so it is a significant program.

Soon after the states started their CZM efforts, they began to involve conservation districts and state soil conservation agencies. The district role included serving on policy and technical committees, accelerating soil surveys and reviewing sediment control plans, furnishing resource data and inventories, and aiding in the installation of erosion control measures and structures to protect the coast lines.

But all was not sweetness and light, as one might imagine. Many districts felt that the CZM planners were a bunch of "paper planners" who were only interested in finding a way to impose more regulations, and many coastal planners either didn't know the districts existed, or felt they were simply a farm organization that had little, if anything, to offer.

NACD's Coastal and Shore Resources Committee met many times with officials from the Office of Coastal Zone Management, and became convinced that districts needed to become a great deal more active in coastal matters. "The expertise, information and assistance at the disposal of districts," said Chairman Stanley R. Christensen of Oregon, "can be highly useful in achieving control of erosion and protection of beneficial values associated with coastal lands."[4]

There were other problems, however. States and conservation districts had been active for some time in shoreline erosion control efforts, cooperating with the Corps of Engineers in many of them, but offering services directly to landowners wherever possible. In addition, the Corps was running a permit program to regulate "dredge and fill" in wetlands and districts were working with many 208 planning agencies that were developing plans to reduce nonpoint source pollution.

The problem was that these efforts could become competitive rather than complimentary in some cases. Shoreline erosion often required structures, or earthmoving. Was this a "fill" in wetlands that required a 404 permit? Whose regulations would prevail in controlling nonpoint source pollution of coastal waters, CZM or 208? The questions weren't easy to answer, and shoreline property owners and conservation districts often found themselves right in the middle of the fray.[5]

In addition, NACD was constantly concerned about the Plant Materials program of the SCS. This program had been instrumental in developing and testing the strains of grass and other plants needed to stabilize dunes and other coastal areas. Budget cuts continually threatened this program, which NACD felt was essential to progress in addressing coastal resource issues.

In 1978, NACD was awarded a $20,000 grant by the Department of Commerce to prepare a manuscript describing the conservation district system and exploring ways for conservation districts to cooperate with federal and state coastal zone management programs. The research was coordinated by Bob Williams of the NACD Special Projects office, with Rosalee Johnson hired as the researcher on the project, and oversight provided by the Coastal and Shore Resources Committee.

The publication, released in December of 1979, portrayed extensive district involvement in coastal and shore erosion control, upland erosion and sediment control, and provided resource data for CZM planners. The state soil conservation district laws, the CZM law, and the authorities contained in Section 208 of the Clean Water Act were compared, and an action program for coordinating the three was proposed. Titled *The Role of Conservation Districts in Coastal Zone Management,* it was distributed to conservation districts, coastal planners, and state and local land use agencies in the coastal areas.

As a result of this effort, the nearly 500 conservation districts in the coastal counties of the nation (where, it is estimated, over half of the people in America reside) seem fairly comfortable with the coastal zone management programs that have emerged from a decade of testing. The federal CZM program remains at a low ebb, and the state programs operate at various levels of intensity. In most coastal states, however, a major element in the protection of coastal waters is an active soil erosion prevention effort, and that effort is assigned to the conservation districts.

The National Watershed Congress

The National Watershed Congress continued its successful annual meetings until 1978, holding 25 meetings in all. Many of the meetings in the 70's were far from placid -- the fight over channelization meant that many of the participants were bitter antagonists in political and legal battles elsewhere. But the Congress was a place where all points of view could be heard, and every organization wanted that chance, even when it meant listening to someone else's far different opinion.

By 1971, the number of participating organizations had grown to 31, with 15 of the originals remaining. Some of the original sponsors had dropped out, or gone out of existence, but others joined to take their place.

In 1978, following a meeting at Toronto, the sponsoring organizations met several times to determine the future of the effort. Large national meetings were getting more and more expensive, and operating budgets were under extreme pressure in virtually every organization, as inflation was driving up costs far faster than memberships and quotas could be increased. As a result, many organizations felt that the large meeting should be replaced with something on a smaller scale, perhaps held in the Washington, D.C. area on an annual basis.

With only hazy plans for the future, the sponsoring committee made a decision and announced that there would be no annual meeting of the scale previously held. At first it was felt that the annual awards program could be continued, with the awards presented at a smaller meeting in Washington. Both the small meeting and the awards program, however, failed to materialize.

The P.L. 566 Small Watershed Program, which benefited so much from the 25-year history of the Congress, was now seen by most to be a mature program. Its directions had been fairly well set, its authority secure, and its policies balanced between resource development, flood protection, and environmental enhancement. Inflation had robbed it of purchasing power, as well, and far fewer new projects could be started each year as a combined result of rising costs and the federal budget crunch.

The sponsoring organizations have kept the basic organization of the Watershed Congress alive, in case the situation changes in the future and calls for a renewal of that communications forum. NACD, through the efforts of Charles Boothby, has retained the proceedings and made them available to interested parties, as well as responding to inquiries about the Congress.

Urban Conservation

The resource needs of urban and urbanizing areas had been growing in importance since the early 1960's, and districts across the nation were undertaking many urban-related tasks. But to many in districts and NACD, the recognition of that effort was lagging. Support for soil and water conservation programs, both in local budgets and at the national level, needed to come from more than the 3 percent of the nation's people who were actually farmers, the argument went.

In some instances, urban-related functions provided a new source of district financing. In 1975, the Lake County SWCD in Lake Zurich, IL, reported that the problems caused by urban sprawl in the Chicago-Milwaukee corridor were a major part of their work. The district furnished natural resource evaluations on all zoning changes, variances, subdivisions, and developments. That workload demanded the hiring of an executive director, but also provided the basis for funds to hire him. Thus, working with urban-related problems provided an income source and staff capability that the district would not otherwise have had. Similar experiences were occurring in many parts of the country.[6]

Another function of districts was to call together various local factions to discuss the problems and potentials of their area. From around the country came stories of districts using their position to start community-wide evaluations of the local cost of sprawl, the wise use of resources, and the need to protect a viable agriculture and a healthy environment in the face of growth and change.

As one result of these new services, urban areas that had never considered soil conservation districts began to form them. Nassau County, New York, established a district with over 1.5 million people in it, to work on problems of landfill location and rehabilitation, critical area seedings, shore erosion control, land use recommendations, and environmental education. The District of Columbia, operating under its unique charter, did the same. Conservation districts were becoming a local natural resource agency -- just as the District Outlook Report had predicted.

In 1979, the NACD Council passed a resolution urging the establishment of an Urban Conservation Committee in NACD to focus attention to the major conservation concerns in urban areas and to try and win support of the vast majority of Americans who call those areas home. They identified the major thrust of the urban conservation program as reduction of erosion and sediment damages in urban and urbanizing areas, and urban storm water management to reduce flooding. This was the culmination of several years of urging by the representatives from the Northeast, led by Director Kenneth Roehrich of New Jersey and others.

Since 1979, the committee has been active in developing informational materials for urban districts, providing assistance in the formation of new districts in urban areas, and helping facilitate information flow between districts facing similar problems in urbanizing areas.

Farmland Retention

The increasing public attention to the loss of prime farmland in urbanizing and developing areas was an issue made to order for the conservation districts, and they became involved at the earliest stages. "Soil is not a second-rate resource," NACD President George Bagley told the National Farm Institute in 1975. "We must find ways to protect the nation's prime and unique agricultural lands wherever they are in danger of being damaged by over-use, or of being converted unnecessarily to non-agricultural uses."

The conservation case was clear: whether the loss of soil productivity was due to soil erosion or to construction of a parking lot, the problem was the same, and NACD would speak out to prevent it where possible.

A small group within USDA had been working to get the Department more interested in the problems afflicting the prime farmlands of the nation, as well, but it was an uphill battle. Coming out of decades of farm surpluses, the last thing USDA policymakers wanted to worry about was land loss. Their major problem for years had been to try to get more of that land used for something besides growing surplus crops. But the pressure for an active role in land use matters was great, and the farmland case was too compelling to ignore.

In 1975, USDA sponsored a "Seminar on Prime Lands" which explored the issues and produced a publication saying that the indiscriminate and unnecessary loss of the nation's best lands was becoming a problem. In 1976, USDA's Land Use Committee worked with the Council on Environmental Quality to draft guidelines to all federal agencies. Prime agricultural lands were valuable, the CEQ memo told agency heads, and the environmental impact statements on federal projects should consider the impact on farmlands as well as on other resources.

Congress got into the act in 1977, when Congressman James Jeffords of Vermont introduced a bill that would establish federal policy discouraging federal agencies from indiscriminately ruining prime farmland with public works projects, initiate a federal study of the farmland situation and report back to Congress, and test a few local programs on a pilot basis to see what could realistically be done to stem farmland losses. In hearings on the bill, Director Kenneth J. Roehrich of New Jersey spoke for NACD. "This bill squarely addresses one of the most important resource issues that America will face," he said. "The land base that supports our food production is America's most basic, most vital resource."[7]

The bill did not make it out of the House Committee in 1977, in the face of strong political pressure criticizing its "land use" implications, but the attention it brought catalyzed other actions. In 1978, the Environmental Protection Agency issued new guidelines, asking project planners to take account of farmland values in siting sewers and other facilities. USDA issued a new land use policy, committing the Department's agencies to "seek to avoid irreversible conversion" of prime and unique farmlands, or encroachment on flood plains, unless there were no viable alternatives.

NACD decided to go straight to the districts themselves, and ask what district officials thought of the issues. In a survey sent to all 3,000 districts, NACD received over 1,900 replies. Over 40 percent said that they viewed farmland loss in their locality as a "serious" or "very serious" problem. The NACD staff displayed these responses on a colored map of the U.S. which showed that, although the concern was most pronounced on the coastal areas, there was no region of the nation untouched by the situation.

In the Administration, USDA Secretary Bob Bergland and CEQ Chairman Charles Warren decided to go ahead with the agricultural lands study proposed in the Jeffords Bill. Named the National Agricultural Lands Study (NALS), it was to be an 18-month attempt to outline the issues and propose policy alternatives. Robert J. Gray, formerly Jeffords' Administrative Assistant, was chosen to direct the study.

One part of the NALS was the report *Soil Degradation: Effects on Agricultural Policy,* developed by NACD under a contract from NALS. The report, which was published as *Interim Report No. 4* in 1980, helped the NALS point out that soil erosion and other forms of soil damage were still serious, and that these forces were adding to the productivity being lost to the nation's future, just as farmland conversion was taking its toll.

As the NALS proceeded, Congress kept considering the bills before it, and NACD continued to support them. President Lyle Bauer reviewed the results of the NACD survey, and told the House Agriculture Committee that "the problem warrants immediate attention from the Congress." He urged Congress to remember the conservation tradition established over 4 decades, and avoid undue regulation. "Our goals today, as they were at the start, are good conservation and wise use of the nation's lands and waters," he said. "We believe that goal can best be accomplished by a free people, working together in a voluntary manner, guided by a sensible land ethic, and supported by adequate research, technical assistance, and economic incentives."[8]

This time, the bill made it out of committee, again with NACD's solid support. President Bauer used the widely-read editorial page in the *Tuesday Letter* to say, "We think this bill meets the requirements that NACD has set forth for any type of legislation that affects the use of land."[9] But the House rejected the bill, largely on the basis of opposition to anything that might smack of "back-door federal land use planning."

Within weeks of the bill's failure, the NALS was released, with a great deal of press attention to its "explosive" findings. Several states had exceptionally high rates of farmland conversion, the 1977 National Resource Inventory (NRI) data showed. On the national scale, the past decade had seen as much as 3 million acres of agricultural land converted to other uses each year.

The findings were attacked by some analysts, who claimed the rate of farmland loss was badly overstated by the SCS data that was used. There is some evidence, since the 1982 NRI has been released, that the 1977 inventory data did overstate urban conversions in some areas, but the NALS results were not hinged entirely on the amount of acres being converted each year. What the study showed graphically was that, whatever the rate of farmland conversion, public funds were significantly and, often, needlessly, financing that destruction.

Finally, in the 1981 Farm Bill, a farmland protection policy based on the Jeffords Bill was enacted. It was aimed mainly at federal agencies, requiring that they conduct their projects and programs in a way that minimized adverse effects on prime farmlands. As of 1984, it is still uncertain how USDA will administer that policy, since the issuance of Departmental regulations is still not complete, having been plagued by serious political controversy from the beginning.

Out in the countryside, however, conservation districts are working on farmland protection in a variety of ways. One district in New Hampshire, and perhaps some others, have accepted donations of "development rights" from farmers who wished to assure that their land would not be taken for development. State and local farmland protection programs have grown up in many states -- Maryland, Massachusetts, New Jersey, New York, Pennsylvania and Wisconsin have been among the leaders. Private nonprofit organizations such as the American Farmland Trust have sprung up, and local "land conservancies" have been formed to protect farmland by entering the market and either buying key farmland parcels or negotiating for the development rights on them. Farmland protection is, in many parts of the country, a resource issue of major magnitude as a result of the work of conservationists during the 1970's.

Pasture and Range Improvement

"The forgotten resource" was the way one person described the situation facing the pasture and rangeland resources of the nation in the 1970's. Both public and private lands were seen to be suffering serious depletion of the grass stands which, while renewable, are also vulnerable to total destruction.

One specialist in rangeland ecosystems, Dr. Harold Dregne of Texas Tech University, estimated in 1977 that 1.1 million square miles of the North American continent's arid lands had already undergone severe desertification. That did not mean that they had turned into deserts overnight, but that the ecosystem had been severely damaged by the depletion of the native grasses and the invasion of undesirable species, accompanied by wind and water erosion that has largely denuded the land of topsoil and, consequently, of vegetation.[10]

A major problem was seen on the public lands, and in 1975

environmentalists sued the Bureau of Land Management, contending that BLM should be forced to prepare environmental impact statements on the grazing leases issued for domestic livestock on the public domain. A federal court agreed, and BLM began the massive undertaking of evaluating some 8,000 leases in 212 separate environmental assessments.

NACD had been concerned about range conditions on the public lands from its earliest days. The organization had worked hard to help establish a cooperative BLM-SCD demonstration program in each of the 11 western states in the early 1960's. These "demonstration districts" were used as showplaces to prove what could be accomplished when the private cattlemen and the federal agency worked together to manage the rangeland properly.

The problem was not limited to the West, as Gordon Zimmerman pointed out to the Western Governors Conference in 1975. "The 1964 Census of Agriculture shows a total of 665 million acres of range, grazed woodland, and pastures," he said, "more than 50 percent of the land area of our nation."

At the 1975 Convention, the NACD Council passed a resolution advocating the development of a long-term program emphasizing pasture and range improvement on all federal, state and private range and pasture lands. NACD would provide leadership, it was stated, and seek the cooperation of all other interested organizations.

In 1976, President George Bagley set a high priority on moving forward with the efforts to formally establish a national Pasture and Range Improvement Program. As a result, he and Pete Jackson of Montana, Chairman of the NACD Public Lands Committee, met in Washington with officials of USDA and USDI, the American Forage and Grassland Council, the Society for Range Management, and representatives of BLM, SCS, and the Forest Service. The participants agreed to move forward, and a series of meetings were held which broadened the group's participants and helped sharpen the focus on what was to be done.

By 1977, a National Coalition for Pasture and Rangeland Improvement was organized with leadership from NACD. Joining NACD were 22 private environmental, agricultural, forestry and rangeland organizations, along with representatives of the Congressional committee staffs and the federal agencies. A 13-member Task Force, with ten additional technical consultants, was named to conduct a study and prepare a report for the group.

The goal of the coalition was to develop a national commitment to conserve, protect, and enhance soil, water, and vegetation resources on range and pasture lands to assure that these resources reach their full productivity.[11] In March, 1979, five national organizations concerned with these issues met in Denver to seek agreement on issues. As a result, the National Cattlemen's Association, Public Lands Council, National Wool Growers, the Society for Range Management and NACD agreed upon a list of ten rangeland issues that should be brought to national attention.[12]

In July, the 38-page Pasture and Range Improvement Report was complete, compiled by Bob Williams of the NACD Special Projects Staff and Chairman of the Rangeland Coalition's Task Force. It listed six major concerns that needed to be addressed, and carried the coalition's recommendations for moving ahead. NACD President Lyle Bauer said that the report demonstrated the need to move forward quickly. "It is time for us to do better," he said. "As exports rise and grain prices follow, more red meat must be produced on the grasslands. We can't gain this productivity together with needed wildlife habitat and environmental improvement, unless a strong national effort is put into grassland programs."[13]

Some signs of movement within governmental circles appeared as a result of the effort. USDA announced formation of a Departmental Committee on improving range and pasture programs in November of 1979. In 1980, the National Governor's Association Committee on Agriculture identified rangeland improvement as one of its top three priorities. In Utah and Montana, state-funded revolving loan funds were created so that ranchers could borrow low-interest money for making rangeland improvements.

But outside those two efforts, the rangeland program has been marked by more talk than action. Restricted federal budgets have held down the federal agencies' abilities to install the needed fencing, water developments, and seedings on rangeland. Even with a provision in federal law that a certain percentage of all grazing fees must now go back into rangeland improvement, the progress is still not adequate according to most observers.

But the pasture and rangeland improvement efforts led by NACD in the late 1970's served to raise the consciousness of many organizations and agencies to the need for better pasture and range treatment. At least in the minds of many, rangeland is no longer a "forgotten resource."

Resource Conservation and Development

In the early days of the Carter Administration, USDA leaders were looking for ways to cut back on programs in order to meet the severe budget restraints they faced. One seen as most vulnerable by the budget analysts was the RC&D program. A study conducted by SCS had found that there was no significant difference in employment or economic statistical trends between RC&D areas and those without the program. Thus, it was reasoned, RC&D could be dropped. The program had always been a thorn in the side of the Rural Development leaders at USDA, as well as the Extension Service, because it was an activity of SCS and districts that often appeared to trample on the other agency's "turf" or take credit for accomplishments that had involved many actors besides SCS. As a result, the notion that RC&D would be discontinued brought few tears in some corridors of USDA.

But out in the countryside, it was a different story. NACD had always been supportive of RC&D, even though many districts (particularly those that were not in RC&D areas) had complained that the program had siphoned off some of the dollars and skilled SCS technicians that had formerly been assigned to help farmers with erosion control efforts. In 1975, an NACD Subcommittee on RC&D had expressed support for the program, but also listed 15 recommendations for changes that needed to be made.

The 1978 decision by USDA to phase out RC&D, however, galvanized national support for the program. NACD began receiving letters and calls from all over the country, urging the organization to come out strongly to prevent the demise of RC&D. Supporters were not just conservation districts, but other local officials and rural organizations who testified that the program was highly beneficial to their areas, even if the benefits were often not the kind that could be readily quantified and picked up in statistical data.

NACD's leaders didn't need much encouragement from others. President Lyle Bauer had been active in regional planning work in Kansas for many years, and was heavily involved in the RC&D program, with an active program in his own region. He reacted strongly to the USDA proposal in a *Tuesday Letter* editorial. "From hundreds of people, we hear how RC&D has helped their communities -- improved their local capability to work together -- carried out needed projects that conserve soil and water -- helped attract business and industry -- assisted in broadening the economic base," he said. "All this on a limited budget, spread among 178 RC&D areas, that has resulted in an increasing backlog of project measures that cannot be funded."

"If RC&D hasn't done what some people thought it could, it is no surprise," he charged. "It is a good idea that has never received adequate support in Washington."

USDA Assistant Secretary M. Rupert Cutler, somewhat taken aback by the ferocity of the reaction, (he had been quoted as saying that RC&D "lacked a national constituency") named a Task Force to study the possibility of redirecting the program, with his Deputy David Unger (previously NACD's Executive Vice President) as Co-Chairman. The Task Force held nine public hearings in seven cities during the summer of 1978 and made five field trips to RC&D areas. As a result, they wrote a report to the Department saying that very strong support for the program existed throughout the country. Secretary Bob Bergland was impressed, and proposed budget increases, but the response of the Office of Management and Budget (OMB) was to cut the RC&D budget still further, continuing the phase-out plan into 1979.

In 1979, the Senate Agriculture Committee's Subcommittee on Environment, Soil Conservation and Forestry got into the act, with hearings on the program and its future. The subcommittee, chaired by Sen. John Melcher of Montana, was urged into action by Sen. George McGovern of South Dakota, long a staunch advocate of the program. Based on the testimony of RC&D officials from all parts of the country, as well as NACD and USDA, the Senators announced that they would oppose any phase-out efforts.[14]

As a result, Congressional budget action continued to keep the program intact, both appropriating funds and instructing that none of the money given to USDA could be used to effectuate a phase-out of the program. In addition, an "organic" act for program was introduced in 1979 and in the House in February of 1980 to provide a better legislative base for the program than had been provided in the brief authorizing clause contained in the 1962 Farm Bill. In 1980, the Administration dropped the phase-out plan and proposed a budget of almost $35 million for RC&D in FY 1981.

RC&D officials Michael Shay, Massachusetts, Peggy McNeill, New Jersey, and J.B. Jones, Georgia, made an impression on the Senate.

The RC&D areas themselves also began to form their own associations. In addition to working with NACD, regional associations of RC&D's began to be formed to assist with the political effort needed to keep the program intact. As a result of these efforts, the "organic" bill was enacted as part of the 1981 Farm Bill.

The program was still not out of trouble, however. After proposing a $26.8 million budget for FY 1982, the Reagan Administration "rediscovered" the fiscal opportunity afforded by an RC&D phaseout. Budgets of $10 million for FY 1983 and $0 for 1984 were the result. Congress has consistently rejected those cutbacks, but the result has been cycles of uncertainty in the program, where SCS would be required to stop all new RC&D activities during the period between the President's budget and the Congressional action, then rush to spend a whole year's funds after the Congress had finally finished work on the Appropriations Bill. It has been frustrating for all the participants in the program, and there are no signs that the frustrations have been eliminated for the future.

Surface Mined Land Reclamation

The challenge of restoring and reclaiming land that had been surface mined had been one that districts had tackled for many years. Some of these lands, reduced to barren rubble piles, were significant eyesores and environmental problems in addition to being totally non-productive. Often the exposed minerals contained significant quantities of acid-forming compounds or heavy minerals which, when exposed to the surface, broke down rapidly into chemicals or particles that could wash or blow readily off the site. Many a stream suffered a complete loss of biological life because of acid coming from an old surface mine.

The problem was fairly significant in scope by the mid-70's when federal action was finally taken. USDA estimated that, by 1965, surface mining had disturbed 3.2 million acres of land. That increased to 4.0 million acres in 1972, 4.4 million in 1974, and 5.7 million acres in 1977.[15] With some 400,000 acres being disturbed each year, and with many millions of acres of lands simply abandoned or "orphaned" after the mining was concluded, Congress moved to remedy the problem.

The issues were difficult and divisive, and Congress worked several years to get a bill that could meet the political tests. When they finally did get a law enacted in the closing days of the session in 1974, President Gerald Ford pocket-vetoed it. That set the stage for two more years of negotiating and wrangling in the Congress. Congressman Morris Udall had a bill (H.R. 25) introduced in January of 1975, and held hearings immediately, but the Senate struck first, passing its version of the bill in March.

NACD was strongly supportive of the legislation. George Bagley told readers of the *Tuesday Letter* that "Conservation districts are especially interested in the section in both bills which establishes a fund to reclaim 'orphan' (abandoned) mined lands." Fees on each ton of coal mined go into the fund, which then must be appropriated out of the fund by Congress before it can be used for reclamation work. The money goes to the Department of the Interior, who can transfer up to 20 percent of it to the Department of Agriculture for use in the Rural Abandoned Mine Program (RAMP) administered by SCS.

In addition, districts in the midwest were particularly interested in sections of the law which specified soil reconstruction standards to return prime farmland to its original productive state following mining. That this was technically possible was strongly argued by the SCS and districts, but the mining industry was bitterly opposed, claiming that such restoration drove up the costs unnecessarily, that few acres were involved on a national scale, and that the loss of prime farmland was a problem of limited national consequence.

In 1976, the political opposition led by the coal industry prevailed again. The bill was passed, but again vetoed by President Ford. Congress was not to be denied, however, and the new 95th Congress pushed the law through one more time. Finally, on August 3, 1977, it was signed into law by President Carter.

In the meantime, the work of the conservation districts had continued. In 1975, a Wyoming law specified that surface mined lands must be reclaimed, and mentioned conservation districts as one of the agencies an applicant could work through to achieve approved reclamation status. In several districts where mining was occurring, assistance to strip miners became one of the district's highest priorities.

In early 1977, NACD sponsored a workshop in Denver to review procedures for coordinating technical assistance in surface mine relamation when the coal is federally owned but the land is in private ownership. This led to a series of state meetings in the western states, where the problem of mixed public-private ownership was particularly severe.

In the Tennessee Valley area, 13 conservation districts cooperated with TVA in reclaiming orphan strip mines and abandoned haul roads in east Tennessee. The districts would select priority watersheds, search out land ownership records and contact the owners, call meetings as needed, find the landowners and get cooperative agreements signed, then help with preparing reclamation plans. The districts would assign and oversee work crews as the sites were reclaimed, then provide follow-up inspections.

Technical assistance for the reclamation plans came from the state's Division of Orphan Land Reclamation and the SCS.[16]

These pilot projects proved that orphan land reclamation was possible, and that districts could provide a very useful service in working between the federal or state agency and the landowners.

By early 1979, the RAMP was ready to be put into action in 29 states and some 377 counties with abandoned coal-mined lands. Districts began receiving applications, screening them for priority, and forwarding the best ones to the SCS state office for funding consideration. The SCS State Conservationist, working with a statewide reclamation committee, established the order in which the projects would be funded.

By June of 1979, SCS reported that a total of 2,500 applications had been received, of which only 70 could be funded in the 1979 fiscal year. The estimated cost of the 481 project applications determined to be in "priority one" (lands which posed a hazard to life or property) was in excess of $30 million, while the agency only had about $14 million to spend. But funding was not the only hang-up. Many contracts were awaiting a ruling from the Internal Revenue Service about the tax treatment to be accorded the RAMP cost-sharing. If the money was to be treated as personal income, many taxpayers would be unable or unwilling to cooperate in the program. Legislation to assure that federal cost-shares would not be treated as gross income was passed in 1978, then improved with technical corrections in 1980. Still, by October of 1980, there was no resolution, and the RAMP was significantly held back as a result.

The IRS situation has still never been fully resolved, as Treasury Department rules have never been finalized, but the RAMP's progress has been impeded more by unwillingness on the part of Congress and the Administration to fund it. Interior has consistently fought against giving funds to USDA, arguing instead that sending the money directly to the states would be preferable. Congressional committees funding Interior's programs have gone along with that position, and for a time it appeared that the RAMP would be allowed to die.

In 1982, NACD formed a special committee on RAMP, with members from each state where the program was in operation. This committee has kept the pressure on Congress to allow the RAMP to continue, particularly in those states where the state agencies have not been able to get ready to cope with the challenge of orphan land reclamation. The solution for the best organizational approach for dealing with this difficult land issue is still far from realized.

Farm Forestry

While farm forestry was not a new subject to NACD by any means, it was given a great deal of attention in the 1970's. A joint Task Force had been established in 1969 by the American Forestry Association, NACD and representatives from Forest Service, Soil Conservation Service and Extension Service to focus directly on the problems facing private forest owners. Entitled "Trees for People," the idea of the group was to mobilize the joint efforts of the organizations and agencies on the need for improved management of the nation's private, non-industrial forests.

The NACD Forestry Committee, under the Chairmanship of Monroe Samuel of Arkansas, conducted a complete study of conservation district forestry programs, discovering that forest management was a major program element in about 2,500 districts and that some 1,500 districts had working agreements with the state forestry agencies. Equipment, crews, and technical assistance for tree planting was a service that many districts already provided.

NACD also took an active role in a program entitled "The South's Third Forest," urging districts to become involved in the 12-state southern effort to replant timberland in the South and manage it so that the region could supply a major share of the forest products needed in the future. These forestry efforts led to the planting of trees on many thousands of acres of formerly eroding crop and pasture land, bringing a multitude of economic and environmental benefits to many communities in the South.

Monroe Samuel, who holds the record for length of service on the NACD Board, was recognized throughout the South, and across the country, as "Mr. Forestry" in NACD, and was an avid promoter of forestry issues in the organization throughout the decade.

Manpower Needs in Districts

A major realization of districts during the era of expansion was that they would not be able to undertake all the new jobs they were considering if they only relied on the technical assistance provided by SCS. As a result, districts and NACD have conducted continuous studies of ways to find more help for districts. In January of 1975, the District Operations Committee of NACD sent each district a survey of manpower needs to be filled out and returned to their state soil conservation agency. The state agencies summarized their state's response and forwarded the state total to NACD.

This survey, which showed that considerable additional assistance was needed, has been repeated annually since, giving a profile not only of what is needed, but of what manpower districts are using in their work.

Public works programs were proving useful, as well. Starting with youth training programs in the 1960's, districts were able to take advantage of such programs as the Comprehensive Employment and Training Act of 1974 (CETA), the Emergency Jobs and Unemployment Assistance Act of that same year, and the Public Works Employment Act of 1976.

At the same time, districts were getting into urban erosion and sediment control programs, surface mine reclamation and other tasks which not only required that they have a skilled staff, but provided the funding source to pay for it, either through fees and permits or through state or county appropriations. As a result of all these activities, the NACD survey for 1978 showed that districts were managing a staff of around 6,000, with additional needs for another 3,725. Compared to a decade earlier, when districts had employed hardly any staff, the increase was staggering. Even compared to a total SCS staff of somewhere in the range of 14,000, the districts were beginning to add a significant dimension to the assistance available to America's land users.

In addition, districts were learning how to combine various federal programs for maximum advantage. There was a senior citizens employment program called Green Thumb, sponsored by federal funds and the National Farmers Union, that employed nearly 14,000 senior rural residents in 1978. There were various youth employment programs, including a Youth Conservation Corps, a Young Adult Conservation Corps, and the Job Corps, to name the most widely known. NACD encouraged districts to take advantage of the combinations that were possible. A senior citizen with experience could be put in charge of a youth crew with strength and energy; the best of both would be achieved. Conservation districts rose to the challenge with vigor, and soon reports began to filter back to NACD of conservation projects under way with these kinds of combined efforts.

But districts were running into management problems, as well. Having never had employees before, and often having very little time on the part of the supervisors for direct supervision, the districts needed help with policy development, benefit packages, and a host of other personnel details. As a result, NACD entered into an agreement with SCS and the National Association of State Soil Conservation Agencies for a special project on manpower needs. In March of 1979, Roger Montague was assigned from SCS to NACD under the terms of the Intergovernmental Personnel Act to carry out a manpower project.

The project, which continued through September 30, 1981, was responsible for the development of a Personnel Handbook which contains basic information, samples, and ideas on all aspects of personnel management. The handbook was distributed on request to state soil conservation agencies and districts to serve as an aid in establishing their own personnel policies. The project (and the handbook) was a complicated one due to the many differences between state laws on districts and employment, but the state administrative officers provided the linkage that allowed NACD to develop the basic document.

·By January, 1979, the NACD survey showed that there were 329 full-time district managers and 474 full-time district technicians hired by state and local funds. The total number of district employees using state and local funds was around 4,100, with another 2,000 or so furnished by the various federal jobs programs. As those federal programs were eliminated after 1980, the total number of district employees dropped slightly, but state and locally-funded positions continued to rise.

NACD's leaders have felt, since the advent of the District Outlook activity, that the future of conservation districts would be largely defined by their ability to identify specific tasks, gain local or state funding to carry out those tasks, and become more of a local resource action agency and less of a local advisory committee for SCS. If that is a true measure of district effectiveness, the history of the past 15 years is a very positive indicator, as districts have, indeed, grown steadily in this manner. That trend, while certainly not universally true for all districts, has been one of the major changes affecting the district movement.

In Summary

As the foregoing has shown, the soil conservation movement is no longer a simple, straightforward effort by a few dedicated scientists and an equally dedicated cadre of lay leaders from the farm community to stem the loss of topsoil from America's farms. The dreams of Hugh Bennett and E.C. McArthur have been vastly expanded and extended into areas that neither probably foresaw. That has not happened without a great deal of controversy on the part of conservation professionals and lay leaders alike.

Some have argued that the new environmental and resource concerns have taken attention, dollars and resources away from the fight against soil erosion. Others have countered with the theory that these expanded concerns have kept the conservation movement in tune with the mood of the times, and attracted dollars and attention to tasks which, had the conservation districts not been willing to undertake, would have been done by some other organizational arrangement, to the ultimate (and perhaps, even fatal) detriment of the district movement.

The fact is that districts are no longer what they once were, let alone what they were originally conceived to be. Neither, for that matter, are the agencies that work with them. Any person, whether deeply involved with a local district, with an agency that works with districts, or with an agency or organization that sees districts as a competitor, needs to be aware of that fact. Actually, many districts today are closer than ever to what Henry Wallace thought they might become -- a local natural resource agency that can help call together a broad array of public agencies and private resources to address the problems of natural resource management and conservation.

But districts are not one entity, for each varies greatly in its program capabilities, leadership, and technical backup skills. Compounding the differences in the 50 state laws are the added differences of districts in such areas as Puerto Rico, the Virgin Islands, the District of Columbia and some of the major Indian Reservations. In 20 states and territories, districts have legal authority to enact and enforce erosion and sediment control legislation. In some states, they are part of the regulatory mechanism that guides growth and development. In one state (Wisconsin), they are a bureau of county government. In some states they are formed on county boundaries; in others they are multi-county in size; in still others they follow watershed or irrigation district boundaries. In all, the conservation districts of America offer an interesting range of characteristics -- a national concept that, while universally adopted, has also been locally shaped to fit local conditions and meet local needs.

The issues, laws, and ideas that have shaped this incredibly complex institutional framework have themselves been shaped significantly by the National Association of Conservation Districts and its leaders. The decade of the 1970's, while certainly not the only time in which this was true, clearly was a decade in which NACD, its leaders, and its ideas, were seriously tested. That the organization emerged from that period as a strong, respected national spokesman for soil conservation is a testimony to hundreds -- perhaps thousands -- whose small and large contributions were part of the total effort.

NACD Today 11

Any attempt to assess an organization's present situation and condition is always more hazardous than looking back into its history. The problem, of course, is that everything one is doing at present looks terribly important; only after a few years will we really know what turned out to be major accomplishments, and which efforts went for naught.

The breadth and nature of the issues addressed by the conservation districts and their national association have had considerable impact on the organization itself. The organization has had an impact on national issues as well, and is in much stronger condition in the 1980's to affect conservation policies than ever before. The work of the past has built toward today's capabilities, a few of which are discussed in the following chapter.

Expanding Capabilities

The major staff expansions after the Regional office expansion of the early 1970's occurred in the Washington office, and were largely related to the Special Projects undertaken by NACD from 1972 onward. The projects have varied in size and number at different times, and the staff capability has varied from one person to as many as five or six at times, depending on the number of projects going on at once.

A major move to expand staff and services came in 1977, with the decision to initiate a national communications program in NACD. This had been one of the goals of the long-range program adopted at St. Croix, but it had necessarily waited until financial abilities improved. Victor E. Muniec of Connecticut was hired as Director of Communications in 1978, and continued in that position until 1980. In 1980, Charlotte Nichols of Illinois was named to the Communications position. She resigned in 1983 to go into television broadcasting.

In the top executive spot, Gordon Zimmerman served from 1958 until 1976. During that time, he was instrumental in shaping the outreach capabilty of NACD. His carefully crafted articles in the *Tuesday Letter* and articulate, compelling testimony (almost always presented by, and attributed to, one of the organization's officers) were highly influential in Washington and throughout the country. A superb writer, he was the author of 21 Soil Stewardship booklets over the years, carrying on as a consultant after his retirement. His final product -- *The Judgment of Nature* -- was the basis for the 1980 observance.

David G. Unger moved into the Executive Vice President's role in January of 1977. He had been in the NACD Washington office since 1964 as Zimmerman's assistant, and knew both NACD and Washington intimately. He, too, was a very skilled writer, who prepared most of the *Tuesday Letter* copy for many years and was the draftsman behind the documents of the District Outlook Committee and the long-range plan adopted in 1970. In addition, he had taken a leading role in establishing relations with EPA and negotiating the work on the special projects that started in 1972. He resigned in February, 1978, to take the position of Deputy Assistant Secretary for Natural Resources and Environment in the Department of Agriculture.

R. Neil Sampson followed Unger into the NACD executive position in April of 1978. He had been in the USDA Office of Environmental Affairs, on loan from the SCS, where he had served for 16 years in the Washington office and at various field offices in the State of Idaho. His years at NACD were marked by a significant growth in information and communications work, as public attention became much more intense on soil and water conservation and NACD stepped up its role as the major private-sector national spokesman on the subject. He, too, was a widely published author, who held the Executive Vice President's position until March of 1984.

Charles L. Boothby, formerly Executive Director of the Maine State Soil and Water Conservation Commission, moved into the Washington office as Unger's assistant in 1977, and remained as Executive Secretary until June of 1984, when he was named Executive Vice President.

Jean Zimmerman, Administrative Secretary from the time the office opened in 1959, retired in 1979. Christina Berger has served as Office Manager since that time.

In addition to focusing on staff at Washington, NACD has aggressively sought to improve the operational capability of the office. In 1978, with the active support of Vice President Milton E. Mekelburg, modern word processing equipment began to be installed. With this equipment, newsletter layouts, multiple letters, or lengthy testimony could be more rapidly and professionally produced. Mekelburg continued to push for improved equipment and technology in the NACD offices, a goal that was also actively supported by Secretary-Treasurer Sam Chinn.

In 1982, Neil Sampson carried his portable personal computer to a meeting in League City, and the NACD officers had the chance to develop an annual budget using the computer's capabilities. The budget preparation session was cut from the normal two days down to one, and the officers made the decision to move ahead with the installation of personal computers in all offices as rapidly as finances would allow.

Rounding out NACD's capabilities have been several faithful consultants, counsels and volunteers. George M. Cason, a League City attorney, (now retired from practice and living on the family farm near Eagle Lake, Texas) has served as NACD's lawyer and Legal Counsel since 1970, working as an unpaid volunteer. Stuart M. Leiss of Houston has handled the auditing tasks for the association since 1965. In the Washington office, Legal Counsels have included Philip M. Glick, who served from 1956 to 1967, and Mary M. Garner, who has worked with NACD since 1975, after retirement from USDA. Each has brought the experience and legal background of the district movement dating back to its very inception to the association.

At the Service Department, the staff has remained stable at around 20-25 people, many of whom have served NACD for 10-15 years or longer. Two employees -- Director of Accounting Sue Wilkinson and Shop Foreman Saul Balderas -- each have over 30 years of service, dating back to the Waters Davis era.

NACD Service Department, League City, Texas

The workload of the Service Department has grown steadily over the years, and has been largely met by upgrading equipment and facilities rather than increasing staff. Two major building expansions have been made to the 9,350 square-foot building given to the Association by Waters Davis. (For many years, the League City Post Office rented about one-fourth of the building, with the Service Department utilizing the remainder. In the early 1960's, the Post Office moved, giving the facility its first space increase.) In 1974, 4,650 square feet of office space was added to the front of the building, and in 1979, a 3,800 square-foot, climate-controlled warehouse was added at the rear.

Under the direction of T. David Stewart, Jr., who has managed the facility since 1961, the Service Department now handles over 1,000 orders a month on the average, ranging from the printing of a district newsletter or meeting program to the publication of large reports. Stewart also serves as financial manager and staff advisor to the Finance Committee.

All typesetting is done on computer-based typesetters now, and with a daily workload of several conservation district newsletters plus the weekly *Tuesday Letter* and an assortment of booklets, programs, and other output, it takes the fastest and most efficient equipment possible, as well as skilled staff.

In the press room, two 17" x 22" 2-color presses roll almost constantly, while three smaller 10" x 14" presses handle small jobs. An electronically-controlled paper cutter, as well as folding, trimming and assembly machines round out a modern printing facility.

In the mailing room, the Elliot Stencil system that Waters Davis installed had been hopelessly outdated for years. At one point, NACD had close to 750,000 of the manual address stencils stored in bank upon bank of filing cabinets. The system has been gradually replaced by computer-based mailing lists. The *Tuesday Letter* mailing list -- almost 30,000 -- was turned over to a computer service bureau in 1979. In 1983, after a year's study, personal computers were introduced in the mailing room and computerization of the hundreds of thousands of names in the individual conservation district mailing lists was begun. This process has resulted in an entirely in-house computerized mailing list capability.

In the Accounting Department, the same transformation has taken place. For years, an outside computer service bureau was used to keep records and prepare reports, but as personal computers came down in price and up in capability, the decision was made to establish an in-house system. The Accounting Department, with only one bookkeeper and a secretary to assist Director of Accounting Sue Wilkinson, now handles between $2 and $3 million annually. As NACD has grown and the number of special projects has proliferated, this work has dramatically increased. Transferring the accounting system to a personal computer program allows the staff to handle the workload and produce the variety of management reports that are needed with greater ease.

The Environmental Film Service issues some 6,500 copies of its catalog each year, sending copies to school districts as well as all conservation districts. A nominal rental charge for the films, as well as profits from the sale of NACD-produced films, helps the service stay self-supporting. New films are added regularly, and slide shows -- often with a coordinated tape narration -- are popular as well.

The Davis Conservation Library has continued to grow, adding yearly to its unique collection of information on soil and water conservation districts, state associations and state soil conservation agencies, as well as a steadily improving collection on general conservation subjects. It fills thousands of requests for conservation brochures and information each year.

Another service that has grown is the sale of awards, signs, and other materials through the Service Department. An annual four-color catalog is sent to all districts, offering products that range all the way from give-away pencils and balloons embossed with the district's name or a conservation message to fancy engraved award plaques for special people or events. Districts can also buy everyday supplies like personalized stationary and billing forms.

The major annual event at the Service Department, however, is Soil Stewardship. Even with the new warehouse, the arrival of the Soil Stewardship material from the printer's means that virtually every square foot of the facility is taken. Over 7 million pieces, ranging from the observance booklet to bookmarks, church program covers, inserts, place mats and posters must be handled. Orders flow in from conservation districts by the hundreds in a few short weeks, and tons of materials are transferred from pallets handled by fork-lift trucks to carefully counted and wrapped small bundles for mailing. Keeping track of all these materials and orders with limited facilities and a small staff, while continuing the normal workload of printing and other activities in the Service Department, is a major accomplishment.

Conservation Tillage Information Center

The most ambitious, and complex, special project ever undertaken by NACD was the establishment in 1983 of the Conservation Tillage Information Center. This project is a joint effort with agricultural industry and government agencies which is dedicated to assisting business, industry, agencies and farmers share information quickly and accurately about the new methods of conservation tillage that have emerged in recent years.

Conservation tillage was not a new subject to conservation districts, NACD, or the professional community. In 1973, NACD had joined with Soil Conservation Society of America, the American Society of Agronomy, and the American Society of Agricultural Engineers to sponsor a three-day meeting on the subject in Des Moines, IA. In the keynote speech at that meeting, NACD Vice President George Bagley had urged conservation districts to take a leading role in encouraging adoption of conservation tillage techniques where they were adapted.

A great deal of research and testing was still needed, however. The system demands planting equipment that can operate dependably through heavy layers of crop residue, methods of weed control to replace cultivation, and different management techniques to handle such things as soil acidity, proper fertilizer timing, placement and amount, and a host of other details. Different soils must be managed differently, and new crop varieties were needed to thrive under the different residue management systems.

This research accelerated through the 1970's, spurred by rising oil prices that made the potential fuel, labor and time savings of various conservation tillage methods, particularly no-till, very attractive to farmers. By the early 1980's, it was apparent that a major revolution in farming technology was under way, and that one of the benefits could be a significant reduction in soil erosion if the systems were properly adapted.

A series of meetings between industry leaders, USDA agency representatives, and Jim Lake of NACD resulted in a plan for an "Information Center" to serve as a catalyst in speeding up adoption of the new conservation techniques. Another major participant was the Environmental Protection Agency, whose Great Lakes office had been sponsoring "no-till" projects in conservation districts in the region. These tests had convinced the EPA scientists that the added emphasis on soil conservation which resulted from the demonstration projects was also reducing the delivery of pollutants to the waters of the Great Lakes.

To guide the Center, the group established an Executive Committee, made up largely of the sponsoring organizations and industries, with an advisory group from the federal and state agencies. The Executive Committee would raise money, determine budgets, and set policies. NACD would administer the daily operations and help find new sponsors and cooperators.

A decision to go ahead was made in September of 1982, and the Center was planned for opening in January, 1983. A $50,000 grant from the Joyce Foundation in Chicago helped pave the way, and agricultural industries put up a matching amount. NACD, EPA and SCS provided staff to open the Center's field office in Fort Wayne, Indiana, and NACD provided the administration, management and information staff resources in Washington. In January, the Center was opened on schedule, and a new monthly newsletter *Conservation Tillage News,* was introduced. Written and produced by consultant Sara Ebenreck, and printed and distributed by NACD's Service Department, it quickly established a reputation as an authoritative, useful information source.

During 1983, James E. Lake, Field Office Coordinator, and Bruce Julian, SCS Conservationist serving on detail to CTIC, coordinated the completion of three national surveys. The first, an estimate of the conservation tillage practices employed in the 1982 crop year, was done on a state-by-state basis. The second, a survey of local attitudes and views on conservation tillage, was done with the 1,500 conservation districts that had joined the Center's efforts. The third, a survey of the conservation tillage practices employed in the 1983 crop year, was done on a county-by-county basis, and is the most authoritative estimate of its kind available. The field work was carried out by SCS, who gathered the information in each county in cooperation with the Extension Service and conservation districts, then forwarded the data to Fort Wayne for analysis.

Handling these major data surveys was accomplished on micro-computers similar to the ones used in other NACD offices. Dr. James Morrison of Purdue University served as a consultant on this aspect of the Center's work, and took the leadership in conceptualizing and overseeing the development of the needed computer programs and data management procedures. Accomplishing so much, in such a short time, was exhausting to the staff, but firmly established the CTIC as a capable, vital force in the field.

In the NACD Washington office, Dr. James Bauder, conservation agronomist, was furnished to the Center by the Cooperative Extension Service to develop the network of scientists and scientific information that could be the basis for the CTIC "referral" service. This was set up on the basis that no one person or organization could possibly help in all the wide variety of field situations that would be encountered. Instead, then, of trying to answer questions from farmers or local technicians, CTIC set out to assemble lists of experts in all fields, in all areas of the country. For example, if a person calls today and wants to know about controlling a certain pest in a certain crop, CTIC can tell them who to call for the answer. In addition, Bauder has established a significant library reference system for local and statewide publications, the kind that do not often get in the national media, but which can be very helpful if the right one can be found by a person when they need the information.

Information and Communications

The late 1970's and early 1980's were marked with intense public interest in the subject of soil and water conservation, perhaps more so than at any time since the Dust Bowl. This brought NACD the opportunity -- and the challenge -- to be a national spokesman on the issues. The organization responded in many ways.

With the establishment of a Director of Communications, a great deal more service to the media was possible, both through the efforts of the Communications Director and through the release of the other professional staff from such tasks as preparation of the weekly *Tuesday Letter.*

Under the guidance of Charlotte Nichols, a major effort to upgrade NACD's brochures and publications led to dozens of new products. In 1982, NACD produced a series of television public service announcements, in cooperation with the Iowa Department of Soil Conservation, that districts can purchase at a nominal fee from the Service Department for use by their home stations.

And the media effort paid off. In 1978, James Risser, a reporter from the *Des Moines Register,* came to the NACD Washington office to get ideas for a story on soil erosion and nonpoint pollution. He left with a bundle of background files and a list of names to contact. Six months later, his 7-part series in the *Register* attracted national attention and, eventually, garnered a Pulitzer Prize. Other reporters (none quite so successful, however) followed by the dozens, and NACD's staff attempted to be responsive and helpful to each. As a result, literally hundreds of newspaper, magazine and book articles were written to tell the conservation story. Several feature films were made for television or educational use, and radio and TV news stories became a regular occurrence.

NACD's bylines appeared as well. Between 1978 and 1984, Sampson authored dozens of book chapters, technical papers, and magazine articles on conservation and resource topics. His 1981 book, *Farmland or Wasteland: A Time to Choose,* was also widely distributed and read.

The *Tuesday Letter* was changed from a 2-page to a 4-page format in 1978, and its editorial thrust changed as well. Instead of the "letter from the President" approach that had been retained since the first Waters Davis letter, a more "news-oriented" approach was taken. The first page generally carries items of national importance on a broad range of resource topics. Pages 2 and 3 carry a variety of information, varying from internal announcements and NACD activities to feature stories on how a district is solving a particular problem. Page 4 carries the President's message, written in first-person, editorial style. This is the most widely-read section of the *Tuesday Letter,* according to reader surveys, and the positions stated in the editorial are widely quoted in speeches, articles and news stories around the country.

The circulation of the *Tuesday Letter* is just under 30,000. It had been as high as 40,000 prior to 1973, when rising costs forced NACD to cut back drastically on the number of complimentary copies mailed. The letter is sent to each conservation district official at their home address, and to each district office. It goes as well to the office of each Member of Congress, Governor, and selected state resource agencies in each state, in addition to the members and offices of each state's soil conservation commission or board. Non-voting membership in NACD is encouraged, and those who donate $25 or more to the organization each year also receive *Tuesday Letter*. A small complimentary list is maintained, largely to swap newsletters with other national organizations and reach specific audiences selected by NACD's staff. In 1982, *Tuesday Letter* was named "Newsletter of the Year" by the Natural Resources Council of America.

Budget and Finances

NACD's financial condition has grown more secure over the years. From a very shaky start in the early years, when donations from industry were absolutely vital in getting the organization started, and making such major moves as becoming established in the Washington office, the organization has continued to build financial capability.

District quotas are now $375 per year, having been increased about every 3-4 years since 1971 in the face of inflationary cost increases. Tight management by the officers and staff, however, has kept expenses controlled in spite of inflation. During the late 1970's, for example, NACD's managers kept expenditures rising at rates of 5-7 percent annually, in spite of double-digit inflation. Financial dependence is based on the quota system, which provides 75 percent of the organization's income. NACD's officers have insisted that special project income be kept small in relationship to quota income so that NACD will not be at the mercy of outside funding sources. As a result, while some national organizations were going out of business in the early 1980's, when high inflation drove up costs as federal budget cut-backs virtually eliminated grant income, NACD was keeping a tight lid on expenditures, but experienced no undue stress.

To provide more financial stability, NACD's officers and directors established an Endowment Fund in 1975 to try to build a significant investment pool that could provide steady income for the future. Earlier attempts to attract major outside contributors to the Conservation

Districts Foundation had met with little success, so a different approach was taken: go to the people who were already giving to conservation districts and NACD, and ask them to give further. All donations would be tax-deductible, and the principal in the fund would be invested and held by NACD in perpetuity. Only the interest earned would be used to help support NACD's programs.

This time it worked. District officials were proud to contribute to their national organization, and many of them were able to make substantial contributions. NACD created a "Century Club" for those who contributed $100 or more, a "President's Club" to honor givers of $1,000, and a "Life Membership in the Presidents Club" for those who contribute $10,000 or more. The officers were quick to meet the $1,000 goal themselves, and they were followed by many others. Conservation districts joined the move, some giving their $1,000 in one check, others pledging $200 per year for five years.

The growth of the Endowment Fund has been steady. It has been a cherished project of the Association of Past Presidents of State Associations, and many individuals have been dedicated to fund-raising for the Endowment. A major pride of Secretary-Treasurer Sam Chinn, the Endowment grew from next to nothing at the advent of his term in 1975 to $250,000 before his retirement in 1984. The first $10,000 donation level was achieved by Betty and Jack Broemmelsiek of Missouri in 1984. Betty is a member of the NACD Board and former Chairman of the Missouri State Soil Conservation Commission who is dedicated to serving conservation in a variety of ways, including financial support. Their contribution has been recognized by renaming the Environmental Film Service in their honor.

The charts below and on the following pages illustrate the steady growth of NACD's net worth, in spite of annual fluctuations in the amount

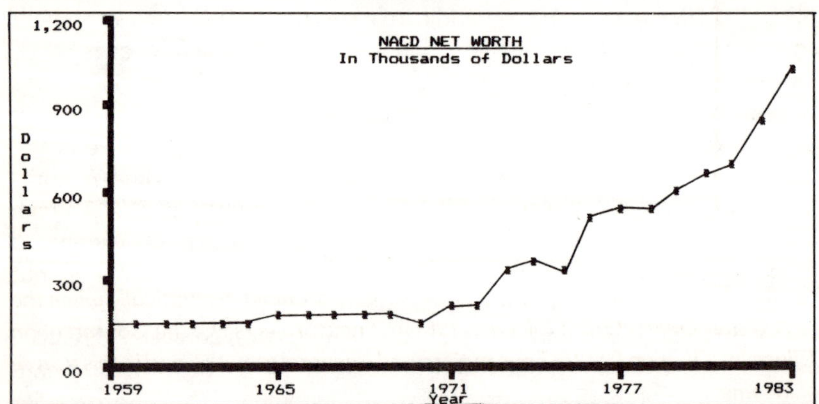

Fig. 1.   *NACD's net worth has grown steadily since 1972.*

of outside special project income and Service Department net profits. This net worth, which is largely tied up in the land and buildings at League City, as well as the equipment both there and in the other NACD offices, indicates the general financial health of the organization and how it has improved over the past decade. The Endowment Fund has also been a substantial contributor, as the chart shows.

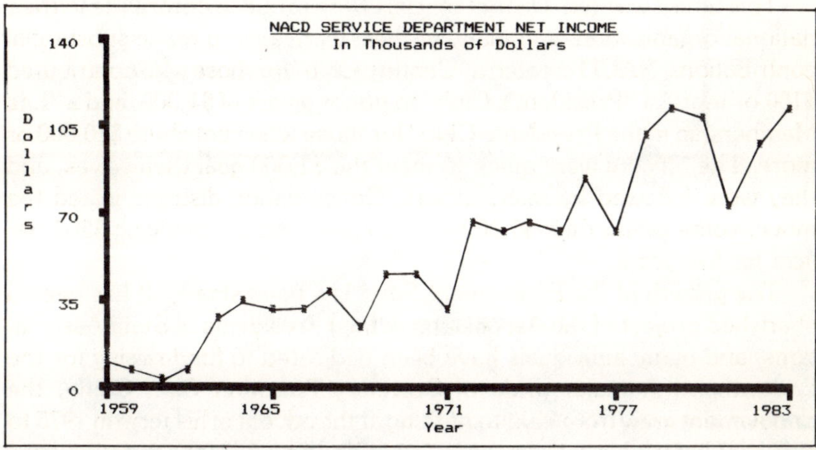

Fig. 2.   *Service Department net income has varied from year to year, but the trend has always been upward.*

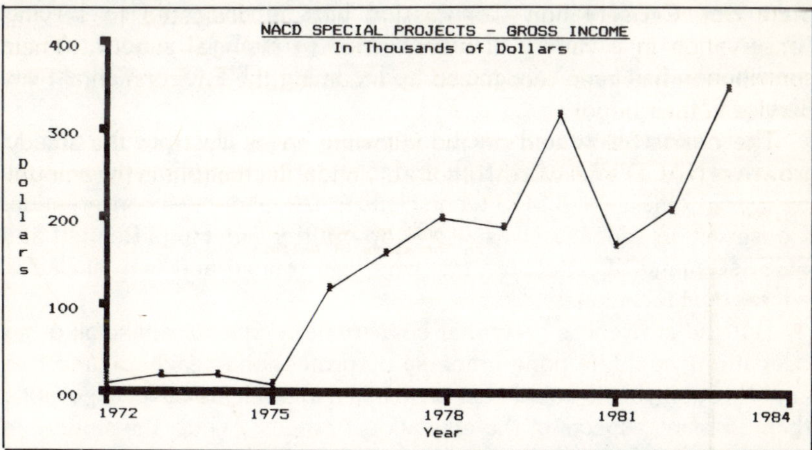

Fig. 3.   *The gross income from special projects dropped dramatically when the EPA Water Quality Grant folded in 1981, but new projects like the Conservation Tillage Information Center have maintained a general growth trend in this source of income.*

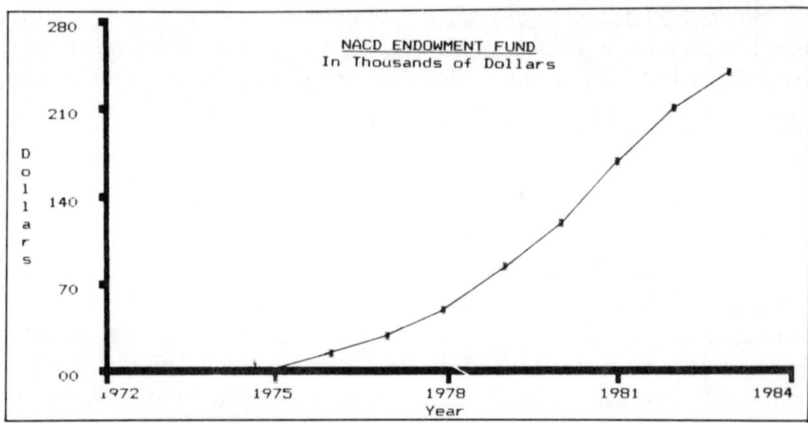

Fig. 4   *The NACD Endowment Fund has grown steadily in the last decade.*

Education and Youth

Concern for conservation education has characterized the soil conservation district movement from the very outset. The first district officials faced the problem of encouraging better land management among farmers who often were not aware of the importance of conservation. One district history said that while early district officials were trying to establish a conservation conscience in their neighbors, "many of their neighbors and acquaintances appeared unconcerned, prompting the hope that the next generation might be more readily susceptible to new ideas and change."[1]

Early efforts in schools included poster, essay and speech contests sponsored by districts; field trips and tours; and classroom appearances by district officials and SCS technicians to talk about soil conservation. Conservation education was also a top priority with Hugh Bennett and SCS, so many SCS technicians were well trained and very skilled in educational techniques.

But the awareness grew that conservation education, like all other education, would be done primarily by professional teachers, and that conservation values could best be instilled in students by incorporating them in many aspects of the educational process. Thus, the student in reading could read classic conservation essays; the biology student could learn the intricacies of maintaining ecological balance; and the science student could learn the importance of topsoil and the details of the water cycle. This was a fine idea, but it meant that teachers had to understand these factors in order to teach them, and textbooks had to include them so that they were part of the normal lesson schedule.

Buoyed by interest generated in the Environmental Decade, a new emphasis on training teachers, developing curriculum guides, and helping establish school-site outdoor education areas swept through the conservation movement in the 1970's. In many states, a State Committee on Environmental Education was established, and state soil conservation agencies, state associations and SCS were deeply involved in the actions of those committees.

In 1974, the Allis-Chalmers Corporation joined with NACD to sponsor an annual Awards Program to recognize the best conservation education programs in America. Teachers and districts are nominated and a state winner selected. These winners are entered in a regional contest managed by the NACD Regional Representatives, and the regional winners are sent to the NACD Washington office, which arranges for national judging. The national winning teacher wins a prize of $1,000 plus an expense-paid trip to the NACD Convention. The second-place award is $500, and the regional winners each get $200 and an engraved plaque. Conservation district winners receive a plaque, but no cash award.

NACD has also operated several special projects to encourage conservation education. A one-year project started in 1977 developed a handbook for district use. The book, *Conservation District Guide for Education Programs* was the subject of regional workshops held throughout 1978 in connection with the NACD Regional meetings. These workshops, conducted by the NACD Education Committee, were intended to improve the education activities of state committees and associations, as well as the programs of individual districts. The guide, which was sent to all conservation districts and sold through the Service Department, contained a step-by-step approach to planning and carrying out an effective educational program.

Many state associations picked up on the program, and followed with training workshops intended to reach individual district supervisors and help them understand how to carry out local education programs. The NACD Ladies Auxiliary also pledged to help, assisting state associations in developing an improved statewide education program, working directly with schools at the district level, and distributing conservation curriculum guides to schools.

Youth activities have also been an important part of the total educational program of NACD. In addition to work with scouts, 4-H groups, and other youth organizations, NACD has encouraged districts to involve local youth in Youth Boards. By watching the district board at work, young people learn how one of their community funtions is carried out, plus they have the chance to help on many specific projects and programs of the district.

In 1975 a quarterly newsletter providing information and news about conservation district youth programs was initiated by the NACD Youth Programs Committee. Edited by Cary Chamblee of the South Carolina Land Resources Commission, the letter attempted to encourage a wider interest in district youth activities. Periodical features in the *Tuesday Letter* have focused on the youth programs as well.[2]

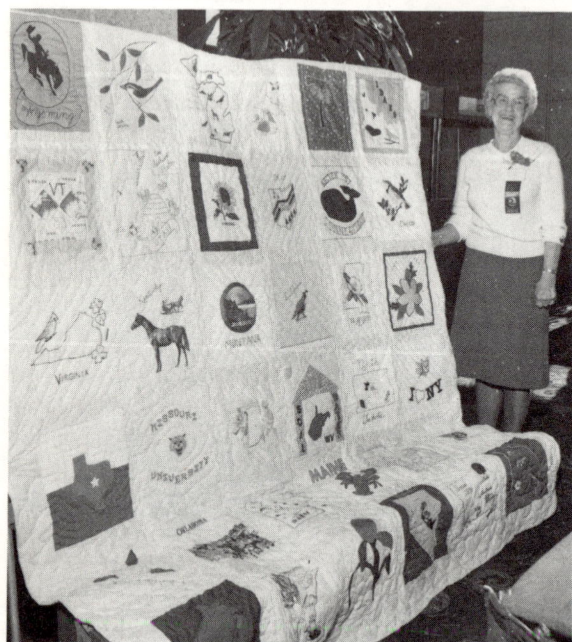

Mary Alice Willett of Kentucky shows off the beautiful quilt made by members of the Ladies Auxiliary for the Denver meeting.

In 1982, the NACD Ladies Auxiliary began a fund-raising project at the NACD Conventions designed to allow them to provide a $500 prize to the District Youth Board chosen as the top board in the nation by the NACD Committee on Education and Youth. (The two committees were merged in 1981.) The ladies make a beautiful patchwork quilt which is the prize in a raffle held at the Convention, and awarded at the Annual Banquet.

Building District Capability

Assisting districts to build their own program capability has been a high priority of NACD's officers for many years, and several cooperative programs are operated to help achieve that goal.

The oldest, and most direct, is the Goodyear Conservation Awards Program. The evaluation guide used by districts to record and evaluate their programs has changed over the years, as issues have shifted, but the basic idea of the program remains the same. Districts win the award on the basis of the quality of their annual program, and their success in carrying it out.

> "Conservation district officials need to recognize that they are in charge of a local unit of government. A district is not a voluntary association, a social organization, or a committee for a government program. A district is a subdivision of state government just like a county, town, township, or school district. And you are local government officials.
>
> "If a district is to function effectively as a local government, it must have the respect of its citizens. They need to know what the district is doing, believe in the merits of its work, and respect its governing officials. This, in turn, requires that district officials take their responsibilities seriously, and that they should expect the public to take them seriously. Only in this way can we move ahead with the job.
>
> John S. Wilder, "Key Issues Ahead,"
> 1971 NACD Convention, Chicago, IL.

NACD leaders have long been convinced that every district that participates in the Goodyear Program is a winner. Filling out the evaluation guide is an excellent way to gain new and valuable ideas for improving programs, and efforts to achieve each year's goals, if they are reviewed at each monthly meeting of the district board, are a good reminder that helps get things done as planned.

Winning districts are still awarded the trip to Litchfield Park, and even though the romance of the week-long charter train trips and first-ever airplane flights are no longer such a prevalent part of the program, the opportunity to see the excellent work done on the Goodyear Farms and spend a few days with district officials from all over the nation is always given accolades by the district winners.

Also still an important feature in NACD's program is the Annual Newsletter Contest sponsored by the Farm and Industrial Equipment Institute (FIEI), which started in 1957. It was estimated in 1975 that only about one-fourth of the conservation districts were publishing newsletters, and NACD and FIEI have concentrated on providing incentives to increase that percentage. In addition to a first prize of $500 for the winning national newsletter, the contest provides the second place winner with $300, the third with $200, and the winning "new" newsletter with a prize of $200. The prizes, as well as plaques to all regional winners, are presented at the Annual Convention.

Leadership Conference

In 1978, President Lyle Bauer initiated a summer leadership conference for the state association presidents. He felt that most of these state leaders needed a structured opportunity to receive formal training in leadership skills, and that the skill of state leaders was one key to the ultimate success of NACD.

The series, which began in League City, has been expanded to include State Administrative Officers and members of State Soil Conservation Commissions. The agenda has been a mixture of issue analysis and discussion on conservation issues and presentations by outside instructors in communications, leadership styles, legislative activities, fund raising, and similar subjects. Around 100 of the nation's top conservation leaders attend the conference each year.

International Travel

In 1973, NACD inaugurated a program of international conservation tours for district officials, cooperators, friends of conservation and their families. The program was called "Con-Tours" (later trademarked as CONTOURS). The purposes of the tours are to exchange ideas and techniques between Americans and citizens of other nations, and to expand knowledge of conservation and agricultural resources both here and abroad. Between 1973 and 1981, the tours were coordinated by Educational Travel Co. of Spokane, Washington, who owns the term "CONTOURS."

Under Coordinator Bob Whitmore and, later, Richard Ellis, tours were arranged to just about every corner of the world. They were ordinarily led by an NACD officer or staff member, although many other leaders were selected by CONTOURS to be a tour leader. Tour members all contributed to a tour diary, which was then reprinted as a permanent record for each tour member.

In 1978, a cherished goal was achieved with the first CONTOUR to visit China, as part of an "around the world" tour led by George and Barbara Bagley. Since then several trips to that vast country have been made, usually under the leadership of Sam Chinn. In 1981, Educational Travel discontinued the CONTOURS program, saying that it was no longer financially profitable for them. Negotiations between NACD and Educational Travel to transfer the "CONTOUR" trademark to NACD were unsuccessful.

In 1983, NACD announced a new international travel program, to be coordinated by GTU, Inc., a San Francisco-based travel agency. The staff advisor for the travel program is Bob Baum, and a special committee to oversee the program was established in 1984.

The Annual Convention

The highlight of the NACD year is the Annual Convention, normally held in the first week of February. At this meeting, the NACD Council (which is made up of one representative of each state and territorial association) meets to consider policy resolutions that will guide the organization's actions for the coming year. These resolutions, normally about 70 in number, originate from conservation districts through their state associations or NACD regional councils. They create about six full hours of deliberation, and often stir up heated debate.

The Council members are broken up into seven NACD regions, which coincide with the old, pre-1953 SCS regional breakdown. SCS long ago abandoned these regional alignments, but NACD has continued to feel that the original regional layout best meets the needs of the district officials in terms of grouping states with common interests. Each regional council meets at the convention to fill vacancies on the Board of Directors.

The Board of Directors is made up of three members from each NACD region, serving three-year terms with a two-term limit. The Board also meets in conjunction with the convention, electing new national officers whenever those terms expire and taking whatever actions are needed to guide the officers or carry out Council policies.

Each national committee sponsors one or more "discussion forums" at the convention, which are panel discussions, speakers, films or other programs on issues that are of current interest in the committee's field. About 8-9 of these forums go on simultaneously for three half-day sessions, and from 50-300 people attend each one, so the convention is a busy, working meeting.

Affiliated organizations meeting in conjunction with the convention include the NACD Ladies Auxiliary, the National Association of State Conservation Agencies, and the Association of Past Presidents of State Associations. These organizations elect officers, review activities, and plan annual programs at this meeting, which is usually the only full membership meeting any of them schedule during the year.

The NACD Business Advisory Committee meets, and hosts the officers and directors and their spouses to an evening social event and dinner. The Goodyear Company hosts an annual breakfast where all the people who have attended the Goodyear Conservation Awards Program tour in the past can meet for a "reunion." In the past two years, the Conservation Tillage Information Center has hosted a major discussion forum and demonstration, and the executive committee holds a policy meeting.

Many of the highlights of the meeting, however, occur in its major events. Starting off the convention on Sunday evening is the annual Inspirational Meeting. Here, the theme for the coming year's Soil Stewardship observance is featured, and speakers use the essays in the annual stewardship brochure as the basis for short messages. Musical entertainment rounds out an evening that gives the convention an inspirational send-off.

On Monday morning, over 1,500 people attend an opening session where major speakers are featured, and the NACD President gives his annual address. The session also includes awards and recognition of NACD's top financial supporters. States who have 100 percent participation in the Goodyear Conservation Awards Program are recognized, as are the winning teachers in the NACD - Allis-Chalmers Conservation Education Awards Program and the NACD-FIEI Newsletter Contest. NACD also provides recognition for states where all districts have paid their voluntary NACD quota, and gives a plaque to the "top ten" states in terms of dollar support for NACD.

In 1984, at the Denver Convention, a major feature during the opening session was an official stamp release ceremony conducted by the U.S. Postal Service. The ceremony, which introduced the 50-year commemorative stamp for soil and water conservation, drew many additional guests to the NACD meeting, and a special postal station set up in the hotel foyer was kept busy for three days, selling and cancelling first-day copies of the new stamp.

Tuesday's luncheon attracts about 1,000 guests for a major speaker and a portion of the NACD awards. At this session, awards are presented for Business Conservation Leadership, Communications, Professional Service, and other special honors. A publication citing all these awards, and their winners throughout NACD's history, is available from NACD.

The convention concludes on Wednesday night with a gala banquet that usually attracts close to 1,500 guests. Awards and entertainment are the order of the evening, with the NACD Special Service and Distinguished Service Awards being presented. If new officers have been elected at the meeting, they are introduced, as are the new officers of the affiliated organizations. Music, comedy, or dancing troupes perform, and the evening concludes with an orchestra and ballroom dancing.

The conventions are scheduled, and the sites selected, many years in advance, with 1985 going to Honolulu, HI; 1986 to Nashville, TN; 1987 to Reno, NV; and 1988 to Little Rock, AR.

Regional and State Meetings

Each NACD Region holds an annual meeting, usually in the summer or early fall, to discuss issues of interest to the region as a whole, and review the policy concerns that have risen in state associations in the region. NACD's officers attend these meetings, and share national concerns with the district officials in attendance, many of whom may be unable to attend the Annual NACD Convention.

The NACD Regional organization, backed up by the staff support provided by the Regional Representatives, has provided a vehicle for internal NACD communications that has been growing since the major thrust forward in 1970. By using regional meetings, seminars, and workshops, NACD's officers have been able to meet face-to-face with district officials on a regular basis, hearing their concerns from the local level, and spreading a common theme in line with national NACD priorities.

Adding to this capability is a very active travel schedule for the top officers in attending state association meetings. Between the President, Vice President, Secretary-Treasurer and Executive Vice President, between 30 and 45 state association meetings are visited each year, with the NACD officer delivering a major speech outlining national goals and concerns in the conservation field. NACD is a communications organization, and thousands of hours, and many nights away from home, are donated each year by the top officers (none of whom are paid, except the Executive Vice President). Because of this dedication and commitment, few district officials, if they have any interest in their position at all, should have to go over two years -- or leave their home state -- to have personal contact with the nation's leaders in soil and water conservation.

"In these last four years, I have been pleased with the growth of NACD's reputation and influence in Washington. It is not influence built with political clout or money. Our influence is built by being helpful, by being willing to develop facts and figures to support our arguments. It is built by thousands of dedicated individuals, each with a somewhat different experience, and different words to explain their views, but with a common set of ideals and goals.

"You believe in the American system, and are willing to devote your time and effort as a working part of that system, either as a public official in a conservation district, as a public servant, or as a volunteer. You believe that government is meant to work for people, not enslave them, and that your contributions to local, state and federal government can benefit all Americans.

"You believe in growth, and change, and development, both in your personal life and in the life of an organization like NACD, for none of us ever stops learning and growing. You believe that each of us who is accorded the privilege of owning land is also given a responsibility for stewardship. You believe that we can work as individuals, in groups, and through government to make this earth a better place when we leave it than it was when we arrived. Those are the kind of ideals that make NACD strong today, and that will help this organization grow in strength and influence in the future."

Lyle Bauer, "Seeking New Visions for Conservation,"
at the 1982 NACD Convention in Phoenix.

Issues of the 1980's

12

The most obvious conclusion to be made from a history of soil conservation in the United States is that the district movement faces a future marked with change and organizational challenge. The basis for this conclusion rests easily on its first half-century, which has been a constant test of organizational capability. The story is one of people testing theories about the best use of organizations and government to solve resource problems. E. C. McArthur was prophetic when he said, "Organization is the answer," but he might also have said that "how to organize may be the most difficult question."

The problems are mainly about method, not substance. There are few technical questions about how to solve a particular soil or water conservation problem that seem worth arguing about; these kinds of questions are simply challenges to be addressed, and energies are generally focused on solving the problem at hand. Whether those energies are expended by government researchers, employees of action agencies, or farmers themselves is of little consequence to most of the participants; solving the problem successfully usually seems to be of more consequence than identifying who designed the solution (which usually ends up as an amalgamation of many efforts, anyway).

Organizational issues, on the other hand, make good political grist. People can argue endlessly about whether or not one approach to solving the problem is better than another; at times such arguments offer a handy substitute for actually getting to work on the challenge itself. And organizational solutions are seldom ever permanent, or neat. Decisions are made, but often they are not final. A new Administration, a new day, a new personality, and the question breaks out all over again.

The role of an organization like NACD is to keep moving forward, constantly articulating the unfinished agenda that the public and private sectors must, somehow, find a way to address. In doing this, the organization works both ways simultaneously. It takes the opinions of its members (normally focused on problems of a local or statewide dimension) and makes them known to national decisionmakers who often concentrate so hard on national problems that they fail to relate to local issues. At the same time, it must also educate its members. District officials do not learn about national problems by magic, and one of the major functions of a national organization like NACD is to help people understand the scope of people's attitudes and problems in other, far away, regions so that a national concensus can be formed on the issues facing everyone.

In attempting to carry out this role, NACD followed up its successful "Resources Agenda for the 70's" with a new version geared to the 1980's. Developed again by the District Outlook Committee, under the Chairmanship of Steve Brunson of Tennessee, the agenda represents NACD's definition of what remains to be done in conservation. It was presented in the hope that it would inspire new debate, new policy, and new action to more effectively manage our natural resources.

A Natural Resources Agenda for the 80's

The following 14 points were adopted by NACD at its 1979 Annual Convention to serve as an outline of the unfinished resources agenda of the nation.

1. There must be a higher national priority for the conservation of the nation's productive soil and water resources.

2. Natural resource conservation programs must be designed and implemented to take advantage of the willingness of private resource users to voluntarily carry out needed conservation measures.

3. Conservation program policies and budgets should be based primarily on the natural resource needs identified by the Appraisal carried out under the Soil and Water Conservation Act of 1977.

4. Federal natural resource programs must be altered to maximize the role of state and local governments and landowners in defining priorities and carrying out action programs.

5. Conservation district legal authority and financial support must be strengthened in most states to provide the district staff and program implementation capability that will be needed.

6. National agricultural programs must be coordinated so that food, agriculture, and natural resource conservation policies will be linked together and provide appropriate private incentives to produce while still protecting resources.

7. More effective procedures for resolving conflicts over resource use are needed to reduce the amount of paperwork, controversy, litigation and delay that has become common during the last decade.

8. Congress should establish a special dedicated revenue source to provide stable, adequate and continuing financing for needed reinvestment in natural resources through conservation programs.

9. Basic and applied research on natural resources management and conservation must be improved.

10. The national cooperative soil survey must be completed as rapidly as possible to provide the basic information for many types of natural resource programs.

11. We need stronger national and local leadership in a concerted private-public, local-state-federal effort to develop new policies and programs to encourage balanced rural and urban growth with less waste and misuse of natural resources.

12. The nation needs new policies and programs -- and a new commitment -- to encourage the conservation and rational development of adequate water supplies.

13. Non-consumptive uses and values of natural resources, whether for wildlife, recreation, scenic beauty or preservation must be considered in making resource management choices.

14. Through effective environmental education programs, every citizen -- both student and adult -- should have opportunities for classroom and field study to acquire the knowledge, skills, values, attitudes, and commitment needed to protect and improve the environment.

These statements will be of interest in another decade or so, just as the "Agenda for the 70's" is of interest now. The agendas have identified what needs to be done. In a few years, we will be able to look back to see how much has been accomplished. That is, in one sense, a reasonably good measure of NACD's contribution to the public debate on resource conservation. Judging from the "1970's Agenda," the organization's effectiveness has been excellent in the past decade. The "Agenda for the 80's" will give a future analyst a measuring stick to make a similar assessment.

Living with the RCA Program

NACD was, as detailed earlier, strongly supportive of the Soil and Water Resources Conservation Act of 1977 (RCA), and in turn, deeply involved in carrying out the process that the RCA set in motion. But neither NACD or conservation districts had control over the final program, and there are aspects of that program that deeply disturb district people. A brief review of the activities leading up to the final program gives some hints about the genesis of the problems encountered.

After the signing of the Act in November of 1977, SCS immediately began to carry out the appraisal it required. NACD began to assist in the public education process by publishing a 4-part series in *Tuesday Letter* during May of 1978 to set out the background of the RCA, outline the public participation process envisioned, and explain how the appraisal and program would be developed. The information was, of course, based on the Act itself and the implementation plans then being developed in SCS.

Basic to the RCA process were to be a series of local public meetings, sponsored by conservation districts, to identify critical local problems, set priorities, and recommend needed programs to USDA. In addition, SCS scheduled 5 major public meetings in regional hub cities during September. The result was a massive effort to gather public opinion, largely through the efforts of the districts. Over 9,000 meetings, involving over 100,000 people, were held by the districts. Public opinion was also gathered from the public meetings held by SCS (which were eventually expanded to 18 in number) and from written opinions received by the agency.

But critics both within USDA and on the outside faulted SCS for seeking local opinion, insisting that a more analytical approach was needed; that the local opinion would only result in recommendations for "more of the same" from national conservation programs. There was also powerful pressure to expand the effort to include all of the USDA programs that affected soil and water conservation, not just the SCS programs.

To stem these critics, Secretary of Agriculture Bob Bergland named an RCA Coordinating Committee in November of 1978 to oversee the RCA process. David G. Unger chaired the effort. In addition to membership from USDA agencies, the committee included representatives from the Council on Environmental Quality and the Office of Management and Budget.

The OMB representative, Donald E. Crabill, who has been involved in natural resource budgets at OMB for over 20 years and is openly opposed to conservation programs that assist private landowners, insisted that the entire RCA study was starting from the wrong premise. Instead of asking what programs were needed to solve conservation problems, he proposed, what must first be done was to prove that there really was any conservation problem at all. What were the rates of resource depletion, he challenged the agency specialists to answer, and what, if anything, did those rates mean to the national economy? Only after those questions were satisfactorily answered, he argued, and proof developed to show that a problem really existed, could one even begin to consider the need for solutions.

The USDA analysts agreed with the logical-sounding challenge, and began to search the data developed from the 1977 National Resource Inventories for the answers. Unfortunately, those answers did not exist, for those questions had not been posed in the data-gathering process. Estimates on soil movement, based on the predictions of the Universal Soil Loss Equation, had been made, as had estimates of wind erosion in the Great Plains. What was not known, however, was the costs being inflicted by those soil erosion rates. It was one thing to tell someone that land was losing 5 or even 15 tons of soil per acre per year on the average; quite something else to estimate what those erosion rates meant in terms of economic or environmental costs. Those questions had not been studied since Bennett's earliest efforts, and that work was hopelessly out of date.

Although the Coordinating Committee generated interagency cooperation that may have been unique in USDA history, the process ground on, for what seemed like endless months. Computer run after computer run ground out streams of paper -- at one time, it was said that over 100,000 pages of computer printout had been produced in the process, but there were no magic answers. So the Coordinating Committee held meetings that accomplished little or nothing except to further frustrate the SCS analysts, and those who were watching the process continued to watch -- and wait.

In late 1978, USDA announced that it had identified policy issues and options that would be the subject of review by 13 Task Forces named within the Department. NACD was represented on several of the Task Forces, which met on issues involving administrative, program and technical questions associated with the USDA programs.

In May of 1979, NACD published a 6-part *Tuesday Letter* series explaining the 1977 NRI data, and what it might mean to the policymakers studying the situation to develop the RCA Appraisal and Program. In that same month, the RCA Coordinating Committee announced that the Appraisal date had been set back from August to September, and the team charged with running the volumes of computer analyses were warning that further delays were more than likely.

In June, the District Outlook Committee began an intensive study of the RCA data and process, charged by President Lyle Bauer with developing recommendations for NACD's positions on the program when it was finally made public. Finally, the program was ready for initial public review, beginning in January, 1980 -- the date set forth in the Act for the completed program to be sent to Congress. Three to five alternative proposals would be circulated, USDA announced.

In response to the USDA draft, NACD developed a set of "general principles and policies" that it felt should be considered in any program. Finally, in late January, the USDA draft was released. NACD immediately published a 12-page special edition of the *Tuesday Letter* (Feb. 5, 1980) to set forth the findings of the appraisal, the conclusions drawn, and the alternative strategies being tested by USDA. Public comments were encouraged, and USDA established a special unit in an unused military building in Athens, Georgia, to receive, catalog, and analyse the public response.

At about the same time, USDA released the results of a public opinion poll on soil conservation that had been conducted by pollster Louis Harris. The poll found that half of the American public considered the abuse of soil and water resources a serious problem, that more conservation was needed, that there should be a partnership between government and the farmer in the implementation cost of conservation systems, and that the public should pay a fair share of the cost.[1]

The first RCA draft documents brought forth some 68,000 comments, as well as some serious political invective. One of the alternatives proposed was for "cross compliance" -- a system whereby a farmer would be required to meet certain conservation standards in order to be eligible for other farm programs. This suggestion brought forth such a violent reaction, largely led or orchestrated by ASC committees and ASCS employees, that in May Congressmen Tom Foley of Washington and Kika de la Garza of Texas felt compelled to call USDA officials into a "dressing-down" session to tell them to "cool it" on the cross compliance and other internally divisive issues. A press release from the two Congressmen said that they would strongly oppose any efforts to establish mandatory conservation programs that would threaten farmers with loss of federal price supports or other farm program benefits if they failed to comply with conservation rules.[2]

In June of 1980, Lyle Bauer explained what was happening to the readers of the *Tuesday Letter*. As a result of a District Outlook Committee review of the RCA process, he pointed out that, while the USDA staff had paid attention to the public comment on the RCA proposals, it was clear that the important decisions on the final RCA program would not be made by the RCA study team or "for that matter, may not be made in USDA at all."

"The RCA proposal is supposed to show what kinds of federal spending and program efforts will be needed to carry out a conservation program that meets the needs of the nation's soil and water resources," Bauer said. "We have seen enough of the data, and heard enough public opinion, to know that the RCA study is proving the nation has a serious problem that needs immediate attention.

"The federal soil and water conservation effort is grossly underfunded. The existing programs need more money, along with some updating to make them more effective. In addition, new approaches are needed to encourage state and local government to participate more fully in the conservation effort.

"All this will take money, and federal budgets are being cut, and cut hard, in Washington these days. The Office of Management and Budget may simply not allow USDA to openly state the facts of the matter: the nation's agricultural productivity is in jeopardy, and federal support of conservation programs must be increased. In this election year, the political factors may outweigh the overwhelming evidence that the RCA has accumulated."[3]

Two weeks later, Bauer concluded his warnings on the RCA process. "I think USDA's RCA proposal will reflect the Administration's current policy on controlling the federal budget," he said. "If it is disappointing, because of the fact that no new money can be proposed, we shouldn't be too surprised. Knowledgeable Members of Congress won't be, I can assure you. They are accustomed to Administration proposals that extol the virtues of conservation, but simultaneously cut back on dollars and manpower in the federal programs that support it."

Bauer noted that in 1980, in the heat of the Carter-Reagan Presidential campaign, budget-cutting political gamesmanship was especially noticeable. He quoted from a speech made at Harvard by former Secretary of State Cyrus Vance, who had strongly warned of the potential problems in this approach. "It is time to set, and stick to, basic goals," Vance had said. "It is far too easy, in an election year, to let what may seem smart politics produce bad policies."[4]

A joint agreement between NACD, SCS, and the National Association of State Conservation Agencies was developed in 1980 whereby NACD would hire a staff person to spend full time monitoring the progress being made in the states to develop state soil conservation programs. These programs, encouraged by SCS as a way of establishing state-level priorities, were being developed with some assistance from federal grant funds from the RCA budget of SCS. The joint agreement project was staffed by William E. "Gene" Lamb, who had been involved in the development of the Florida state plan.

A series of "RCA Notes" were developed which kept state soil conservation agencies and other interested parties up to date on the details of the RCA process and the state planning progress.

In September of 1980, NACD published the results of the public comment on the RCA proposals, after they had been analysed in USDA. Not too surprisingly, most of the respondents favored redirecting the current conservation programs, along with a set of conservation bonuses for those who practice good conservation. Least favored were the alternatives suggesting cross compliance or a regulatory approach. In looking at the proposed objectives for the USDA conservation programs, respondents expressed strong support for objectives aimed at reducing soil erosion, maintaining soil quality, and retaining prime farmland in agriculture.[5]

NACD's suggestions, based on the District Outlook Committee, were not too different: USDA should propose new programs that support the goals and objectives of state and local programs, require all USDA farm programs to support conservation objectives, create a Special Areas Conservation Program, create a Conservation Loan Program, and test the "Green Ticket" concept of conservation incentives that NACD had proposed for some time.

But the election in November signalled a change in Administrations, so the proposed RCA program languished in USDA, awaiting the arrival of new leadership. Everyone connected with the program knew it would be foolish to go forward with a plan under a lame duck Administration. After three years of study and frustration, the realization had firmly taken hold: the RCA process was a *political* process, not an *analytic* one.

The action quickened in 1981. In March, Congressmen Ed Jones of Tennessee and James Jeffords of Vermont introduced the Soil Conservation Act of 1981, a conservation package destined to become the conservation title in the 1981 Farm Bill. It contained provisions for a Special Areas Conservation Program, matching grants for local conservation activities, conservation loans, an Agricultural Land Resources Policy, an organic act for the Resource Conservation and Development Program and other details. Many of these tracked the RCA alternatives that had been studied at length by USDA and which were favored by NACD.

As the Reagan team was installed at USDA -- Secretary John Block, Assistant Secretary John Crowell, and Deputy Assistant Secretary Richard Siegel -- the staff began to unveil the RCA proposals and get the guidance of the new leaders. They needed time to study the issues, and become comfortable with the alternatives to be proposed. Another round of public comments was sought, received, and studied, this time with more specific program proposals. Again, the public was fairly specific -- the ongoing programs were not all that bad. Properly funded, they would be both acceptable and effective, was the general response. This put USDA officials in a bind. They could not propose that more money was needed, that was against the political grain. So the delay continued.

But Congress was in no mood to wait. Over the objections of the Administration, they passed the entire conservation package in the Farm Bill, giving the USDA new conservation tools it had not requested, did not want, and have yet to use. In this Farm Bill, more than ever, NACD was a major actor in helping get the pieces drafted properly, introduced, and publicized. Following Lyle Bauer's strategy, NACD was trying to provide a leadership role rather than simply reacting to the initiatives of others.

A recommended RCA program was unveiled by Secretary John Block October 28, 1981. It set forth four national priorities: (1) reducing excessive soil erosion that would impair agricultural productivity; (2) reducing flood damages in small, upstream waterways; (3) conserving and enhancing water quality and supply; and, (4) improving fish and wildlife habitat. Because of fund limits, Block said, USDA would give major attention to the first two objectives. A new set of "coordinating committees" would be created at the state and local level to help set program priorities, and USDA funds would be "targeted" to the areas suffering the worst soil erosion damages. Grants to states would be made, but at the expense of ongoing soil conservation programs.

In November, the *Tuesday Letter* again carried a full explanation of the USDA proposal, in an 8-page special edition, but the organization's assessment of the program, printed on December 8, 1981, was critical. In a letter to Secretary Block, Bauer indicated the areas of concern: (1) reducing ongoing conservation programs to get the money for grants to states; (2) creating local and state coordinating boards, who would be given priority-setting roles previously held by conservation districts; and, (3) "targeting" conservation funds to certain areas at the expense of ongoing programs in other areas.

What Bauer had foreseen in the editorials aimed at the Carter Administration had come true in the Reagan Administration. Instead of the RCA program being a document to guide the budget process, it was a document dictated by the budget limits. As a tool to encourage more rational budgeting of natural resource programs, it had failed.

As a result of the criticisms of NACD and others, Block amended the RCA program significantly before issuing it in final form. Gone were the coordinating committees, and three objectives had been accepted, including an objective to address soil erosion problems on range and pasture lands. The "water" objective had been broadened to include both flood control and water quality.

But the "targeting" concept remained, as did the notion that any new programs such as grants must be done at the expense of ongoing conservation programs. In other words, a great deal of concern over conservation had been created, and the Administration's response would be to shift a shrinking amount of dollars to different areas that could show a higher numerical payoff in terms of tons of soil saved. In an article published in the *Journal of Soil and Water Conservation,* Neil Sampson called it an attempt to solve the problem using "blue smoke and mirrors."

The targeting efforts have continued since 1980, increasing each year, and the dual effects of the targeting, along with other funding adjustments and inflation, is taking its toll in many conservation districts. Districts with urbanizing areas, those whose lands are used mainly for range or forest production, and areas where erosion rates are not high have felt the worst pinch. NACD's leaders are dedicated to doing something to keep the thin veneer of conservation assistance from being completely torn apart by these shifts, but are so far unable to find a solution.

The federal soil conservation program is now being directed more and more from priorities set in Washington, and less and less by priorities established by the conservation districts. This trend, which really started back in the 1950's, when SCS was directed by Congress to furnish technical services to ACP participants whether or not they were a cooperator with the district, has been gradually increasing each year, and there is little to suggest that it will change in the near future.

That has caused serious concerns among conservation district leaders, and NACD has been attempting to articulate those concerns in a way that illustrates the dangers of allowing the conservation program to wither and die in some parts of the country based on today's priorities. The institutional framework and capability that has been built over 50 years can be dismantled much more rapidly, it is feared, if USDA allows the very thin layer of soil conservation programs to be completely moved out (or even seriously reduced) in many areas. How NACD, states, and conservation districts cope with that situation may have an overwhelming influence on the soil conservation programs in their second half-century.

Milton E. "Bud" Mekelburg

In 1982, at the Phoenix Convention, the Board elected Milton E. "Bud" Mekelburg of Yuma, Colorado, to the Presidency. Clarence Durban of Plain City, Ohio, was elected Vice President, and Sam Chinn of California was re-elected Secretary-Treasurer.

Secretary of Agriculture John Block travelled to Phoenix to address the Wednesday evening banquet, telling the delegates about the major features of the Department's new RCA program and assuring them of his support for the conservation districts and their goals. Within a month, Block and NACD were at swords point over Block's appointment of a political appointee as head of the Soil Conservation Service. This was a move that NACD opposed vigorously, so Mekelburg was not given much time in office before becoming involved in a political confrontation with

Milton E. "Bud" Mekelburg is a native of Yuma, raised on a ranch near that small eastern Colorado farming community. He was educated in the local school system there.

Mekelburg was an original supervisor with the Yuma Soil Conservation District, and has been Chairman of that district for 21 years. He was Vice President of the Colorado Association of Soil Conservation Districts from 1970 to 1972, and President of that association from 1973 to 1975.

He was elected to the NACD Board of Directors in 1977 and became Vice President in 1978. He was elected President in 1982.

Bud and his wife Genevieve have developed a wheat, cattle and corn farm, now operated in partnership with their sons. He was also active in a local feedlot partnership, and served as President of that operation for a term.

Mekelburg's community affiliations include the Yuma Chamber of Commerce, the Colorado Cattlemen's Association, and the Soil Conservation Society of America. He was chosen Outstanding Young Farmer of Yuma in 1969 and Colorado Conservationist of the Year in 1975. He won the Honor Award from the Soil Conservation Society of America in 1975.

USDA.

A tireless worker, Mekelburg is on the phone at all hours, and travels almost constantly in his NACD role. His farming operations at Yuma are in conjunction with his sons and daughters, so the family holds down the farm while Bud donates most of his time to conservation.

Relationships with the Soil Conservation Service

Conservation districts have always worked very closely with the SCS technicians assigned to the district, as might be expected, and NACD has always had a close relationship with the leaders of SCS. That relationship has, however, been made more balanced in recent years. At the outset, SCS had all the money, all the capability, and all the organization. Pioneering district officials have always seen, however, that a solid partnership between unequals is difficult. The history of districts and NACD is replete with efforts to increase the capability and role of the private, local, state, and national partners who work with USDA and SCS.

The changes have occurred in many ways. At the district level, administration of local ordinances was a task that could not legally be done by a federal employee, and districts in that role hired professional technicians of their own. At the state level, state soil conservation agencies became stronger, better funded, and more capable of carrying out programs to build district strength. NACD, with its efforts in communications between local leaders and national issues, developed its own staff and analytic strength.

For the most part, SCS leaders saw these efforts as beneficial to the entire movement, not competitive. Other agencies saw more and better opportunities to work with districts, as well. In programs like Coastal Zone Management and water pollution control, state and federal agencies were finding that the legal powers of districts were exactly what was needed to provide a link between the public program and the private landowner who would need, in the end, to actually accomplish the goals of the program.

The public was made more aware of the need for improved conservation programs, as a result of the environmental movement, the increased attention focused by the RCA activity, and the intensified communications efforts of NACD and other conservation organizations on the topic. This raised the political pressures, both in Congress and the Administration, to "do something."

In March of 1982, Secretary of Agriculture John Block "did something" that revealed the intensely increased political nature of the conservation program. Norman Berg, the Secretary announced, would be replaced at the helm of SCS with a political appointee, Peter C. Myers, a Missouri farmer.

There was nothing new about this idea. From Hugh Bennett forward, the top man at SCS had been vulnerable to political appointments. That had been avoided over the years by a combination of events, and heavy pressure from NACD and other conservation organizations who lobbied hard to keep career professionals at the leadership of all the natural resource agencies, in both USDA and USDI. Norm Berg was no newcomer to this situation. He had sat through weeks of uncertainty while he and Ken Grant's resignations sat on Earl Butz's desk, before the Secretary decided to forego the option of making changes.

During Robert W. Long's tenure as Assistant Secretary of Agriculture, the SCS Administrator's job (along with the Forest Service Chief's position) was moved out of the political category, and placed as a career position. This solidified the actual practice that had extended from Bennett, and gave the agency heads more stability. Long believed firmly that the agencies needed to respond to political leadership, but he felt just as strongly that the task of providing that leadership belonged with the Secretary and Assistant Secretary. The agency heads, he felt, needed to be expert in the operation of the agency.

But this was changed by the Civil Service Reforms carried out by the Carter Administration. Agency heads, and all managers above GS-16, were to eventually become part of the Senior Executive Service, open to transfer anywhere in government that their skills were needed. Using this authority, Secretary Bergland had transferred R. M. "Mel" Davis from the SCS Administrator's job in 1979 and named Norm Berg as his successor.

In 1982, Secretary Block carried the process one step further, going outside the career ranks to select Peter C. Myers as the new Chief. NACD, along with many other conservation organizations, reacted in violent opposition, but there was nothing that could be done. The Secretary was operating within his authorities, and felt very strongly that SCS would be improved with the views of a farmer at the helm. A tradition of professional leadership in the SCS dating back to Hugh Bennett had been broken, perhaps permanently.

Bud Mekelburg spoke out against the principle of political leadership in *Tuesday Letter,* making it clear that he held no personal animosities toward Peter Myers, but that NACD had strong feelings about the need to retain professional, career leadership in agencies such as SCS, Forest Service, and others of a similar nature.

Secretary Block continued to request NACD's acceptance of his choice, and involved Mekelburg in several top-level meetings or "round-tables" held by the Secretary to seek advice from leaders of agricultural organizations.

As with many current issues, it is far too soon to evaluate how these moves may ultimately affect the national soil conservation effort and the role that NACD can play on the national scene. Both the increase in "targeting" of federal programs and the conversion of the SCS leadership to political appointees spell a greater federal control of the program's elements. NACD has opposed both, with some success in helping make targeting criteria more sensitive to local needs, but no success in slowing down the trend to more and more federally-directed priorities.

The Commodity Conflict Continues

The abuse of soil and water that results from the federal commodity programs has been a continued cause of concern within NACD, as well as many other conservation and agricultural organizations, and many ideas have surfaced that might have some positive effect on the situation.

One idea that NACD developed was for a "green ticket" incentive program that would provide benefits to conservation farmers that might offset some of the disincentives in the current programs. Such an approach would allow conservation districts to identify those farmers who were carrying out an approved conservation program on their land and give them a certificate of approval. The farmer could then take this "green ticket" to the USDA agencies administering farm programs and use it to claim differential incentives set aside for conservation farmers.

In this way, income support, commodity stabilization, farm loan, crop insurance, and other farm programs could contain a built-in "conservation incentive" without the program administering agency being burdened with the requirement of establishing whether or not a particular farmer was truly carrying out a good conservation program on his land. The idea gathered considerable support within NACD, and has been proposed in various forms as part of legislative packages. No incentive package has been built into any USDA program yet, however, so the use of the "green ticket" has been limited to a few local tests.

Another suggestion was for "cross-compliance," forcing farmers to meet conservation standards before they would be eligible for any USDA program benefits. This idea was pushed by many environmental and conservation groups, but was felt by many in NACD to be too "compulsory" in nature to be accepted by American farmers.

What was clear, however, was that conservation and production policies could not be divorced. "The strength of the dollar depends on the strength of the land," President Lyle Bauer told the House Appropriations Committee in 1980. "If the productivity of the land is depleted, every bushel of wheat or corn, every pound of milk, and every bale of cotton produced will cost more than it did this year . . . and add to the inflation spiral," he said. "The rising cost will continue each year, so long as the land is allowed to get less and less productive."[6]

These concerns continued to build as each year passed. In 1979, the USDA announced that Russia might buy up to 10 million metric tons of grain, and so there was no need for a program to set aside acres. Conservationists, as well as Members of Congress, worried that such an announcement was an invitation to bring land formerly set aside for conservation use back into cultivation.[7]

But there were no real ways that the situation could be averted. NACD called on districts to make an extra effort to try to convince farmers that expansion of cultivation should be done with the land's capability in mind, but Lyle Bauer pointed out the limits involved. "We cannot force farmers to take proper care of their land," he said in a *Tuesday Letter* editorial. "But this country cannot afford to let its productive capability wash away, either, and if farmers cannot or will not take proper care of their land on a voluntary basis, the pressures for stronger national action will grow."[8]

In a response reminiscent of Earl Butz's "plant-fence-row-to-fence-row" exhortation, followed by the "production with protection" USDA campaigns of the early 1970's, Bergland followed the announcement that there would need to be no set-aside in 1980 with a telephone call to a selected group of NACD and ASC Committee leaders, telling them that USDA would embark on a "policy of persuasion" and a strong new information campaign to keep farmers from abusing the land.[9] It was the same old story. USDA policy and national economic conditions would be driving farmers to exploit the land and take advantage of the situation, while the best conservation policy that could be generated was a little hand-wringing and a few press releases.

In the fall of 1980, as the election signalled a change in Administrations, the international grain supply looked very favorable for the producing nations. In spite of the 1980 grain embargo placed on the Russians by President Carter, the world stocks were fairly low, and weather conditions were not particularly favorable. It looked like 1981 would be a banner year for grain producers, and a fine time for a free-market oriented Administration to let federal farm policy drift for a while. That was not to be a lasting situation, however.

A sudden weather reversal in 1981 brought out a bumper crop, as a worldwide recession dampened export demand. Suddenly American farmers were up to their eyebrows in grain, and prices dropped through the floor. By the end of 1982, the situation was clearly an emergency. President Ronald Reagan and USDA Secretary John Block responded with a "Payment-In-Kind" program for 1983, where if farmers agreed not to plant wheat, corn, cotton or rice they could be compensated with an amount of that commodity equal to some percentage of what they might otherwise have grown. They would be free to use, sell or keep the commodity, as they wished. It was a program aimed at two problems: getting some income to farmers and cutting down on government-held commodity stocks.

Conservationists saw a marvelous opportunity. Farmers signed up to set aside over 80 million acres -- one-fourth of the normal planted acreage. USDA policy said that these acres would be seeded to grass or otherwise protected from erosion. The situation was a significant, one-time opportunity to enhance soil conservation, wildlife habitat, and watershed values.

But the program happened too fast. The grass seed wasn't available to plant that many acres, and farmers were told by many local ASC Committees that seeding the land wasn't necessary. If they left the land alone, weed growth would be adequate for soil protection, they were told. As a result, less than 20 percent of the land was seeded to grass in most areas, and in some areas there simply were no acres seeded. About one-quarter of that land was left in condition to suffer serious soil erosion, a survey conducted by NACD revealed. The whole affair was simply another example of a commodity program that paid little more than lip service to its effect on soil and water resources.

Public recognition of the problem, spurred by NACD's persistence in calling the matter to public attention, seems to be making a difference, though. Studies of agricultural policy now routinely contain a section on the effects on natural resources, and many observers feel that the 1985 Farm Bill will pay serious attention to this situation as it outlines a new set of farm policies for the remainder of the decade.

Conservation Districts in the Information Age

Another major challenge to districts, SCS, Extension, and anyone else who works with farmers is to learn how to cope in the "Information Age" that is upon us. Successful farmers are now as well educated as most agency technicians, and more skilled in most aspects of their farming operation. They no longer rely on the county agent for farming advice. They read as many magazines, go to as many technical seminars, and can talk directly to as many specialists as he can.

The same holds true for soil conservation technicians. It is no longer a matter of educating uneducated farmers, as the pioneers faced the challenge 50 years ago. Today it is a matter of convincing a busy, hard-driving farmer that your information is better than his, that a good conservation system will save his soil, and make him money -- either in the long- or short-run.

Information is the key to that process, and districts have been both aggressive and successful in reaching out with conservation information in the past. Two recent developments may prove to be helpful in that regard.

In 1983, after a considerable effort by Bud Mekelburg, Mary Garner, and David Stewart, NACD was successful in getting a favorable U.S. Postal Service ruling that allows conservation districts to qualify for lower rates on certain types of bulk mail. The issues were complex, but through application of the Postal Service's own regulations, districts were interpreted to be special units of local government engaged in improving agriculture, and, as such, qualified to be considered for the nonprofit mailing rates.

The practical difference, for districts with newsletters, amounts to many thousands of dollars each year, and a good district information program is now within the reach of many more districts than would have otherwise been the case. The victory, while fairly typical of the service provided by any effective national association for its members, was one of the few opportunities NACD had realized in many years to get something done in Washington that would so directly, and positively, hit the treasury of each of its local member districts.

The other trend, far too new for any evaluation, is the rapid adoption of microcomputer technology by NACD, conservation districts, and SCS. As more farmers turn to microcomputers to assist in their own decision-making process, conservation districts and technicians are finding that to be a necessity as well. As foreign as these machines are to many who were schooled before their emergence, they are the tool of the future, and learning how to use them is rapidly becoming a necessity for technical survival. A survey of districts by NACD in 1983 indicated that over 100 already had computers, and hundreds more were planning to purchase machines as soon as possible.

It has been said, however, (only partly in jest) that computers do not prevent mistakes, they only help people make them faster. For that reason, a great deal of work is needed to develop conservation planning tools that conservation districts and the technicians that work with farmers can rely upon for accurate, usable information. A great deal of confusion, wasted effort, and frustration seems inevitable as conservationists and others fight their way into this new "Information Age".

But these new tools may fundamentally change the ways in which information can flow to landowners, and assist in getting conservation on the land. SCS has been losing field engineers for years, as budgets have shrunk in the face of inflation and federal spending controls. If a $3,000 computer can reduce the design time on a channel from days to hours, as seems to be the case, the increased efficiency will hopefully result in more practices being designed and more land users being assisted.

They may also change the manner in which an organization like NACD can reach out with its communications capability. Already, the advent of word processing capability has helped NACD produce more printed material, of higher quality, at a faster pace. This has been helpful many times; crucial in a few instances. As other new innovations such as electronic mail become more common, it may become easier to get the "full story" on an upcoming political issue out to NACD regional offices, state soil conservation agencies, and state association leaders themselves.

With timing and facts as the two most important weapons in any political battle, the better an organization can inform its members, the more effective they (and it) can be. Whether or not this will actually occur is yet to be seen, but NACD and districts are moving forward aggressively to take whatever advantages these new technologies can offer.

The Bottom Line: People

In the final analysis, however, it will be people and ideals that define the success of NACD. For it is surely true, as Sam Studebaker told the 1967 Annual Convention of NACD: "Soil and water conservation does not start with land treatment. It starts in the mind of the landowner." Conservation districts, and conservation district officials, because of their ability to communicate with the landowners of America, have filled a key role in building the bridge that can bring the technical knowledge of the scientist and the ethics of the conservationist into the mind of the landowner in a compelling way.

Conservation districts have, for a variety of reasons, been consistently successful in attracting community leadership to their boards of supervisors. The combination of a highly altruistic set of goals and objectives, a local platform of some prestige, and a chance to contribute time and talent pretty much at each individual's chosen pace, have no doubt helped attract leaders. For the most part, district officials receive no compensation at all for their efforts. That may serve to discourage young people who need to solidify their personal financial position, but it is a positive attraction for people seeking an independent platform from which to speak their mind and contribute to their community's welfare.

The transition of a local leader to a national leader is usually gradual, but an organization like NACD encourages those who would seek such growth. District board decisions force a person to look beyond their own farm, or community, and become knowledgable about issues that may never touch their personal lives in any direct way. Working day and night to get a watershed project so that the people on the other end of the county can be protected from flood damages is an experience in social growth that has affected thousands of district officials.

In addition, the active district official learns about dealing with government agencies. No longer are the local offices simply a place full of nameless people who fill out forms. District officials learn why these offices work the way they do, who sets the policies, and how citizens can make a difference in their operation.

When these talents are coupled with political savvy, the state, regional, and national organization of NACD offers an exceptional career opportunity in which a person can contribute, and learn, every step of the way. Only a very few make it to national office, but hundreds serve on national committees, on the NACD Council, on the Board of Directors and, in other ways, bring their talents to the conservation district movement.

Holding all these diverse talents together is the central core of the conservation ethic. Conservation district officials believe, and act, because they are deeply convinced that they are dealing with the right issues -- the fundamental issues of life. As Sam Studebaker said, "Some call this improving the quality of our environment. Others use the term conservation and resource development. Whatever it is called makes little difference. The objective is the same: protecting, preserving, maintaining, developing, and using our natural heritage in ways that will enable us and our children to enjoy the richest and fullest life possible."[10]

This is the central idea that has moved men and women to donate tremendous amounts of time and talent. People come because they care, and they participate and contribute because of the infectious enthusiasm that grows when hundreds of caring people work together in a cause they feel is right. From E.C. McArthur to Bud Mekelburg, that commitment has been reflected in the first 50 years of the soil and water conservation district movement in America. The results, as we have seen, have been impressive.

But the story of NACD and its leaders only touches the surface of what is happening, for behind these leaders are similar stories of commitment, sacrifice, leadership and innovation that have moved state legislatures, county courts, town councils, citizen groups, and individuals to conservation action. The history of such a movement can never be fully recorded, it is too complex and far-reaching throughout society.

As a result, it seems clear that NACD will continue to be a strong, vibrant factor on the national policy scene. Not because of the organization so much, or because of any particular personalities who may share center stage now or in the future, as because of the thousands of people who share a common belief in the basic concepts of resource conservation and wise use for which the organization stands. Those thousands of men and women, working in their own communities, in their own ways, continue to shape ideas, mold decisions, and directly affect the attitudes with which all Americans view their stewardship responsibilities in today's world.

The accomplishments of the first half-century are impressive, but the challenges ahead seem equally awesome. The public is more concerned about resource management and conservation than at any time since the 1930's. There are more activists involved, more organizations, more technical studies, and more "experts" on soil conservation than ever before. To many, the challenge seems to be primarily a technical one. The history of the conservation movement suggests, however, that such is not the case. The challenge is one of moving people to constructive action. Anyone who would seek to understand the political forces that move Americans to action on soil and water conservation issues would do well to understand the potential that lies in the dedication, commitment and skill of those who love the land -- the people of the soil conservation districts.

Consider Our Commitment

What beauty abounds here on God's green Earth!
    And who can begin to measure its worth?
What price a sunset, a blossom-filled spring;
    A moonlit lake, a butterfly wing?

God gave all these and so much more;
    There are beautiful harvests, too much to store.
All this He meant for us here to treasure.
    How fortunate we are, enriched beyond measure!

But there is the danger that we might forget
    That for all this beauty we do owe a debt.
For, as He gave to us His world to share,
    He also committed it to our care.

When God made the Earth, before it He stood.
    He looked His work over and said, "It is good."
Do you wonder sometimes what God has to say
    When He looks down upon His world today?

Man's obsessions have upset nature's balance.
    Today costly mistakes are taxing our talent.
We mustn't forget Earth's not ours alone;
    That we're only mortal and soon will be gone.

We each have a duty to God our Creator
    To protect Earth's resources for those to come later.
Yes, its time our commitment went even deeper,
    If we are to be our brother's keeper.

Consider our commitment; consider it well.

1984 Soil Stewardship Brochure

APPENDICES

APPENDIX A
Those Who Have Served

Out of love for the land, eighteen men founded the National Association of Conservation Districts on July 25, 1946. They added fresh vitality to American democracy and launched an enduring campaign to elevate concern for the nation's resources. The following lists those who have served the NACD as officers and directors in the ensuing years.

ALABAMA
W.M. Hodgson*
P.G. Compton*
A.D. Holmes
F. Mooney Nalty

ARIZONA
Frank Gyberg*
Moroni M. Larson
J. David Lee
John Olsen
TL Meredith
Desmond Wood
Hank Raymond
James K. Henness

ARKANSAS
Reece Caudle
John Faulkner
R. Sloan Rainwater
Monroe Samuel
Robert P. Lewis
William F. Teeter

CALIFORNIA
A.N. Chamness
J. Max Wilson
W.E. "Ted" Silverwood
Francis C. Lindsay
Lorin Trubschenck
Sam Chinn

COLORADO
Walt A. Groom*
Clarence Svedman
L.B. Casselman
George Weaver
Quincy Cornelius
Ross E. Chambers
Milton E. Mekelburg**

CONNECTICUT
Daniel McKeon
John Breakell

DELAWARE
Irving Hudson
Cashar Evans
Isaac Thomas

FLORIDA
Thomas Ford

GEORGIA
W.F. Hall
W. Houser Davidson
David Kistner
Joe Hawkins

HAWAII
Jay Sasan

IDAHO
Milton Branch
Don G. Frederickson
Lowell C. Moore
Earl McClellan
James Busch.

ILLINOIS
Willard Cook
Richard Grob
Hillard Morris

INDIANA
Lloyd Arbuckle*
Lawrence McKinney
Russell Reiff
Harold Wilson

IOWA
Don Anderson
R. Edward Baur
Joe O'Hara
Ervin J.J. Koos

KANSAS
Fred Prell*
Laurence Rittenoure
Roger W. Lemon
Leon Trumbull
Lyle Bauer**
Harold Johnson

* Founder   ** President

KENTUCKY
A. Threlkeld*
Fred Pace
Hugh Jones
Ken Bean

LOUISIANA
R.D. Conly*
W.T. Nolin
Tom P. Moore
Marion S. Monk, Jr.**
Richard Thompson
George R. Bagley**
Richard Hollier, Jr.

MAINE
Dennis Getchell*
Ray Thurston
Willis Lord
Robert W. Spear

MARYLAND
Walter Burrall*
Wm. R. Powel
Harry Rieck
T. Walter Denny

MASSACHUSETTS
Hans Van Leer
George Hartley

MICHIGAN
R.L. Hill*
Herb Van Aken
R. Wally Petersen
Randel Burson
Warren Suchovsky

MINNESOTA
Wm. A. Benitt*
Alfred Wiger
Alf Larson
Cy P. Crawford
Del Krenik
Robert Wetherbee

MISSISSIPPI
A.B. Adams
Sam Thompson
P.T. Eubanks

MISSOURI
Ancel Webb
Harley E. Bogue
Betty Broemmelsiek

MONTANA
Guy Van Cleve
Gordon McGowan
Oscar Hippe
Peter Jackson
John Vanisko

NEBRASKA
Everett M. Barr*
Bill Richards**
Milton Fricke
Warren Patefield

NEVADA
Harvey Hale
Albert Romeo
Maurice Bidart

NEW HAMPSHIRE
Hugh C. Tuttle

NEW JERSEY
Newton Layton
Kenneth J. Roehrich

NEW MEXICO
W.A. Williams, Jr.
E.O. Moore
Lewis Merritt
Willam G. Patton
David King
James W. Harrison

NEW YORK
Kent Leavitt**
Harold S. Wright
Silas Eakins
William F. Chamberlain

NORTH CAROLINA
Charles M. Ladd
James Bellamy

NORTH DAKOTA
Otis Tossett
Osborne Galde
William Bosse
Ray Reich

OHIO
Allen Craig*
Clay Stackhouse
Herbert Eagon
Orran Hofstetter
Sam Studebaker**
Clarence Durban

OKLAHOMA
Nolen J. Fuqua**
A.P. "Red" Atkins
R.C. Longmire
Wallace Denny
Leonard Graumann

OREGON
Forrest Scroggin
Ralph Saylor
Elmer Peterson
Stanley R. Christensen
Ernest Josi

PENNSYLVANIA
W. Clayton Jester
Raymond Shaffer
Donald Stephens
Robert Lott
William D. Lange

SOUTH CAROLINA
E.C. McArthur* **
Joe B. Douthit
Newman D. Buck
L.H. Hicks

SOUTH DAKOTA
Tony Krebs
Leonard Schultz

TENNESSEE
John Wilder**
Steve Brunson

TEXAS
R.M. Boswell*
Waters S. Davis, Jr.**
John D. Faught
W.C. Howard
John D. Wells
A.L. Black
Doyle Hutcheson
Kenneth Kuykendall

UTAH
Parley P. Smith
George Barton
Lawrence E. Thorderson
James Nessen
Leo P. Harvey
Thaine Taylor
Kenneth Cardon
Dale P. Bateman

VERMONT
Robert Graf

VIRGIN ISLANDS
Hans Lawaetz

VIRGINIA
Russel J. Fisher
J. Gilbert Cox
Edward L. Felton
R.E. Wilkinson

WASHINGTON
R.L. Rutter, Jr.*
Dave J. Doneen
J. Wes Cornwall
Conrad Hougen
John Snider
Charles W. O'Neill, Jr
Gerald B. Digerness

WEST VIRGINIA
D.T. Paugh*
George R. Heidrich
Howard Thornburg
Edward M. Bumgarner

WISCONSIN
Oscar Laper
Byron Berg

WYOMING
Orr Garber
Walt Dimond
Donald Fraker
Richard N. Donelson

Appendix B
Points in Time

1946

January - Forty-nine conservation district officials met at Washington, D.C. in a fruitless effort to get legislation passed transferring surplus military equipment to conservation districts. The group, after suffering defeat, drafted Edgar C. McArthur, Gaffney, S.C., to organize a national association.

July - McArthur and 17 selected associates, meeting at Chicago on July 24-25, organized the National Association of Soil Conservation District Governing Officials. They adopted a constitution, and elected McArthur temporary President and Robert L. Rutter, Jr., Washington, temporary Vice President.

August - Organization issued first general publication, a brochure entitled "National Association of Soil Conservation District Governing Officials."

December - Organization changed name to National Association of Soil Conservation Districts.

1947

January - The original constitution of NASCD was developed.

February - First annual meeting attended by 69 conservation district officials from 42 states, at Chicago, Feb. 25-26. McArthur elected President, Rutter Vice President.

April - McArthur sent the first communication letter to Directors and Council, along with a plan of action, April 1. First Information Letter was sent out April 30, planned as bimonthly feature.

July - Information Letter of July 24 reported Cooley bill would eliminate Soil Conservation Service and transfer functions to state extension services.

August - First Goodyear Awards Programs began in districts in eight states of SCS Upper Mississippi Region, Aug. 1.

September - McArthur killed in automobile accident, Sept. 8, 1947. Directors met at Chicago, Sept. 11; elected Kent Leavitt, Millbrook, N.Y., to fill unexpired term.

November - Leavitt issued his first newsletter, Information Letter No. 5, Nov. 1, and changed to monthly schedule.

1948

February - Second annual meeting, Des Moines, Feb. 27-28, attended by 165 from 40 states. Thirteen committees made reports. Many delegates flew to Washington and made congressional contacts following convention.

March - NASCD supported the National Land Policy bill introduced by Rep. Clifford

Hope, Kansas.

June - Mrs. Ellen S. Cobb resigned, and was succeeded as Executive Secretary by Morris E. Fonda.

October - Fonda resigned, and was succeeded by Robert S. Calkins.

1949

February - Third annual meeting, Denver, Feb. 15-17, attended by 334 from 42 states.

June - USDA Appropriation Act for fiscal year 1950 provided that 5% of ACP allocation in any county could be allotted to SCS for technical services to ACP.

1950

February - Fourth annual meeting, Atlanta, Feb. 28-March 2, attended by 1,200. Waters Davis, Texas, elected President; Clay Stackhouse, Ohio, Vice President. A new constitution was adopted, providing for Area Vice Presidents.

July - "Information Letter" becomes "District News" and goes to quarterly schedule.

November - Executive committee approved sale of signs identifying district cooperators and Program for Greater Service.

Don Daily, Colorado, succeeded Robert S. Calkins as Executive Secretary.

1951

February - Fifth annual meeting, Oklahoma City, Feb. 20-23: Board adopted slogan, "Conservation - Development - Self-Government." Secretary of Agriculture Charles F. Brannan was keynote speaker.

Hugh Hammond Bennett, SCS Chief, received NASCD's Distinguished Service Award.

Secretary Brannan issued Memorandum 1278 stating unified USDA conservation policy and making SCS responsible for permanent-type conservation practices of ACP.

The Ladies Auxiliary of NASCD was organized to encourage involvement of farm women in conservation programs, focus on conservation education, community planning and promotion.

April - Secretary Brannan's April 9 memorandum stressed the role of conservation districts in national programs of SCS and ACP.

June - The Board, at Kansas City, began the custom of regular conferences with Agriculture and Interior agencies.

1952

February - Sixth annual meeting at Cleveland, Feb. 25-29. Board accepted Don Daily's resignation as Executive Secretary effective May 1.

June - The Board formalized a District-Dealer Program providing for cooperative efforts between local conservation districts and 17,000 retail farm equipment dealers.

William L. Southworth became Program Advisor, headquartered at League City.

July - "District News" became a monthly publication, listing 3 functions of NASCD: (1) channeling helpful information to districts; (2) "A Program for Greater Service;" and (3) representing individual districts nationally.

October - Secretary's Memorandum 1318, Oct. 14, placed responsibility for all USDA soil survey activities in SCS and consolidated soil survey staffs of ARS and conservation surveys of SCS in SCS, effective Nov. 15. Also transferred to ARS all SCS research activities except those relating to soil formation, soil geography, and laboratory analysis.

Waters Davis issued first *Tuesday Letter,* Oct. 21. "District News" was soon phased out. The first TL offered to print and mail similar newsletters for individual districts. A small building at League City, TX, was rented to provide an office to produce TL and provide services to districts.

1953

January - *Tuesday Letter,* Jan. 1, published summary of NASCD's gross receipts: 1946-47, $16,009; 1948, $23,846; 1949, $28,645; 1950, $39,325; 1951, $68,981; 1952, $81,727.

February - Seventh annual meeting, Omaha, Feb. 3-5.

Francis Coxe, South Carolina, proposed establishment of Soil Conservation Districts Foundation. The Conservation Districts Foundation was to gather funds and provide capital reserve funds for NASCD.

April - April 14 *Tuesday Letter* printed on new offset press instead of mimeograph. June 9 mailing list was 19,364.

October-November - Representatives of NASCD, state associations and local districts appeared before Rep. Clifford R. Hope's House Agriculture Committee at field hearings in 10 states.

Secretary Benson's reorganization plan for SCS was announced Nov. 2.

The Goodyear Conservation Awards Program was extended nationwide to recognize outstanding districts for their programs and accomplishments.

1954

February - Eighth annual meeting, New Orleans, Feb. 23-25. The Board adopted a constitution change placing limit of five years on tenure of national officers.

March - President Davis, in a letter to Secretary Benson, urged appointment of national soil and water conservation advisory committee.

April - Gordon Webb became field representative for NASCD's Northeastern, Southeastern and Upper Mississippi areas out of Spartanburg, S.C., April 5.

May - Waters Davis invited leaders of major conservation organizations and watershed associations to meet in Washington, D.C. to plan the first National Watershed Congress.

August - National Watershed Protection and Flood Prevention Act, Public Law 566, became law, Aug. 4.

October - The Board at Galveston, Oct. 28-31, voted to sponsor annual Soil Stewardship Sunday observance.

December - The First National Watershed Congress at Washington, D.C., Dec. 6-7

1955

February - Ninth annual meeting at San Diego, Feb. 10-15. Nolen J. Fuqua, Oklahoma, elected President; William E. Richards, Nebraska, Vice President, Waters Davis named Treasurer. Bob Hope's radio program was broadcast live from the convention.

May - First Soil Stewardship Sunday under sponsorship of NASCD, May 15. President Fuqua spoke on National Farm & Home Network broadcast, May 14. Secretary Benson issued Soil Stewardship statement. Soil Stewardship booklets distributed through local districts.

Fuqua was one of a dozen guests at President Eisenhower's stag dinner, May 5.

June - Governors of 10 Plains states and conservation district leaders from Nebraska, Kansas, Oklahoma, Colorado, New Mexico, and Texas met at Denver June 1 with Secretary Benson to discuss drought and dust storm problems.

July - *Tuesday Letter,* July 19, announced sponsorship of Soil Stewardship Week in 1956 beginning with Sunday, May 6, and running through Saturday, May 13.

Fuqua, Richards, Colorado President Clarence Svedman, and Wyoming President John Snyder met with the Great Plains Council to make recommendations to USDA for Great Plains Conservation Program.

October - Secretary Benson appointed 18-member soil and water conservation advisory committee, called first meeting for Oct. 27-28. Appointees included two NASCD directors, A.D.Holmes, Jr., of Alabama and R. Edward Baur of Iowa.

November - The Board at Galveston, Nov. 14-17, voted to keep business office at League City on recommendation of committee headed by Marion Monk.

Monk presented the Board with deed to part of a new building to be used as an NASCD office, gift of Mr. and Mrs. Waters Davis.

1956

January - Receipts in 1955 were $176,398.56, compared to $140,224.93 in 1954 and $119,103.00 in 1953.

February - 10th annual meeting at Boston, Feb. 6-9.

Waters Davis enlarged NASCD office space in new building by 1,500 square feet before moving day.

April - Clair P. Guess, Executive Secretary, South Carolina State Soil Conservation Committee and former State Association President, became a Program Advisor, headquartered in League City.

August - The Great Plains Conservation Program, P.L. 1021, was enacted by Congress.

October - In a dedication ceremony at League City, the Board accepted the gift of a new business office building from Mr. and Mrs. Waters Davis.

December - Secretary Benson assigned program responsibility for the Great Plains Conservation Program to SCS, and announced that districts would have prominent role, and that the program would be geared to a basic soil and water conservation plan.

1957

January - Jan. 1 issue of *Tuesday Letter* went to mailing list of 27,523. NASCD receipts in 1956 were $224,623.50.

NASCD formed an action committee to implement the Great Plains Conservation Program in a Denver meeting with Don Williams, SCS Administrator, and Assistant Secretary Ervin L. Peterson of USDA.

February - 11th annual meeting at St. Louis, Feb. 4-7. First annual Soil Stewardship inspirational meeting held.

Directors approved Farm Equipment Institute proposal to provide $2,500 in cash prizes for district newsletter contest.

March - The Board endorsed Future Farmers of America land judging program sponsored by Bankers Service Life Insurance Co., urged expansion.

June - Robert S. McClelland, Columbia, Mo., became a Program Advisor, June 15, stationed at Duncan, Oklahoma.

Program Advisor William Southworth resigned to enter private business.

1958

February - 12th annual meeting at Minneapolis, Feb. 16-20. First district newsletter prizes awarded, first grand prize to Harris Conservation District, Texas. Norway red pine planted on state capitol grounds in soil from all states taken to convention by district officials in 3,750 bags.

New "rurban" problem presented to Council by Hans Van Leer, Massachusetts, who recommended appointment of special committee to explore ways of dealing with non-farm land users.

The Board gave the official title of "NASCD Service Department" to League City Office.

April - Governor Happy Chandler, Kentucky, signed bill amending districts law to authorize county courts to levy up to two cents an acre for use by conservation district boards.

June - East Corson Conservation District, South Dakota, dissolved at instigation of anti-district organization called "F.A.R.M."

July - The Board, July 21, disregarded committee report recommending Omaha as site of national office, chose Washington D.C. instead, authorized Fuqua to negotiate with Gordon K. Zimmerman for position of Executive Secretary.

Fuqua announced employment of James C. Hart, Atlanta, in editorial position, effective

Sept. 1.

September - Zimmerman became NASCD Executive Secretary the day after Labor Day, and, by early October, had Washington office in operation in room 305, Washington Bldg., 15th and New York N.W., Washington, D.C., with Jean Sullivan as Office Secretary.

October - Board authorized Zimmerman to be administrative head of organization under directors.

USDA 1958 Yearbook, "Land," included chapter on conservation districts and their accomplishments.

November - Waters Davis , district official since 1944, Texas President, 1947-50, national President, 1950-55, Treasurer, 1955-58, died at League City, Texas, Nov. 15.

1959

February - 13th annual meeting at Houston, Feb. 1-5. William E. Richards, Nebraska, elected President; Gilbert Cox, Virginia, Vice President; Marion Monk, Louisiana, appointed Treasurer.

The NASCD Distinguished Service Award was presented to C. R. "Pink" Gutermuth, Vice President of the Wildlife Management Institute of Washington, D.C.

Amendments to constitution were adopted providing

(1) that officers be President, national Vice President, Area Vice Presidents, Executive Secretary, Treasurer;

(2) that Executive Secretary be Secretary to Council, directors, executive committee, and, under direction of President, supervise all employees and offices;

(3) that President be elected by directors for two years and may succeed himself once;

(4) that national Vice President and Area Vice Presidents serve at will of directors but no longer than seven consecutive years;

(5) that Executive Secretary and Treasurer be nominated by President and elected by directors and hold office until removed by President with advice and consent of directors.

Directors voted to establish Waters Davis Memorial Library at suggestion of Vice President Cox, $1,000 being contributed for that purpose by Alabama State Association.

The NASCD Ladies Auxiliary elected Mrs. Henry Bethea of Florida as President, Mrs. George Montgomery of Missouri as Vice President and Mrs. Oscar Camp of Washington as Secretary-Treasurer.

Women in Soil and Water Conservation, an 11-page brochure outlining the Auxiliary's history written by Mrs. Pearl Frederickson of Idaho, was released.

March - Regional office for NASCD's Northern Plains, Southwestern, Pacific areas opened in Denver with Bob McClelland in charge as Western Program Advisor.

Clair Guess was named Service Department Manager.

August - The Post Office Department issued world's first commemorative soil conservation stamp, Aug. 26.

October - Board appointed Philip M. Glick as NASCD General Counsel, noting his services for three years without charge.

1960

January February 14th annual meeting at Louisville, Jan. 31-Feb.4. Richards and Cox were re-elected to office. The banquet speaker was Fred A. Seaton, Secretary of the Interior. A highlight of the meeting was the premier showing of "The Earth is the Lord's," film produced under guidance of Soil Stewardship Advisory Committee by Farm Equipment Institute.

Nine original founders and the first Executive Secretary, Mrs. Ellen S. Cobb, honored in special ceremonies. Founders present were Lloyd Arbuckle (IN), Everett Barr (NE), R.D. Conly (LA), Frank Gyberg (AZ), R. Lester Hill (MI), W.M. Hodgson (AL), D.T. Paugh (WV), Fred Prell (KS), and August Threlkeld (KY).

Sixty-two ex-presidents of 32 state associations formed the Association of Past Presidents of State Associations, named Otis Tossett, North Dakota, acting Chairman; Cy Crawford, Minnesota, Secretary.

A. H. "Don" Settle, Director of Goodyear Conservation Awards Program, was presented the Distinguished Service Award. W. H. Edmund, Executive Consultant to Goodyear Tire & Rubber, was the luncheon speaker.

April - Post Office Department issued commemorative water conservation stamp at National Watershed Congress, Washington, D.C., April 18.

May - NASCD sponsored observance of 25th anniversary of Soil Conservation Service, National Press Club, Washington, D.C., and presented bronze plaque to SCS Administrator Don Williams, commemorating quarter century of SCS service to people.

June - Urbanization caused dissolution of Arcadia SCD, Arizona's smallest, located at south toe of Camelback Mountain in heart of growing residential and resort area.

July - Hugh Hammond Bennett, 79, died in North Carolina, July 7; buried in Arlington National Cemetary, July 12.

October - Board, meeting in Amarillo, TX, took no action on proposal by General Counsel Glick recommending fund-raising amendment to constitution providing for associate memberships in NASCD by individual residents of conservation districts.

1961

February - 15th annual meeting at Memphis, Feb. 5-9. Richards was re-elected President and W.A. Williams, Jr., New Mexico, was elected national Vice President. Monk was reappointed Treasurer.

Rev. E. W. Mueller, Secretary of Church in Town and Country for the National Lutheran Church, received NASCD's Distinguished Service Award.

New Auxiliary officers elected were Mrs. Charles Gotthard, Michigan, President; Mrs. James Setters, Washington, First Vice President; Mrs. Archie McIntosh, Illinois, Second Vice President; and Mrs. Oscar Hippe, Montana, Secretary-Treasurer.

Zimmerman distributed first copies of watershed newsletter, reported contributions of $1,000 from Oklahoma State Association and $700 from Arkansas State Association to help finance expanded watershed activities.

March - Graham Hollister, former Nevada State Association president, former state committee chairman, former NASCD Council member, district supervisor for 14 years, appointed special assistant to Interior Secretary Udall.

David Stewart became Service Department Assistant Manager.

Otis Tossett gave Directors first copies of NASCD history, "Land, Water & People."

NASCD and National Reclamation Association jointly sponsored National Water Research Symposium at Washington, D.C., March 28-30.

April - 8th National Watershed Congress, Tucson, AZ.

June - NASCD Business Advisory Committee formally organized at Chicago, June 15. Stanley Learned, Executive Committee Chairman and Assistant to President of Phillips Petroleum Co., elected Chairman.

1962

January - NASCD announced seven Philmont (New Mexico) training scholarships for B.S.A. Scoutmasters in each NASCD area in 1962.

February - 16th annual meeting at Philadelphia, Feb. 4-9. Secretary of Agriculture Orville L. Freeman, in keynote speech, asked conservation districts to update programs, enter into new cooperative agreements with USDA.

NASCD presented an oak tree as a gift to the Independence National Historical Park, and Secretary Freeman and Governor David Lawrence officiated at the planting ceremony.

Marion S. Monk, Jr., Louisiana, was elected President; Sam Studebaker, Ohio, national Vice President, and Max Wilson, California, was appointed Treasurer. Kent Leavitt, second President of NASCD, received the Distinguished Service Award.

Name changed to National Association of Soil and Water Conservation Districts, with NACD as the official abbreviation.

The Association of Past Presidents of State Associations of Soil Conservation Districts was officially organized. L. B. Casselman of Colorado was elected President, Cy Crawford of Minnesota, Secretary-Treasurer.

March - The Natural Resources Council of America, an organization of 37 scientific and conservation organizations, including NACD, sponsored banquet at National Press Club, Washington, D.C. on March 19, commemorating 25th anniversary of first conservation district in nation -- Brown Creek, N.C.

April - Southeastern Conservation District, North Carolina, first in nation to negotiate new agreement with USDA in response to Secretary Freeman's challenge at Philadelphia annual meeting.

May - Concurrent resolution adopted by Congress commemorating 25th anniversary of conservation districts, praising their accomplishments.

Clair Guess transferred to Washington office as Eastern Program Advisor; David Stewart named Service Department Manager and South Central Program Advisor.

June - 9th Annual Watershed Congress, Columbus, OH.

October - Davis Conservation Library dedicated, League City, Oct. 23.

1963

January - Southeastern district leaders celebrated 25th anniversary of nation's first cooperative agreement between a conservation district and a farmer-cooperator on farm of Mrs. Ploma M. Adams, Seneca, S.C. Agreement was signed February 4, 1938. Permanent marker placed on highway in front of Adams home.

February - 17th annual meeting at Denver, Feb. 3-7. Secretary of the Interior Stewart L. Udall was keynote speaker. The NACD constitution was amended to make Association of Past Presidents and Ladies Auxiliary affiliated organizations of NACD.

Auxiliary officers elected were Mrs. Gladys Hippe of Montana, President; Mrs. Melva Pancoast, Oklahoma, 1st Vice President; Mrs. Adeline Krenik, Minnesota, 2nd Vice President; and Mrs. Lucille Thompson, Louisiana, Secretary-Treasurer.

The Distinguished Service Award was presented to Susan Myrick, Associate Editor of the *Macon (GA) Telegraph*. The Right Reverend George J. Hildner of Missouri was given the NACD Special Service Citation.

March - Special monthly newsletter called "Report" launched for officers and directors, state association presidents, state commission administrative officers, and others to keep them informed on proposed legislation, other current issues.

May - 10th National Watershed Congress, Philadelphia, PA.

October - Massachusetts legislature broadened jurisdiction and responsibilities of conservation districts by empowering them to deal with conservation and development of natural resources, serve all citizens of the state, both town and country.

1964

January - Special Committee on District Outlook formed with John Wilder of Tennessee as Chairman. Members included NACD Directors R. Wally Petersen of Michigan and Raymond D. Shaffer of Pennsylvania, SCS members Norman A. Berg, Hollis Williams, Val Silkett, Darnell Whitt, and Harper Simms. NACD participants were Gordon Zimmerman, David Unger, Clair Guess and Phil Glick. Added later from state soil conservation agencies were William Greiner, Iowa; Ewing Kinkead, Arkansas; Art Darsey, California; and Grant Walton, New Jersey.

February - 18th annual meeting at Kansas City, Feb. 2-6. Orville L. Freeman was the keynote speaker and ex-President Harry Truman was the luncheon speaker. Three Governors, John Dalton of Missouri, John Anderson of Kansas and William Scranton of Pennsylvania, attended.

Monk and Studebaker were re-elected to office and John Wilder, Tennessee, was named Treasurer to succeed Max Wilson, who resigned.

Charles H. Stoddard, Director of the Bureau of Land Management, received the NACD Distinguished Service Award and Everett M. Barr of Nebraska, one of the 18 NACD

Founders was given the Special Service Award.

New Past Presidents Association officers elected were James R. Setters of Washington, President; Dan Sparks of Texas, Vice President; and W.S. Gibbs, Texas, Secretary-Treasurer.

March - Brazoria-Galveston Conservation District officially renamed Waters Davis Conservation District in honor of its Chairman from 1944 to 1958.

April - Nolen Fuqua named Watershed Man of the Year at the 11th National Watershed Congress, Little Rock, Ark.

Richard Longmire, Chairman of the Legislative Committee, and Milton Fricke, Chairman of the Watersheds & Water Resources Committee, testified before the House Appropriations Subcommittee and protested the Budget Bureau's proposed cutback on SCS funding for technical assistance to districts.

May - David G. Unger, for eight years Soil Conservation Director, Pennsylvania Department of Agriculture and Executive Secretary, State Soil and Water Conservation Commission, became NACD Assistant Executive Secretary.

October - Over 75,000 turned out for the Conservation Field Days and Plowing Matches in North Dakota.

1965

January - President's budget called for 20 percent cut in SCS technical assistance to conservation districts, 40 percent cut in ACP cost-sharing; and proposed a revolving fund through which districts and their cooperators would pay $20 million to federal government for technical assistance.

February - 19th annual meeting at Portland, Oregon, Feb. 7-11. Proposed revolving fund requiring payment for technical conservation services decried in speeches by Senator George McGovern, Oregon Governor Mark Hatfield, and A. Lars Nelson, National Grange. Sam Studebaker was re-elected Vice President.

Herb Plambeck, Farm Service Director for WHO, Des Moines, won the NACD Distinguished Service Award, and Frank Gyberg of Arizona, an NACD Founder, won the Special Service Award.

New publication, "America's Soil Conservation Districts," distributed.

Mrs. Gladys Hippe was re-elected President of the Auxiliary, Mrs. Adeline Krenik of Minnesota elected Vice President; Mrs. Thelma McClellan of Idaho, Secretary-Treasurer.

The Past Presidents named Dan Sparks of Texas, President; Thad Kinnaman, Kansas, Vice-President; and Robert Graf, Vermont, Secretary-Treasurer.

March - SCS reported 2.3 million acres damaged in January dust storm in the Great Plains, worst in 10 years.

Joiners in opposition to President's user fee-revolving fund proposal included National Grange, National Farmers Union, many State Farm Bureaus, American Forestry Association, National Wool Growers Association, state and local rural electric cooperatives, National Reclamation Association, Wildlife Management Institute.

Director Elmer E. Peterson, Oregon, received Soil Conservationist of the Year award from National Wildlife Federation.

The NACD Shore Erosion Committee, chaired by Walter Denny of Maryland, held its first meecommittees.

May - NACD was represented at the White House Conference on Natural Beauty, Washington, D.C., May 24-25.

October - The Board met in Nassau Bay, TX, and accepted the report and recommendations of the Special Committee on District Outlook.

1966

February - 20th annual meeting at New Orleans, Feb. 6-10. Sam S. Studebaker, Ohio, was elected President, John S. Wilder, Tennessee, Vice President; George Bagley, Louisiana, was appointed Treasurer.

The Council ratified the Outlook Committee's report.

William J. Klein, Vice President of the Allis-Chalmers Manufacturing Company, was given the NACD Distinguished Service Award and Nolen J. Fuqua, NACD Past President, Oklahoma, was awarded the Special Service Award.

The Past Presidents elected Thad Kinnaman, Kansas, President; Robert Graf, Vermont, Vice President; and Richard Thompson, Louisiana, Secretary-Treasurer.

Director Edward L. Felton, Virginia, received Soil Conservationist of the Year Award from National Wildlife Federation.

The 13th National Watershed Congress, meeting in Oklahoma City, named Elmer Smith of Caterpillar Tractor Company as Watershed Man of the Year.

Director Bob Graf tesified in support of successful legislation to allow SCS to provide soil surveys and interpretations in non-agricultural areas.

May - President Johnson appointed Executive Secretary Zimmerman to Citizens Advisory Commission on Recreation and Natural Beauty chaired by Laurance Rockefeller.

June - West Virginia's conservation districts and State Health Department signed memorandum of understanding, believed to be first of its kind in nation, agreeing to exchange information concerning public health aspects of recreational development, community planning, watershed development.

July - NACD reported 54 new agreements in 17 states between districts and Interior Department agencies, bringing total to 386 in 41 states, Puerto Rico.

August - Louisiana became first state to amend districts law in directions outlined by NACD District Outlook Committee.

September - Over 150,000 people attended the National Conservation Field Days and Plowing Matches at Jefferson, Iowa, September 8-9.

1967

February - 21st annual meeting at Cincinnati, Feb. 5-9. Secretary of Agriculture Orville L. Freeman was keynote speaker; gave the third in a series of Agriculture/2000 speeches outlining where American agriculture was going in the next 33 years. John Wilder was re-elected Vice President.

New officers for the Auxiliary were Mrs. Adeline Krenik, Minnesota, President; Mrs. Thelma McClellan, Idaho, Vice President; and Mrs. Glenda Bauer, Kansas, Secretary-Treasurer.

New officers for the Past Presidents were Robert Graf, Vermont, President; Richard Thompson, Louisiana, Vice President; and George S. Hartley, Massachusetts, Secretary-Treasurer.

The NACD Distinguished Service Award went to Herbert B. Eagon, Water Resources Coordinator, Corps of Engineers, Cincinnati, Ohio. Three Special Service Awards went to WLW Radio and TV, Cincinnati; J. W. "Wes" Cornwall of Washington, a delegate to the first NASCD meeting in 1947; and Daniel T. Paugh of West Virginia, an NASCD Founder.

A tentative organization of Executive Secretaries of State Soil & Water Conservation Committees was agreed upon at a meeting held during the convention

April - Monthly water resources newsletter and bi-monthly Great Plains newsletter absorbed by *Tuesday Letter*.

July - Clair Guess resigned as Eastern Program Advisor to become Executive Director of South Carolina Water Resources Board.

Philip Glick resigned as General Counsel to become Assistant Director for Policy and Legal Advisor of Federal Water Resources Council. John Heimberger, retired after serving as General Counsel to House Agriculture Committee, 1951-1966, retained as NACD General Counsel.

Joe Novak hired as Assistant Service Department Manager and Mrs. Shirley Parks as Librarian at League City.

October - The Board, meeting in Omaha, heard a report from Executive Secretary

Zimmerman on water pollution control and the role of districts in the effort.

1968

January - Director Lyle Bauer, Harper, Kansas, elected to Board of Governors, Agricultural Hall of Fame, Bonner Springs, Kansas.

February - 22nd annual meeting at Dallas, Feb. 4-8. Congressman Jim Wright was keynote speaker. Sam Studebaker was re-elected President, John Wilder was re-elected Vice President, and George Bagley was reappointed Secretary-Treasurer.

Officers elected for the Past Presidents were Richard Thompson, Louisiana, President; Sterlin Hurley, Arkansas, Vice President; and Edward L. Felton, Virginia, Secretary-Treasurer.

The Association of State Soil Conservation Administrative Officers was formally organized and elected Floyd Heft, Ohio, President. The basic purposes of the organization were to: (1) help strengthen conservation districts; (2) to help guide the executive secretaries of state committees in methods that would be more effective in helping districts; and, (3) to parallel the interests of NACD in strengthening communications which, in turn, would keep strong lines of liaison between districts through their state committees.

The Distinguished Service Award went to A. D. Holmes, Jr., of Alabama, a long-time NACD Director. Special Service Awards went to Walter A. Groom of Colorado and Ruel D. Conly of Louisiana, both NACD Founders. The first NACD Communications Award went to Walter R. Humphrey, Editor of the Fort Worth *Press*.

March - Area Vice President Richard C. Longmire, Oklahoma, Legislative Committee Chairman, selected for National Conservation Achievement Award in soil by National Wildlife Federation.

May - Enoch M. Olson, Brule - Buffalo SCD, South Dakota, operator of 1,120 acre farm, long-time district cooperator, became 30,000th participant in Great Plains Conservation Program.

July - President Johnson approved amendment to P.L. 566 Watershed Protection and Flood Prevention Act allowing Federal Government to provide contracting services in watershed projects if requested by local sponsors.

August - Malcolm P. Crooks, Executive Secretary, New Jersey State Soil Conservation Committee since 1966, appointed NACD Eastern Program Advisor, headquarters, New Hope, Pa., effective Sept. 1.

September - Secretary Freeman announced appointment of Kenneth E. Grant, SCS Associate Administrator, to succeed Administrator Don Williams, retired, effective in January.

October - Officers and Directors, meeting in Las Vegas, NV, began consideration of a Resources Agenda for the 70's suggested by Special Committee on District Outlook; approved schedule of seminars for state district leaders.

November - *Tuesday Letter*, Nov. 5, reported appropriations for conservation district work by state legislatures were $31.7 million, an increase of about 20 percent over previous year.

1969

January - All conservation district board members began receiving SCS monthly magazine, *Soil Conservation*.

February - 23rd annual meeting at Atlanta, Feb. 2-6. Herman E. Talmadge of Georgia was keynote speaker. John Wilder was re-elected Vice President.

The Council adopted "A Resources Agenda for the 70's" as presented by the Special Committee on District Outlook and directed the committee to carry out a new study of conservation districts to assess their growth, methods of operation, and needs for support from the national association. The Council also approved the concept of a Water Bank Program to compensate landowners who preserve wetlands.

The Auxiliary re-elected Adeline Krenik, Thelma McClellan and Glenda Bauer to the three top offices. The Past Presidents re-elected Richard Thompson, Sterlin Hurley, and

Edward Felton.

The Distinguished Service Award went to Victor Holt, Jr., President of Goodyear Tire & Rubber Co. NASCD founders William A. Benitt, R. Lester Hill and W. M. "Mack" Hodgson received NASCD Special Service Awards. The Communications Award went to Leland DuVall, farm and business editor of the *Arkansas Gazette.*

February - Feb. 25 *Tuesday Letter* reported contributions of funds and services to district programs from state, local, and private sources increased four-fold in last decade, amount to more than $95 million per year.

April - Ninety-six watershed projects, on shelf more than two years in dispute between Johnson administration and Congress, released on orders of President Nixon.

The 16th National Watershed Congress was held in Louisville, Kentucky.

June - Legislation to implement NACD's water bank proposal introduced by North Dakota's Senator Young and Rep. Mark Andrews.

July - Former NACD Counsel Philip Glick appointed General Counsel to National Water Commission.

National task force for private forest management, Trees for People, organized by NACD and American Forestry Association, Washington, D.C., June 18. Gordon Zimmerman and Malcolm Crooks represented NACD; Kenneth Pomeroy, AFA Chief Forestor, elected Chairman, Crooks, Secretary.

Lewis Merritt, Russ Reiff, and T L Meredith drafted an extensive position paper on public land issues that was submitted to the Public Land Law Review Commission.

Work began to identify sites for shore erosion control projects, as authorized under legislation that had been pushed hard by NACD's Shore Erosion Committee.

Director Donald Fraker won an American Motors Conservation Award. Gordon Zimmerman was elected Vice-Chairman of the Natural Resources Council of America.

September - NACD, National Association of Counties, and Soil Conservation Society of America sponsored First National Conference on Sediment Control at Washington, D.C., Sept. 14-16, attended by 300 invited conservation district and county officials and representatives of state agencies. Cooperators were USDA, HUD, and USDI.

Twenty-five minute color slide presentation, "With One Voice - The Story of NACD," became available for loan.

October - Nebraska legislature enacted bill to consolidate state's 150 soil and water conservation districts, watershed conservation districts, watershed districts, watershed advisory boards, watershed planning boards, mosquito abatement districts into 25-50 Natural Resource Districts, effective in 1972. Bill supported by Nebraska State Association.

November - President Nixon signed law extending Great Plains Conservation Program to Dec. 31, 1981 and broadening program. This law also included conservation districts by name and gave them added authority, a significant gain.

December - M.L. Wilson, former Assistant Secretary of Agriculture, generally considered originator of soil conservation districts idea, died.

1970

January - American Farm Bureau Federation policies for 1970 affirmed role of conservation districts as desirable approach to soil and water conservation, recommended larger share of federal water resource funds for small watershed projects under P.L. 566, and support of state farm bureaus for these programs.

February - 24th annual meeting at San Francisco, Feb. 1-5. John S. Wilder, Tennessee, was elected President; George R. Bagley, Louisiana, Vice President; and Lyle Bauer, Kansas, was appointed Treasurer.

Actor Eddie Albert, principal speaker, gave a strident environmental message that shocked many in attendance.

The Distinguished Service Award went to Clifford R. Hope of Kansas, former Chairman of the Committee on Agriculture in the U.S. House of Representatives. Francis C. Lindsay of California won the Special Service Award, and Ed Wilborn, Editor of *The Progressive Farmer,* won the Communications Award.

The name was changed from National Association of Soil and Water Conservation Districts to National Association of Conservation Districts.

Membership on Council changed from one representative of each state association to one representative from each state, commonwealth, and territorial association in order to clearly recognize Puerto Rico and the Virgin Islands on the Council.

Officers of the Association of State Administrative Officers were William H. Greiner, Iowa, President; Charley S. Staples, Louisiana, Vice President; Charles L. Boothby, Maine, Secretary; and Ole M. Ueland, Montana, Treasurer.

The Past Presidents elected Sterlin Hurley, Arkansas, President; Edward L. Felton, Virginia, Vice President; and Ray Shaffer, Pennsylvania, Secretary-Treasurer.

March - NACD issued leaflet "Environmental Action Guide" suggesting how people can work through conservation districts to improve the environment. Also issued were "Accelerating America's Watershed Program," and "America's Conservation Districts."

Board voted to set up an office for the Foundation in Washington Headquarters and change the name to the Conservation Districts Foundation, Inc.

April - Vice President Bagley named Soil Conservationist of the Year by the National Wildlife Federation.

Maryland enacted legislation, first of its kind in the nation, prohibiting disturbance of land for most construction purposes until an erosion control plan is approved by the local conservation district.

First Earth Day, called "Environmental Teach-In," observed April 22.

May - New Iowa act incorporated all cities and towns in conservation districts and gave department status to State Soil Conservation Committee, renaming it Iowa Department of Soil Conservation. Also provided that any voter can nominate, vote for and serve as commissioner, a privilege previously limited to landowners.

NACD sponsored regional District Leadership Seminars in New Hampshire, Missouri, Montana, Texas, Nevada and West Virginia to discuss key issues with district leaders and officials of state soil conservation agencies. Mary Garner, USDA, reported that over 100 new state laws had been passed in 40 states in the five-year period since the District Outlook Committee had urged district leaders to seek such changes.

June - 17th National Watershed Congress held in Denver, Colorado.

August - Past President Sam Studebaker elected to Ohio Agricultural Hall of Fame.

NACD broke new ground by participating in a request for a grant from the Federal Water Quality Administration to help conduct a series of 25 Sediment Control Institutes with the National Association of Counties.

December - NACD changed its quota basis, effective January 1, to $150 per year for each district and $200 per year for each state association. Previous quotas were on a sliding scale based on number of cooperators in each district, from $60.50 to $302.50 per year.

Water Bank Act, P.L. 91-599, long sought by district leaders, signed by President Nixon. Law provides reimbursement to landowners in the pot hole country who refrain from draining valuable waterfowl habitat through long-term contracts with USDA based on conservation plans approved by local conservation districts. It was the second piece of national legislation to specifically mention conservation districts as an integral part of the functioning of the program.

1971

January - "History of the Soil Conservation Service" by D. Harper Simms, published.
NACD published 16-page brochure, "Guide to Conservation Careers."

February - 25th annual meeting at Chicago, Feb. 7-11. Clifford M. Hardin, Secretary of Agriculture, was keynote speaker. The Annual Luncheon featured a live radio broadcast by Orien Samuelson of Station WGN, Chicago. George Bagley was re-elected Vice President.

The Auxiliary elected Mrs. Thelma McClellan, Idaho, President; Mrs. Glenda Bauer, Kansas, Vice President; and Mrs. Wilma Garman, Michigan, Secretary-Treasurer.

The twenty-fifth anniversary of NACD was featured at the annual banquet with a historical documentary illustrated with film, color slides, recordings and talks by Past

Presidents Leavitt, Fuqua, Richards, Monk, and Studebaker. A plaque commemorating the work of the NASCD founders was presented by the Past Presidents of State Associations for placement in Davis Conservation Library, League City, TX.

Philip M. Glick was the recipient of the Distinguished Service Award, Marion S. Monk, Jr., received the Special Service Award, and Carl E. Carlson, *Colorado Rancher and Farmer,* was presented the Communications Award.

The Council approved the long-range program, "NACD in the Seventies - Goals and Objectives," as proposed by the Board. This program proposed new emphasis on communications, NACD staff support to committees and affiliated organizations, and a continuation of the effort to strengthen districts through the approaches set forth by the District Outlook Committee.

Vice President George Bagley was named Louisiana Man of the Year by *Progressive Farmer* magazine.

March - Goodyear CAP celebrates 25 years.

April - Milton H. Fricke, Papillion, Neb., former NACD Water Resources Committee Chairman, received Army's Patriotic Civilian Service Award for pioneering work in soil and water conservation developments.

May - Oklahoma revised state enabling act establishing conservation districts as primary local unit of government responsible for renewable natural resources and reconstituting State Board as Oklahoma Conservation Commission.

Robert C. Baum, Director of the Oregon State Soil and Water Commission since 1952, appointed NACD Program Advisor for Pacific area, with headquarters in Portland, effective in July.

June - Soil Stewardship Week proclaimed most successful yet. Material requested: 251,000 church program blanks; 621,000 church bulletin covers; 2,287,000 church program inserts; 562,000 place mats; 11,000 posters; 644,000 copies of litany.

The Auxiliary conducted a major project to distribute conservation curriculum guides to schools in cooperation with the National Council of State Garden Clubs.

The House rejected, 278 to 129, amendment to appropriations act proposed by Rep. Henry Reuss, Wisconsin, to withhold P.L. 566 watershed funds for projects involving channel work.

The 18th Annual Watershed Congress was held in Tampa, FL.

July - A special memorial ceremony in Gaffney, S.C., honored E. C. McArthur on the 25th anniversary of NACD's founding and erected a roadside monument as a permanent memorial.

New act in Iowa increased the responsibilties of the state's 100 conservation districts greatly by authorizing them to establish regulations governing erosion control and to establish soil loss limits.

The new NACD quota system made it possible for several national committees to hold summer meetings for the first time in many years.

September - NACD Service Department inaugurated a new film rental service featuring 2,000 prints of 150 of the nation's best conservation sound movies obtained from SCS, which dropped its regional film libraries for budgetary reasons.

October - NACD Executive Secretary Zimmerman was elected Chairman of Natural Resources Council of America, a federation of private organizations including NACD.

David L. Firor, President of Georgia State Association, became NACD Program Advisor for Southeastern and South Central areas, with headquarters at Athens, Georgia.

David Stewart, former South Central Area Program Advisor, was reassigned to spend full time as Manager of Service Department at League City, TX.

Mrs. Florence Kemmerer became Librarian of Waters Davis Conservation Library, succeeding Mrs. Shirley Parks, now working full time in Service Separtment.

Malcolm Crooks was named Director of Development, with the assignment to seek outside funds such as grants to help finance NACD projects or build the Foundation's funding base.

1972

January - Latest count: 3,027 CD's covering 1,824,400 ac.

February - Annual meeting at Washington, D.C., Feb. 13-17, first time in nation's capitol, marked by the largest attendance to date, total registration 2,275. Wilder, Bagley and Bauer were re-elected to NACD's top offices.

Hon. Jamie Whitten of Mississippi, Chairman of the Subcommittee on Agriculture, Environmental and Consumer Protection of the House Committee on Appropriations, was the principal banquet speaker and recipient of NACD's Distinguished Service Award.

Over 1,200 NACD women were entertained at White House tea by Mrs. David Eisenhower substituting for her mother, Mrs. Richard Nixon, an event sponsored by NACD Ladies Auxiliary. Thelma McClellan presented Mrs. Eisenhower with a sheath of red carnations, the NACD official flower, as a gift of the Auxiliary.

The Past Presidents elected Edward L. Felton, President; Raymond Shaffer, Vice President; and Ervin J.J. Koos, Iowa, Secretary-Treasurer.

Milton Fricke of Nebraska won the Special Service Award and Barry Bingham, publisher of the *Courier-Journal* and *Louisville Times,* won the Communications Award.

NACD Director William Bosse of Cogswell, N.D. was appointed to National Water Bank Advisory Board to advise USDA concerning the new program to preserve waterfowl habitat by reimbursing landowners who refrain from draining valuable wetlands.

March - NACD Executive Secretary Zimmerman appointed to Secretary of State's advisory committee on the 1972 United Nations Conference on the Human Environment.

April - Robert S. McClelland, NACD Program Advisor since June, 1957, retired, and was succeeded by Marvin Cronberg, for past four years Executive Secretary of Wyoming Conservation Commission.

Effective April 17, William J. Horvath, Executive Secretary of the Wisconsin State Soil Conservation Board, formerly a field representative of the Pennsylvania State Soil and Water Conservation Commission and Executive Secretary of the Maryland State Soil Conservation Committee, became NACD Program Advisor for the Upper Mississippi states of Illinois, Indiana, Iowa, Michigan, Minnesota Missouri, Ohio, and Wisconsin, with headquarters at Stevens Point, Wisc.

Fifty-five counties in 13 states had been selected to participate in the Water Bank Program: 15 in North Dakota; 10 in Minnesota; 12 in South Dakota; six in Montana; two each in Wisconsin, California and Nebraska; one each in Louisiana, Maine, Oregon, Mississippi, Washington, and Vermont.

June - NACD Director Richard Longmire of Oklahoma, Chairman of Legislative Coordination Committee, named Watershed Man of the Year at 19th National Watershed Congress, San Diego, June 4-7.

First in a series of State Sediment Control Institutes sponsored by NACD/EPA held in Salina, KS. Nine of these institutes were held during the year.

October - Study conducted by Mary M. Garner, USDA Office of General Counsel, showed CD's had strengthened capabilities through changes in state laws.

Thelma McClellan reported that the Auxiliary had assisted in distributing over 150,000 copies of *People and Their Environment,* the environmental education curriculum guides published by the Ferguson Publishing Company.

A building fund was established to seek $100,000 to finance enlargement of the Service Department facility in League City, TX.

December - Project SOAR (Save Our American Resources), sponsored by Boy Scouts of America, included NACD as co-sponsor.

1973

January - Administration proposed to abolish REAP cost-sharing and the Water Bank Program.

NACD protested proposed EPA guidelines on point source pollution in relation to agriculture.

February - 27th Annual Convention, Las Vegas, NV. William D. Ruckelshaus, Administrator of the Environmental Protection Agency, was keynote speaker. George Bagley was re-elected Vice President and Lyle Bauer was elected Treasurer under new bylaw provisions that provided for two-year terms.

Thelma McClellan, Glenda Bauer, and Wilma Garman were re-elected to Auxiliary leadership. In the Past Presidents Association, Edward Felton, Raymond Shaffer and Ervin J.J. Koos were re-elected.

Mary M. Garner, USDA Office of General Counsel, was awarded the Distinguished Service Award. Charles M. Ladd of North Carolina won the Special Service Award and Ernest Douglas, *Arizona Farmer-Ranchman,* won the Communications Award.

George Bagley delivered the keynote address at "National Conference on Conservation Tillage," March 28-30, in Des Moines.

April - Kent Leavitt, 2nd President, died.

May - EPA outlined proposed criteria for agricultural operations, requiring permits for discharges to streams; NACD protested the inclusion of drainage outlets, diversion terraces, channels and ditches as point sources that would have required permits.

June - 20th National Watershed Congress, Wichita, KS

NACD initiated an international travel program "Contours," with a tour of Europe and Russia.

NACD testified in favor of H.R. 1904 "Forestry Incentives Act of 1973," said "incentive is key to upgrading America's privately-owned non-industrial forests."

July - Senate approved increases for technical assistance and cost-sharing, called for restoration of cutbacks in personnel assisting districts.

August - NACD prepared to conduct the first nationwide inventory of private and semi-private outdoor recreation facilities.

September - Slide show "With One Voice - The Story of NACD" produced and made available for use.

October - The Board changed several staff titles. The Executive Secretary became the Executive Vice President, and the Assistant Executive Secretary became the Executive Secretary. The Program Advisor title was changed to Regional Representative.

December - Butz proposed consolidation of 8,000 USDA offices into a far fewer number of "USDA Service Centers."

1974

January - USDA agreed, at NACD urging, to consider Conservation Districts' needs in USDA Service Centers.

February - 28th Annual Convention, Houston, TX, Feb. 10-14, 1974. Representative W.R."Bob" Poage of Texas and Secretary of Agriculture Earl L. Butz were keynoters. George Bagley of Louisiana was elected President; Lyle Bauer of Kansas, Vice President; and T L Meredith of Arizona, Treasurer.

W.R. "Bob" Poage won the Distinguished Service Award. Sam S. Studebaker and William E. Richards, Past Presidents, won Special Service Awards. Orion Samuelson, Station WGN, Chicago, won the Communications Award.

The addition to the Service Department was dedicated in special ceremonies, and hundreds of district officials got to visit their Service Department for the first time.

The Past Presidents elected Ray Shaffer, Pennsylvania, President; Ervin J.J. Koos, Iowa, Vice President; and Milton Fricke, Nebraska, Secretary-Treasurer.

President Nixon proposed merger of GPCP with RECP; NACD testified against that proposal and stopped it.

April - Federal reorganization proposed: SCS & FS would be moved to a new Department of Energy and Natural Resources; NACD opposed, the Administration backed down.

June - 21st National Watershed Congress, Pittsburg, PA.

The House killed the Udall Land Use Bill; NACD supported the House action.

July - NACD and six other national organizations sponsored a National Conference on

Flood Plain Management, Washington, D.C.

NACD and Allis-Chalmers Co. began a new Environmental Conservation Education Awards Program to recognize conservation districts and teachers who have outstanding programs.

NACD coordinated a district-by-district inventory of private recreation facilities, the first comprehensive survey of this kind.

August - NACD opposed additional wildlife coordination provisions in federal water resource programs.

House restored funds for ACP, WB, & GPCP; also increased funds for personnel in SCS, as requested by NACD.

September - NACD studied principle occupation of district officials, as part of District Outlook study.

The Phillips Petroleum Company, working through the Business Advisory Committee, prepared a new logo for NACD and Conservation Districts.

October - President Ford signed the "Forest and Rangeland Renewable Resources Planning Act of 1974."

The Board, meeting in Spokane, accepted the new NACD logo design.

George M. Cason, Jr., League City, TX, named NACD General Counsel.

November - Bill Bosse, NACD Director from North Dakota, represented NACD on National RECP Advisory Board.

The series of 40 State Sediment Control Institutes held in cooperation with EPA was completed.

December - USDA proposed designation of 1,000 Ag Service Centers by July, 1975.

1975

February - 29th Annual Convention, Denver, CO, February 2-6, 1975. Senator Gale McGee of Wyoming was keynoter and recipient of NACD Distinguished Service Award.

Edward L. Felton of Virginia received the Special Service Award and Lynn Adair, Farm News Director for KSL-TV and Radio, Salt Lake City, won the Communications Award. A new award, the Business Conservation Leadership Award, was presented to the Goodyear Tire and Rubber Company.

The first NACD-Allis Chalmers Environmental Conservation Education Awards were presented by P.T. Eubanks, Chairman of the NACD Education Committee, and Charles W. Parker, Jr., Vice President of Allis-Chalmers Corporation.

The Auxiliary elected Mrs. Glenda Bauer, Kansas, President; Mrs. Jessie Chambers, Colorado, Vice-President; and Mrs. Peg Jones, Kentucky, Secretary-Treasurer. Mrs. Darlie Britton was appointed Historian.

The Association of State Soil Conservation Administrative Officers elected Sam Race, New Jersey, President; Bud Svalberg, Oregon, Vice President; W. C. Gayle, Secretary; and Walter Peechatka, Pennsylvania, Treasurer.

March - Rep. Udall introduced new version of land use bill, H.R. 3150.

NACD Board adopted long-range development program.

April - NACD urged Appropriations Subcommittee to appropriate $1 million to begin implementing the "Shore Erosion Demonstration Act of 1974."

NACD requested that federal funds be made available for conservation district programs before House Appropriations Subcommittee on Agriculture.

June - R. M. "Mel" Davis was named 5th SCS Administrator, replacing Kenneth Grant who retired.

July - "Land and Water Resource Conservation Act of 1975" introduced in Senate (S. 2081) to upgrade attention to land and water conservation.

September - New sediment control manpower project began in NACD, under an EPA grant. Project Director was Robert E. Williams, formerly Assistant to the Adminstrator of SCS for Environmental Development.

Tuesday Letter carried major series on "Districts and Nonpoint Pollution Control."

October - Sam Chinn of California was elected Treasurer, replacing T L Meredith. The

Board, facing a deficit in 1975, voted to raise quotas from $150 to $200 per district and from $200 to $250 per state association.

NACD published a history of the Past Presidents Association, entitled *Many Hundred Strong . . . Still Serving,* compiled by Robert McClelland.

December - EPA published a memorandum supporting the role of conservation districts in nonpoint source pollution control.

President Ford asked for $36 million deletion from conservation program budgets. House rejected recission proposal.

1976

February - The 30th Annual Convention in Honolulu, HI, February 1-6, was the largest ever, drawing over 3,000. Governor George Ariyoshi and USDA Assistant Secretary Robert W. Long were the keynoters.

The Distinguished Service Award went to Warren D. Fairchild, Director of the U.S. Water Resources Council, the Special Service Award went to Robert J. Bowers of North Carolina, the Communications Award went to Ben R. Leonard, Farm News Director of WFBC-TV and Radio of Greenville, South Carolina, and the Business Conservation Leadership Award was presented to the Eaton Corporation of Marshall, Michigan.

The Past Presidents elected Ervin J.J. Koos, Iowa, President; Milton Fricke, Nebraska, Vice President; and Lewis Merritt, New Mexico, Secretary-Treasurer.

The State Administrative Officers elected Sam Race of New Jersey, President; Charles McKee, Indiana, Vice President; Walter Peechatka, Pennsylvania, Secretary; and Gary Puppe, North Dakota, Treasurer.

The Auxiliary began a project entitled "Our Natural Neighborhood," encouraging auxiliaries to begin a natural resource assessment of their communities with the goal of spurring local interest in resource development projects.

April - NACD received a grant from EPA to encourage conservation district involvement in 208 water quality planning.

May - Butz policy memo strengthened role of CD's in ACP & Title X of the 1972 Farm Bill.

August - NACD Executive Secretary David Unger named Fellow by SCSA.

October - President Ford vetoed Agricultural Resources Conservation Act of 1976 (S. 2081). Bill was NACD's top legislative priority.

Gordon Zimmerman retired; David Unger named Executive Vice President; Charles Boothby of Maine named Executive Secretary.

NACD experienced its best financial year in history, with an excess of income over expenses of $170,000. Several contributing factors were the response of districts to the quota increase, the financial success of the Honolulu convention (including some NACD-arranged travel packages), high net profits in the Service Department aided by the bicentennial year celebration, and large jump in special project income.

1977

January - The NACD President's Club was established to recognize substantial contributors to NACD Endowment Fund. Twenty-five people were recognized in Atlanta as charter members who had given $1,000 or more to the Endowment Fund.

Robert Raschke of South Dakota, formerly Manager of the Oahe Conservancy Sub-District, was named Western Regional Representative for NACD. His experience included work with U.S. Forest Service and SCS in Oregon and South Dakota.

February - The 31st Annual Convention was held in Atlanta, GA, February 6-11. Senator Herman E. Talmadge of Georgia was keynoter and recipient of the Distinguished Service Award.

Special Service Awards went to Gordon K. Zimmerman and A.L. Black of Texas. Morris G. Hallock, newspaper publisher in South Dakota, received the Communications Award and the Caterpillar Tractor Company received the Business Conservation Leadership Award.

NACD received the Dr. William F. Hornaday Conservation Trust Award for its work in conservation education.

Sue Wilkinson, NACD Director of Accounting, and Saul Balderas, Foreman, were honored for 25 years of service to NACD.

The Auxiliary elected Mrs. Glenda Bauer, Kansas, President; Mrs. Peg Jones, Kentucky, Vice President; and Mrs. Catherine Trubschenck, California, Secretary-Treasurer.

The State Administrative Officers elected Charles McKee, Indiana, President; Walter Peechatka, Pennsylvania, Vice President; Gary Puppe, North Dakota, Secretary; and Doyle Scott, Idaho, Treasurer.

March - NACD completed study of erosion and sediment control programs in six states.

Report published on manpower needs for administering erosion and sediment control programs (SCAMP).

May - The publication "Conservation District Involvement in Water Quality Management," prepared under EPA-funded special project, was released.

October - NACD published first full scale inventory of private-sector recreational facilities.

Sam Studebaker, NACD's 7th President, died.

Jim Lake of Indiana joined NACD staff as water quality specialist with NACD-EPA special project.

November - Congress included Rural Clean Water Program in amendments to P.L. 92-500 (Culver Amendment).

President Carter signed Soil & Water Resources Conservation Act of 1977 (P.L. 95-192).

1978

January - Victor E. Muniec of Connecticut was hired as NACD Director of Communications, stationed in Washington, D.C.

February - The 32nd Annual Convention was held at Anaheim, CA, February 5-9, 1978. Senator John Culver of Iowa and Douglas M. Costle, Administrator of the Environmental Protection Agency, were keynote speakers. Lyle Bauer, Kansas, was elected President; Milton E. "Bud" Mekelburg, Colorado, Vice President; and Sam Chinn, California, Secretary-Treasurer.

David G. Unger, Executive Vice President, announced his resignation to accept a position as Deputy Assistant Secretary of Agriculture for Natural Resources and Environment.

Revised bylaws were adopted, establishing a limit of two 3-year terms for Directors; two 2-year terms for President and Vice President; no limit on 2-year terms for Secretary-Treasurer.

The Distinguished Service Award went to Donald A. McAllister, International Harvester Company, Chicago; and the Special Service Award was awarded to Richard C. Longmire of Oklahoma. Marvin L. Perry, Jr., of KTBS-TV, Shreveport, Louisiana, won the Communications Award and the Big Stone Power Plant, Big Stone City, South Dakota, won the Business Conservation Leadership Award.

The Past Presidents elected Hugh Jones, Kentucky, President; Milton Fricke, Nebraska, Vice President; and Lewis Merritt, New Mexico, Secretary-Treasurer.

April - R. Neil Sampson, formerly SCS employee in Washington Office and State of Idaho, was hired as Executive Vice President.

Tuesday Letter was changed in format from a 2-page, "Letter from the President" style to a 4-page, "newsletter" style. The first 3 pages began being written as a national soil conservation newsletter, with the back page being the President's editorial page.

June - An NACD President's Select Task Force was formed to study connections between agricultural policy and natural resource issues.

The 25th -- and final -- National Watershed Congress was held in Toronto.

July - An NACD Task Force chaired by Vice President Mekelburg developed two publications to provide ideas for developing and updating state and district long-range programs.

August - The first International Rangeland Congress was held in Denver, CO, with NACD as co-sponsor.

The first NACD Leadership Conference was held in League City, TX.

October - NACD received 2nd year funding from EPA to continue 208 nonpoint source education and training program.

November - The American Land Forum was established, with Executive Vice President Neil Sampson as a member of Board of Directors.

1979

February - The 33rd Annual Convention in Washington, D.C., February 10-14, had Secretary of Agriculture Bob Bergland and Congressman Thomas S. Foley of Washington as keynote speakers.

The "Conservation Tree," a Green Mountain Sugar Maple, was presented to the people of America by NACD. It was planted near the Jefferson Memorial with a soil sample from each of the 52 states and territories to nourish it.

"A Resources Agenda for the 80's," as developed by the Special Committee on District Outlook, was adopted by the Council.

Senator John Culver of Iowa won the Distinguished Service Award and Dave J. Doneen of Washington won the Special Service Award. The Communication Award went to Robert G. Rupp, Editor of *The Farmer* magazine, and the McIlhenny Company of Avery Island, Louisiana, won the Business Conservation Leadership Award.

The Auxiliary elected Mrs. Peg Jones, Kentucky, President; Mrs. Lucille Thompson, Louisiana, Vice President; and Mrs. Agnes Wilson, Secretary-Treasurer.

The Past Presidents retained Hugh Jones as President and elected Dwight Spuller, Michigan, Vice President; and A.K. McCalla, Tennessee, Secretary-Treasurer.

The State Administrative Officers elected Gary Puppe, North Dakota, President; Leonard Solomon, Oklahoma, Vice President; Charles Liles, Oregon, Secretary; and Stanley Head, Kentucky, Treasurer.

March - A Multi Association/Society meeting in Denver, CO, reached agreement on 10 rangeland issues that form the core of NACD's Pasture and Range Improvement Program.

The Board created a Special Committee on Urban Conservation in response to Council request.

May - NACD publicized the results of the 1977 National Resource Inventories completed by SCS in a special series in *Tuesday Letter*.

October - NACD opened a 3,500 square-foot warehouse addition to the Service Department.

November - NACD, SCSA and USDA co-sponsored the "Conference on Soil Conservation Policies" in Washington, D.C., Nov. 15-16.

1980

January - A national poll conducted by the Louis Harris organization, found widespread public support for soil and water conservation, including expenditure of additional public monies.

February - The 34th Annual Convention was held in Houston, TX, February 10-14. Jane Yarn, Council on Environmental Quality, and Jim Williams, Deputy Secretary of Agriculture, were the keynote speakers.

Actor Eddie Albert spoke at Film Night about soil erosion and its threat to civilization.

The Distinguished Service Award was presented to Floyd E. Heft of Ohio, and Special Service Awards were given to John Wilder of Tennessee and Doyle Hutcheson of Texas. A Special Honor Award was presented to Gordon Zimmerman at the Inspirational Meeting in honor of his 21 years of authorship of the annual Soil Stewardship booklet.

R. M. "Mel" Davis, former SCS Administrator, was presented with a Special NACD Award. Michael Garner, Editor of the Des Moines *Register* was the winner of the Communications Award and Pennsylvania Power and Light Company won the Business Conservation Leadership Award.

Gordon Zimmerman, former Executive Vice President, was selected for the Natural Resource Council of America's "Award of Honor for 1979."

March - NACD entered into a joint agreement with the Association of State Soil Conservation Administrative Officers and the SCS to evaluate the progress in the development of state soil and water conservation programs, and help assist the states in that process.

April - Robert S. McClelland, former NACD Regional Representative, died in Denver.

May - The Great Plains Conservation Program was extended until September 30, 1991.

July - NACD produced a slide-tape presentation entitled "Hazardous Wastes" for distribution to states and districts.

NACD issued a report on new legislative changes and new conservation programs in Georgia, Idaho, Iowa, Kansas, Missouri, Montana and New Jersey.

Charlotte Nichols joined NACD as Director of Communications, replacing Victor Muniec, who had resigned.

1981

January - Eugene Lamb, formerly with Florida Dept of Agriculture, joined NACD staff as State Programs Specialist, working with joint agreement between SCS, NASCA & NACD.

Sam Chinn, NACD Secretary-Treasurer, received the U.S. Forest Service's 75th Anniversary Award for his outstanding service and contribution to conservation and forestry.

February - The 35th Annual Convention was held in San Francisco, CA, February 1-5. Robert J. Gray and Fred Winthrop were the keynote speakers.

The Board consolidated the Education and Youth Programs Committees into one committee, and established a new Information and Communications Committee.

H. Wayne Pritchard, retired Executive Vice President of SCSA, was awarded the Distinguished Service Award and Stanley R. Christensen of Oregon won the Special Service Award. In two new awards categories initiated in 1981, T. Ed Garrison of South Carolina was presented with the NACD Special Recognition Award and Dr. Maurice K. Goddard, Pennsylvania, received the NACD Professional Service Award. Thomas W. Sharp, Green Forest, Arkansas, won the Communications Award and the Drummond Coal Company, Jasper, Alabama, won the Business Conservation Leadership Award.

NACD's new film "Your Land, My Land, Our Water," narrated by Eddie Albert, was premiered during Showtime. The film was produced by NACD with a supporting grant from the Environmental Protection Agency through the Black Creek Project, sponsored by the Allen County SWCD in Indiana.

The Past Presidents elected Charles Ladd, North Carolina, President; William Bosse, North Dakota, Vice President; and A.K. McCalla, Tennessee, Secretary-Treasurer.

The Auxiliary elected Mrs. Peg Jones, Kentucky, President; Mrs. Lucille Thompson, Louisiana, Vice President; and Mrs. Renie Adams, California, Secretary-Treasurer. They presented the first "Woman of the Year" award to Carolyn Oglesby, Mississippi.

Vice President M.E. "Bud" Mekelburg addressed the National Agricultural Lands Conference in Chicago.

March - The Soil Conservation Act of 1981 (H.R. 2261) introduced by Reps. Ed Jones (TN) and Jim Jeffords (VT).

Gordon K. Zimmerman, former NACD Executive Vice President who opened the Washington office in 1958, died after a prolonged illness.

President Lyle Bauer testified on 1981 Farm Bill before Senate Committee on Agriculture, Nutrition and Forestry.

May - EPA approved $750,000 in funds for No-Till demonstration projects, managed by districts, in 3 states.

June - The Supreme Court upheld the Surface Mine Reclamation Law in a major victory for agricultural and soil conservation interests.

July - Bob Baum, NACD Pacific Regional Representative, was named President of SCSA.

NACD completed study and paper for EPA on "The Role of Conservation Districts and the Agricultural Community in Cleaning up America's Lakes."

August - The Great Plains Conservation Program celebrated its 25th Anniversary.

September - Farmland or Wasteland: A Time to Choose, by Neil Sampson, was published by Rodale Press.

October - The Board established a quota of $375 per district and state association for 1982.

1982

January - Final version of 1981 Farm Bill passes Congress. Major conservation title contains several new programs formulated or supported by NACD, including Grants to States and Districts, Farmland Protection Policy, Special Areas Conservation Program, Volunteers in Conservation, Resource Conservation and Development, Loans for Soil Conservation, and others.

February - The 36th Annual Convention was held in Phoenix, AZ, February 7-11, 1982. Secretary of Agriculture John Block addressed the banquet session.

Milton E. "Bud" Mekelburg, Colorado, was elected President, Clarence Durban, Ohio, Vice President; and Sam Chinn, California, was re-elected Secretary-Treasurer.

George M. Cason, Jr., announced his resignation as General Counsel, in order to spend more time on private and family matters.

The Distinguished Service Award was presented to Senator Robert J. Dole of Kansas and the Special Service Award went to Ervin J.J. Koos of Iowa. Leonard E. Solomon of Oklahoma won the Professional Service Award, Mary Roesner, Farm Editor of the *Daily Dispatch,* Moline, Illinois, won the Communications Award, and the Colowyo Coal Company of Meeker, Colorado, won the Business Conservation Leadership Award.

The Past Presidents elected William Bosse, North Dakota, President; William Sullivan, North Carolina, Vice President; and John Snider, Washington, Secretary-Treasurer.

The State Administrative Officers elected Stanley Head, Kentucky, President; Eugene Savage, Wisconsin, Vice President; Larry Vance, Ohio, Secretary; and Herman Bowers, Florida, Treasurer.

President Mekelburg named a task force to study NACD operations and bring recommendations for change to the Board and Council. It was chaired by Vice President Durban and consisted of Directors James Bellamy, Betty Broemmelsiek, William Chamberlain, James W. "Bill" Harrison, Robert Lewis, Charles O'Neill and Warren Patefield.

Past President Lyle Bauer was named to the National Advisory Council on Rural Development.

May - NACD testified before Senate Ag Committee in favor of S.1825, the "Sodbuster Bill."

June - The National Endowment for Soil and Water Conservation was formed by group of private industries and organizations, in cooperation with Members of Congress.

August - NACD helped co-sponsor the National Congress for Environmental Education.

The 5th Annual NACD Leadership Conference was held in Wheeling, West Virginia, August 25-27.

George R. Bagley, NACD Past President, received the Hugh Hammond Bennett Award from the SCSA.

NACD received a $50,000 grant from the Joyce Foundation to establish the Conservation Tillage Information Center. James Lake was named to head the CTIC Field Office in Fort Wayne.

November - NACD produced and released a television PSA (public service announcement) taken from one originally designed by the Iowa Department of Soil Conservation.

December - Bruce Julian of SCS was detailed to Fort Wayne office to assist with CTIC staffing.

1983

January - The Conservation Tillage Information Center opened for operation January 1; published its first newsletter in mid-January, with Sara Ebenreck, consultant, as Editor.

February - The 37th Annual Convention was held in New Orleans, LA, February 6-10,

1983. Governor Allen Olson of North Dakota was keynote speaker.

Senator Jennings Randolph of West Virginia won the Distinguished Service Award and Monroe Samuel of Arkansas was the winner of the Special Service Award. NACD Special Recognition Awards were presented to Ray Oviatt, Director of the Goodyear Conservation Awards Program and to The Joyce Foundation of Chicago, Illinois. The Communications Award went to Gay Cook of the *Denver Post,* the Professional Service Award was presented to William R. Ratledge of Delaware, and the Business Conservation Leadership Award was given to the Chevron Chemical Company.

The first NACD Youth Board Contest winner was recognized, with the Newberry SCD Youth Board of Newberry, South Carolina, receiving the top prize of $500. This contest is sponsored by the Education and Youth Committee, with the financial support for the prizes coming from the NACD Auxiliary.

Showtime featured "The Price of Abundance," a film produced by the Shawnee RC&D of Illinois, which was narrated by Eddie Albert and carried significant segments featuring NACD Director Hillard Morris of Illinois and Executive Vice President Neil Sampson.

The Auxiliary elected Mrs. Lucille Thompson, Louisiana, President; Mrs. Renie Adams, California, Vice President; and Mrs. Carolyn Oglesby, Mississippi, Secretary-Treasurer.

The State Administrative Officers elected Larry Vance, Ohio, President; Herman Bowers, Florida, Vice President; Vernon Reinert, Minnesota, Secretary; and Wayne Reid, Washington, Treasurer.

The Past Presidents started a "seed money" program for the Endowment Fund. If any state association raises $900 toward a President's Club membership, the PPA will add $100.

March - CTIC completed the first survey of conservation tillage practices in the United States, providing state-level data on five defined tillage types.

Director Warren Suchovsky of Michigan was appointed to the Secretary of the Interior's Council on Protecting Our Wetlands and Duck Resources.

April - NACD testified before the Senate Agriculture Appropriations Subcommittee to urge funding for conservation programs, including grants to states and districts.

NACD testified in favor of S. 663, the "Sodbuster Bill."

Tuesday Letter received the 1983 "Best Newsletter" award and *Farmland or Wasteland* was chosen "Outstanding Book" for 1983 by the NRCA Awards Program.

July - After a considerable effort on the part of NACD, the Postmaster General, William Bolger, issued a clear decision making conservation districts eligible to qualify for special third class bulk postage rates. This decision will mean many dollars to districts who have a regularly published newsletter.

August - The 6th Annual NACD Leadership Conference was held at Traverse City, Michigan, August 17-19.

In cooperation with SCS, NACD produced a booklet "50 Ways to Celebrate the 50th Anniversary of Soil and Water Conservation."

Hurricane Alicia hit League City, TX, and the Service Department suffered $53,000 in damages to the roof, windows, carpets, drapes and trees.

September - James Bauder began work as Extension Liaison with the CTIC, in the NACD Washington office.

October - The Board met in League City, TX, and charged the District Outlook Committee with conducting an extensive survey of conservation district authorities, programs, and priorities both now and for the future.

The joint agreement between NACD, NASCA, and SCS was re-negotiated for another year, with the principle task for 1984 to be the survey of conservation districts, district officials, and state soil conservation agencies being undertaken by the District Outlook Committee.

The first travel project under the new NACD-GTU International Travel Program went to the People's Republic of China under the leadership of Robert Baum.

NACD President Bud Mekelburg participated in a Roundtable discussion at Agriculture Secretary John Block's farm in Illinois.

November - Willard Snyder was hired as CTIC Director, stationed in the Washington office of NACD.

December - Director Betty Broemmelsiek and husband Jack of Missouri became the first Life Members of the NACD President's Club when they gave a donation raising their total contributions to $10,000.

At year's end, the Endowment Fund was nearing the $250,000 goal that had been established for this year by Secretary-Treasurer Sam Chinn.

The Service Department stocked a variety of items in preparation for the celebration of the 50th Anniversary of Soil and Water Conservation.

In response to requests from NACD and others involved in soil conservation, the U.S. Postal Service announced the planned release of a special stamp honoring the 50th Anniversary at the 1984 NACD Convention in Denver, Colorado.

Notes and References Cited

Chapter 1 -- Hugh Bennett's Idea

1. Wellington Brink, *Big Hugh: The Father of Soil Conservation* (New York: Macmillan, 1951), p. 3.

2. Gladys L. Baker, Wayne D. Rasmussen, Vivian Wiser and Jane M. Porter, *Century of Service: The First 100 Years of the United States Department of Agriculture* (Washington: Centennial Committee, USDA, 1963), p. 51.

3. Charles M. Hardin, *The Politics of Agriculture: Soil Conservation and the Struggle for Power in Rural America* (Glencoe, IL: The Free Press, 1952), p. 22.

4. D. Harper Simms, *The Soil Conservation Service* (New York: Praeger, 1970), p. 6.

5. Robert J. Morgan, *Governing Soil Conservation: Thirty Years of the New Decentralization* (Baltimore:Johns Hopkins Press, 1965), p. 6.

6. Murray R. Benedict, *Farm Policies of the United States: 1790-1950* (New York: The Twentieth Century Fund, 1953), p. 317.

7. *The Soil Conservation Service*, p. 9

8. Ibid., p. 9

9. National Resources Board, *A Report on National Planning and Public Works in Relation to Natural Resources and Including Land Use and Water Resources with Findings and Recommendations* (Washington: U.S. Government Printing Office, 1934), p. 17.

10. Stuart Chase, *Rich Land, Poor Land* (New York: McGraw-Hill, 1936), pp. 94-5

11. *Farm Policies of the United States*, p. 318.

12. Santford Martin, "And History is Already Shining on Him," Reprint D-1-59 from *Better Crops with Plant Food* (Washington: The American Potash Institute, no original publication issue cited.), p. 4.

13. Charles W. Collier, personal correspondence to Douglas Helms, Historian, Soil Conservation Service, July 21, 1981.

14. *Governing Soil Conservation*, p. 10.

15. C.W. Warburton, C.B. Manifold, Charles E. Kellogg and C.P. Barnes, "The Remedies: Education and Research," *Soils and Men: Yearbook of Agriculture, 1938* (Washington: U.S. Government Printing Office, 1938), pp. 205-211.

16. Hal Jenkins, draft manuscript, quoting from a speech given by Hugh Bennett on May 4, 1960, at a dinner commemorating the 25th anniversary of the SCS, National Press Club, Washington, D.C.(There are no known written copies or transcripts of this speech.)

17. "And History is Already Shining on Him," p. 5.

18. *Governing Soil Conservation*, p. 15.

19. Personal correspondence, President Franklin D. Roosevelt to Harold L. Ickes, Secretary of the Interior, March 22, 1935.

20. *The Soil Conservation Service*, p. 17.

21. *Governing Soil Conservation*, p. 26.

22. *Farm Policies of the United States*, p. 394.

23. Laurence Drake, Leonard A. Solomon and Harry Birdwell, *The History of Conservation in Oklahoma* (Oklahoma City: Oklahoma Association of Conservation Districts, 1977), p. 15.

24. Philip M. Glick, Oral History interview with Douglas Helms, SCS Historian, Washington, D.C. (In publication).

25. *The Politics of Agriculture*, p. 65.

26. W. Robert Parks, *Soil Conservation Districts in Action* (Ames: Iowa State College Press, 1952), p.6.

27. *Governing Soil Conservation*, p. 39.

28. Ibid., p. 15.

29. Committee on Soil Erosion, "Report to the Secretary of Interior on the Soil Erosion Service on a Permanent Coordinated Program of Soil Erosion Control," mimeographed, December 18, 1934.

30. *Governing Soil Conservation*, p. 21.

31. Ibid., p. 33.

32. Ibid., p. 39.

33. Ibid., p. 50.

34. Hugh H. Bennett, "To the Rescue of Soil Conservation," Address before the National Association of Soil Conservation Districts, San Diego, CA, Feb. 2, 1955.

35. Ibid.

Chapter 2. The Emergence of Districts

1. Gordon J. Swearingen, *History of the Soil and Water Conservation District Movement in Arkansas* (Little Rock: Arkansas Association of Conservation Districts, 1970), p. 7.

2. *Governing Soil Conservation*, p. 77.

3. Ibid., p. 71.

4. Ibid., p. 64.

5. Ibid., p. 40.

6. *The Politics of Agriculture*, p. 74.

7. Philip M. Glick, "Soil Conservation: Highlights of Political and Legal Arrangements," *Soil Conservation Policies: An Assessment* (Ankeny, IA: SCSA, 1979), p. 21.

8. *The Soil Conservation Service*, p. 79.

9. *Governing Soil Conservation*, pp. 92-97.

10. *History of the Soil and Water Conservation District Movement in Arkansas*, p. 17.

11. George R. Bagley, "Evolution of Institutional Arrangements: A Nongovernmental View," in *Soil Conservation Policies: An Assessment* (Ankeny, IA: SCSA, 1979), p. 26.

12. R. Neil Sampson, *Farmland or Wasteland: A Time to Choose* (Emmaus, PA: Rodale Press, 1981), p. 262.

13. Nolen J. Fuqua, Original transcript of oral history interview with Douglas Helms, SCS, September 16, 1983, p. 5.

14. Philip M. Glick, "The Politics of Conservation," *Journal of Soil and Water Conservation*, V. 37, No. 5 (September-October 1982), p. 258.

15. *Soil Conservation Districts in Action*, p. 11.

16. *History of the Soil and Water Conservation District Movement in Arkansas*, p. 10.

17. Otis Tossett, *Land, Water and People* (League City, TX: Conservation Districts Foundation, Inc., 1961), p. 8.

18. Ibid., p. 10.

19. Nolen J. Fuqua, *Interview*, May, 1984.

20. *Land, Water & People*, p. 10.

21. Ralph H. Musser, "Why Another Society?," *Journal of Soil and Water Conservation*,

V. 1, No. 1 (July, 1946), p. 3.
  22. Ibid., p. 3.
  23. *Land, Water & People,* p. 11.

Chapter 3. Birth of an Organization

1. Most of the quotations and facts in Chapter 3 come directly from the minutes of the various meetings in which the situation occurred. These minutes are contained in bound volumes in the Davis Conservation Library, League City, Texas. It is seldom done these days, but most of the early meetings were completely transcribed, and the minutes of a one-day NASCD meeting could run to as much as 150 pages of transcribed copy. Because the text adequately documents the particular meeting from which most of the quotes and facts emerged, footnotes have been minimized in this chapter.

2. Interviews with David Unger and others, who related the story as having been told by Gordon Zimmerman at various times over the years. In his oral history interview with Douglas Helms, SCS historian, in 1981, Zimmerman said he went up to New York on Saturdays, to help Leavitt with "newsletters and correspondence," and was assigned to work with the Agriculture Committee of the American Bankers Association because "my job was information and education and that came as close as anybody came to working with other organizations."

3. *Farm Policies of the United States,* p. 497.

4. Gordon K. Zimmerman, Oral History Interview with Douglas Helms, SCS Historian, February 18 and February 27, 1981, p. 55.

5. Ibid., p. 55.

6. U. S. House of Representatives, *Hearings before the Committee on Agriculture, House of Representatives, Eightieth Congress, on H.R. 6054,* May 4, 1948.

7. *The Politics of Conservation,* p.89.

8. *Governing Soil Conservation,* p. 131.

Chapter 4. Growth in Service

1. *Land, Water & People,* p. 76.

2. Nolen J. Fuqua, *Oral Interview,* (Washington, DC: Soil Conservation Service, Oral History Series), page 32, original transcript.

Chapter 5. Districts Fight to Survive

1. Michael K. Childs and J. C. Headley, "Soil Conservation and Extension in Missouri: A Study of Conflict," *Journal of Soil and Water Conservation,* V. 37, No. 4, July-August, 1982, p. 200.

2. "Soil Conservation and Extension in Missouri," p. 202.

3. *The Politics of Agriculture,* p. 33.

4. Ibid., p. 72.

5. House *Hearings,* Agricultural Appropriations Act, Fiscal 1952, Part 2, pp. 688-9.

6. "Soil Conservation and Extension in Missouri," p. 203.

7. "Farmers Flock to District Referendum," *Soil Conservation,* August, 1944.

8. Russell G. Hill, "Out of the Dust Bowl," *Journal of Soil and Water Conservation,* Vol. 39, No. 1, January-February, 1984, p. 10.

9. *Tuesday Letter,* April 22, 1958.

10. *Tuesday Letter,* April 22, 1958.

11. *Tuesday Letter,* July 22, 1958.

12. Personal correspondence from LeAnn M. Harner, Executive Secretary, South Dakota Association of Conservation Districts, April 25, 1984.

Chapter 6. National Issues Heat Up

1. Charles F. Brannan, "Working Together for Conservation," speech before the National Association of Soil Conservation Districts, Feb 20, 1951 (League City: NACD), p. 89 of meeting transcript.

2. Hugh H. Bennett, "They've Cut the Heart out of Soil Conservation," *Country Gentleman*, January, 1954.

3. U.S. House of Representatives, *Hearings*, Agricultural Appropriations, fiscal 1952, Part 1, p. 547.

4. "Working Together for Conservation," p. 98.

5. Nolen J. Fuqua, "Out of the Dust Bowl," *Journal of Soil and Water Conservation*, Vol. 39, No. 1, January-February, 1984, p. 11.

6. Nolen J. Fuqua, Oral Interview with Douglas Helms, SCS historian, p. 24 of original transcript.

7. Ezra Taft Benson, "A Dynamic National Program for Soil and Water Conservation," *Proceedings, Eighth Annual NASCD Convention* (League City: NACD), p. 17.

Chapter 7. Broadening the Base

1. R. Burnell Held and Marion Clawson, *Soil Conservation in Perspective* (Baltimore: Johns Hopkins Press, 1965), p. 74.

2. *Tuesday Letter*, March 6, 1962.

3. *Tuesday Letter*, May 15, 1962.

4. *Tuesday Letter*, April 3, 1962.

5. *Tuesday Letter*, June 19, 1962.

6. George S. McGovern, "Conservation: A National Imperative," *Proceedings, 19th Annual NACD Convention, Portland, Oregon,* (League City: NACD, 1965), p. 10.

7. *Tuesday Letter*, May 1, 1962.

8. A.K. Booher, "Hull-York-Lakeland RC&D Project," *Journal of Soil and Water Conservation*, May-June 1971, pp. 93-94.

9. *Tuesday Letter*, August 6, 1963.

Chapter 8. Finding a Leadership Role

1. *Tuesday Letter*, May 2, 1972.

2. Personal interview with Lyle Bauer, May 30, 1984.

3. *Report*, Vol. 6, No. 4, (Washington: NACD, May 27, 1970), p. 1.

4. *Tuesday Letter*, December 1, 1970.

5. Ibid.

6. *Tuesday Letter*, December 8, 1970.

7. Personal interview with Lyle Bauer, May 30, 1984.

8. John Wilder, "Key Issues Ahead," *Proceedings of the 25th Anniversary Convention, Chicago, Illinois, February 7-11, 1971.* (League City: NACD), p. 16.

9. *Tuesday Letter*, December 15, 1970.

10. Jamie L. Whitten, "Agriculture and Resource Development in a Growing Economy," *Proceedings of the 26th Annual Convention, Washington, D.C., February 13-17, 1972* (Washington: NACD), p. 18.

11. *Tuesday Letter*, August 28, 1973.

12. *Tuesday Letter*, September 18, 1973.

13. *Tuesday Letter*, October 9, 1973.

14. *Tuesday Letter*, November 6, 1973.

15. *Tuesday Letter*, March 19, 1974.

16. *Tuesday Letter*, July 23, 1974.

17. *Tuesday Letter*, May 18, 1976.

18. Lyle Bauer, "Conservation in the 1980's," *Proceedings of the 33rd Annual Convention, Washington, D.C., February 10-14, 1979* (Washington: NACD), p. 42.

19. *Tuesday Letter,* May 23, 1978.

20. *Tuesday Letter,* June 13, 1978.

Chapter 9. The Decade of the Environment

1. Rice Odell, *Environmental Awakening: The New Revolution to Protect the Earth* (Washington: The Conservation Foundation, 1980), p.5.

2. Eddie Albert, "The End of Man," *Proceedings of the 24th Annual Convention, San Francisco, California, February 1-5, 1970* (Washington: NACD), p. 23.

3. Charles E. Little, *Shifting Ground: New Priorities for National Land Use Policy* (Washington: Congressional Research Service [IPP 76-13], 1976), p. 7.

4. *Tuesday Letter,* December 11, 1973.

5. *Land Use Planning Act of 1974,* Hearings before the Subcommittee on the Environment of the Committee on Interior and Insular Affairs (Washington: House of Representatives, April 23-25, 1974), p. 120.

6. *Tuesday Letter,* May 21, 1974.

7. *Minutes, NACD Board of Directors, Washington, D.C., March 17-20, 1975.* (Washington: NACD).

8. *Tuesday Letter,* March 25, 1975.

9. *Land Use Planning Act of 1974,* Hearings before the Subcommittee on the Environment of the Committee on Interior and Insular Affairs (Washington: House of Representatives, April 23-25, 1974), p. 333.

10. Sam Studebaker, "The Critical Resource Issues of 1968," *Proceedings of the 22nd Annual Convention, Dallas, Texas, February 4-8, 1968* (Washington: NACD), p.16.

11. *Tuesday Letter,* August 22, 1972.

12. U.S. Council on Environmental Quality, *Environmental Quality: The Third Annual Report of the Council on Environmental Quality* (Washington: U.S. Government Printing Office, 1972), pp. 170-171.

13. Mary M. Garner, "Strategies for Conserving Soil and Water," *The Agricultural Law Journal,* Vol. 3, No. 4, 1982, p. 556.

14. *Tuesday Letter,* May 23, 1972.

15. *Tuesday Letter,* November 28, 1972.

16. Environmental Protection Agency, *Report on State Sediment Control Institutes Program* (Washington: EPA-440/9-75-001, April 1975).

17. *Tuesday Letter,* July 24, 1973.

18. *Tuesday Letter,* October 7, 1975.

19. *Tuesday Letter,* March 20, 1973.

20. *Tuesday Letter,* May 11, 1976.

21. *Tuesday Letter,* August 19, 1975.

22. *Tuesday Letter,* May 18, 1976.

23. *Tuesday Letter,* June 8, 1976.

24. *Tuesday Letter,* April 12, 1977.

25. *Tuesday Letter,* November 15, 1977.

26. *Tuesday Letter,* April 19, 1977.

27. *Tuesday Letter,* September 6, 1977.

28. *Tuesday Letter,* May 2, 1978.

29. *Tuesday Letter,* April 2, 1974.

30. *Tuesday Letter,* April 25, 1978.

31. *Tuesday Letter,* January 23, 1979.

32. *Tuesday Letter,* December 4, 1973.

33. *Tuesday Letter,* January 22, 1974.

34. *Tuesday Letter,* September 14, 1976.

35. *Tuesday Letter,* September 6, 1977.

36. *Tuesday Letter*, March 19, 1974.
37. *Tuesday Letter*, October 12, 1971.
38. *Tuesday Letter*, May 14, 1974.
39. *Tuesday Letter*, October 26, 1976.

Chapter 10. Expanding The Agenda

1. *Tuesday Letter*, July 18, 1972.
2. *Tuesday Letter*, August 7, 1973.
3. *Tuesday Letter*, October 4, 1977.
4. *Tuesday Letter*, July 15, 1975.
5. *Tuesday Letter*, August 3, 1976.
6. *Tuesday Letter*, March 11, 1975.
7. *Tuesday Letter*, June 21, 1977.
8. *Tuesday Letter*, July 31, 1979.
9. *Tuesday Letter*, November 13, 1979.
10. Harold E. Dregne, "Desertification of Arid Lands," *Economic Geography*, Vol. 3, No. 4 (1977), p. 329.
11. NACD, *Pasture & Range Improvement Report* (Washington: NACD, July, 1979), p. 23.
12. *Tuesday Letter*, April 10, 1979.
13. *Tuesday Letter*, October 23, 1979.
14. *Tuesday Letter*, March 27, 1979.
15. R.I. Dideriksen, A.R. Hidlebaugh, and K.O. Schmude, "Trends in Agricultural Land Use," *Farmland, Food and the Future.* (Ankeny, IA: SCSA, 1979), p. 23.
16. *Tuesday Letter*, March 8, 1977.

Chapter 11. NACD Today

1. W. B. Wilkerson, et.al., *Keepers of the Land: A History of Soil and Water Conservation Districts in South Carolina* (Columbia: South Carolina Association of Soil Conservation Districts, 1972), p. 60
2. *Tuesday Letter*, June 27, 1978.

Chapter 12. Issues of the 1980's

1. *Tuesday Letter*, January 22, 1980.
2. *Tuesday Letter*, May 6, 1980.
3. *Tuesday Letter*, June 17, 1980.
4. *Tuesday Letter*, July 8, 1980.
5. *Tuesday Letter*, September 30, 1980.
6. *Tuesday Letter*, April 1, 1980.
7. *Tuesday Letter*, September 18, 1979.
8. *Tuesday Letter*, October 30, 1979.
9. *Tuesday Letter*, November 9, 1979.
10. Sam Studebaker, "Key Resource Issues of 1969," *Proceedings of the 23rd Annual Convention, Atlanta, Georgia, February 2-6, 1969,* (Washington: NACD, 1969), p. 13.

INDEX